TSUKASA SAIMURA
KOZO TAKAHASHI

CRUELER THAN DEAD

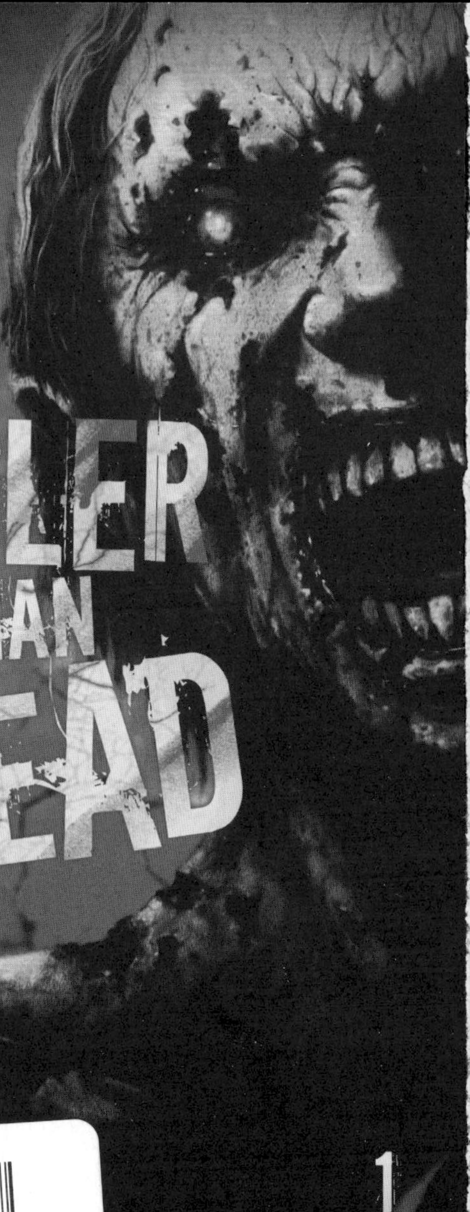

1

CONTENTS

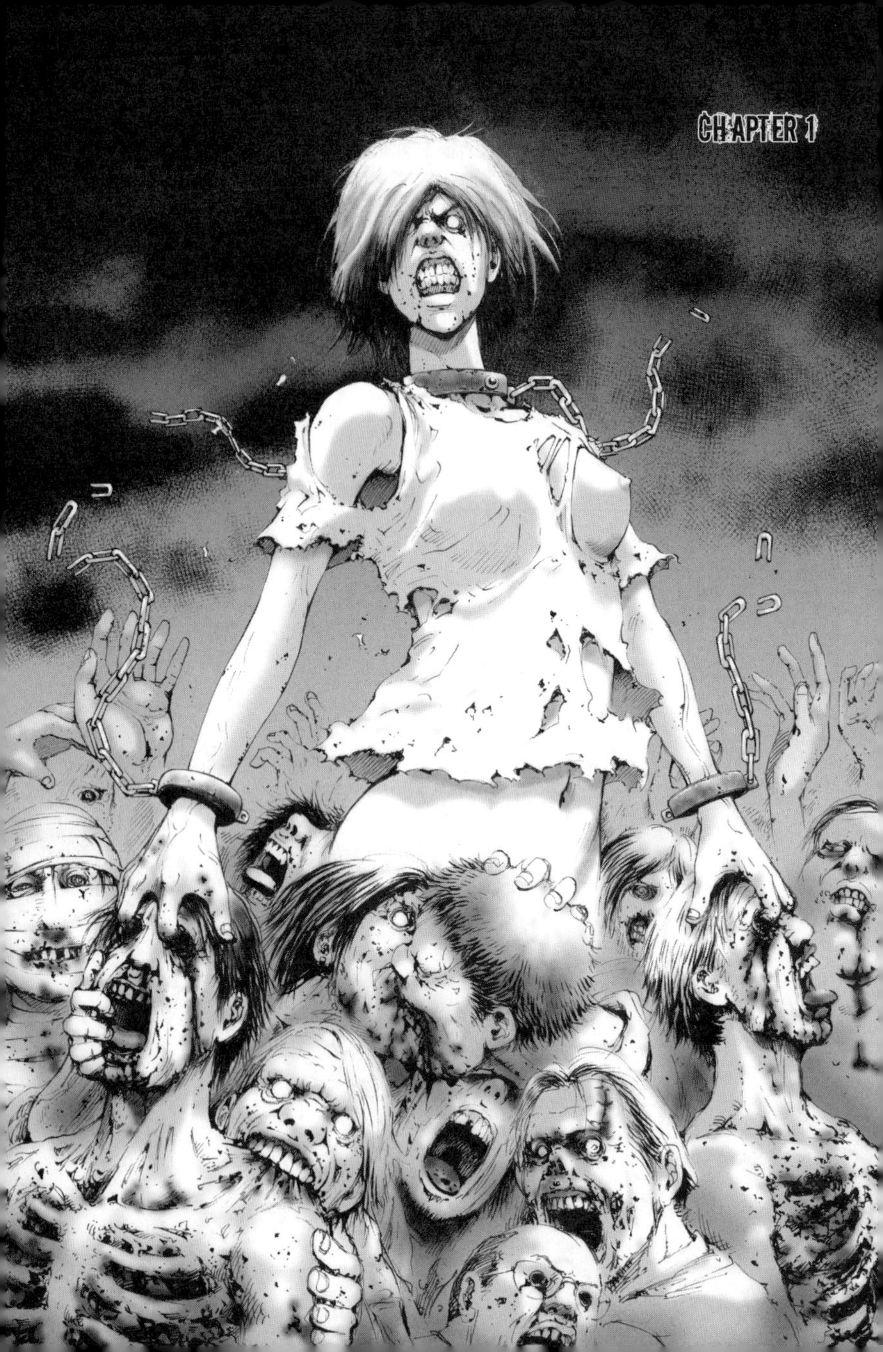
CHAPTER 1

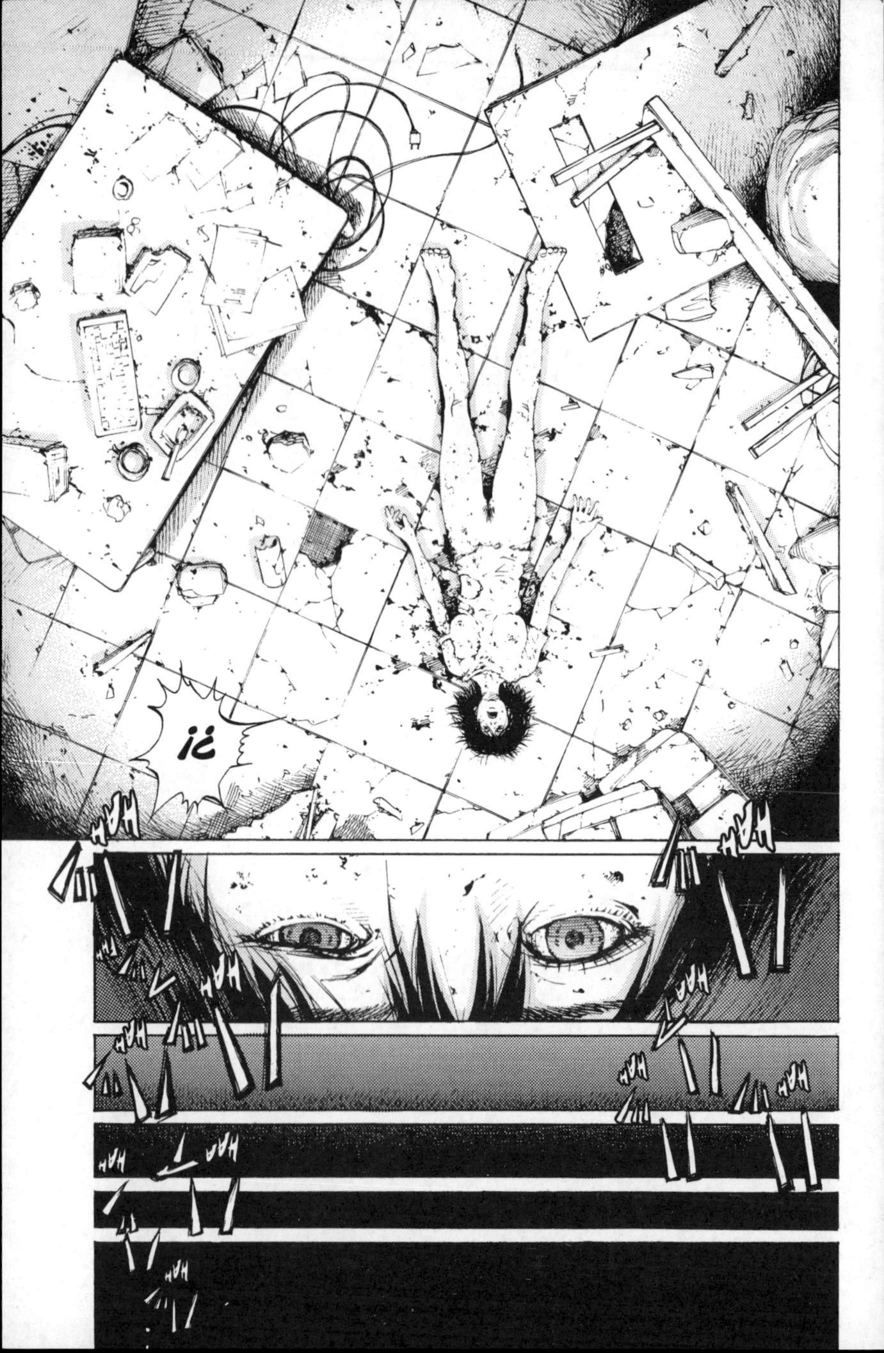
?!
HAH
HAH
HAH
HAH
HAH
HAH
HAH
HAH
HAH
HAH
HAH

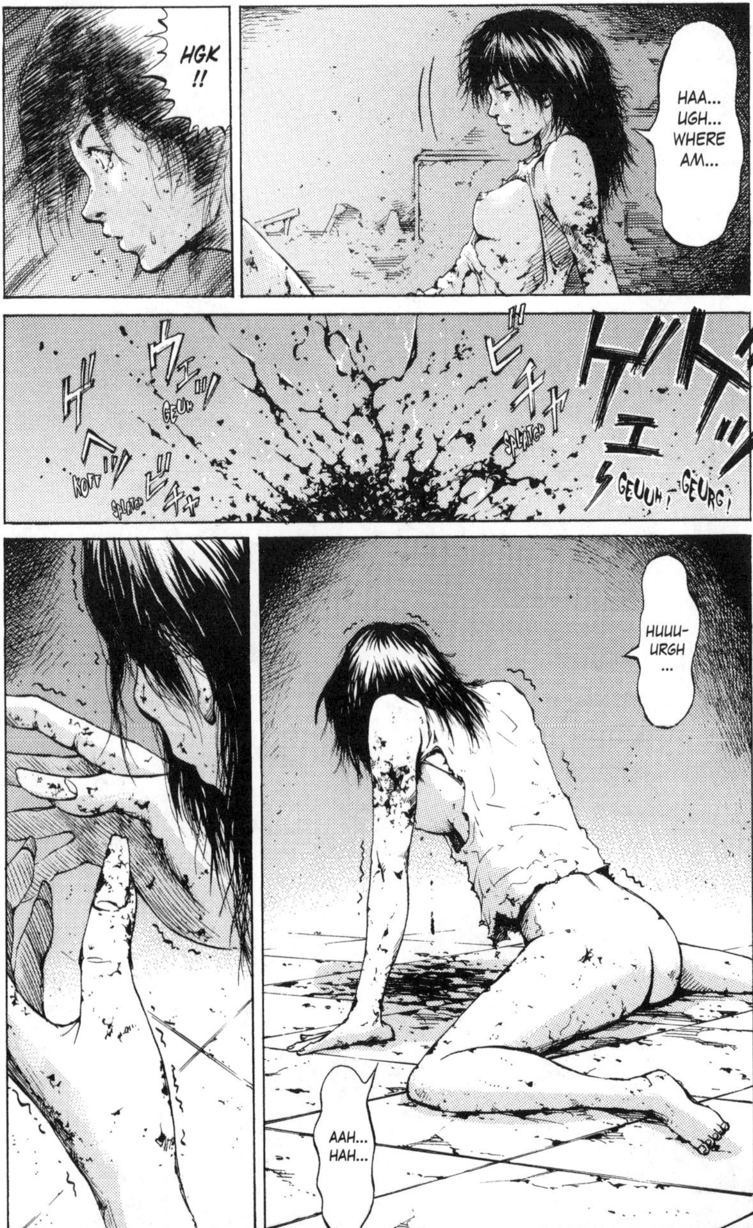
HAA... UGH... WHERE AM...
HGK !!
ゲゲェッ
GEUUH! GEURG!
ビチャ
SPLATCH
ウェッ
GEUH
ゲヘッ
KOFF
ビチャ
SPLATCH
HUUU-URGH ...
AAH... HAH...

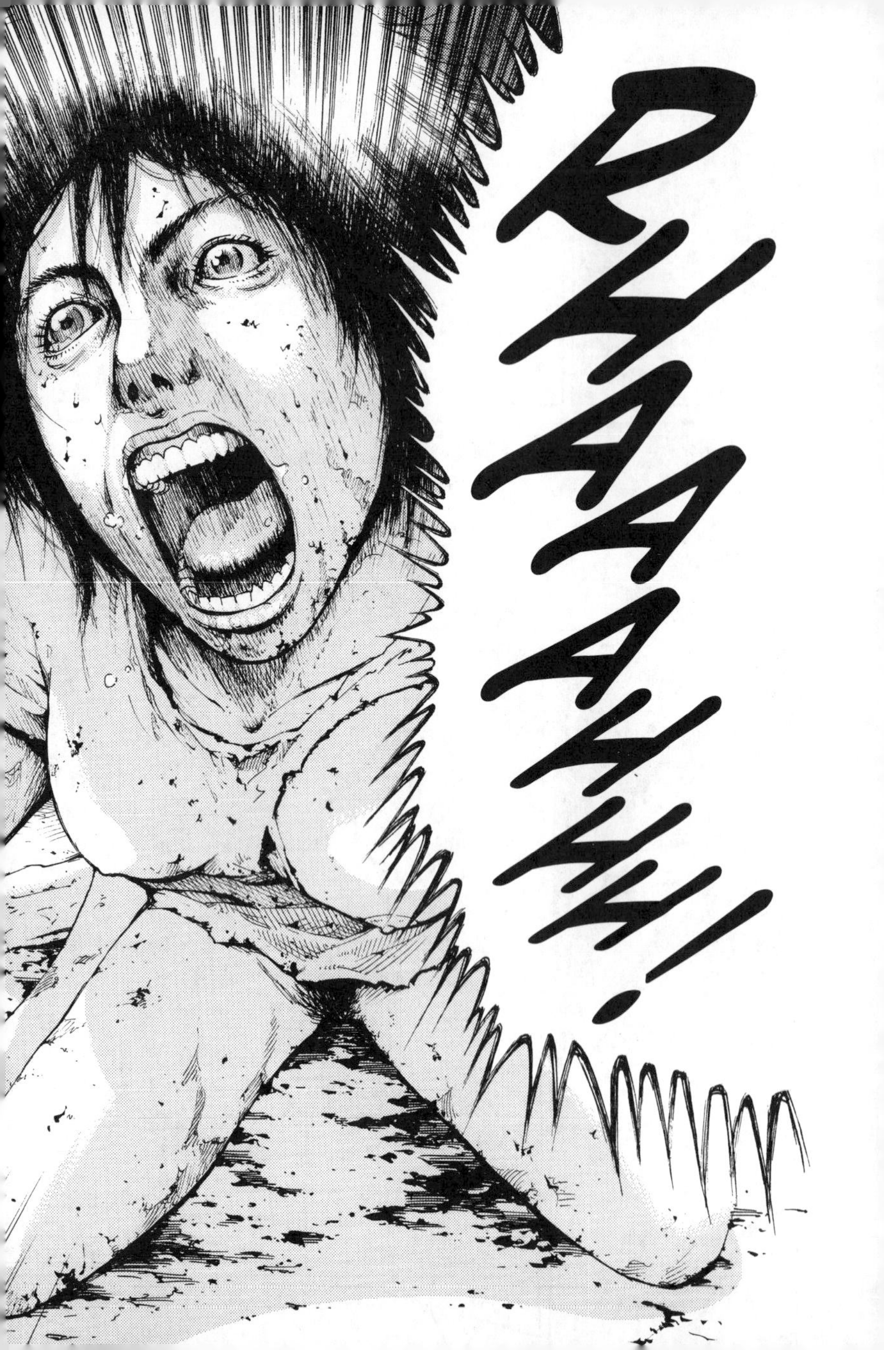
RHAAAHHH!

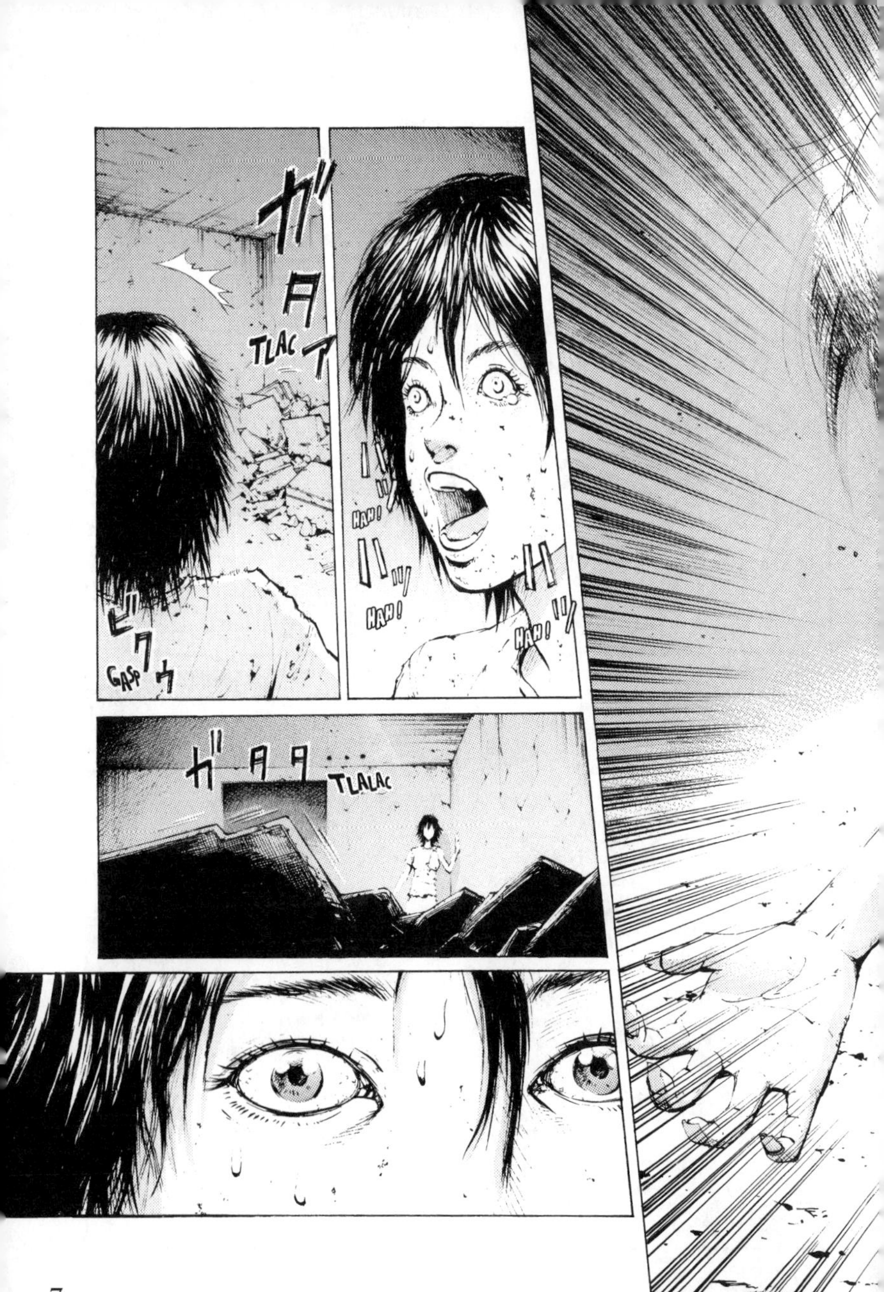
ハッ
HAH!
ハッ
HAH!
ハッ
HAH!
ガタァ
TLAC
ビクゥ
GASP
ガタタ…
TLALAC

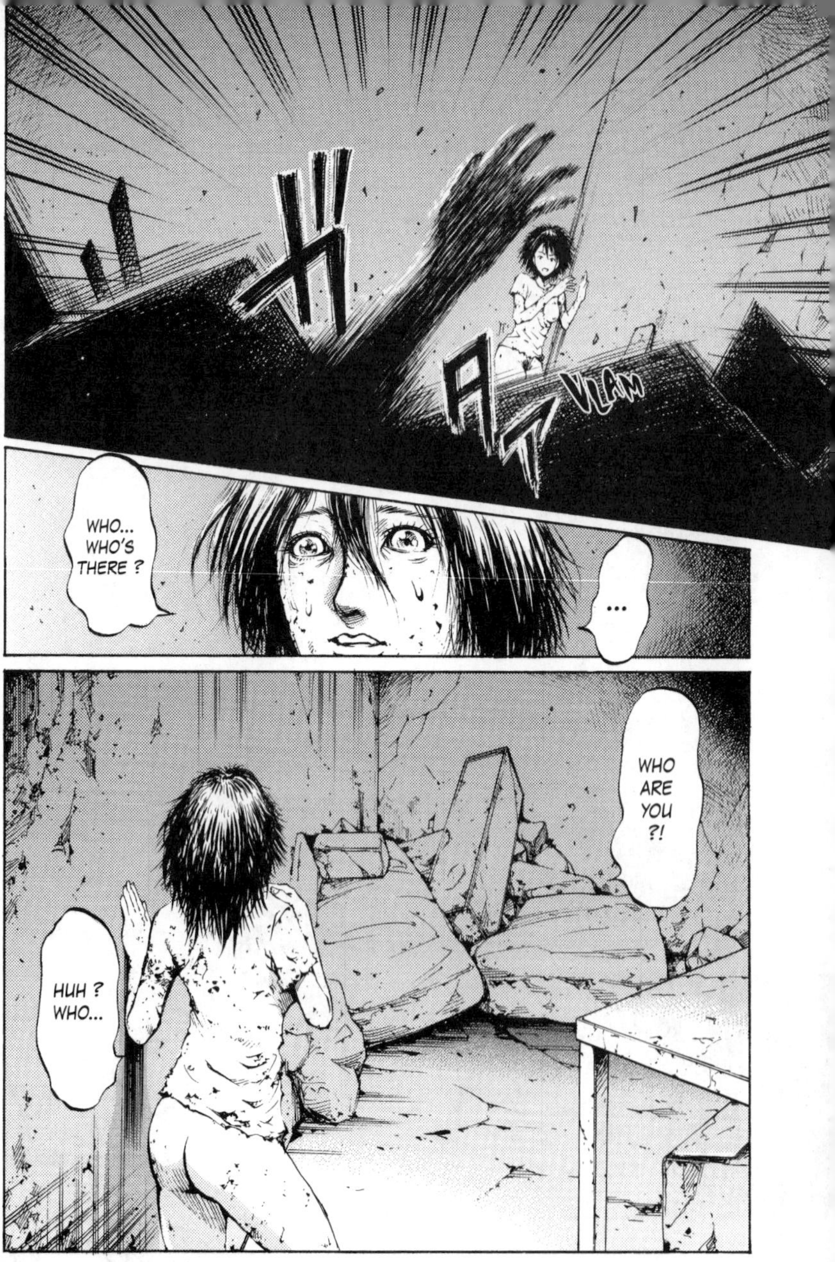
VLAM
...
WHO... WHO'S THERE ?
WHO ARE YOU ?!
HUH ? WHO...

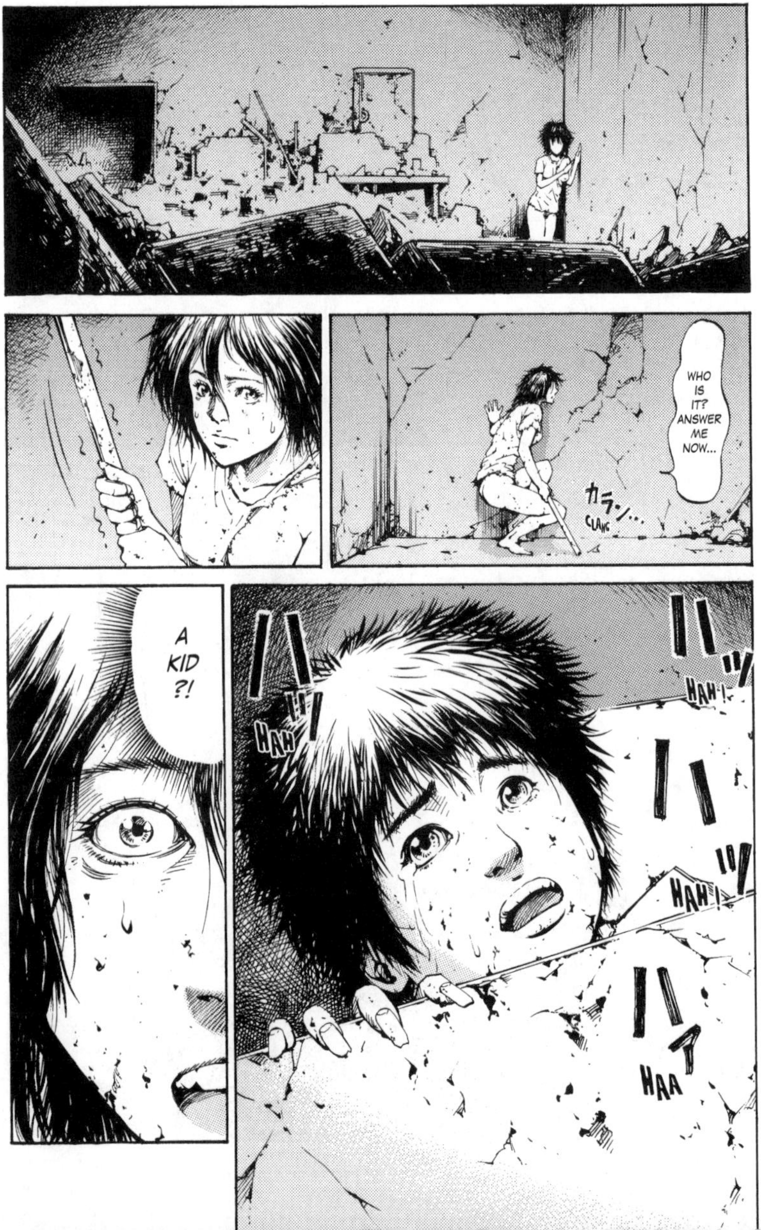
WHO IS IT? ANSWER ME NOW...
カラン…
CLANG
HAH!
HAH
HAH!
HAA
A KID?!

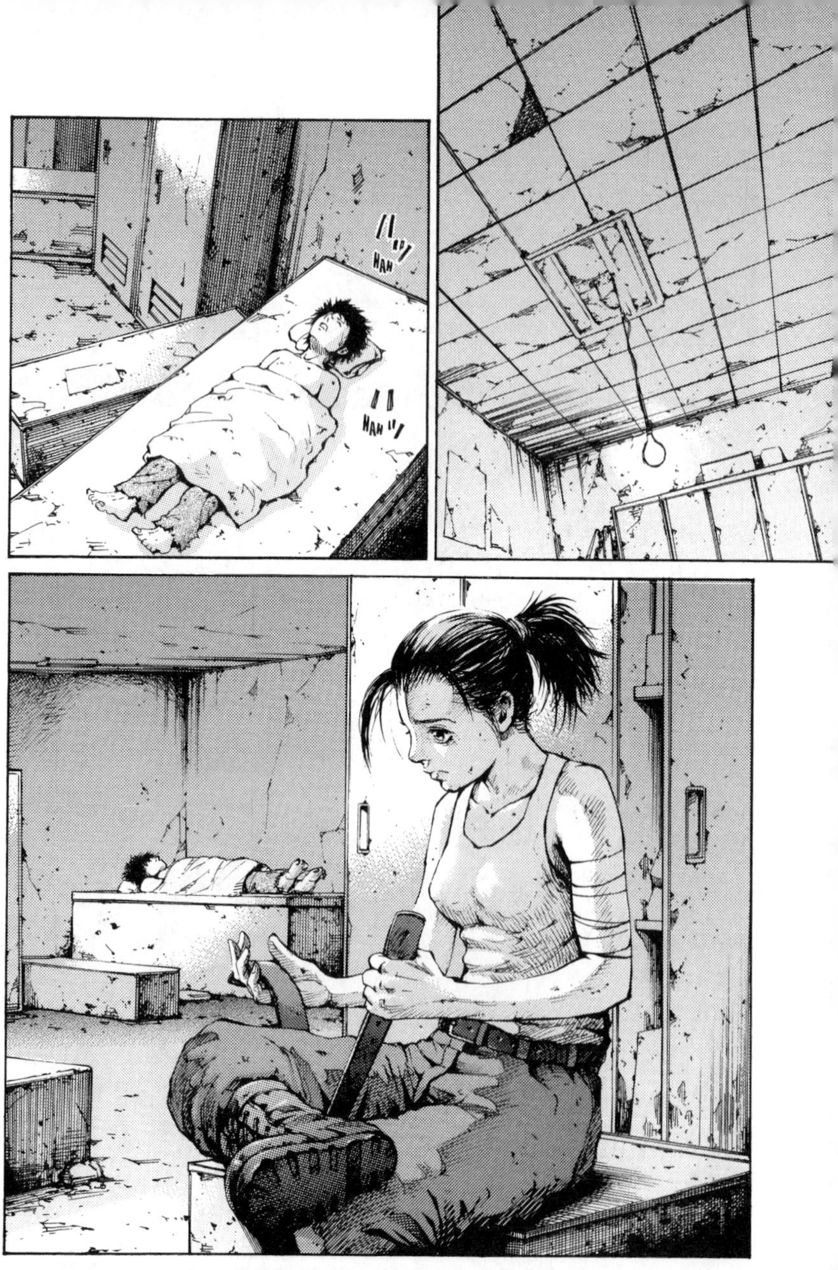
HAH
HAH

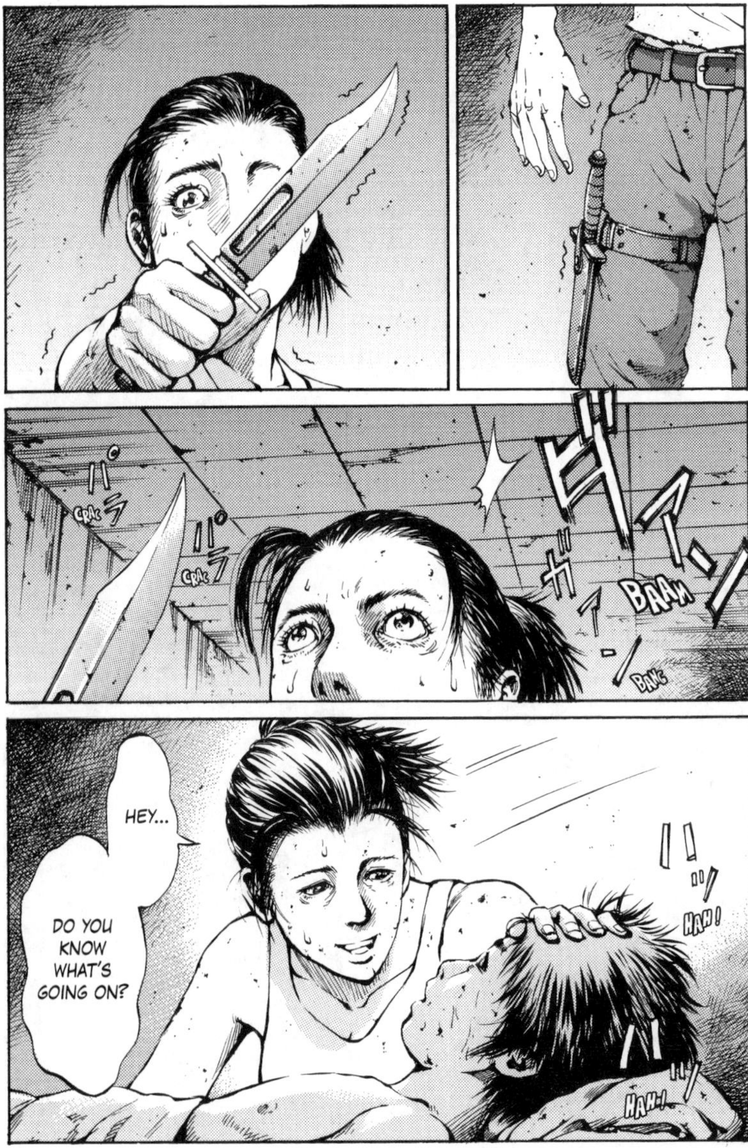
BAAM
BANG
パラ
CRAC
パラ
CRAC
HEY...
DO YOU KNOW WHAT'S GOING ON?
HAH!
HAH!

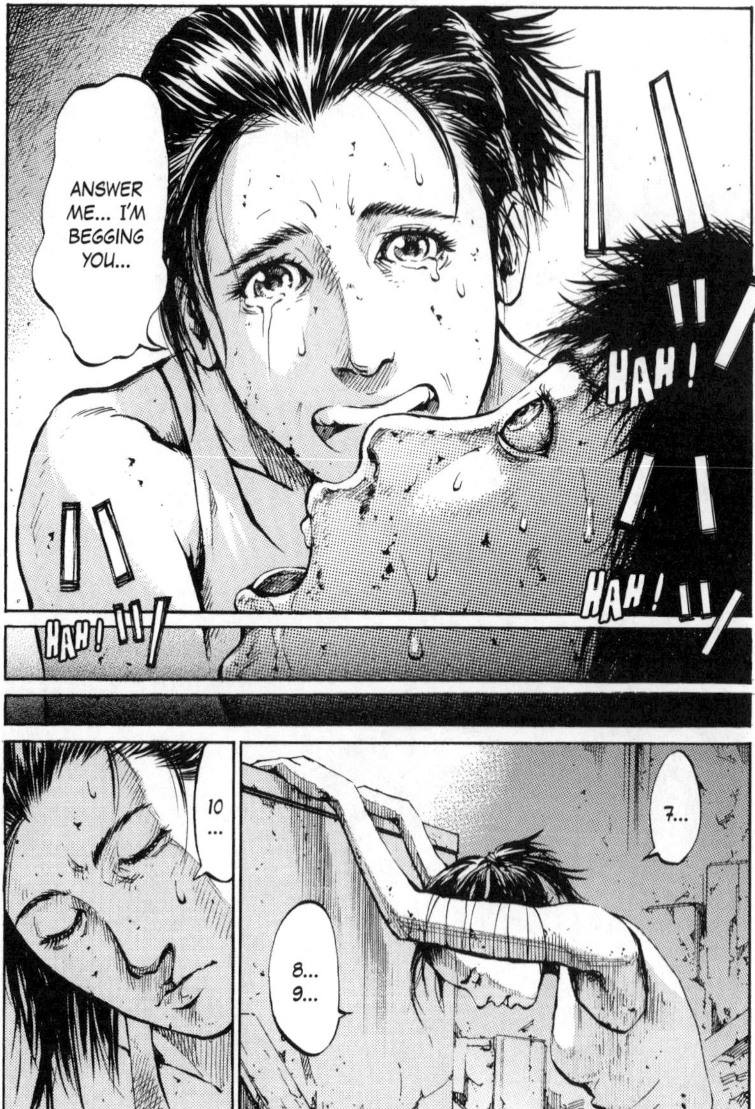
HAH!
ANSWER ME... I'M BEGGING YOU...
HAH!
HAH!
7...
8... 9...
10 ...

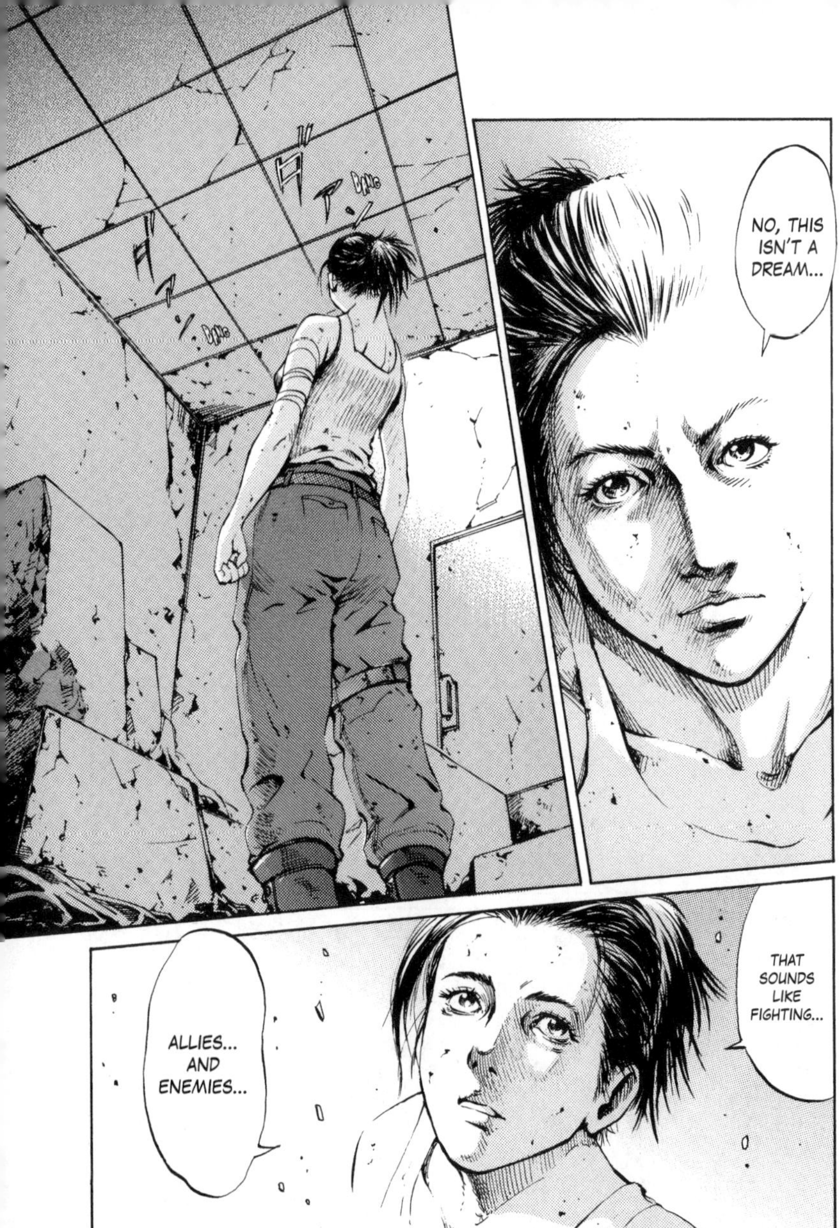
NO, THIS ISN'T A DREAM...
DANG
DANG
THAT SOUNDS LIKE FIGHTING...
ALLIES... AND ENEMIES...

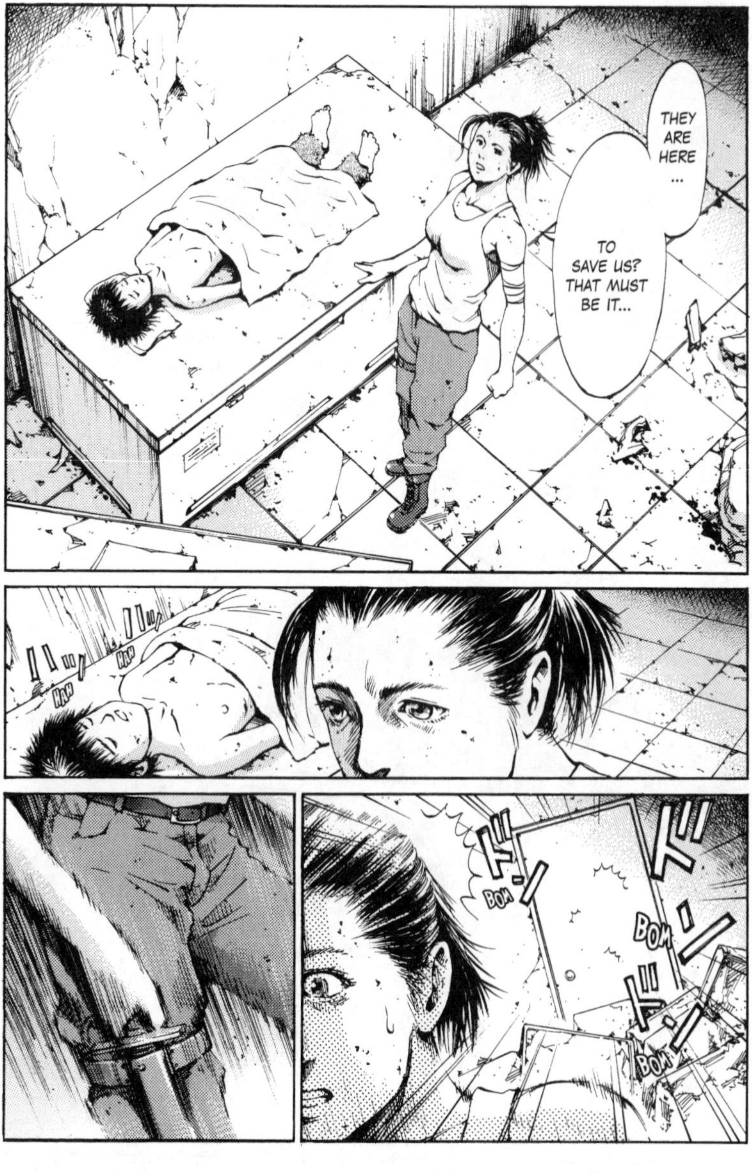
THEY ARE HERE ...
TO SAVE US? THAT MUST BE IT...
HAH
HAH
BOM
BOM
BOM

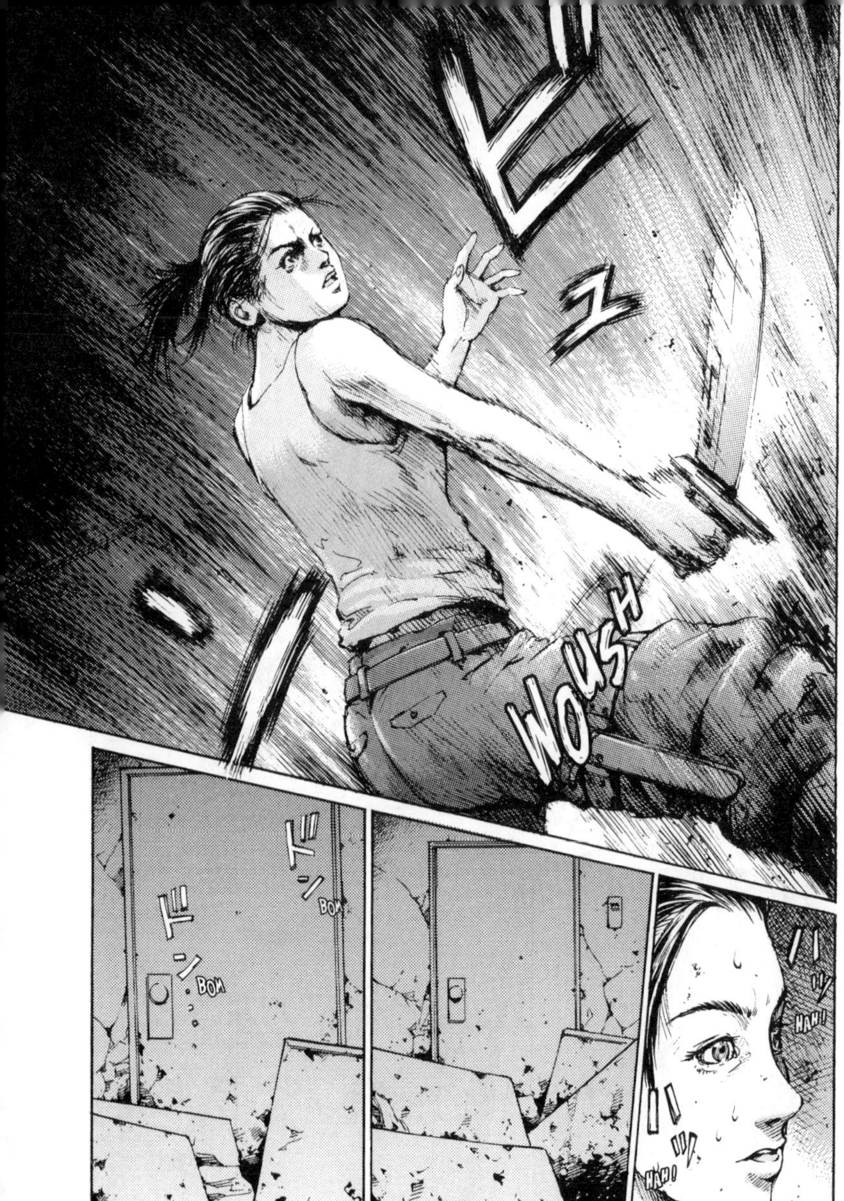
WOUSH
HAH!
HAH!
BOM
BOM

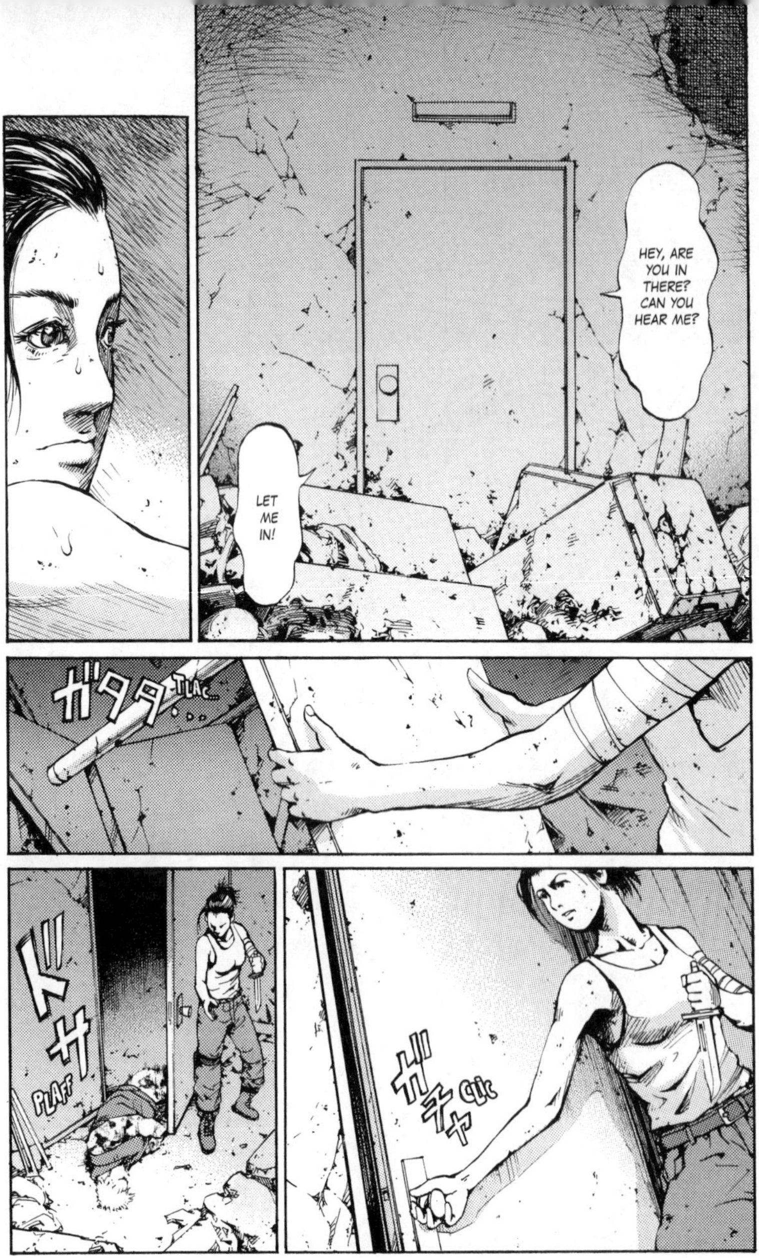
HEY, ARE YOU IN THERE? CAN YOU HEAR ME?
LET ME IN!
ガタタ TLAC...
ガチャ CLIC
ドサ PLAFF

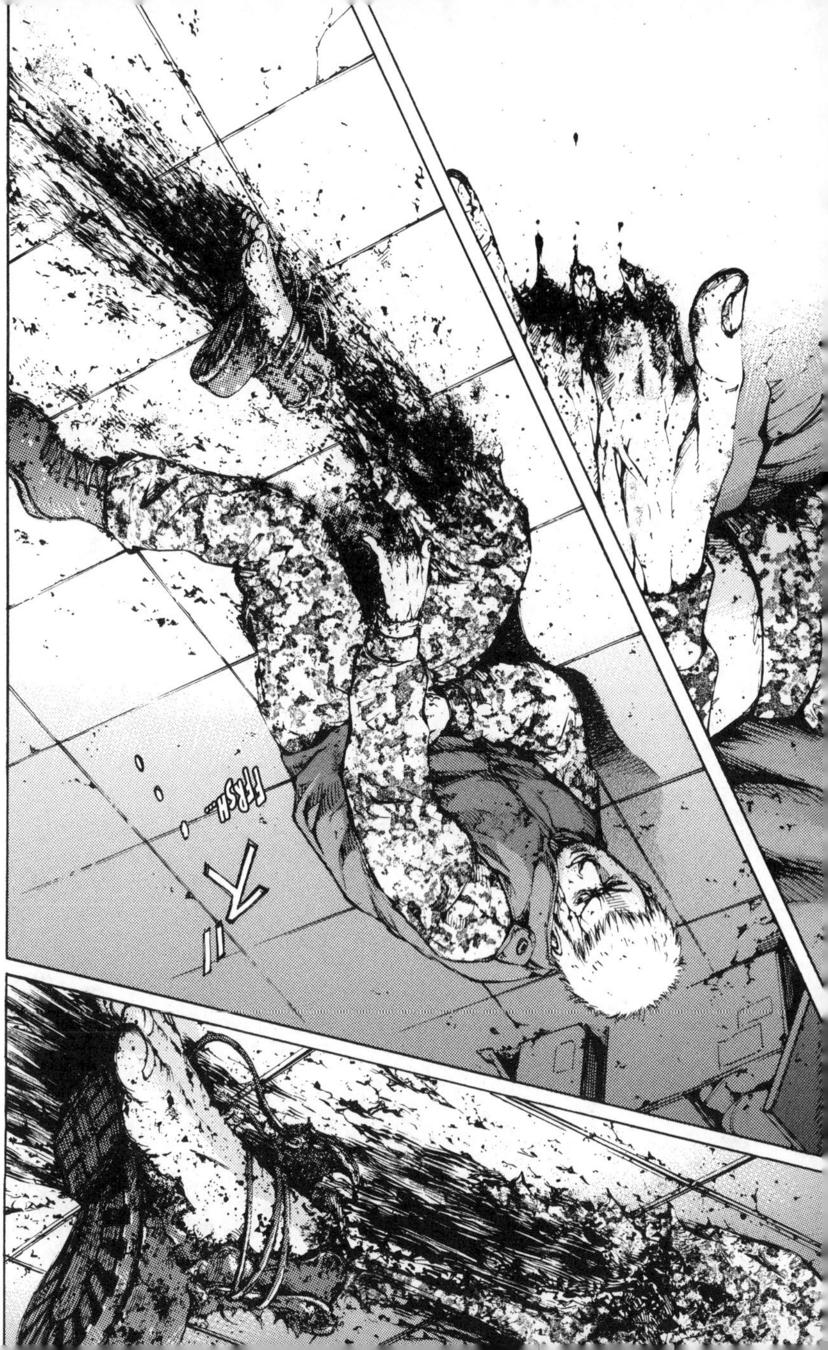
FFRSH...

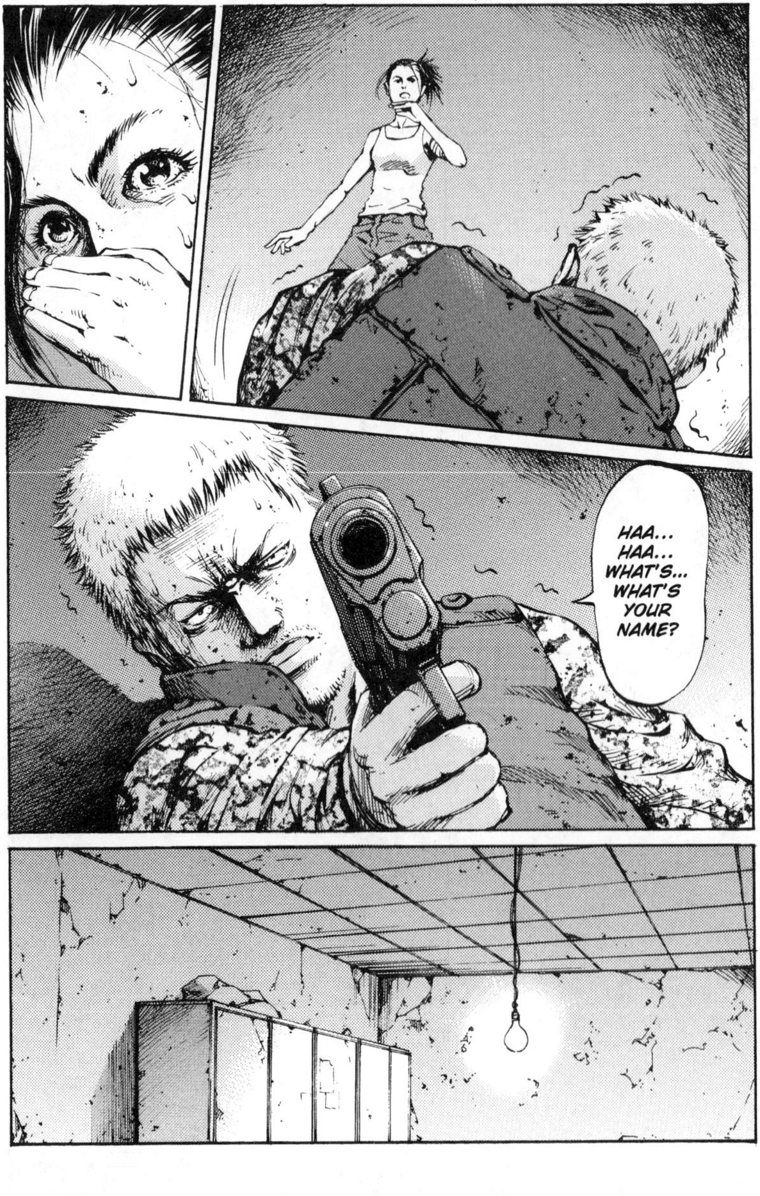
HAA... HAA... WHAT'S... WHAT'S YOUR NAME?

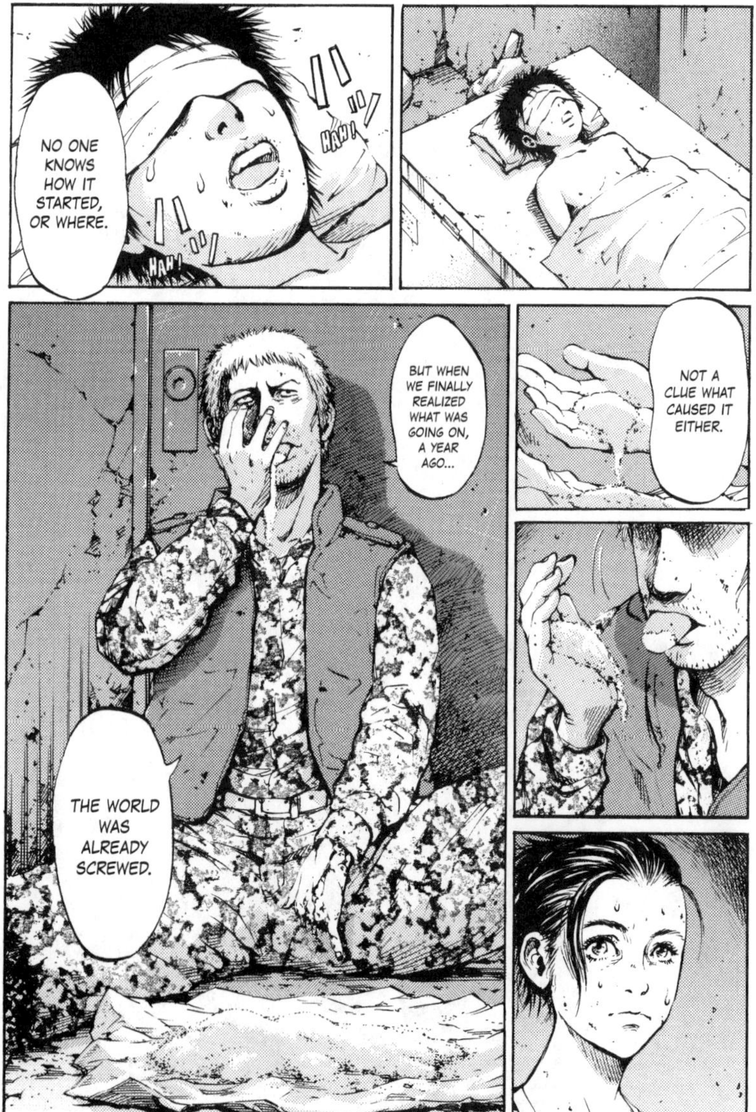
NO ONE KNOWS HOW IT STARTED, OR WHERE.
HAH!
HAH!
NOT A CLUE WHAT CAUSED IT EITHER.
BUT WHEN WE FINALLY REALIZED WHAT WAS GOING ON, A YEAR AGO...
THE WORLD WAS ALREADY SCREWED.

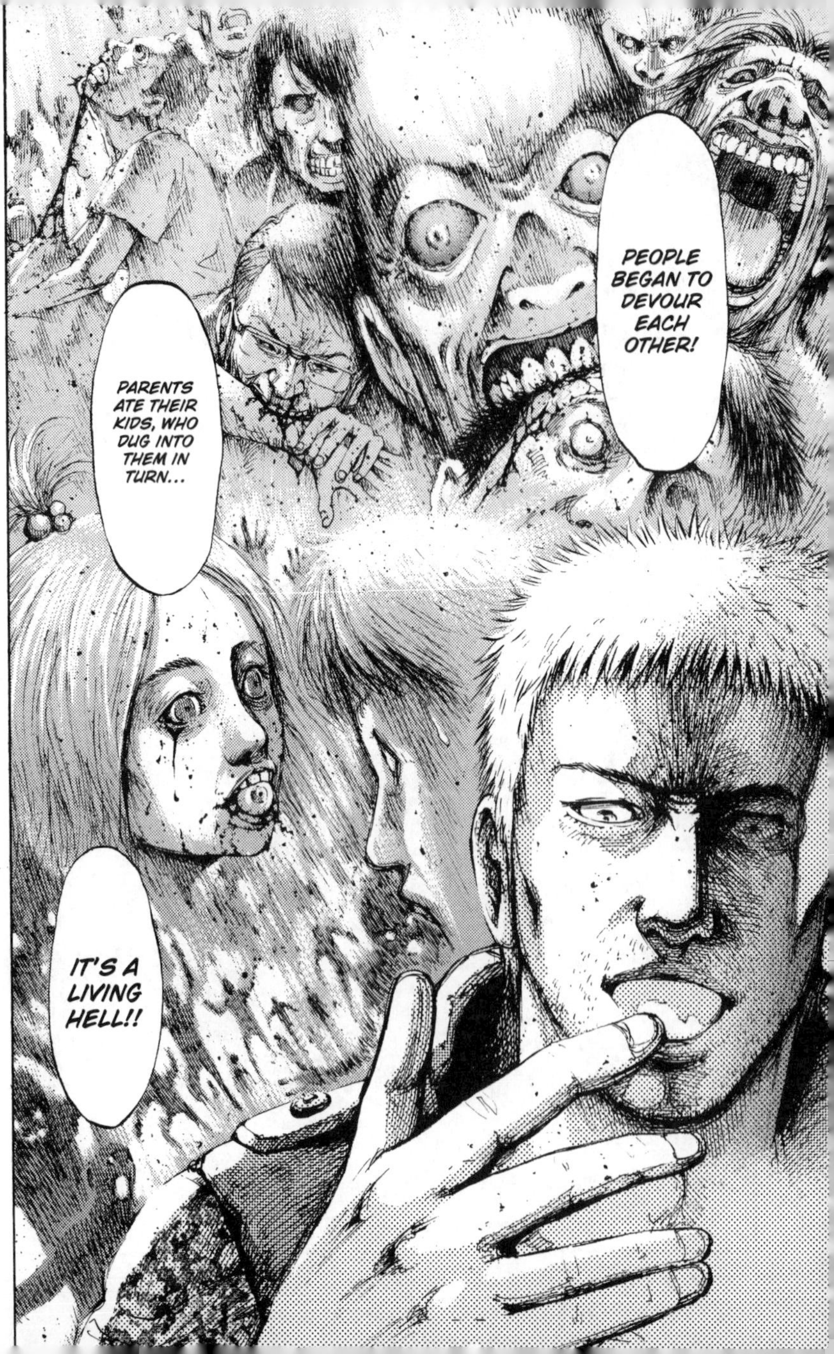
PEOPLE BEGAN TO DEVOUR EACH OTHER!
PARENTS ATE THEIR KIDS, WHO DUG INTO THEM IN TURN...
IT'S A LIVING HELL!!

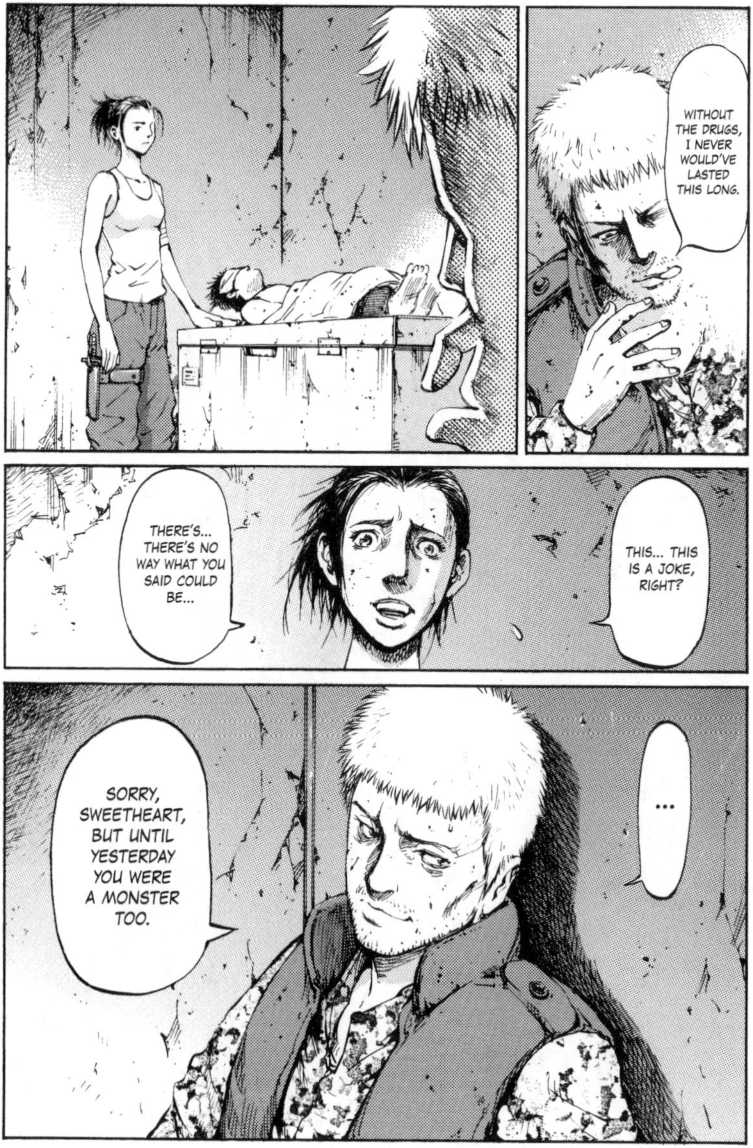
WITHOUT THE DRUGS, I NEVER WOULD'VE LASTED THIS LONG.
THIS... THIS IS A JOKE, RIGHT?
THERE'S... THERE'S NO WAY WHAT YOU SAID COULD BE...
...
SORRY, SWEETHEART, BUT UNTIL YESTERDAY YOU WERE A MONSTER TOO.

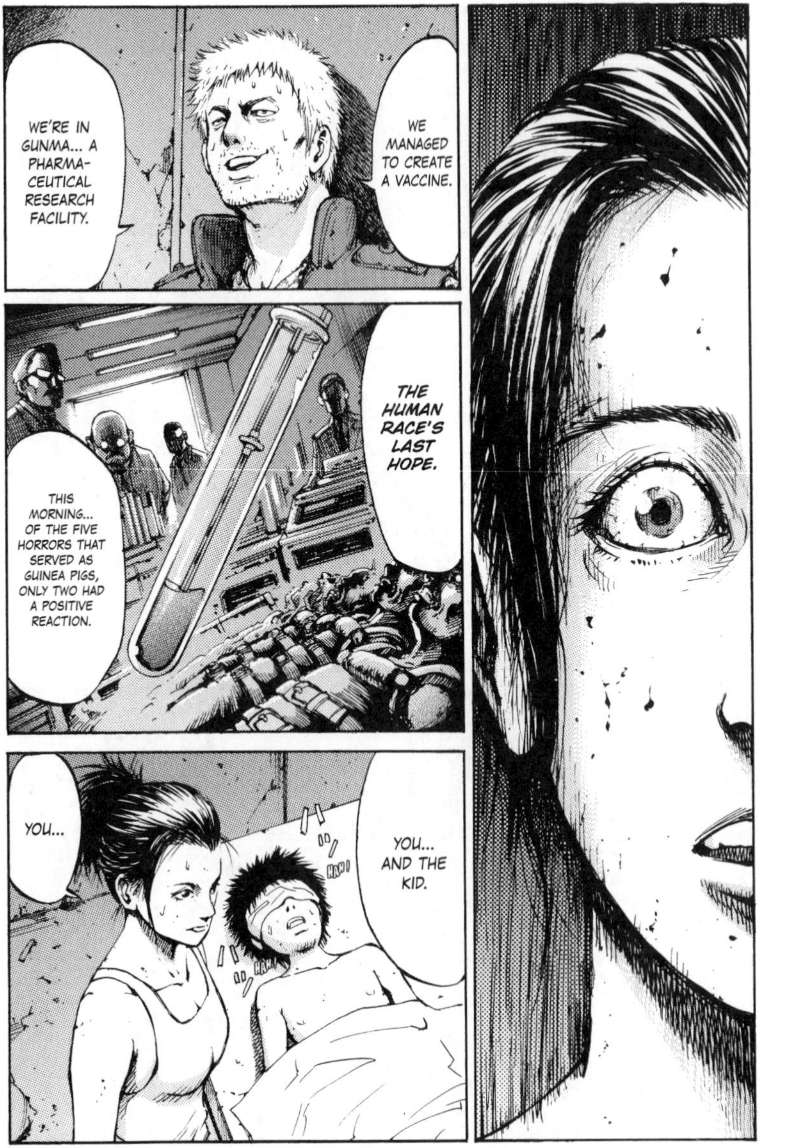
WE MANAGED TO CREATE A VACCINE.
WE'RE IN GUNMA... A PHARMA-CEUTICAL RESEARCH FACILITY.
THE HUMAN RACE'S LAST HOPE.
THIS MORNING... OF THE FIVE HORRORS THAT SERVED AS GUINEA PIGS, ONLY TWO HAD A POSITIVE REACTION.
YOU... AND THE KID.
HAH!
HAH!
YOU...

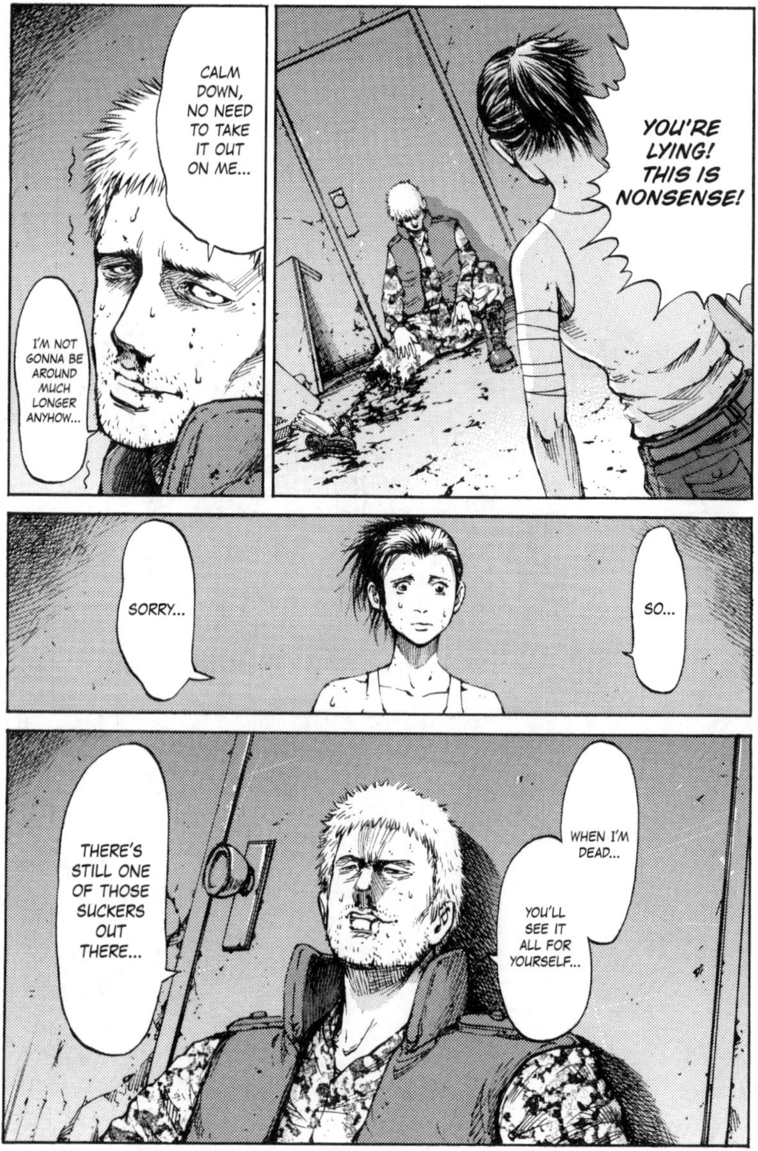
YOU'RE LYING! THIS IS NONSENSE!
CALM DOWN, NO NEED TO TAKE IT OUT ON ME...
I'M NOT GONNA BE AROUND MUCH LONGER ANYHOW...
SO...
SORRY...
WHEN I'M DEAD...
YOU'LL SEE IT ALL FOR YOURSELF...
THERE'S STILL ONE OF THOSE SUCKERS OUT THERE...

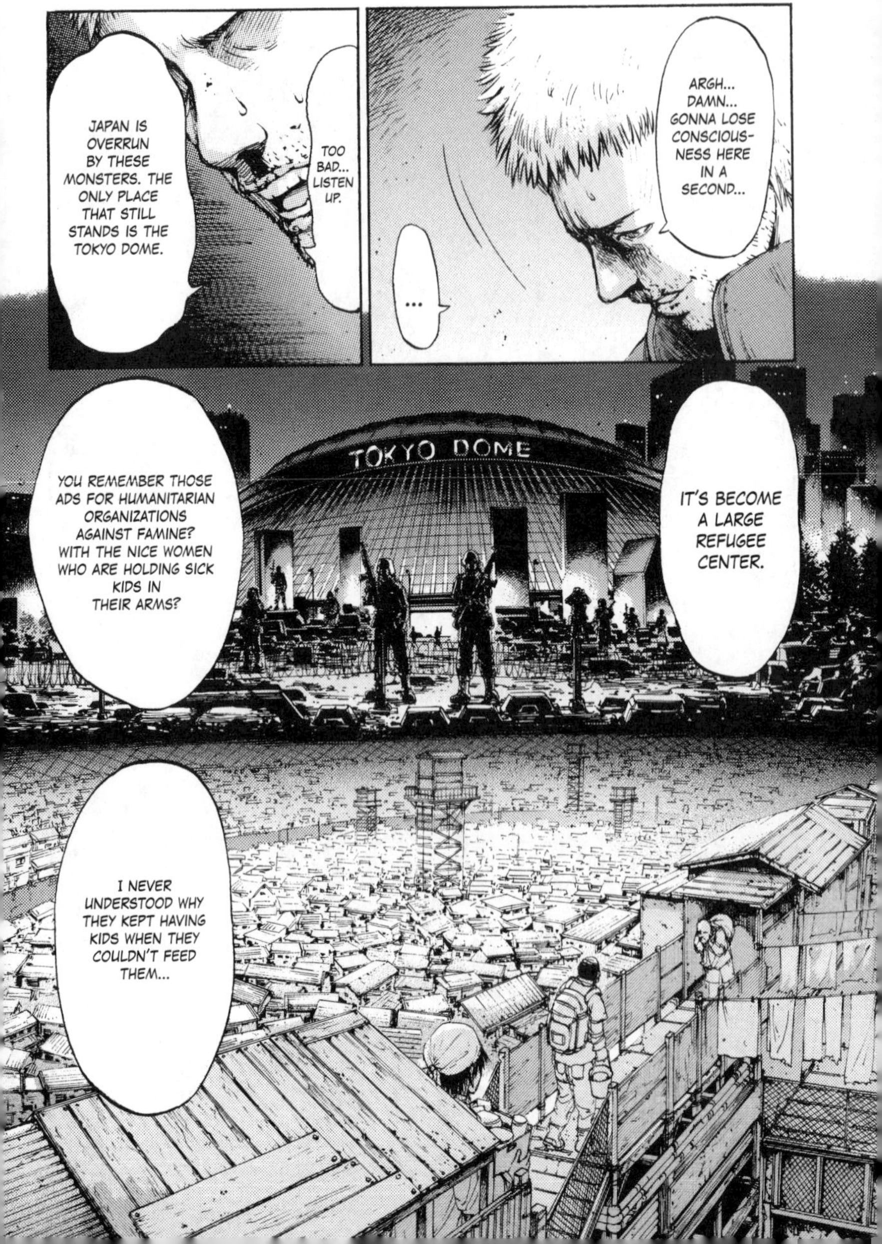
ARGH... DAMN... GONNA LOSE CONSCIOUS-NESS HERE IN A SECOND...
...
TOO BAD... LISTEN UP.
JAPAN IS OVERRUN BY THESE MONSTERS. THE ONLY PLACE THAT STILL STANDS IS THE TOKYO DOME.
TOKYO DOME
IT'S BECOME A LARGE REFUGEE CENTER.
YOU REMEMBER THOSE ADS FOR HUMANITARIAN ORGANIZATIONS AGAINST FAMINE? WITH THE NICE WOMEN WHO ARE HOLDING SICK KIDS IN THEIR ARMS?
I NEVER UNDERSTOOD WHY THEY KEPT HAVING KIDS WHEN THEY COULDN'T FEED THEM...

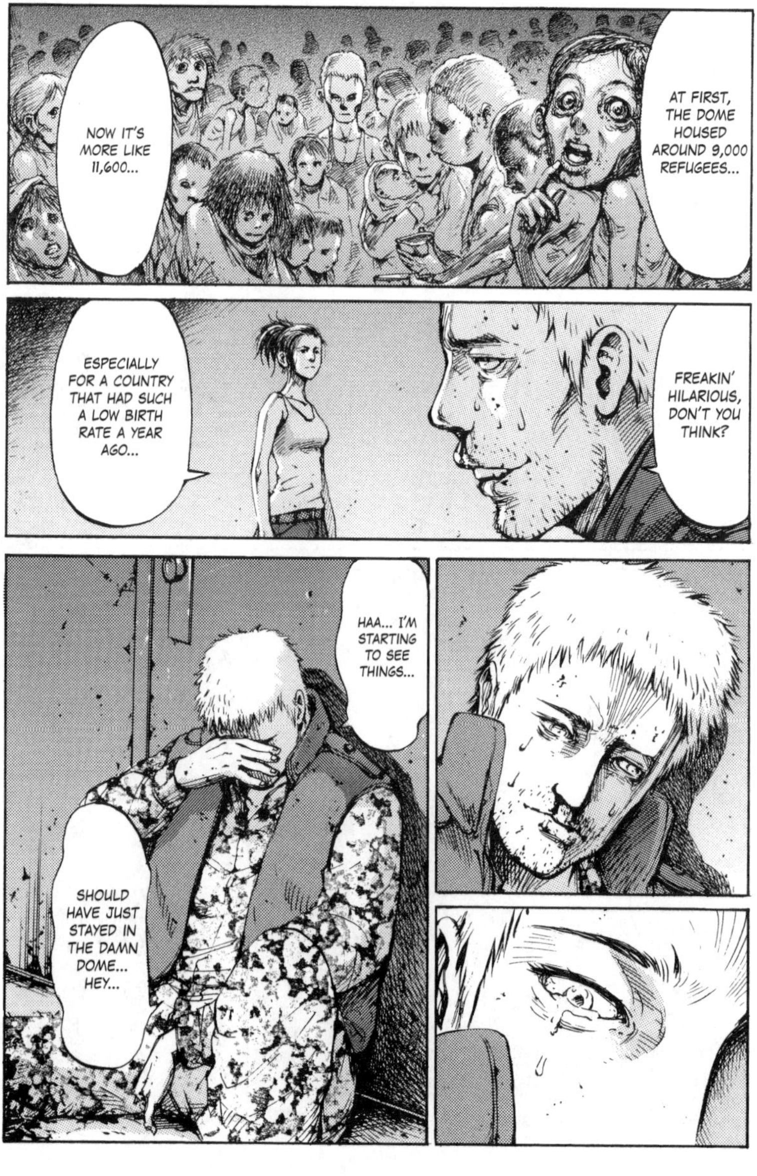
AT FIRST, THE DOME HOUSED AROUND 9,000 REFUGEES...
NOW IT'S MORE LIKE 11,600...
FREAKIN' HILARIOUS, DON'T YOU THINK?
ESPECIALLY FOR A COUNTRY THAT HAD SUCH A LOW BIRTH RATE A YEAR AGO...
HAA... I'M STARTING TO SEE THINGS...
SHOULD HAVE JUST STAYED IN THE DAMN DOME... HEY...

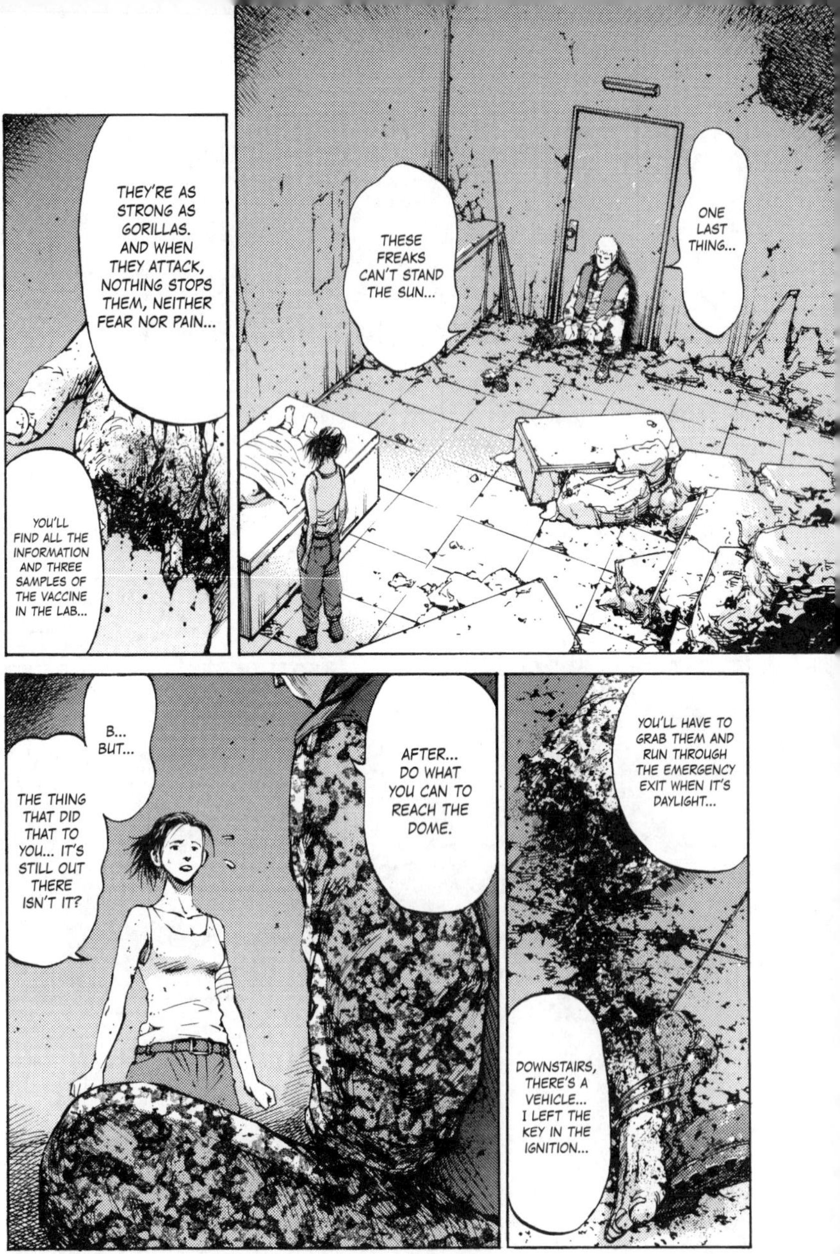
ONE LAST THING...
THESE FREAKS CAN'T STAND THE SUN...
THEY'RE AS STRONG AS GORILLAS. AND WHEN THEY ATTACK, NOTHING STOPS THEM, NEITHER FEAR NOR PAIN...
YOU'LL FIND ALL THE INFORMATION AND THREE SAMPLES OF THE VACCINE IN THE LAB...
YOU'LL HAVE TO GRAB THEM AND RUN THROUGH THE EMERGENCY EXIT WHEN IT'S DAYLIGHT...
DOWNSTAIRS, THERE'S A VEHICLE... I LEFT THE KEY IN THE IGNITION...
AFTER... DO WHAT YOU CAN TO REACH THE DOME.
B... BUT...
THE THING THAT DID THAT TO YOU... IT'S STILL OUT THERE ISN'T IT?

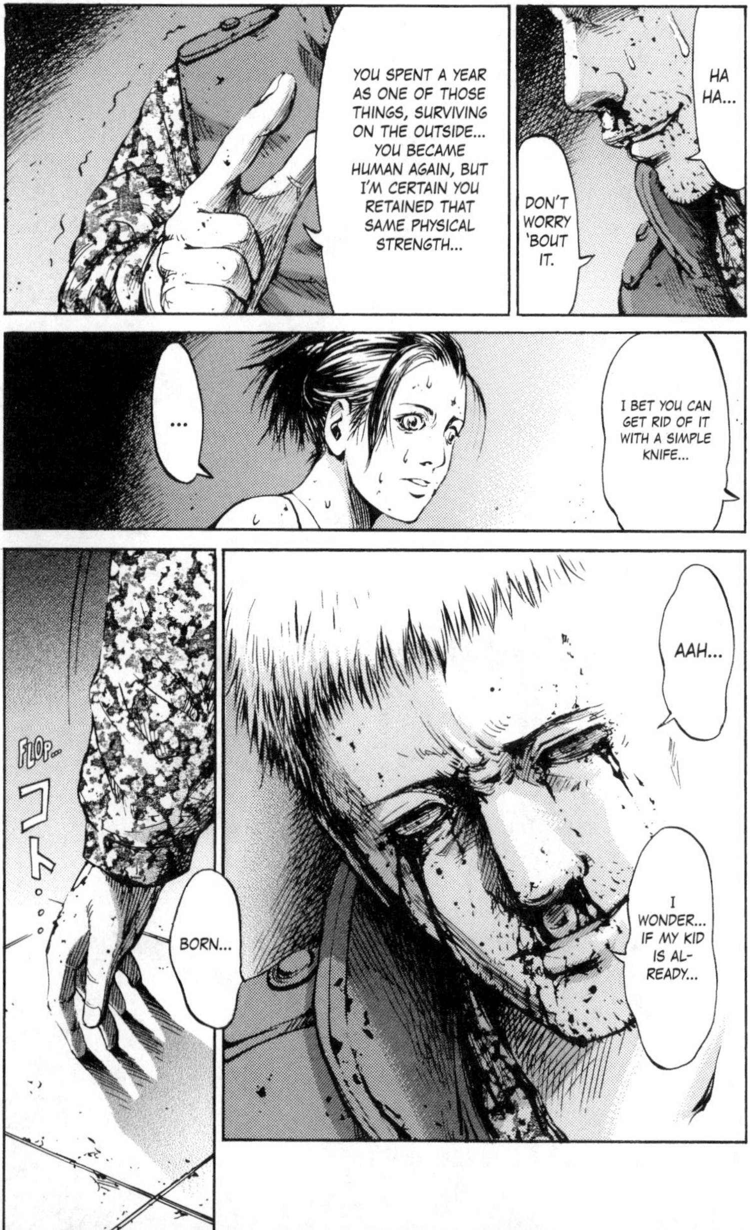
HA HA...
DON'T WORRY 'BOUT IT.
YOU SPENT A YEAR AS ONE OF THOSE THINGS, SURVIVING ON THE OUTSIDE... YOU BECAME HUMAN AGAIN, BUT I'M CERTAIN YOU RETAINED THAT SAME PHYSICAL STRENGTH...
I BET YOU CAN GET RID OF IT WITH A SIMPLE KNIFE...
...
AAH...
I WONDER... IF MY KID IS AL-READY...
BORN...
FLOP...
コト...

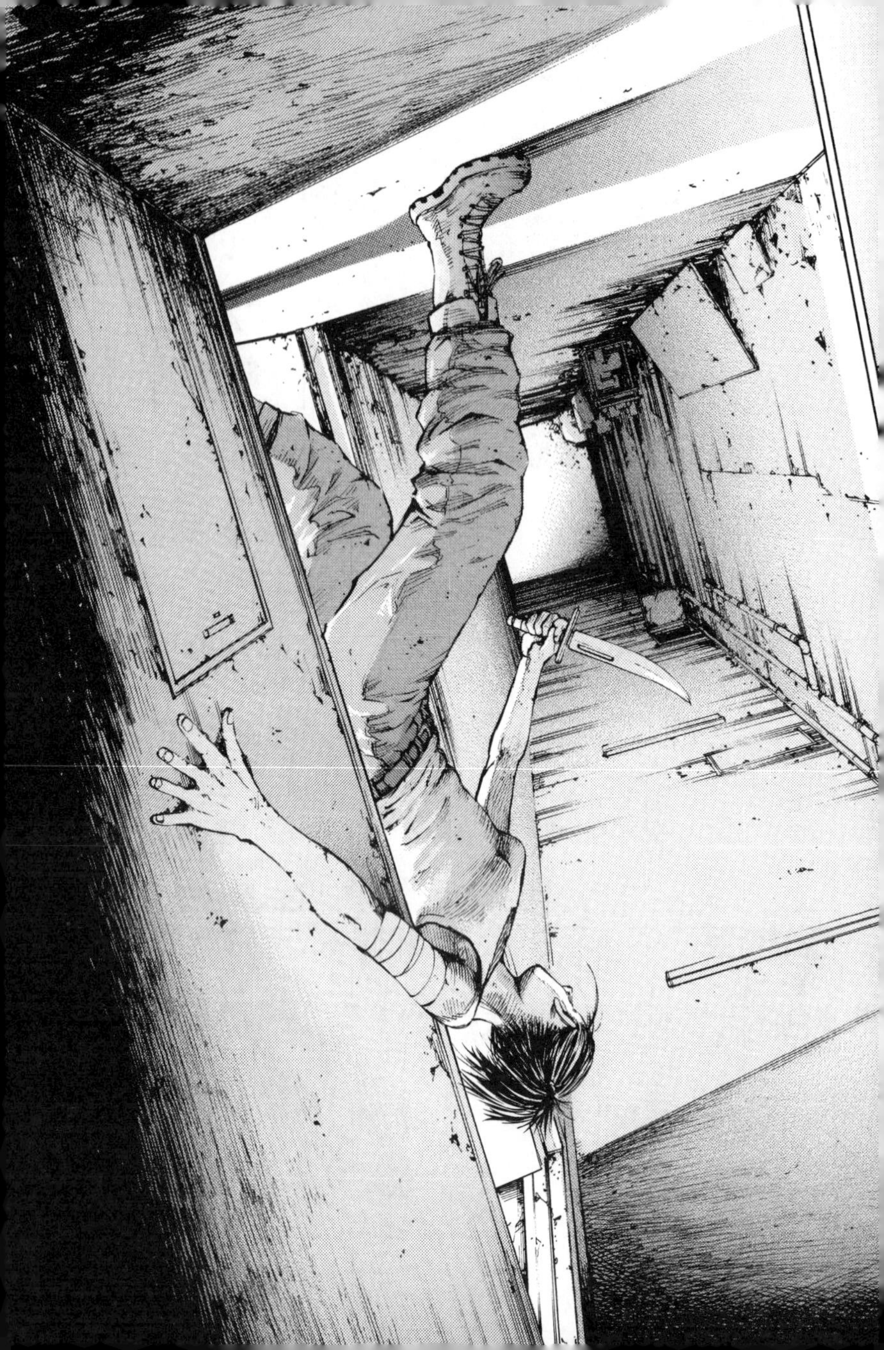

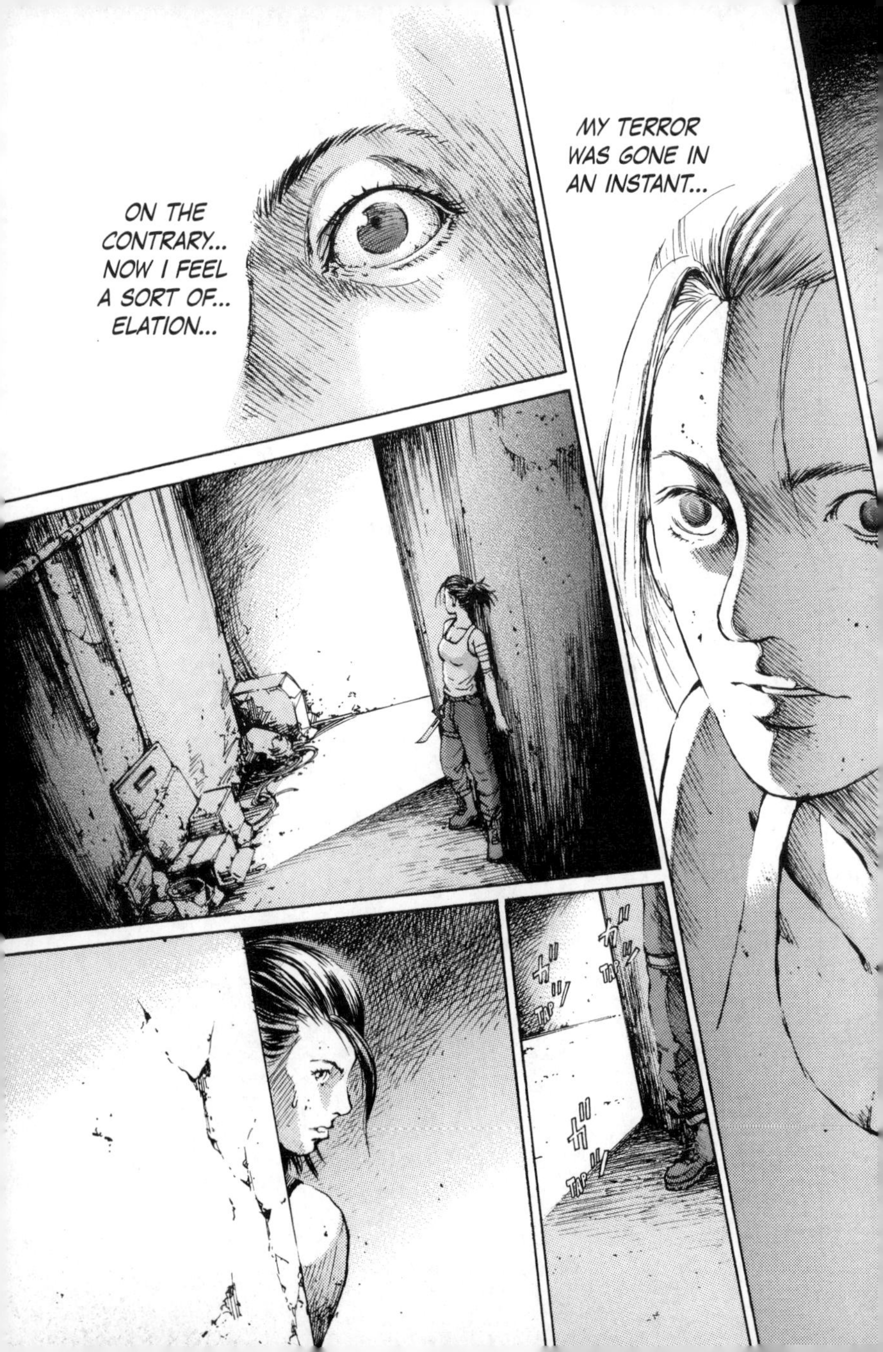
MY TERROR WAS GONE IN AN INSTANT...
ON THE CONTRARY... NOW I FEEL A SORT OF... ELATION...
TAP
TAP
TAP
TAP

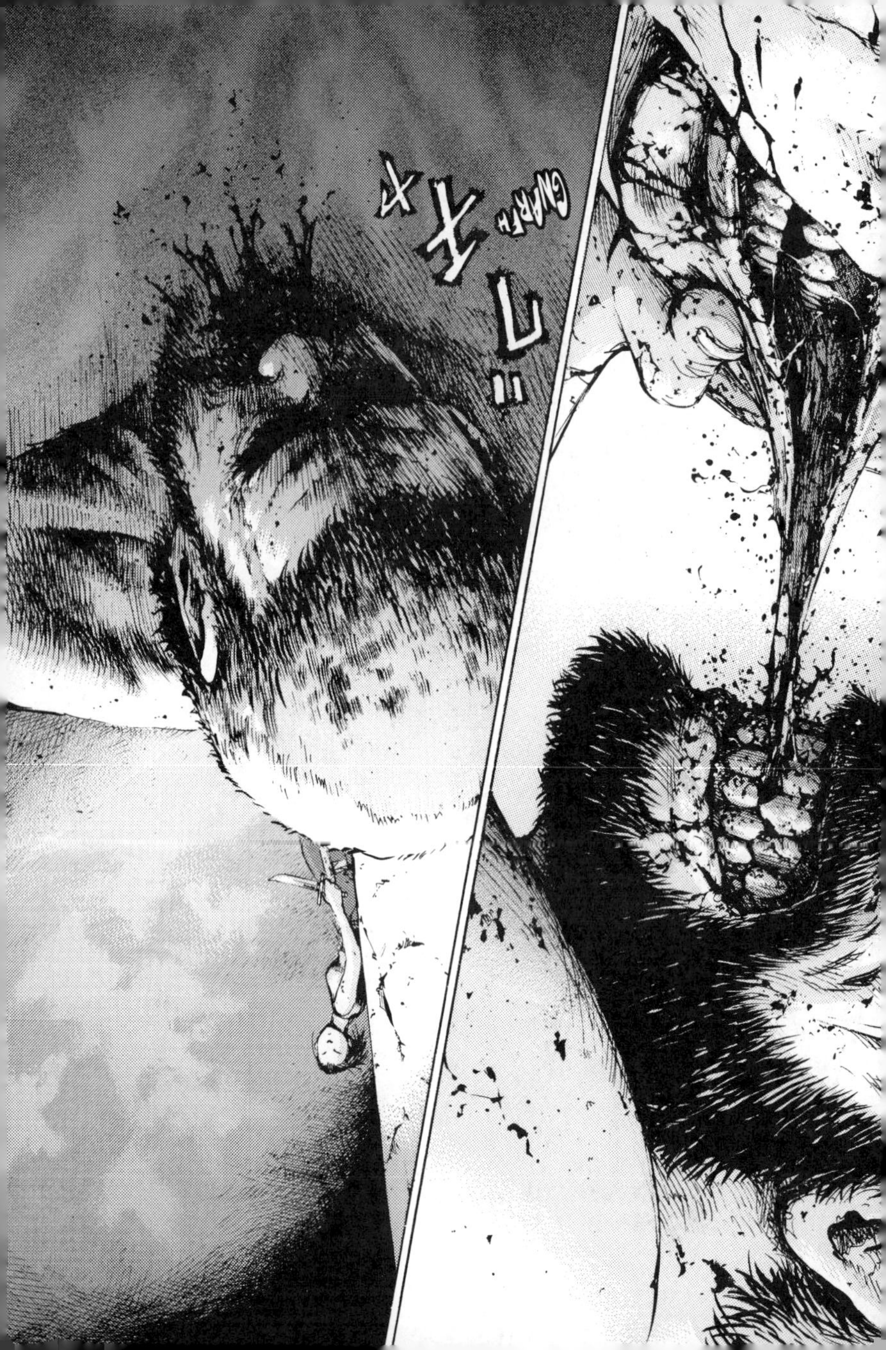
GNARTH

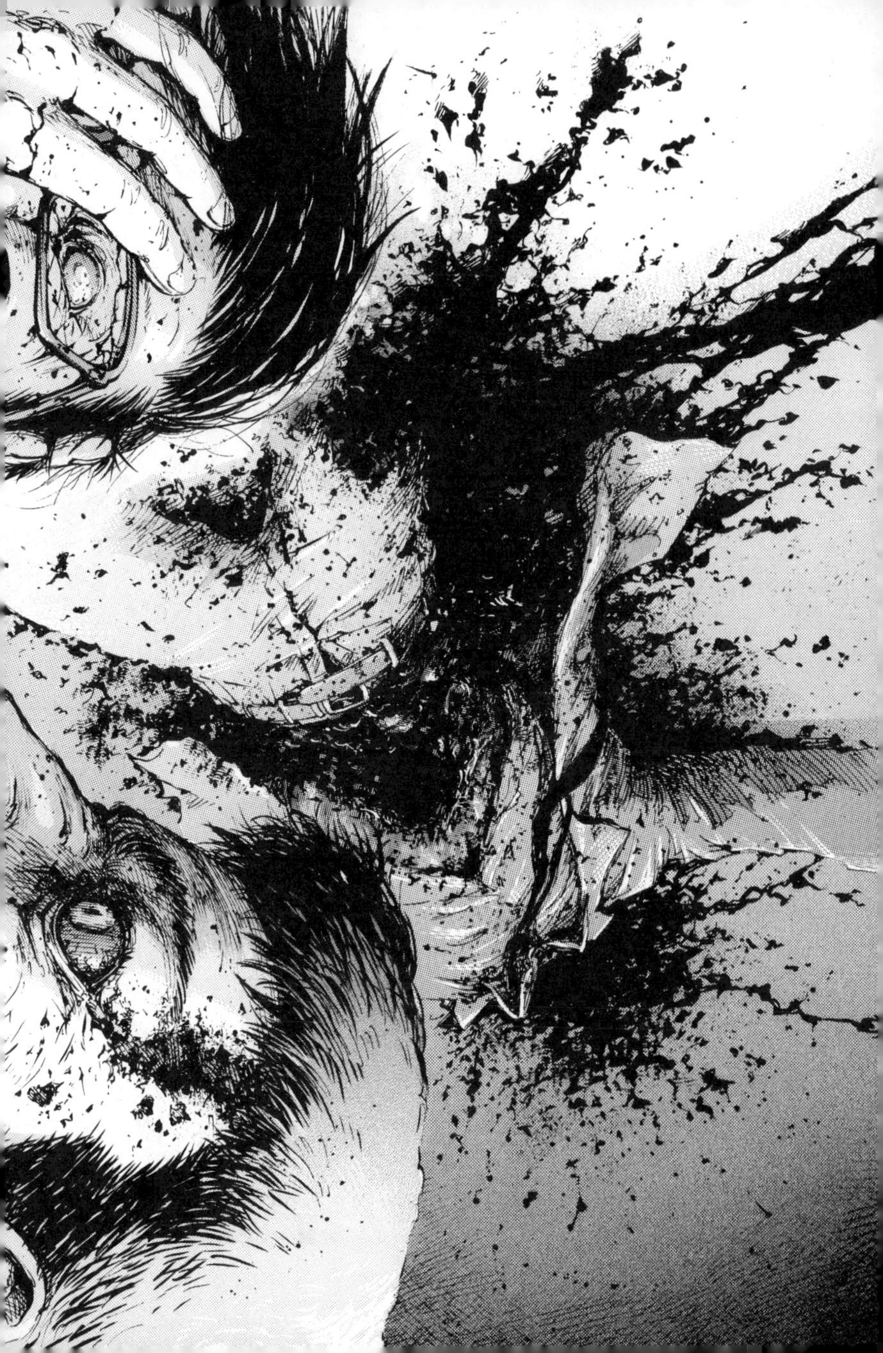

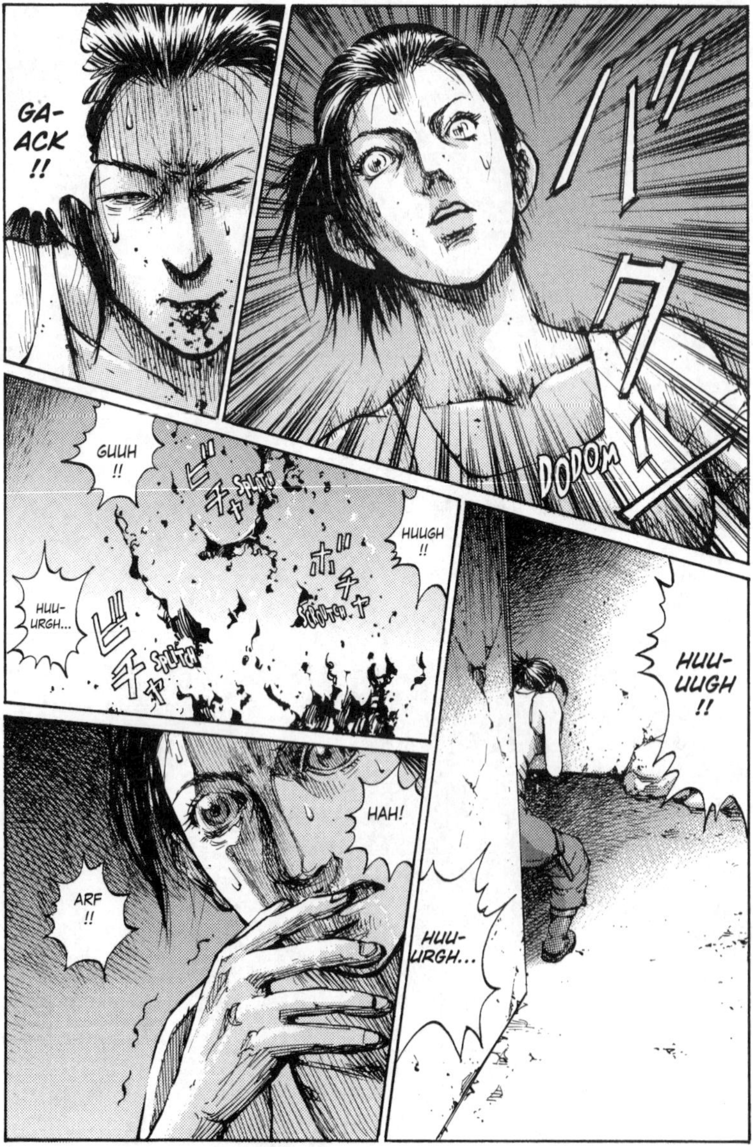
DODOM
GA-ACK!!
HUU-UUGH!!
HUU-URGH...
HUUGH!!
ボチャ SCHLUTCH
GUUH!!
ビチャ SPLTCH
ビチャ SPLTCH
HUU-URGH...
HAH!
ARF!!

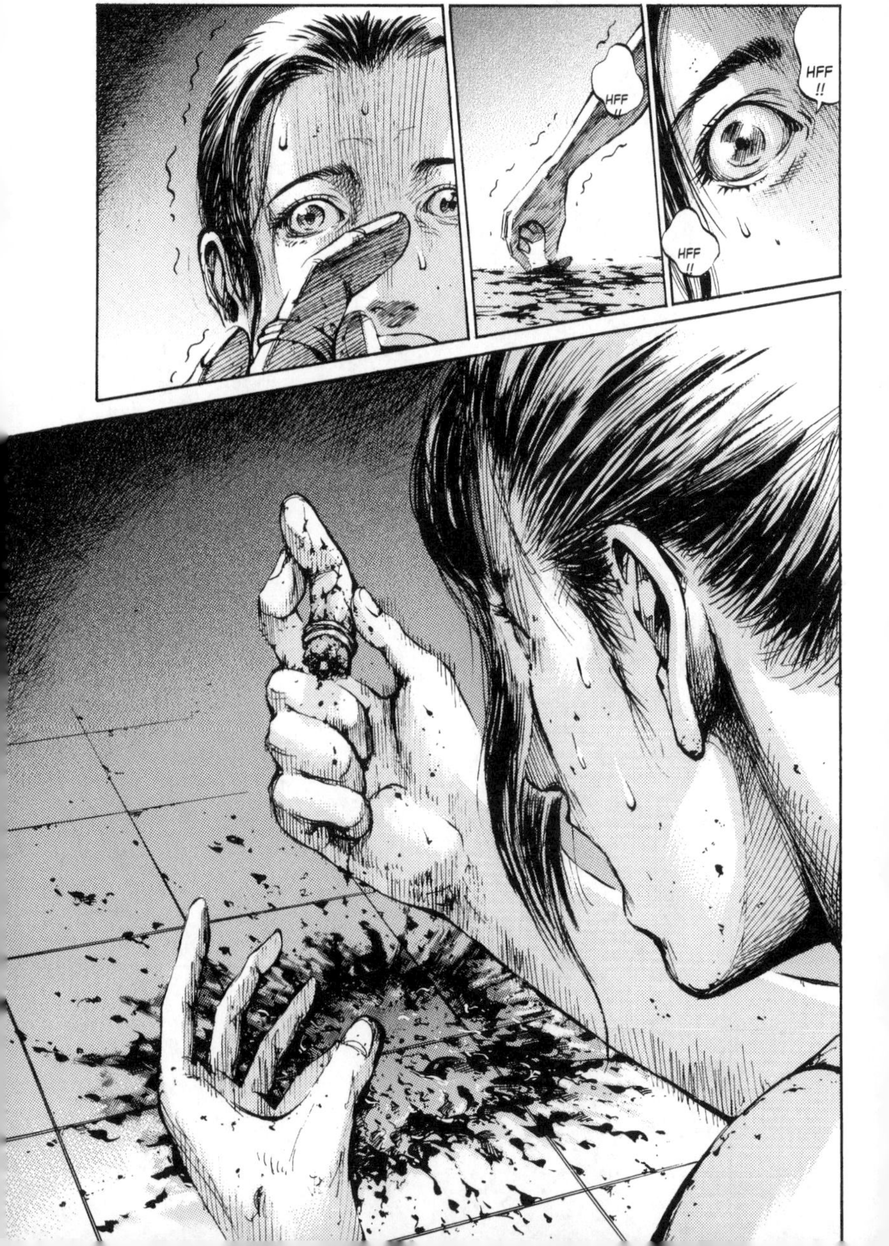
HFF !!
HFF !!
HFF !!

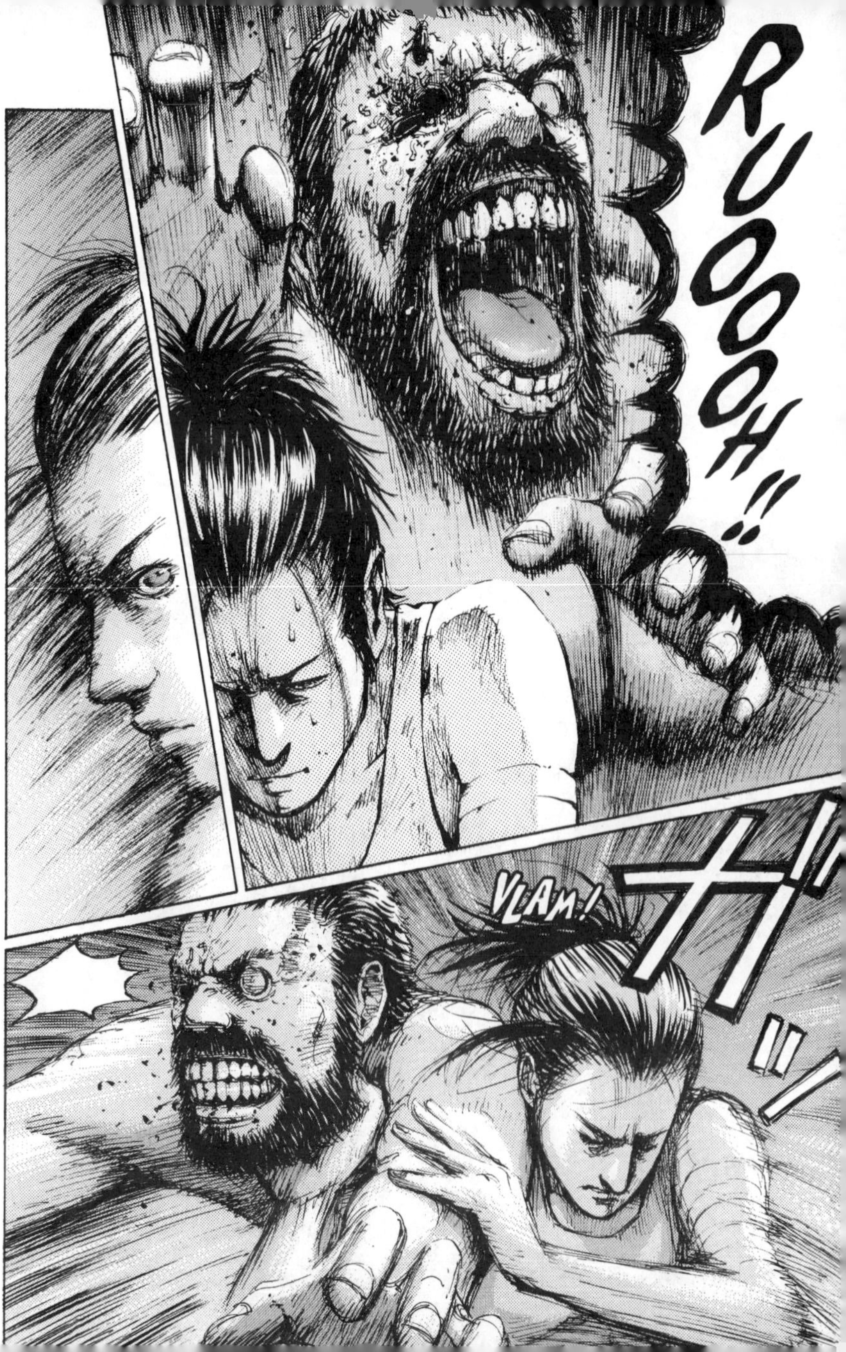
RUOOOOH!!
VLAM!

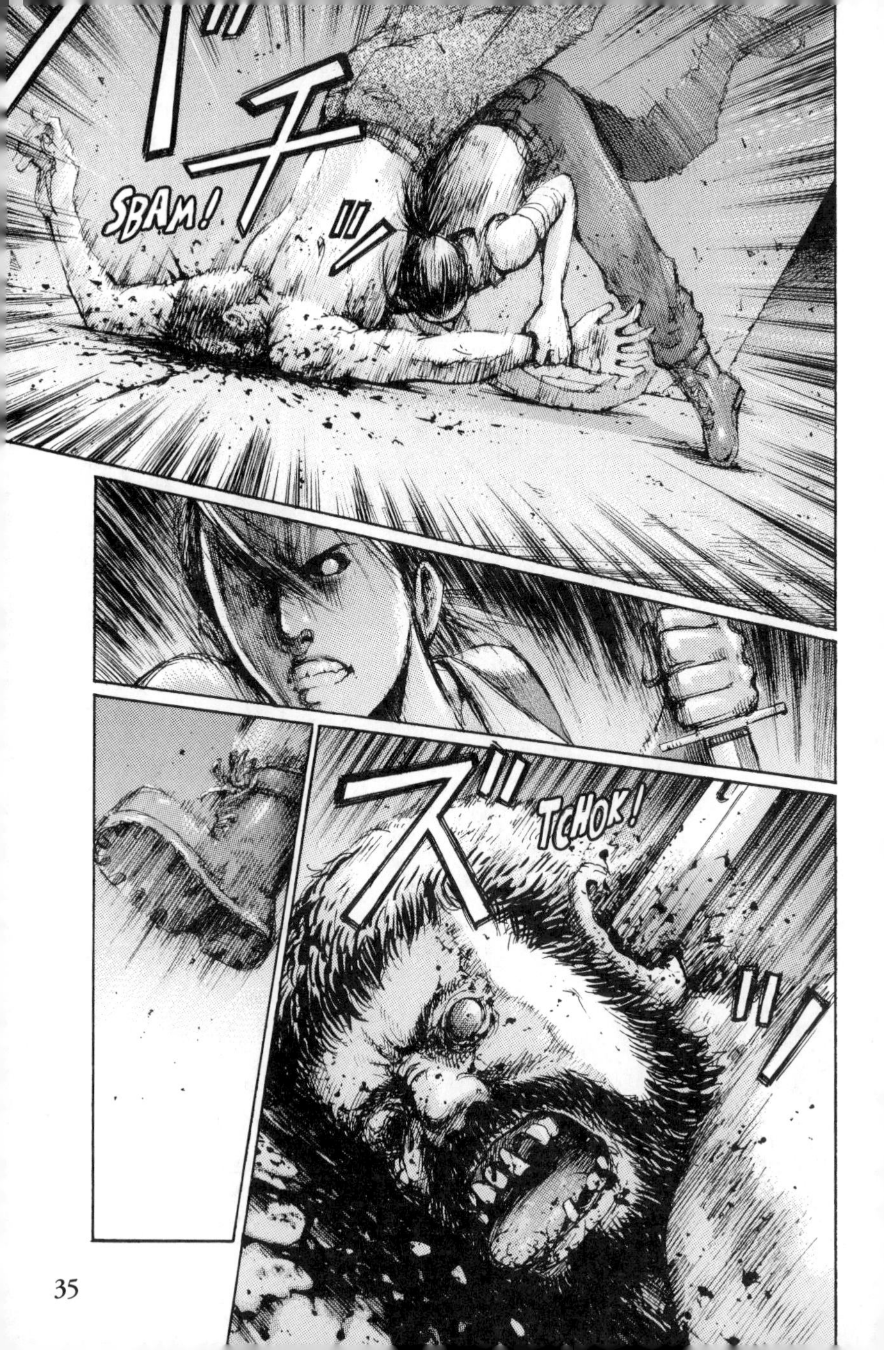
SBAM!
TCHOK!

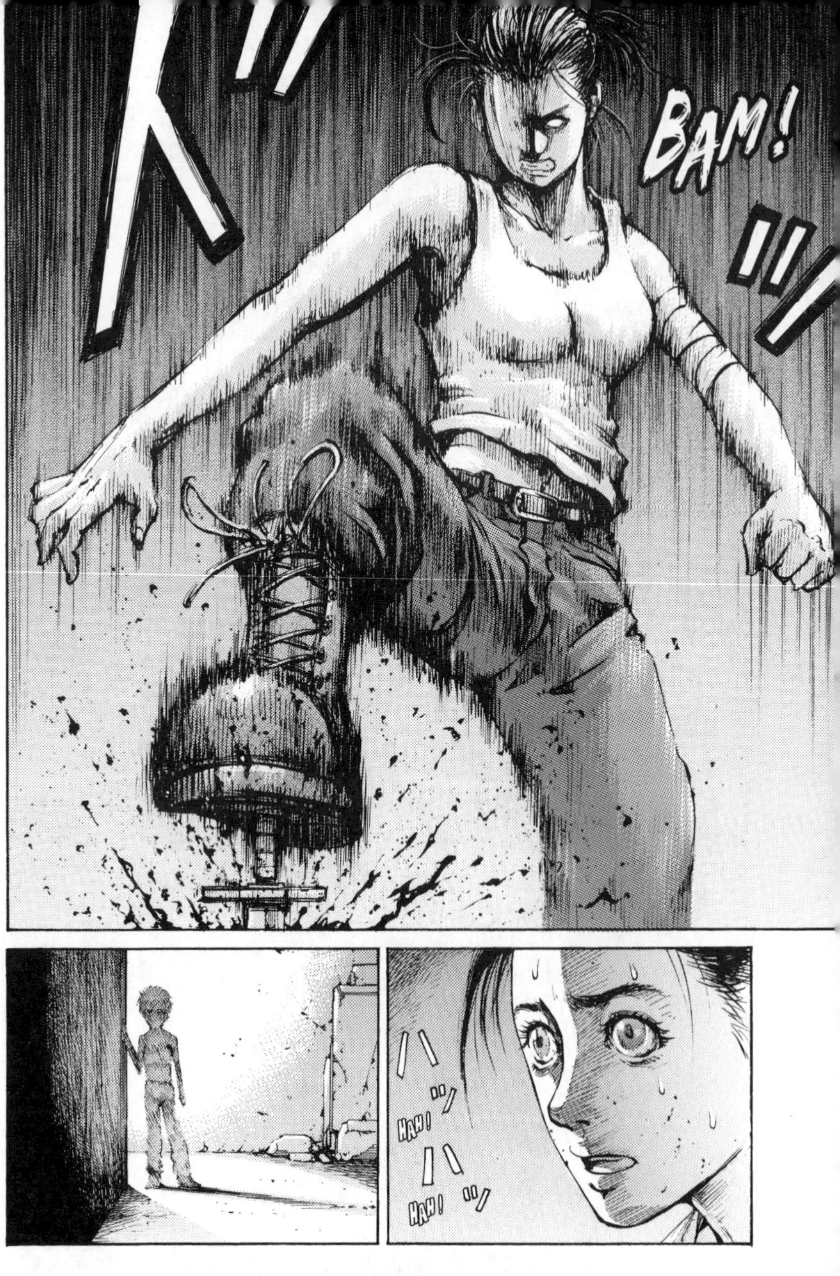
BAM!
HAH!
HAH!

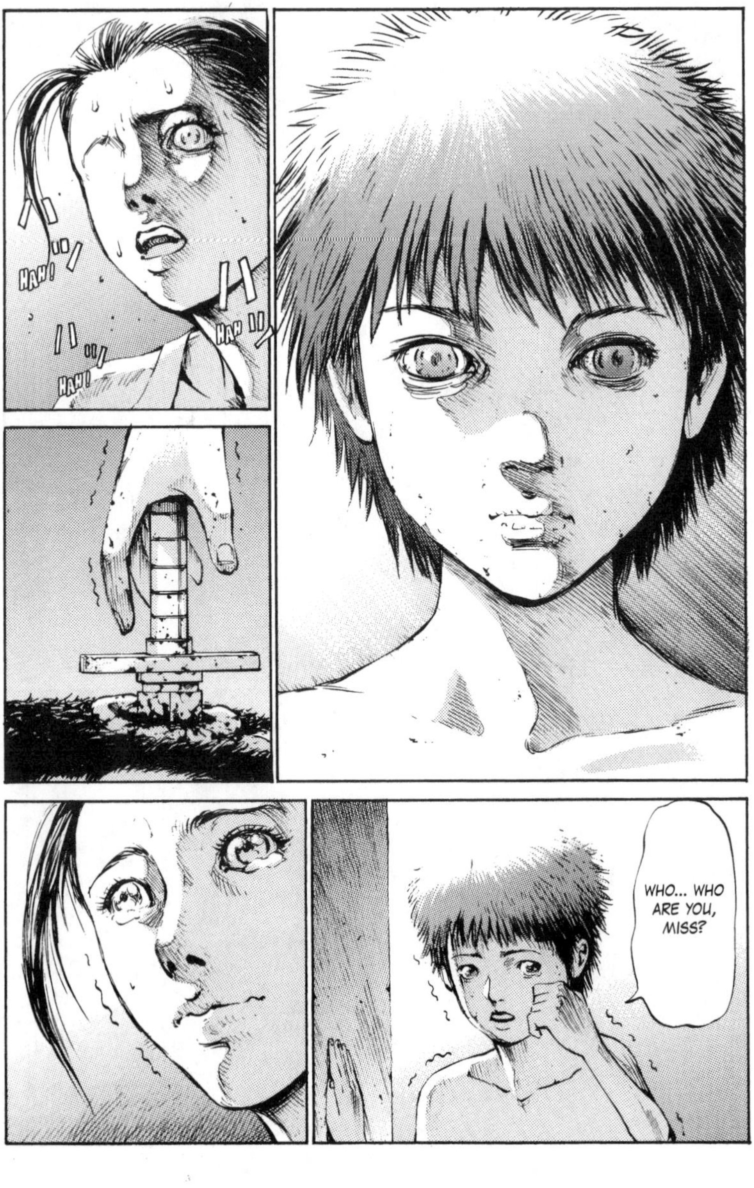

HAH!
HAH !!
HAH!
WHO... WHO ARE YOU, MISS?

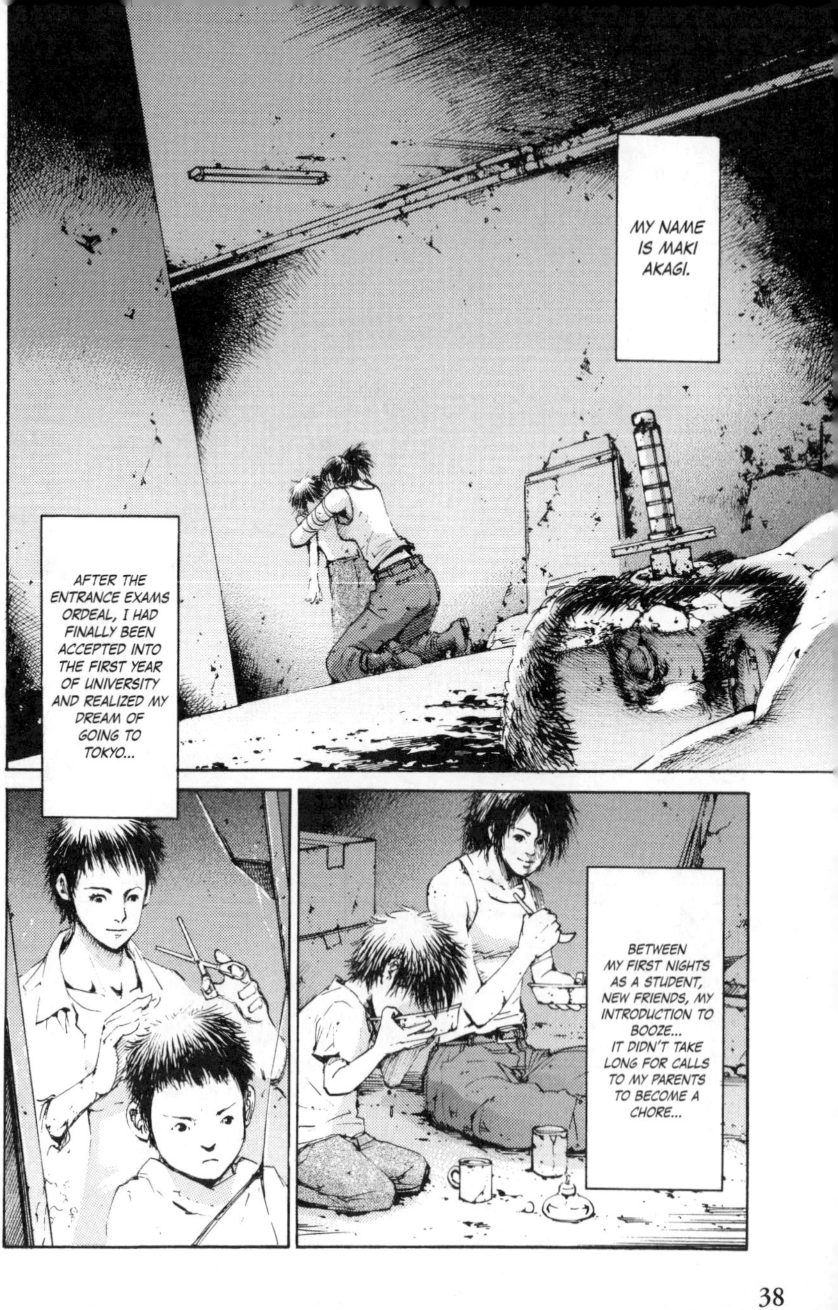
MY NAME IS MAKI AKAGI.
AFTER THE ENTRANCE EXAMS ORDEAL, I HAD FINALLY BEEN ACCEPTED INTO THE FIRST YEAR OF UNIVERSITY AND REALIZED MY DREAM OF GOING TO TOKYO...
BETWEEN MY FIRST NIGHTS AS A STUDENT, NEW FRIENDS, MY INTRODUCTION TO BOOZE... IT DIDN'T TAKE LONG FOR CALLS TO MY PARENTS TO BECOME A CHORE...

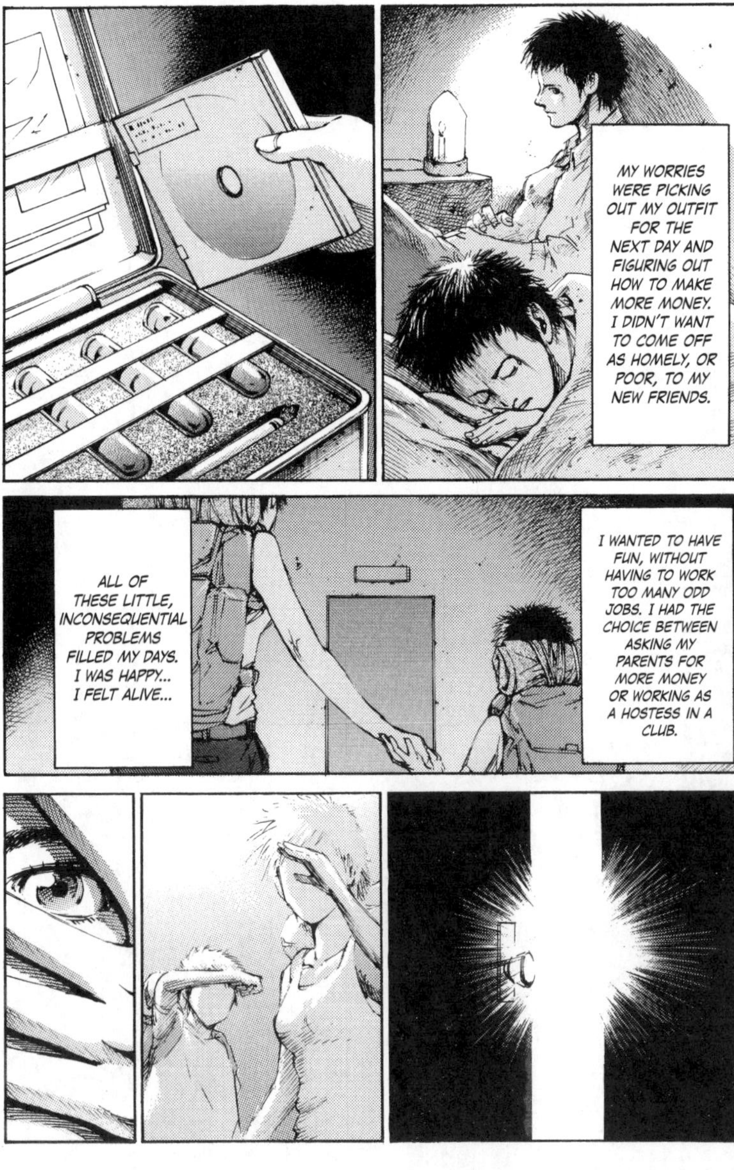
MY WORRIES WERE PICKING OUT MY OUTFIT FOR THE NEXT DAY AND FIGURING OUT HOW TO MAKE MORE MONEY. I DIDN'T WANT TO COME OFF AS HOMELY, OR POOR, TO MY NEW FRIENDS.
I WANTED TO HAVE FUN, WITHOUT HAVING TO WORK TOO MANY ODD JOBS. I HAD THE CHOICE BETWEEN ASKING MY PARENTS FOR MORE MONEY OR WORKING AS A HOSTESS IN A CLUB.
ALL OF THESE LITTLE, INCONSEQUENTIAL PROBLEMS FILLED MY DAYS. I WAS HAPPY... I FELT ALIVE...

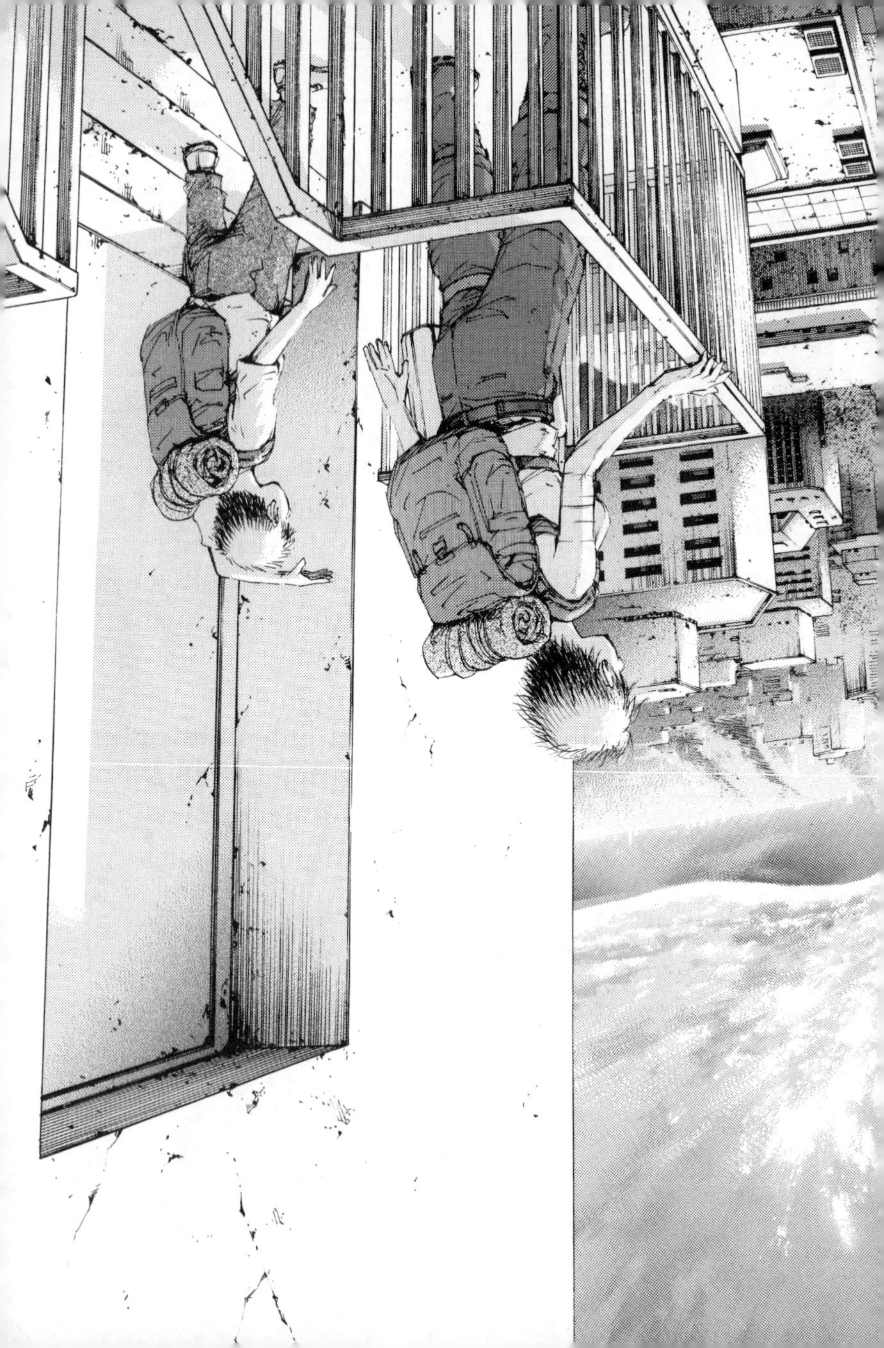

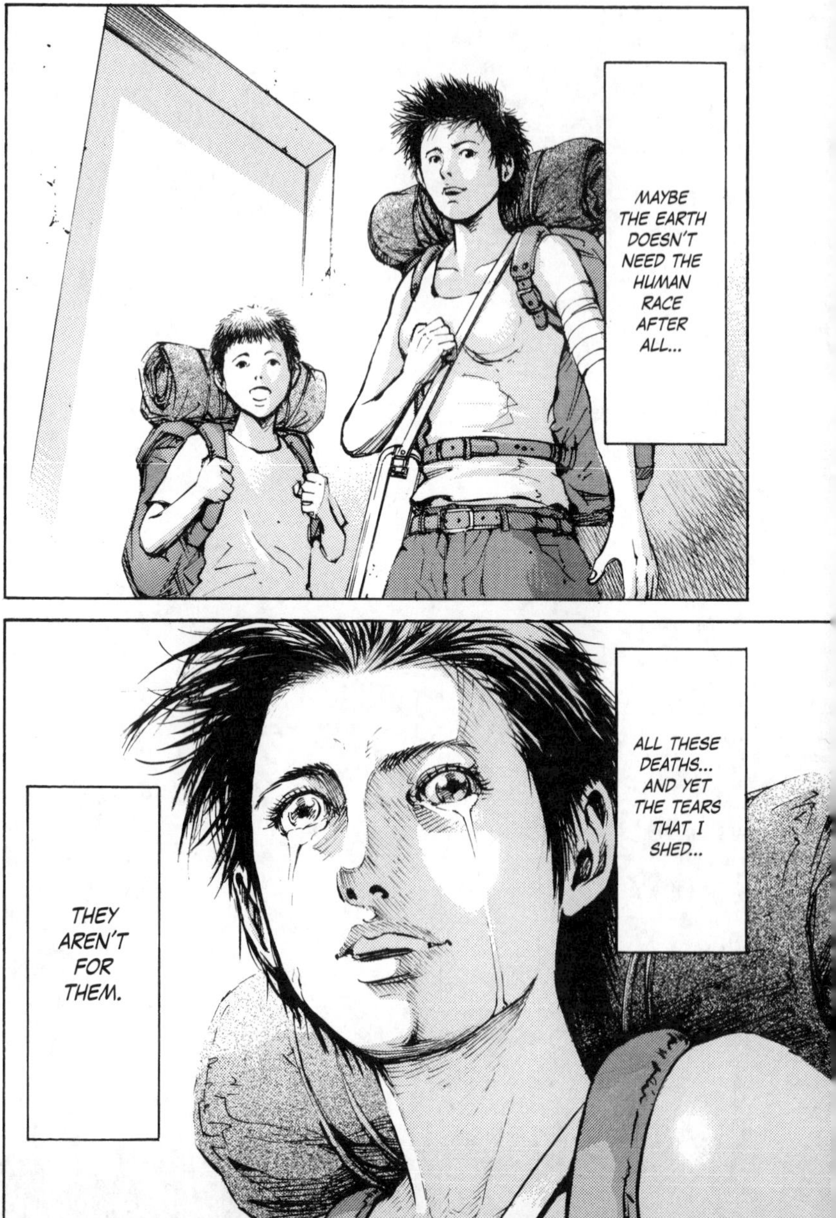
MAYBE THE EARTH DOESN'T NEED THE HUMAN RACE AFTER ALL...
ALL THESE DEATHS... AND YET THE TEARS THAT I SHED...
THEY AREN'T FOR THEM.

CHAPTER-2

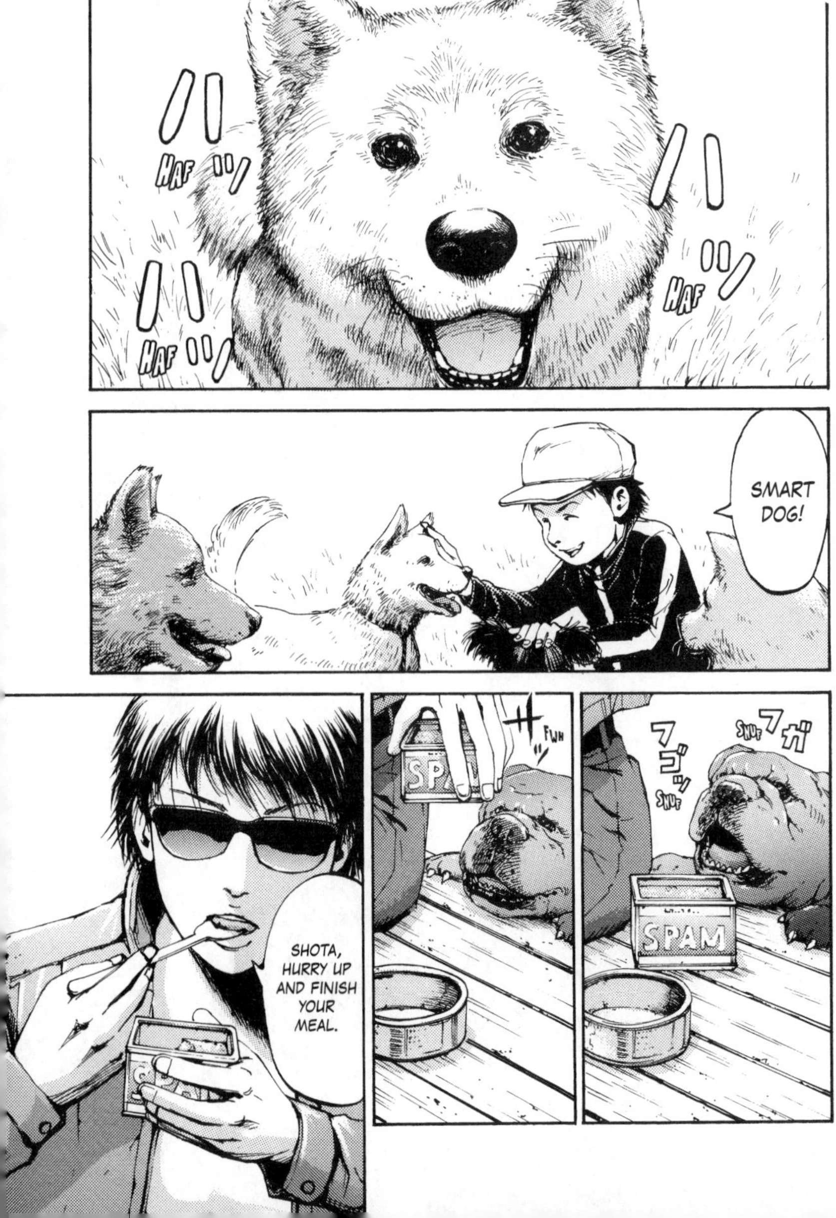

HAF
HAF
HAF
SMART DOG!
SNUF フガ
フゴッ SNUF
FWH
SHOTA, HURRY UP AND FINISH YOUR MEAL.
SPAM

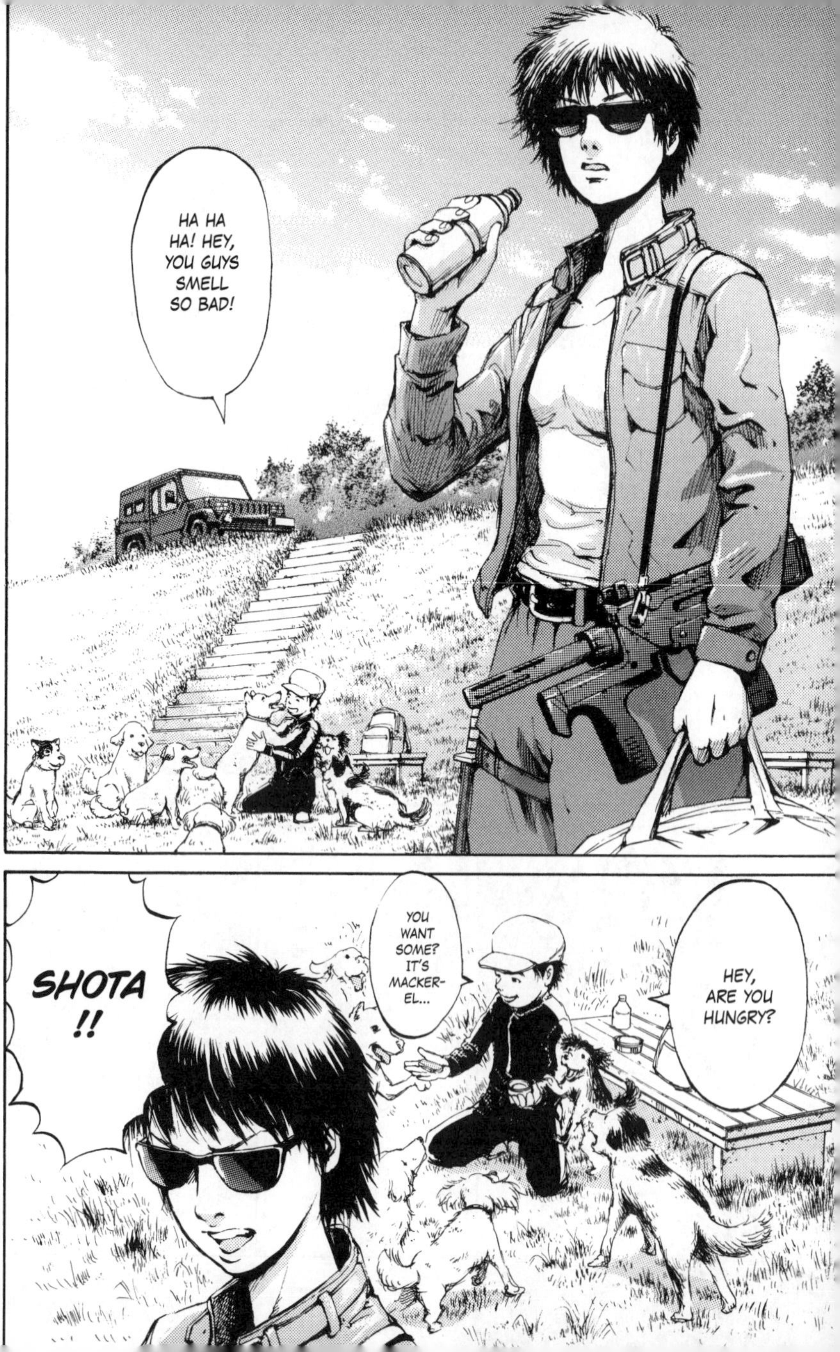
HA HA HA! HEY, YOU GUYS SMELL SO BAD!
HEY, ARE YOU HUNGRY?
YOU WANT SOME? IT'S MACKER-EL...
SHOTA !!

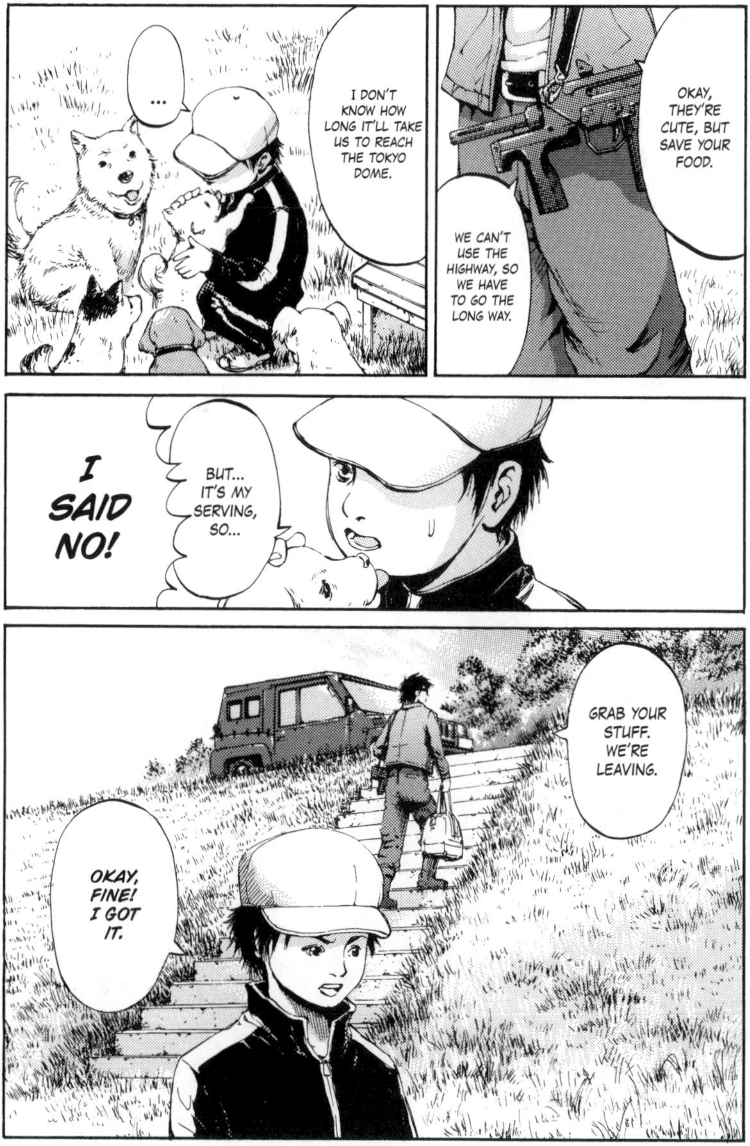
OKAY, THEY'RE CUTE, BUT SAVE YOUR FOOD.
WE CAN'T USE THE HIGHWAY, SO WE HAVE TO GO THE LONG WAY.
I DON'T KNOW HOW LONG IT'LL TAKE US TO REACH THE TOKYO DOME.
...
BUT... IT'S MY SERVING, SO...
I SAID NO!
GRAB YOUR STUFF. WE'RE LEAVING.
OKAY, FINE! I GOT IT.

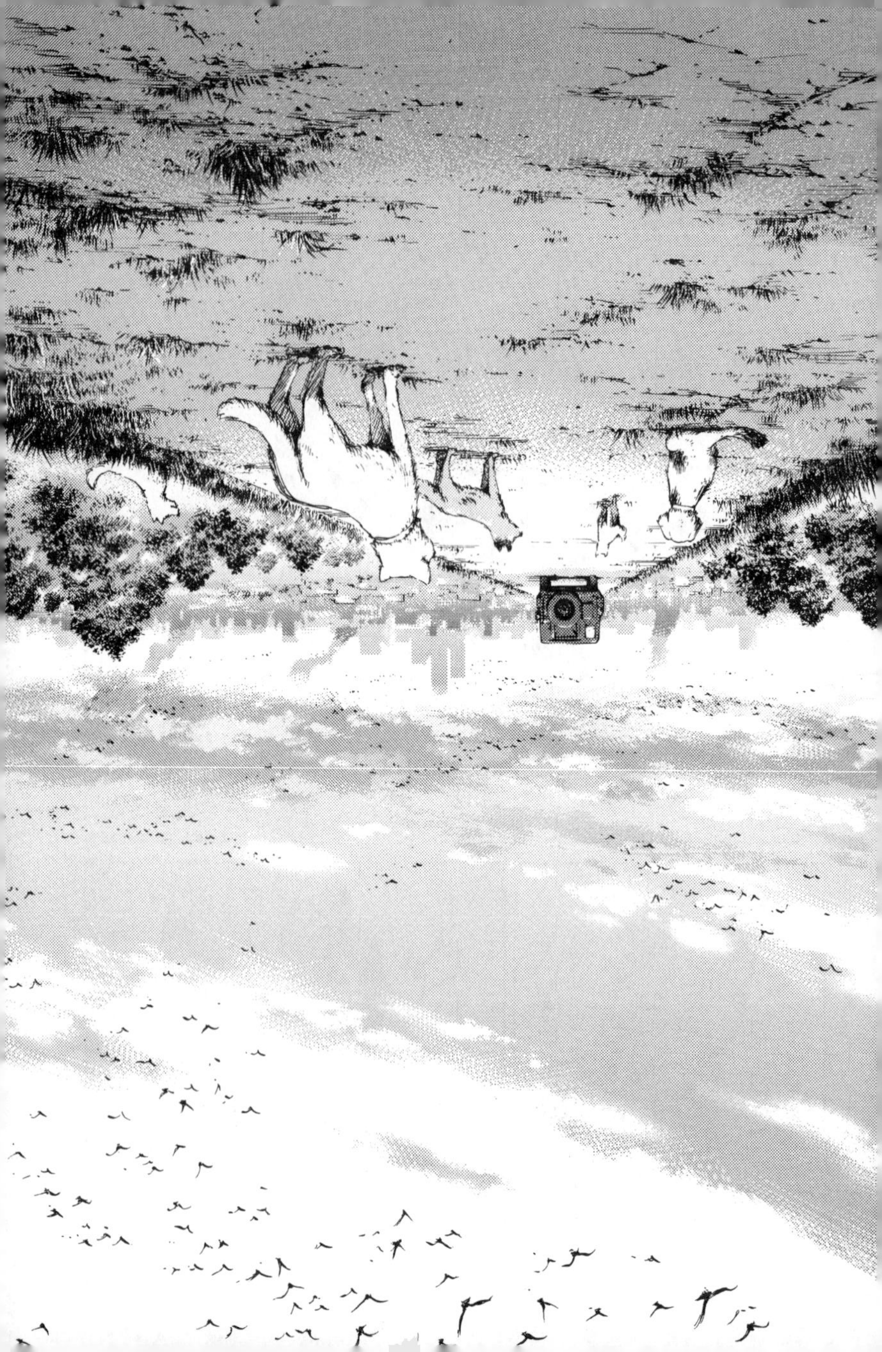

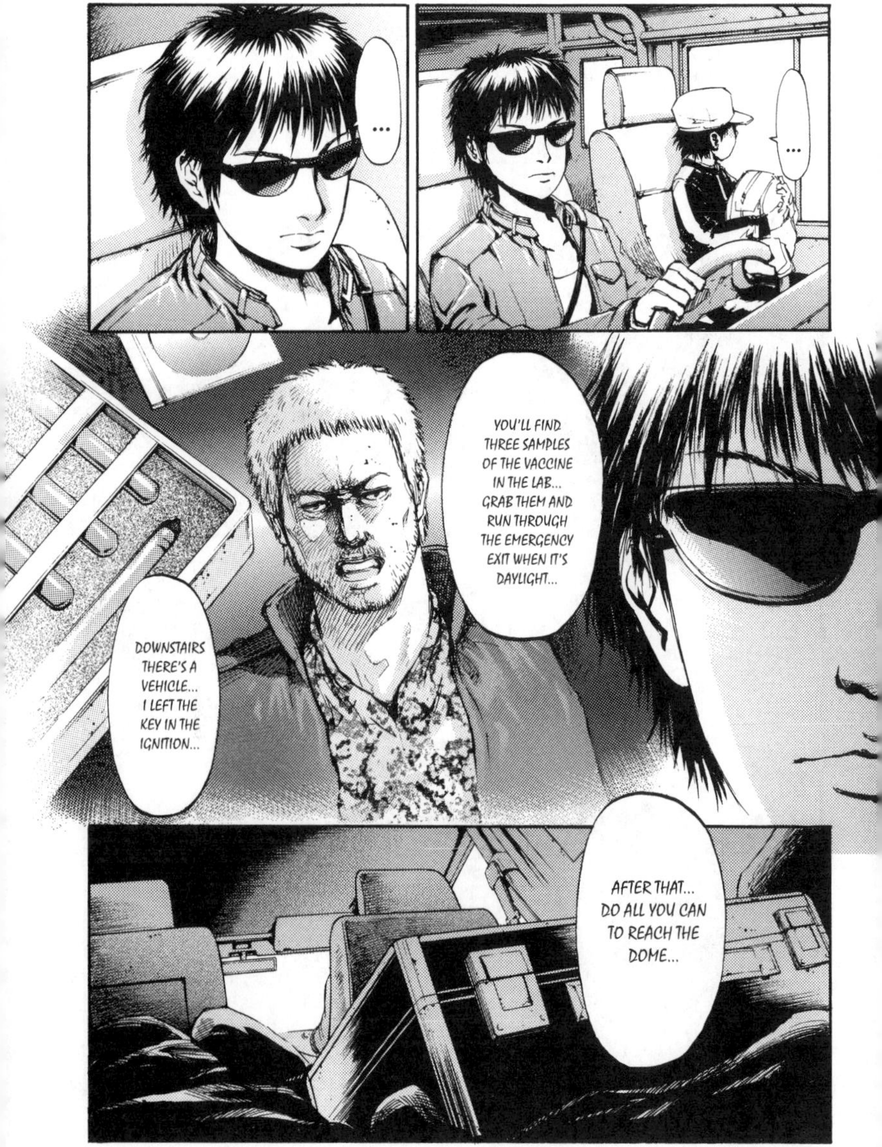
...
...
YOU'LL FIND THREE SAMPLES OF THE VACCINE IN THE LAB... GRAB THEM AND RUN THROUGH THE EMERGENCY EXIT WHEN IT'S DAYLIGHT...
DOWNSTAIRS THERE'S A VEHICLE... I LEFT THE KEY IN THE IGNITION...
AFTER THAT... DO ALL YOU CAN TO REACH THE DOME...

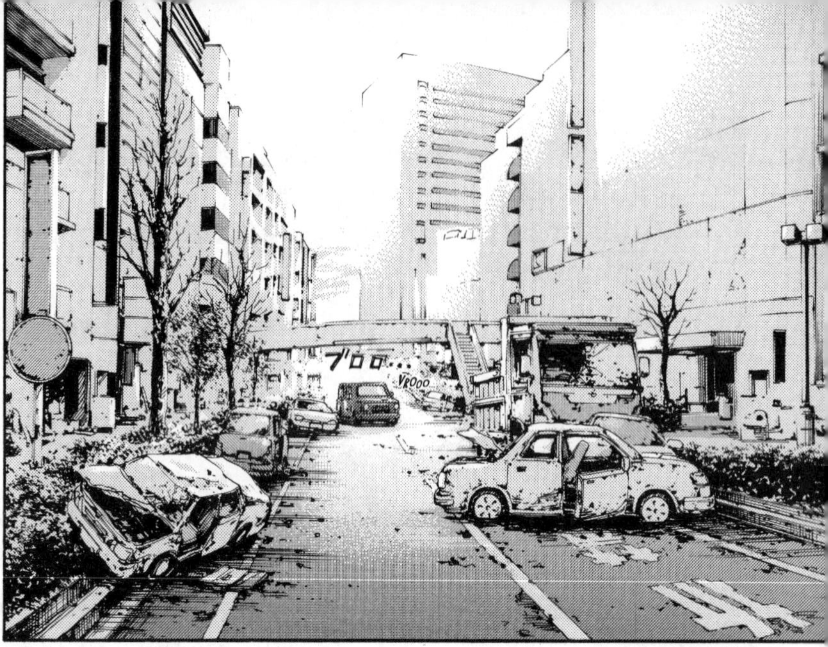
ブロロ…
VROOO

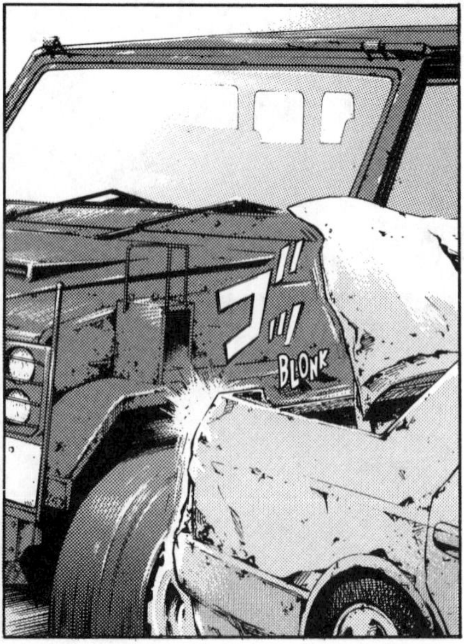
ゴッ
BLONK

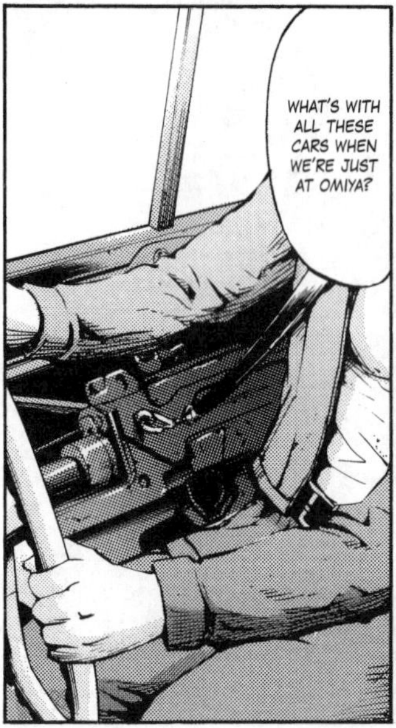
WHAT'S WITH ALL THESE CARS WHEN WE'RE JUST AT OMIYA?

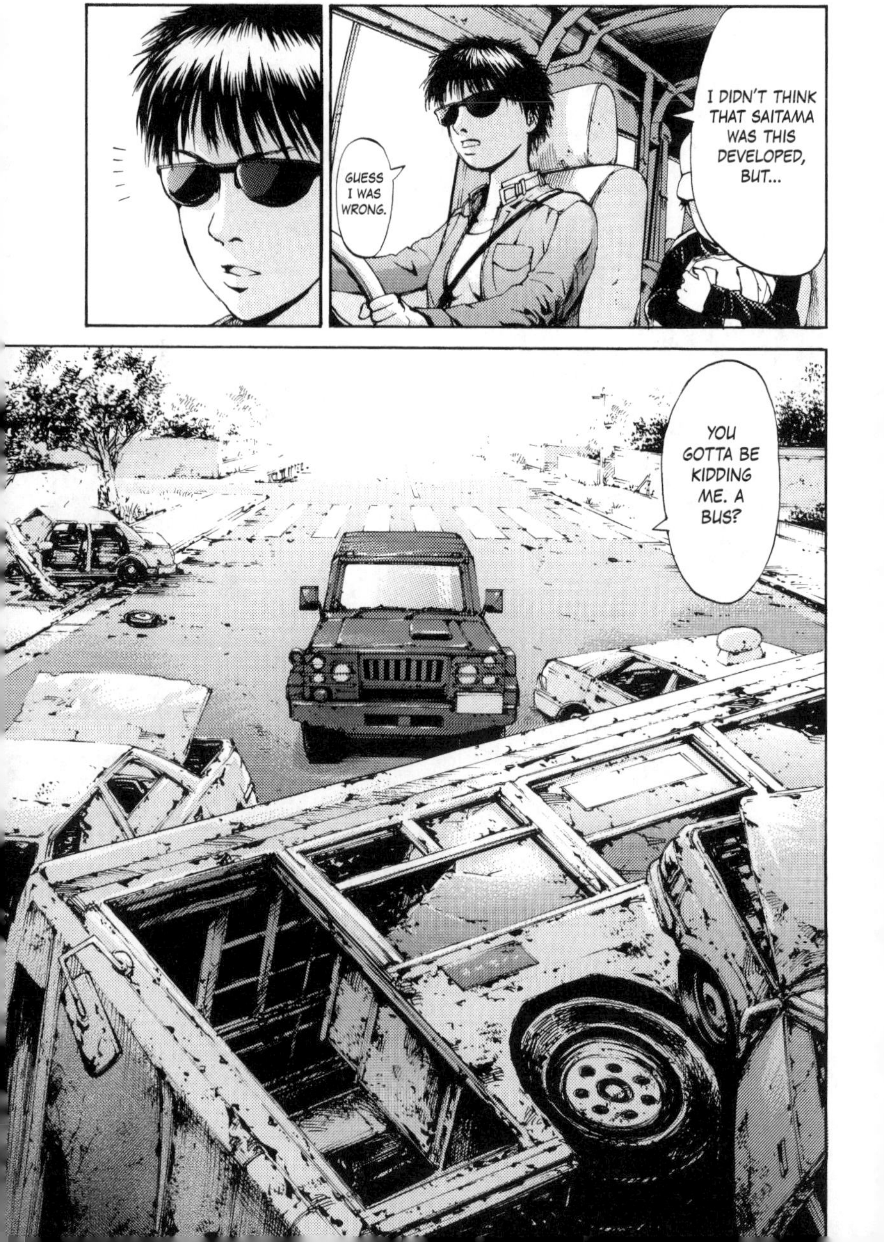
I DIDN'T THINK THAT SAITAMA WAS THIS DEVELOPED, BUT...
GUESS I WAS WRONG.
YOU GOTTA BE KIDDING ME. A BUS?

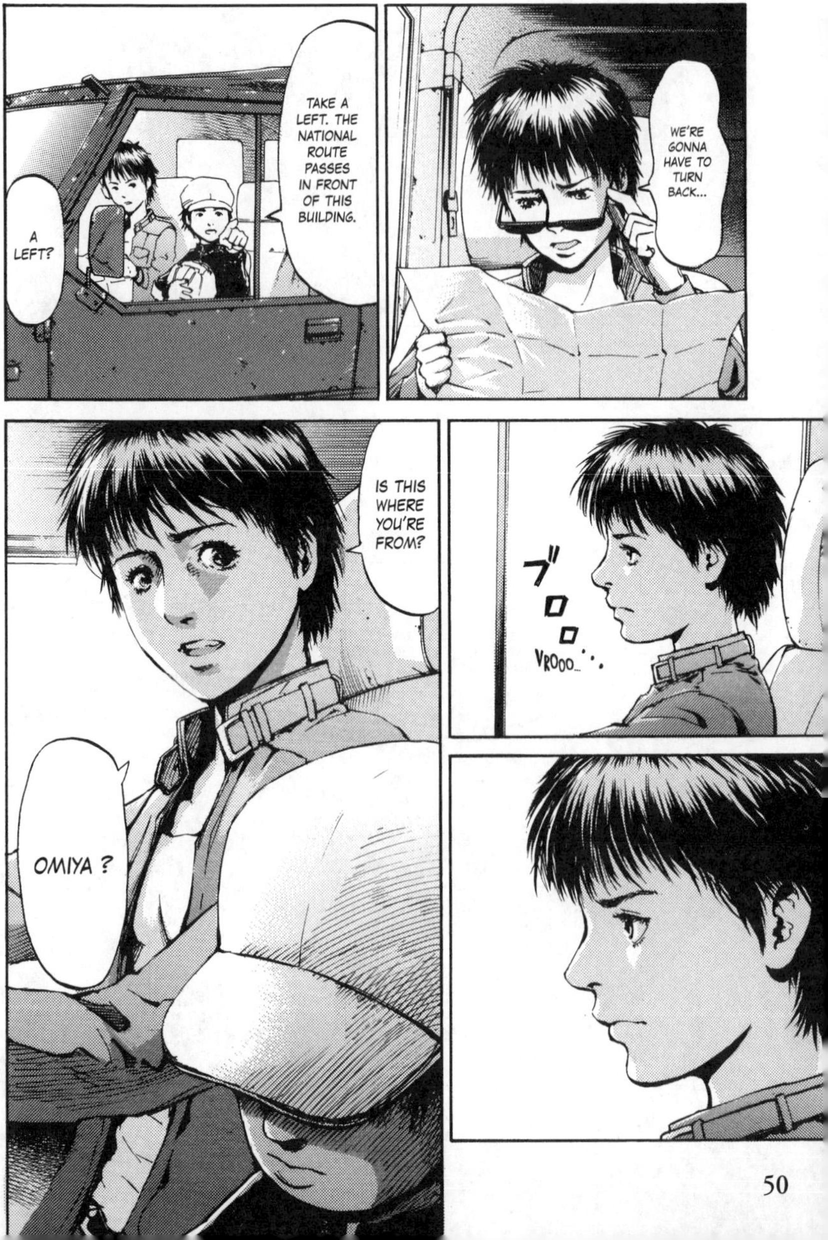
WE'RE GONNA HAVE TO TURN BACK...
TAKE A LEFT. THE NATIONAL ROUTE PASSES IN FRONT OF THIS BUILDING.
A LEFT?
ブロロ
VROOO...
IS THIS WHERE YOU'RE FROM?
OMIYA ?

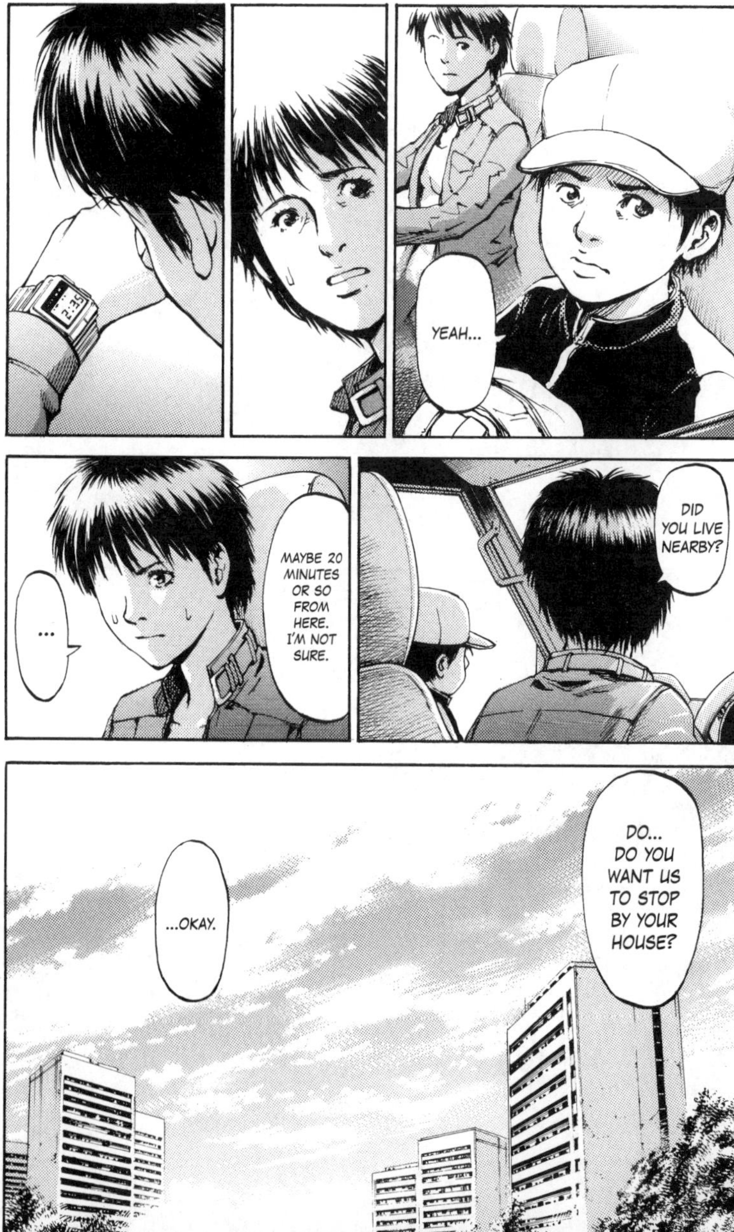
YEAH...
DID YOU LIVE NEARBY?
MAYBE 20 MINUTES OR SO FROM HERE. I'M NOT SURE.
...
DO... DO YOU WANT US TO STOP BY YOUR HOUSE?
...OKAY.

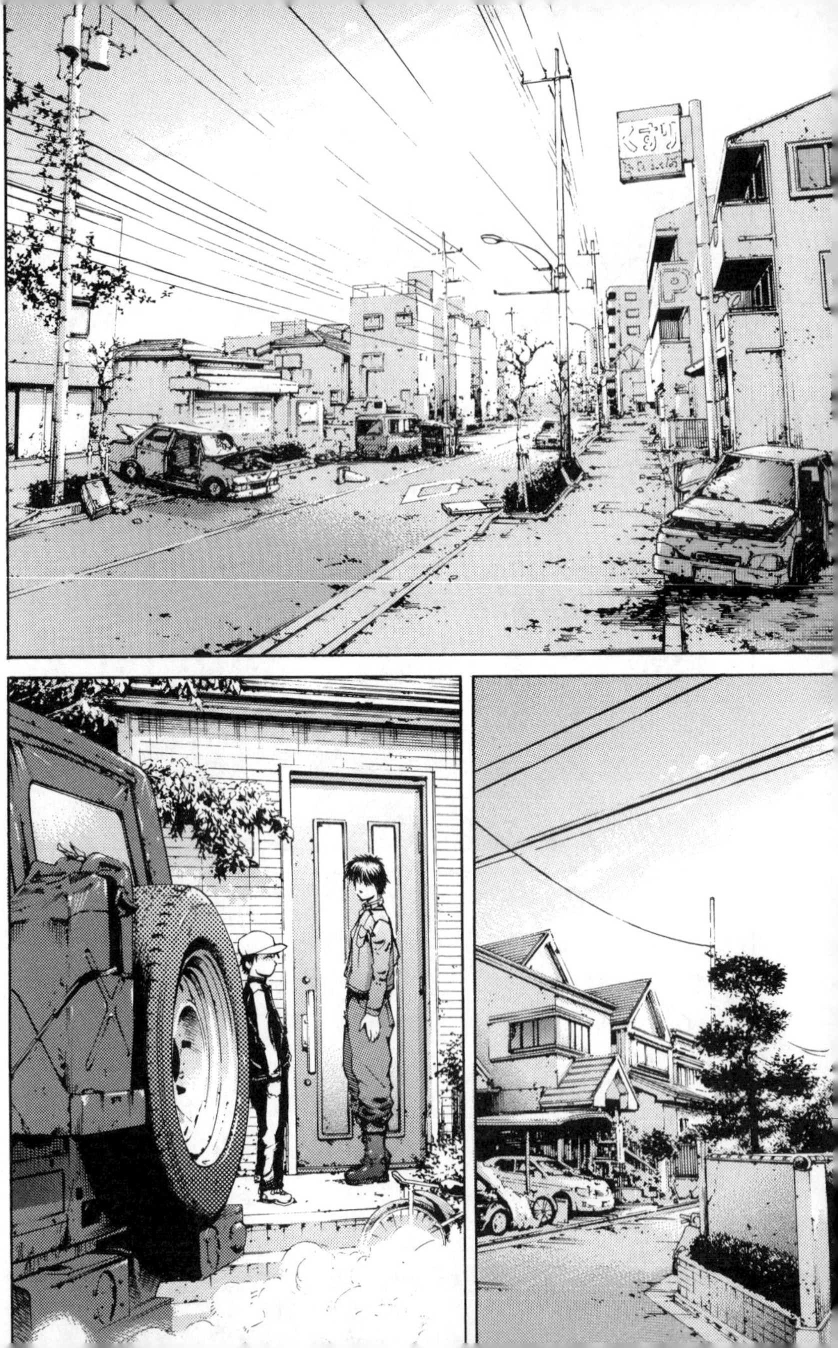
くすり
P

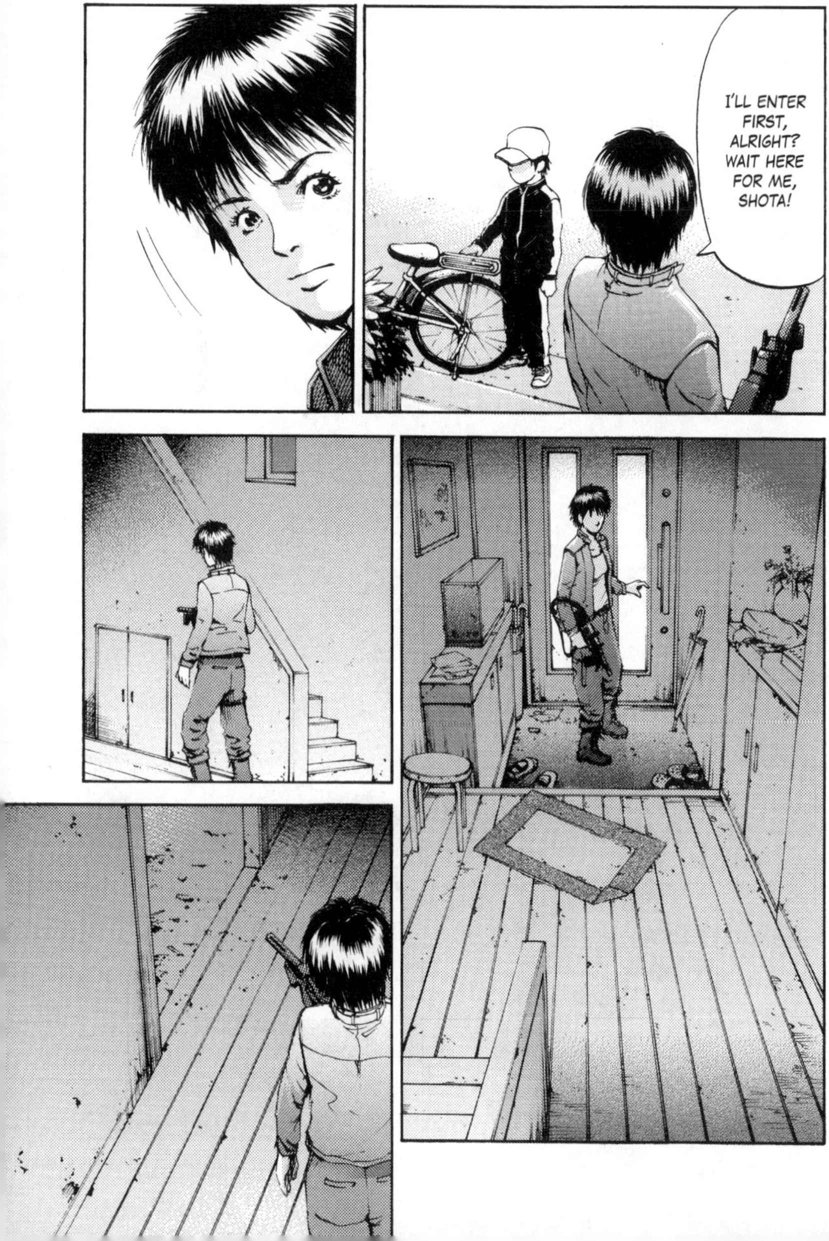
I'LL ENTER FIRST, ALRIGHT? WAIT HERE FOR ME, SHOTA!

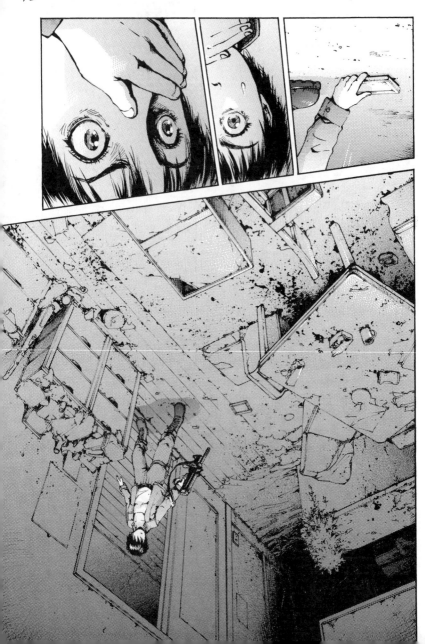

ガチャ
CLAC

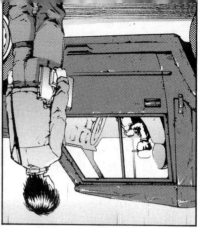

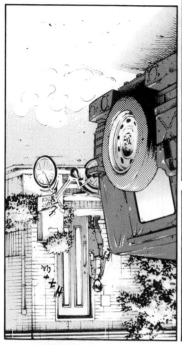

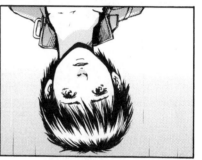

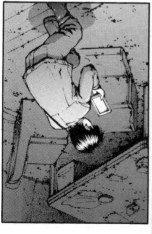

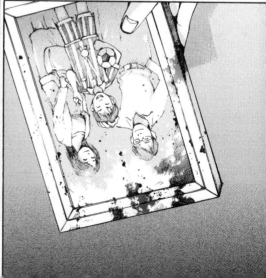

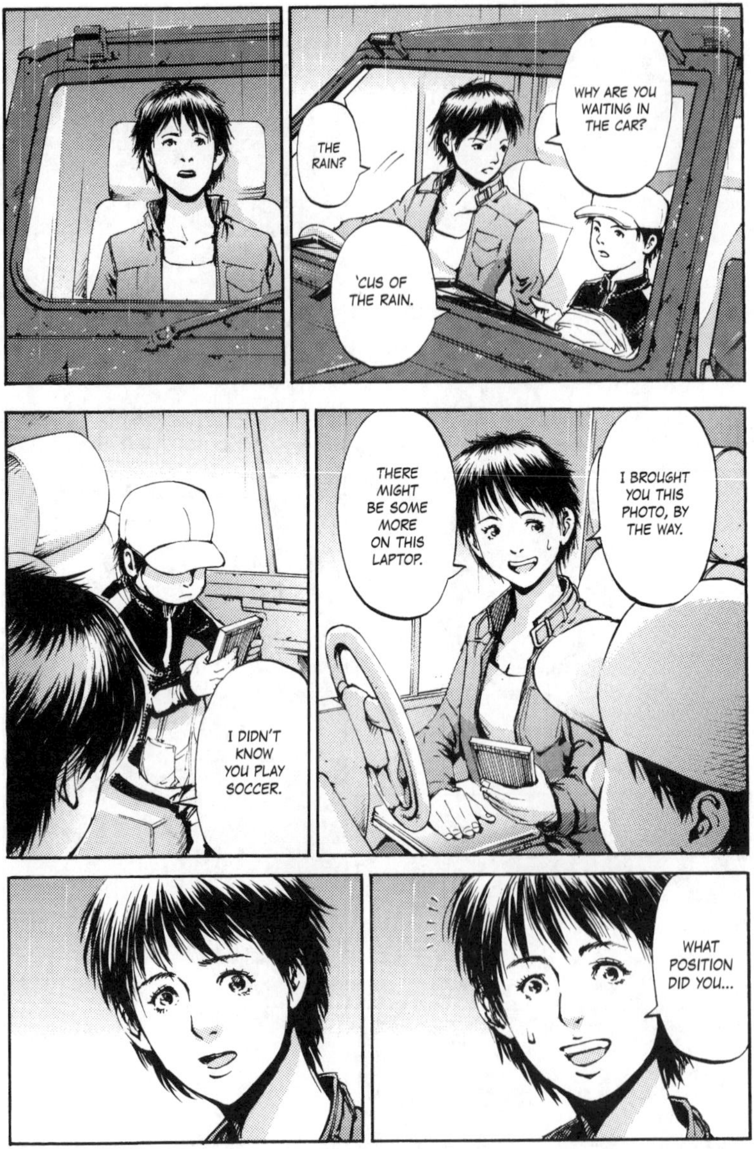
WHY ARE YOU WAITING IN THE CAR?
THE RAIN?
'CUS OF THE RAIN.
I BROUGHT YOU THIS PHOTO, BY THE WAY.
THERE MIGHT BE SOME MORE ON THIS LAPTOP.
I DIDN'T KNOW YOU PLAY SOCCER.
WHAT POSITION DID YOU...

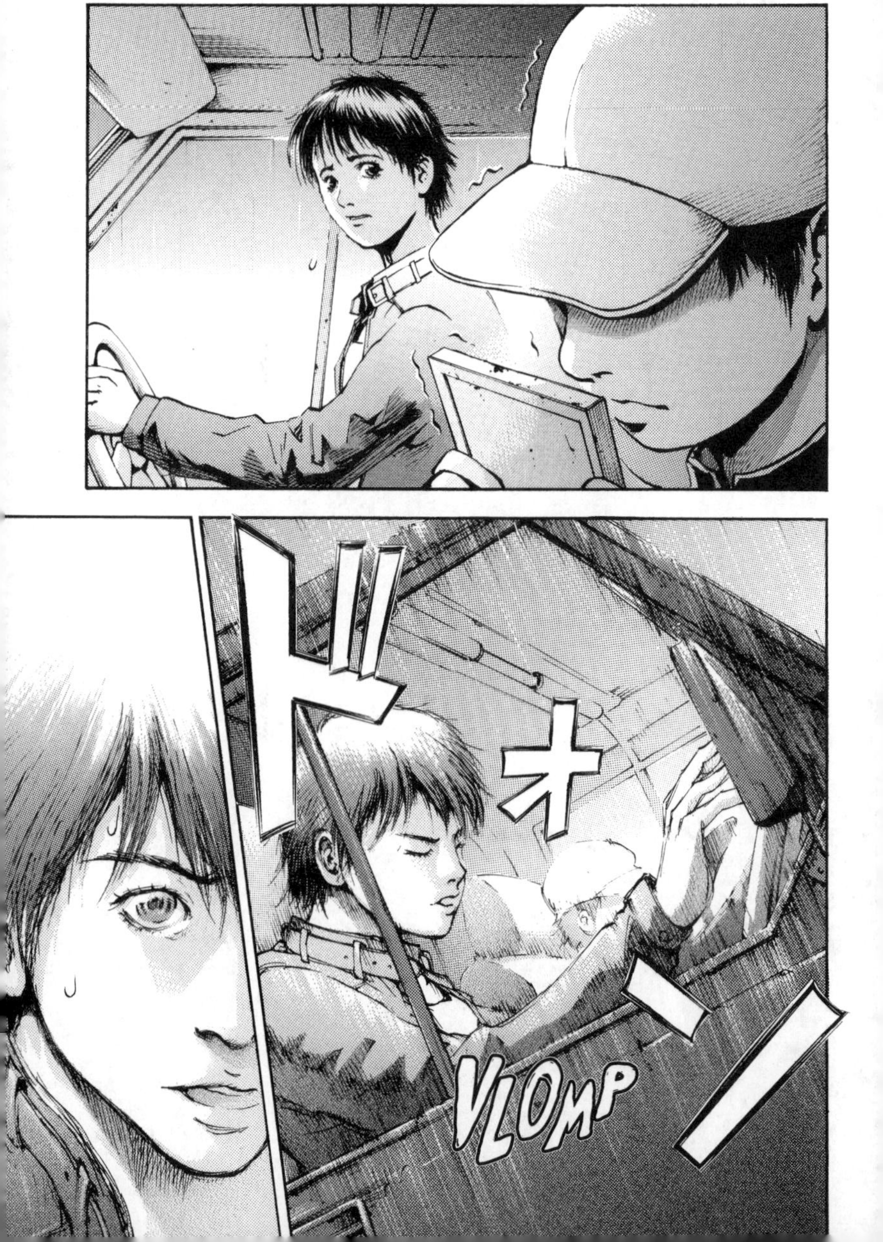
ドオーン
VLOMP

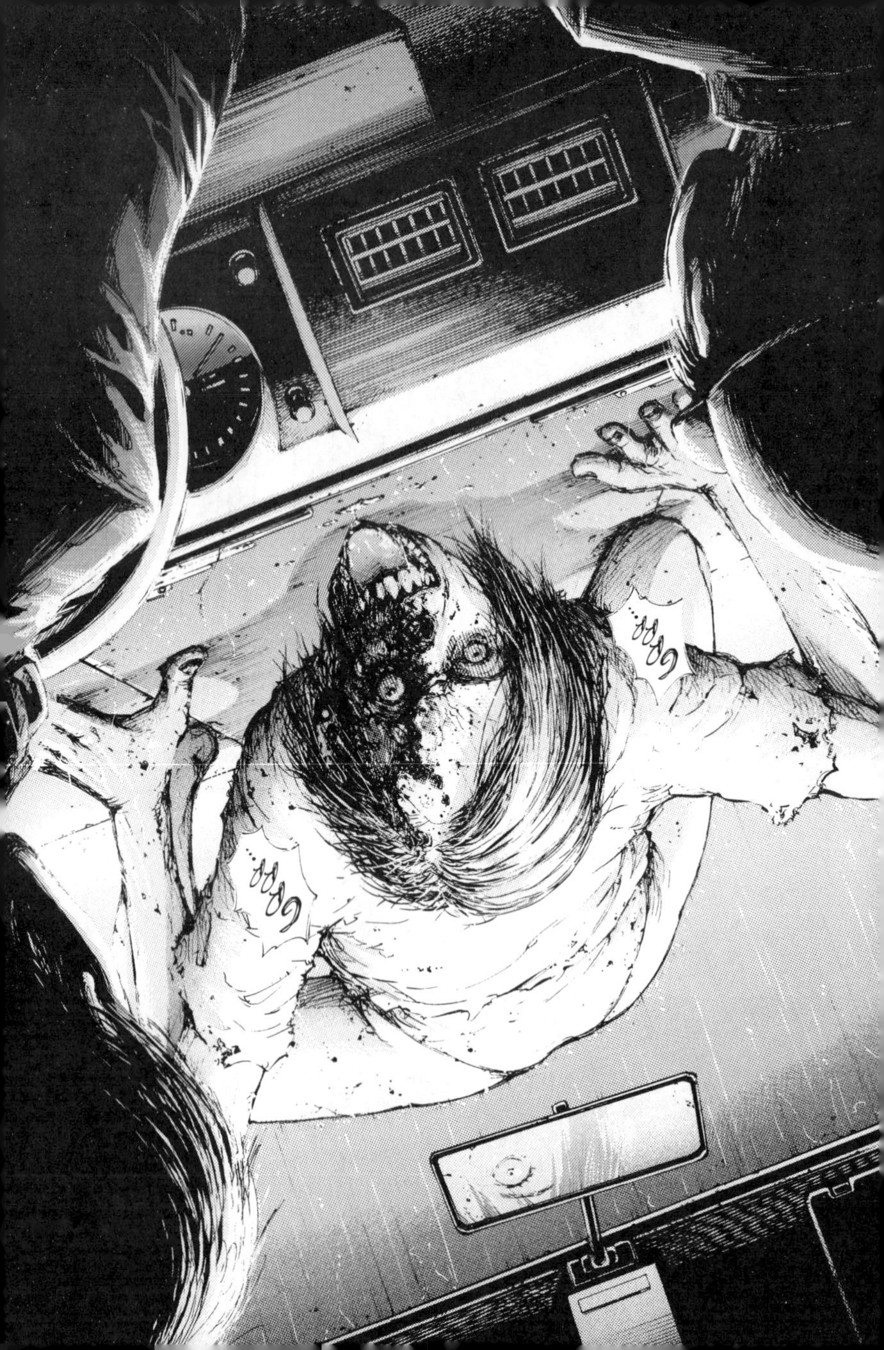
GRRR...
GRRR...

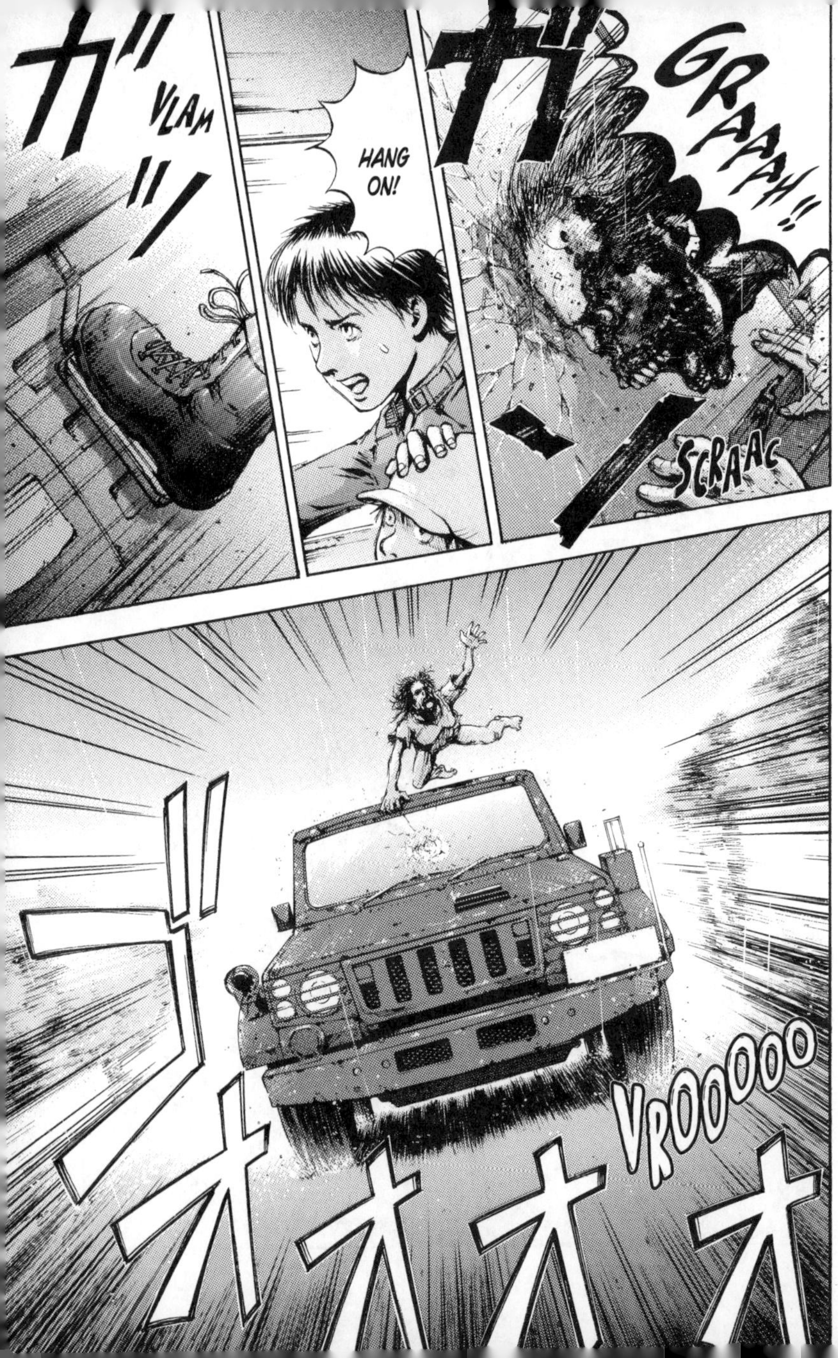
GRAAAH!!
ガ
SCRAAC
HANG ON!
ガ
VLAM
ゴオオオ
VROOOOO

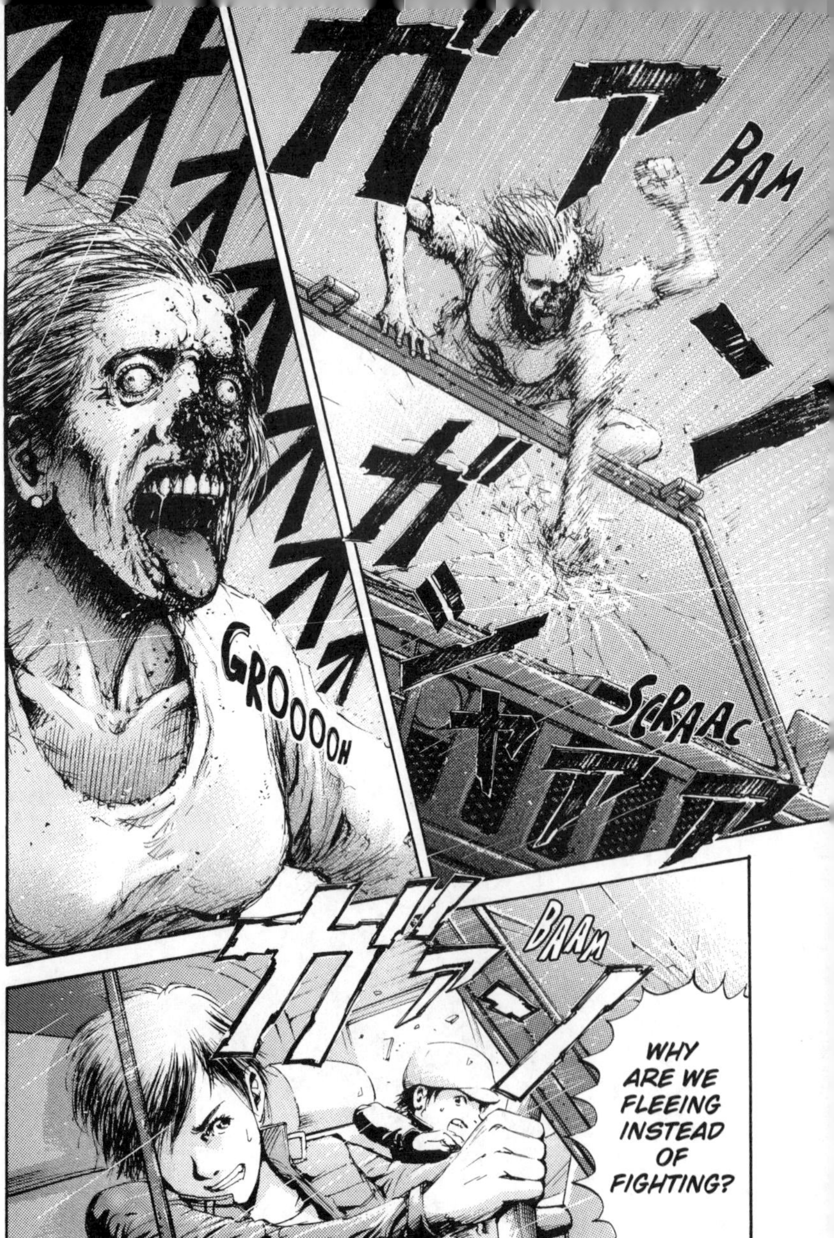
BAM
SCRAAC
GROOOOOH
BAAM
WHY ARE WE FLEEING INSTEAD OF FIGHTING?

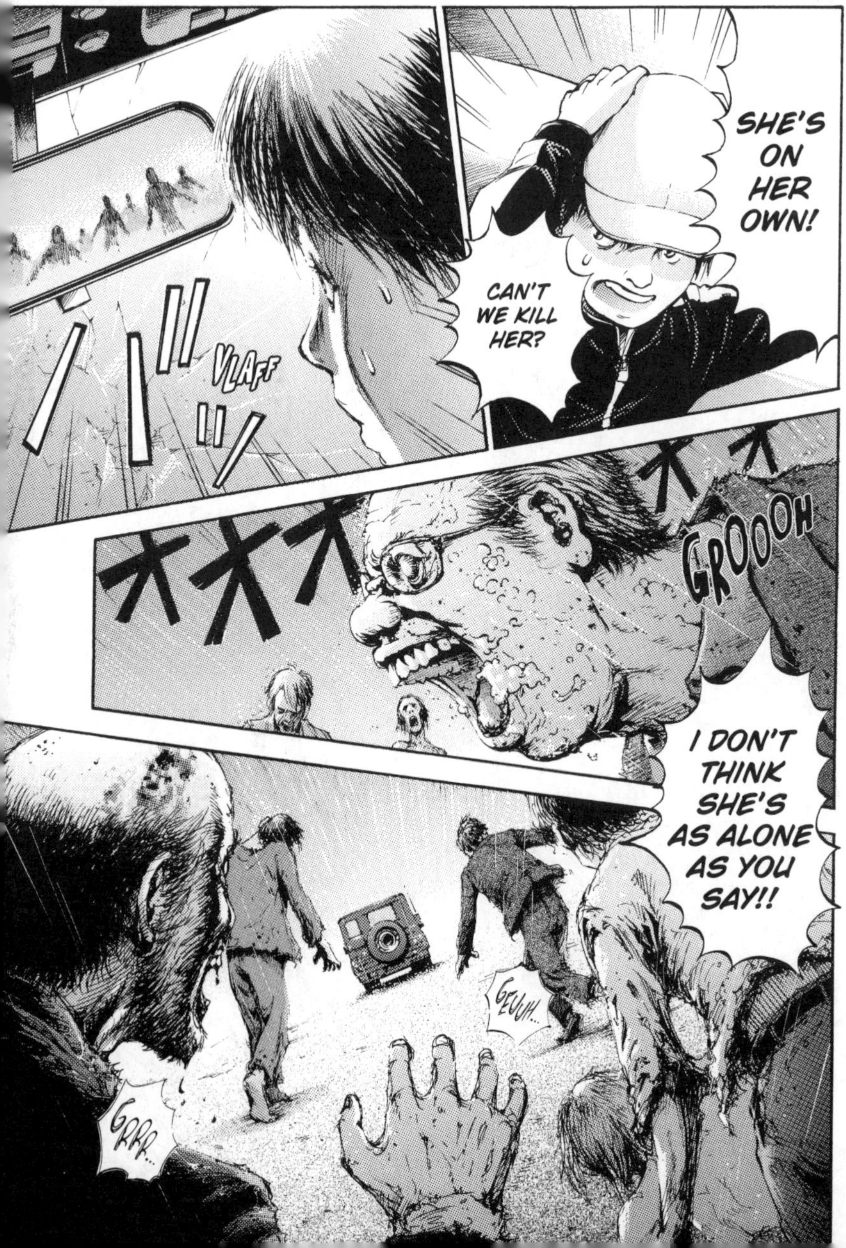
SHE'S ON HER OWN!
CAN'T WE KILL HER?
VLAFF
GROOOH
I DON'T THINK SHE'S AS ALONE AS YOU SAY!!
GEUUH...
GRRR...

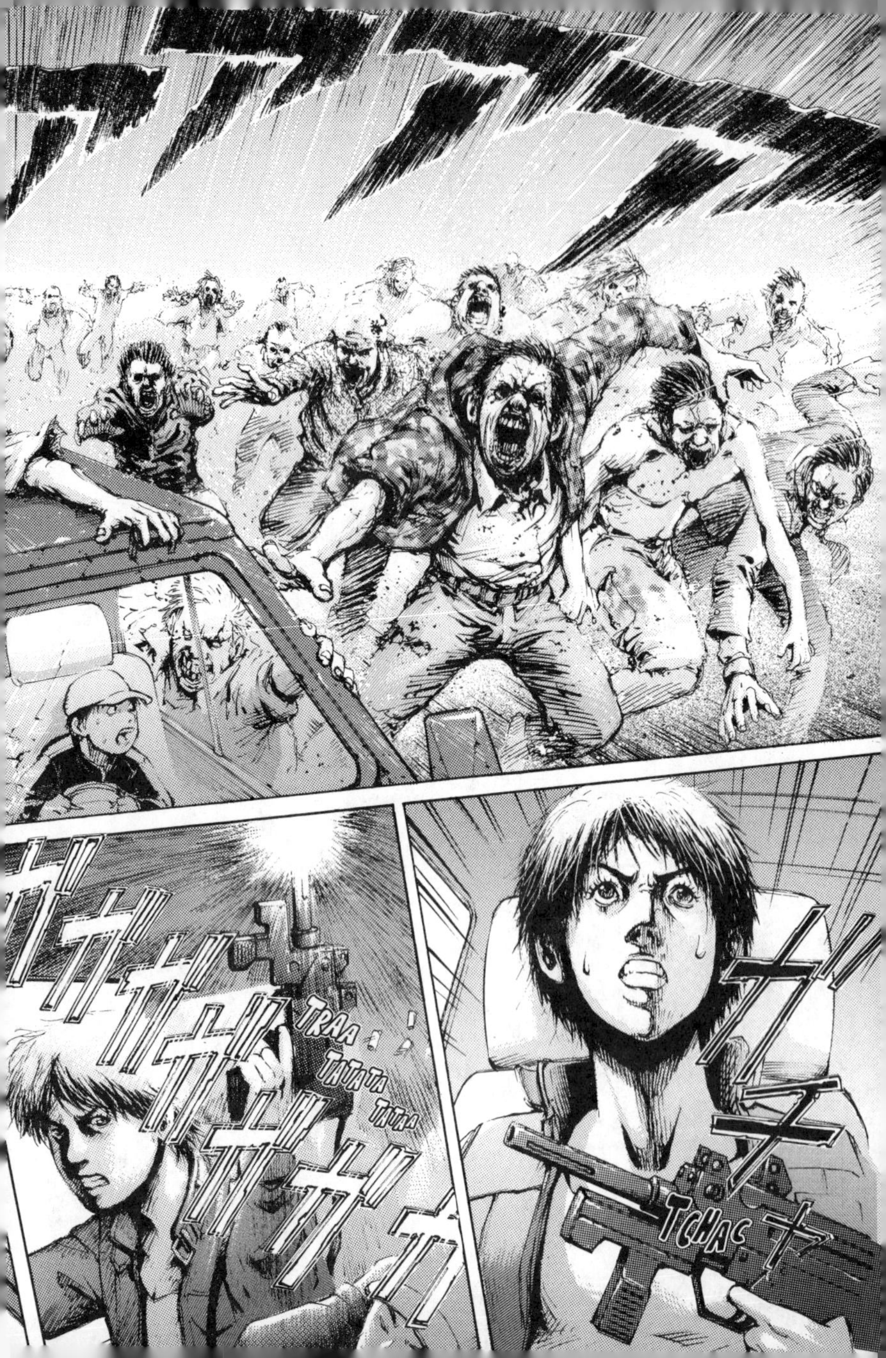
TCHAC
TRAA TATATA TATAA

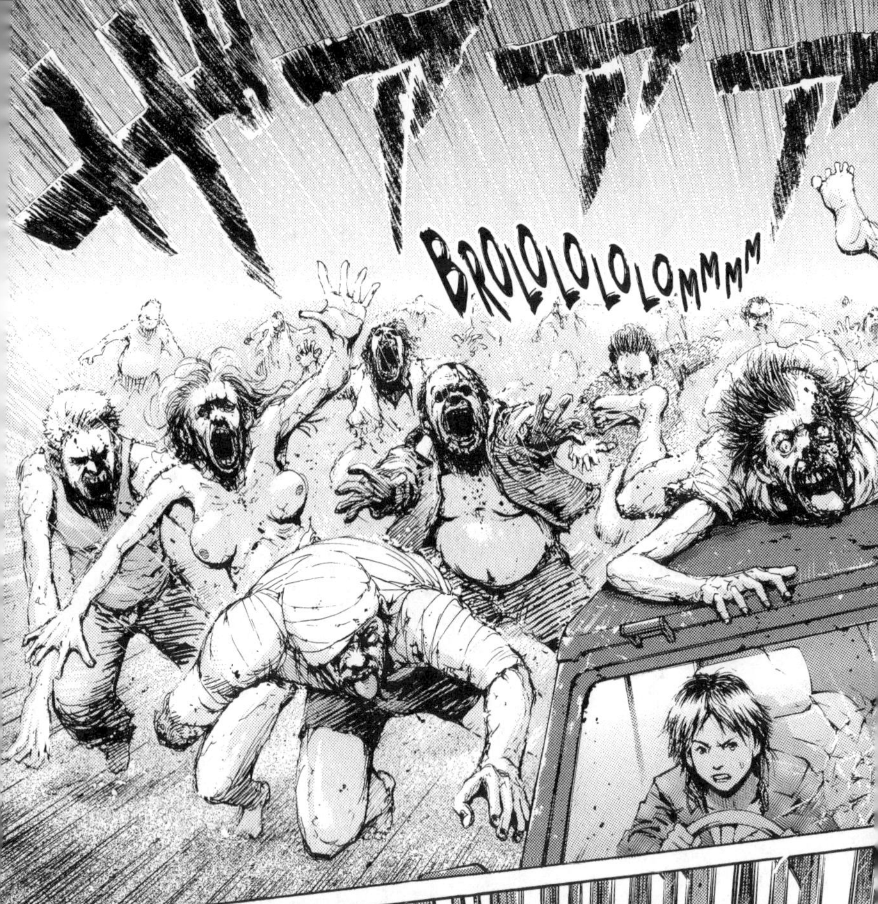
BROLOLOLOLOMMMM
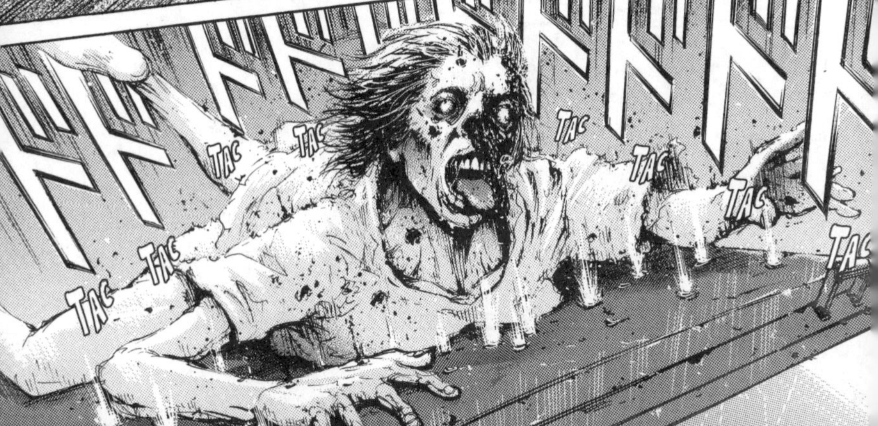
TAC
TAC
TAC
TAC
TAC
TAC
TAC
TAC

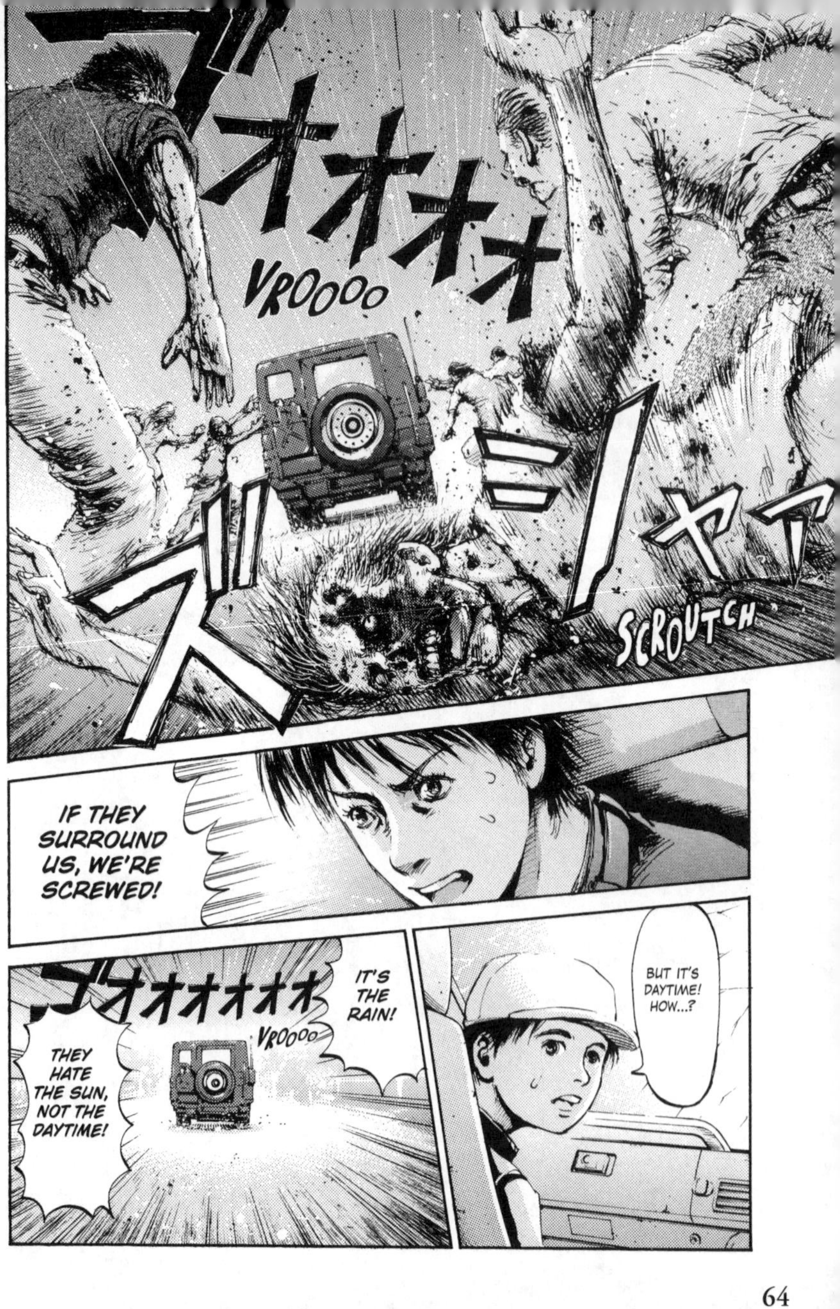
ブオオオオ
VROOOO
ズシャア
SCROUTCH
IF THEY SURROUND US, WE'RE SCREWED!
BUT IT'S DAYTIME! HOW...?
IT'S THE RAIN!
ブオオオオオオオ
VROOOO
THEY HATE THE SUN, NOT THE DAYTIME!

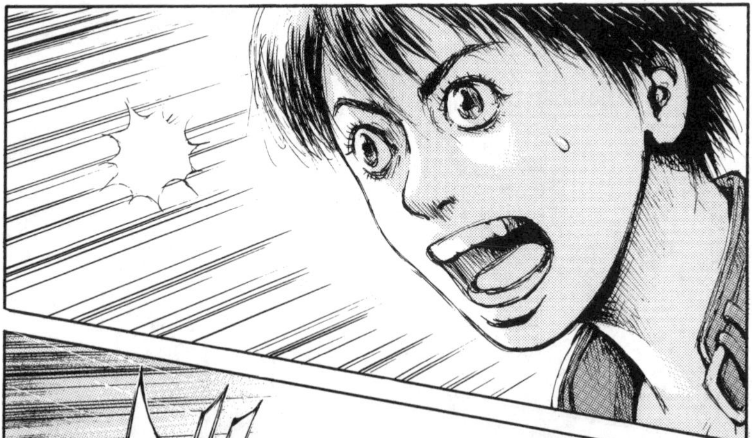

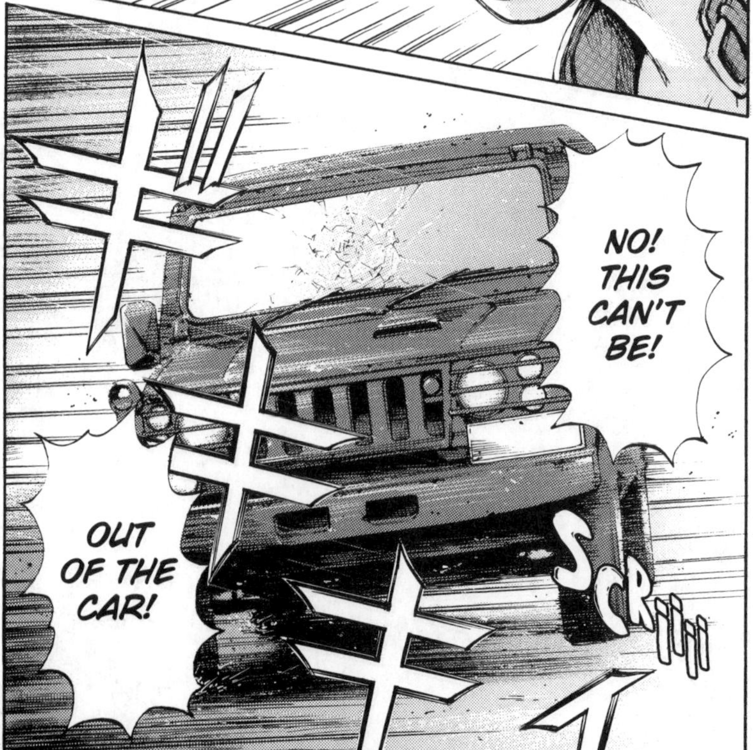
NO! THIS CAN'T BE!
OUT OF THE CAR!
SCRiiii

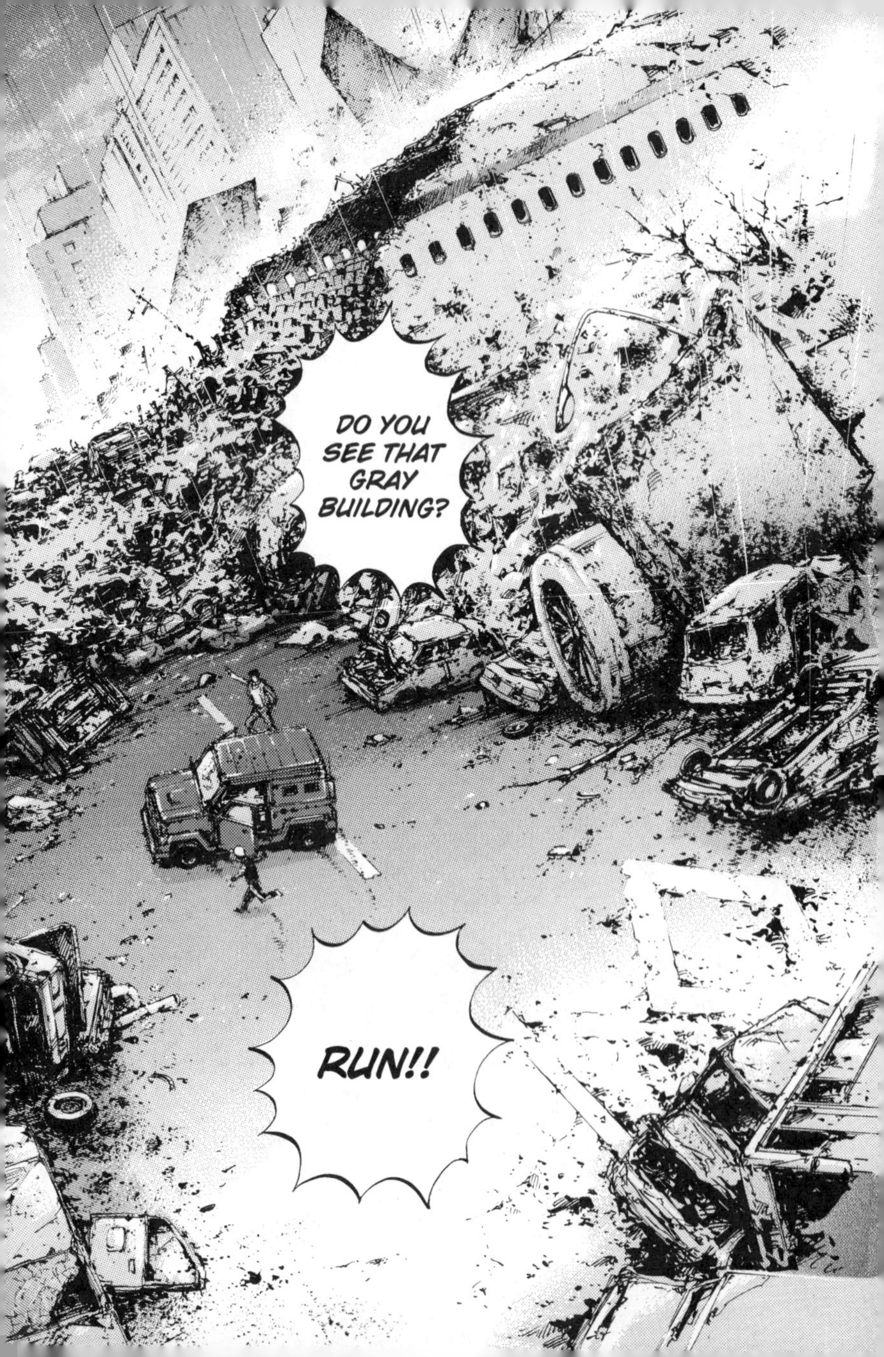
DO YOU SEE THAT GRAY BUILDING?
RUN!!

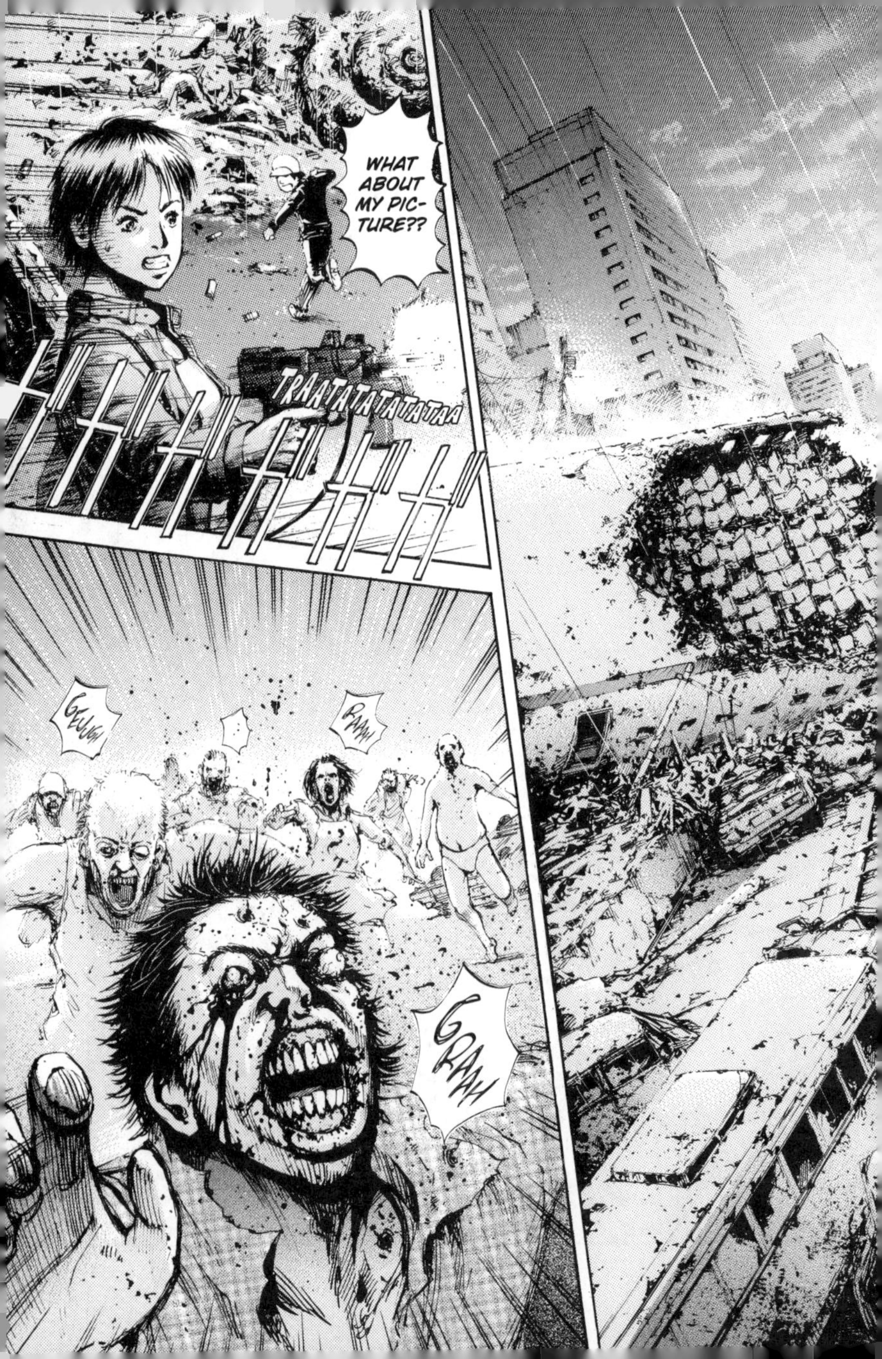
WHAT ABOUT MY PICTURE??
TRAATATATATATATAA
RAAAH
GEUUGH
GRAAH

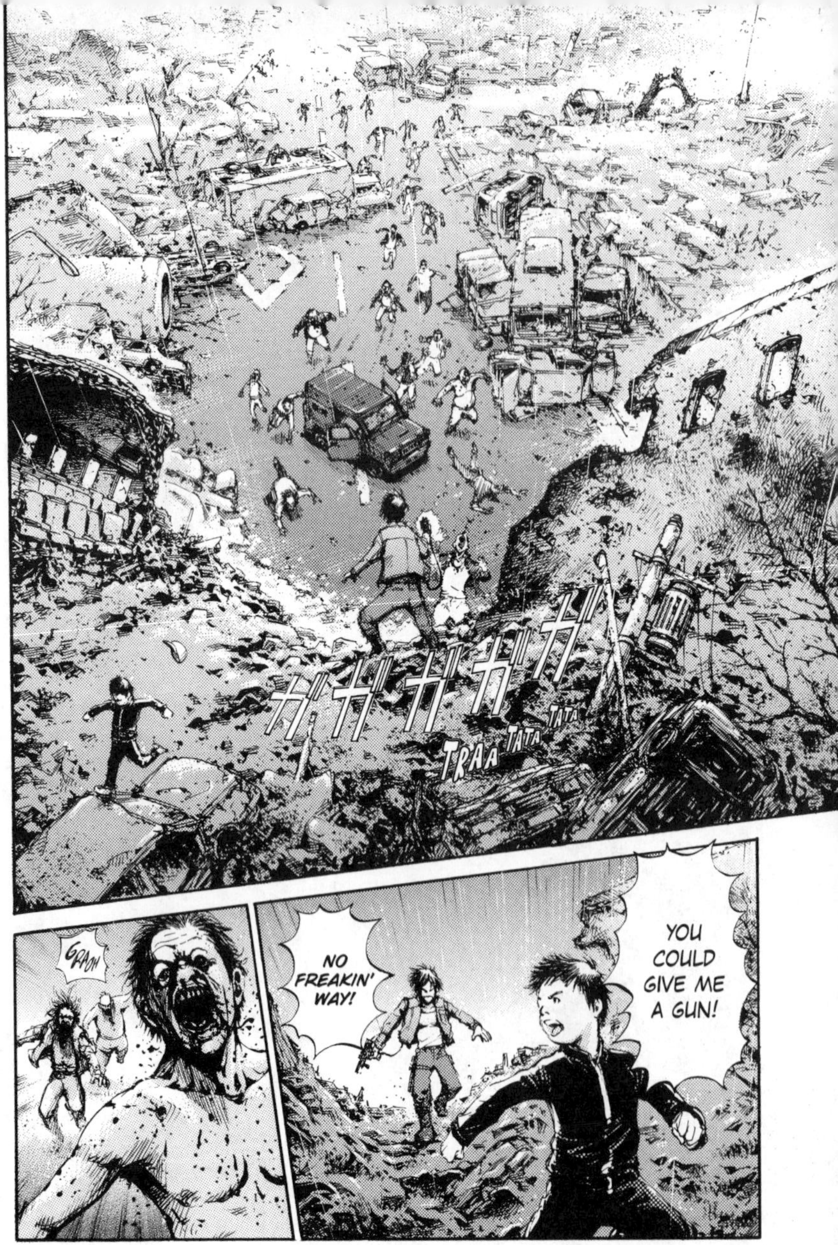
ガガガガガ
TRAA TATA TATA
YOU COULD GIVE ME A GUN!
NO FREAKIN' WAY!
GRAON

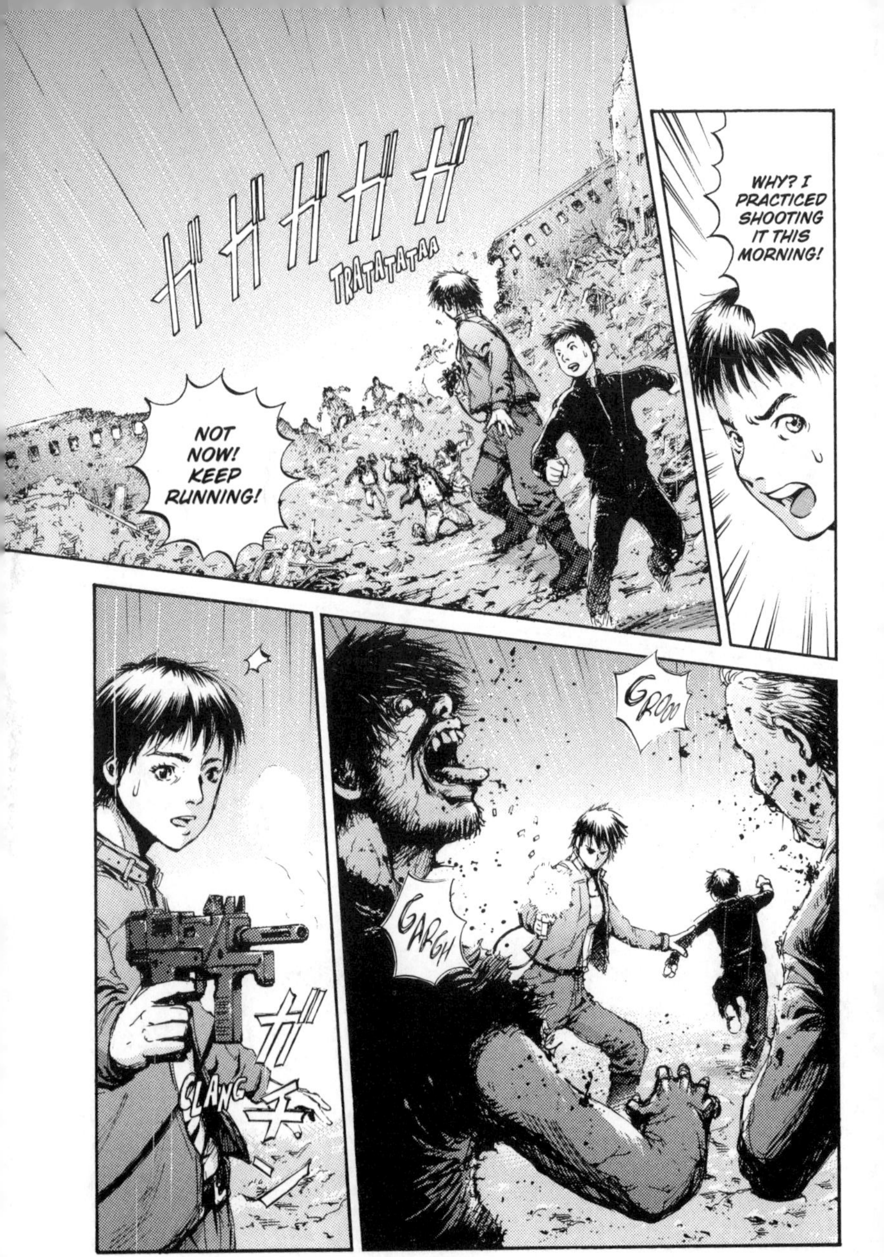
WHY? I PRACTICED SHOOTING IT THIS MORNING!
ガガガガガ
TRATATATAA
NOT NOW! KEEP RUNNING!
GROOO
GARGH
ガ
CLANG
チ

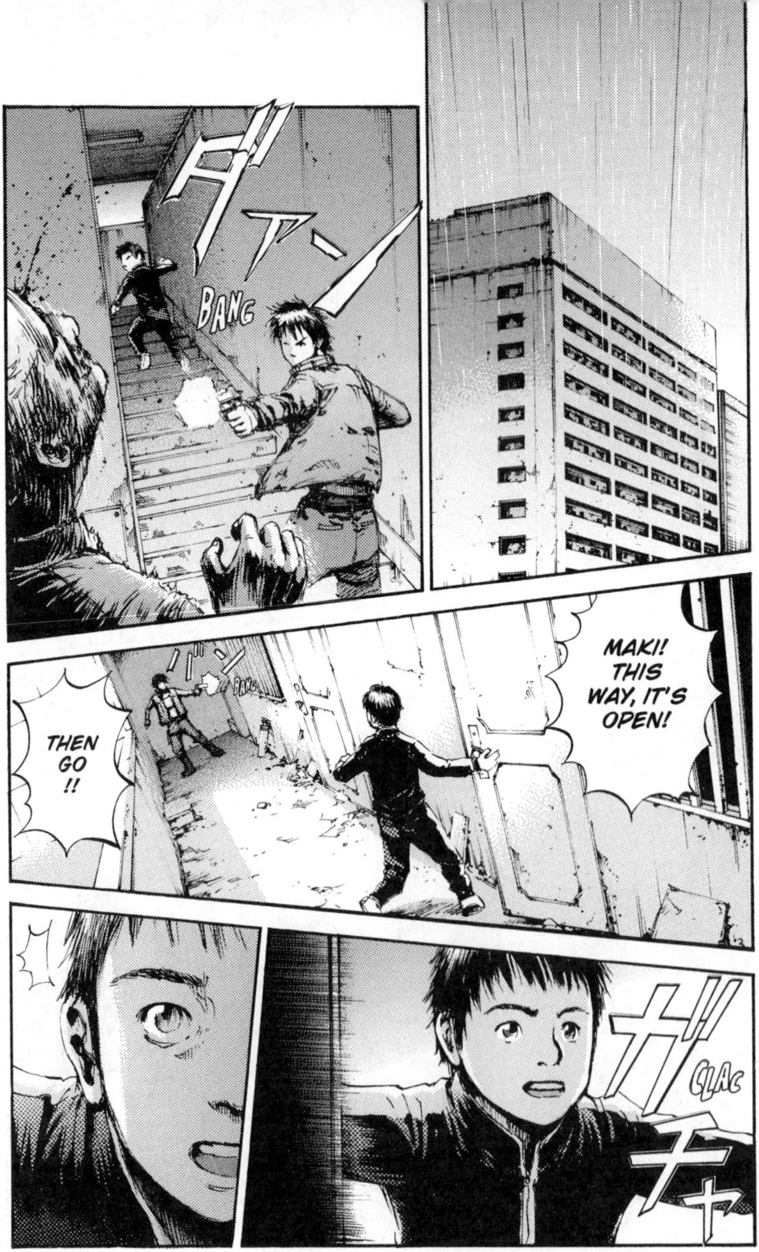
ダアーン
BANG
MAKI! THIS WAY, IT'S OPEN!
BANG
THEN GO !!
ガチャ
CLAC

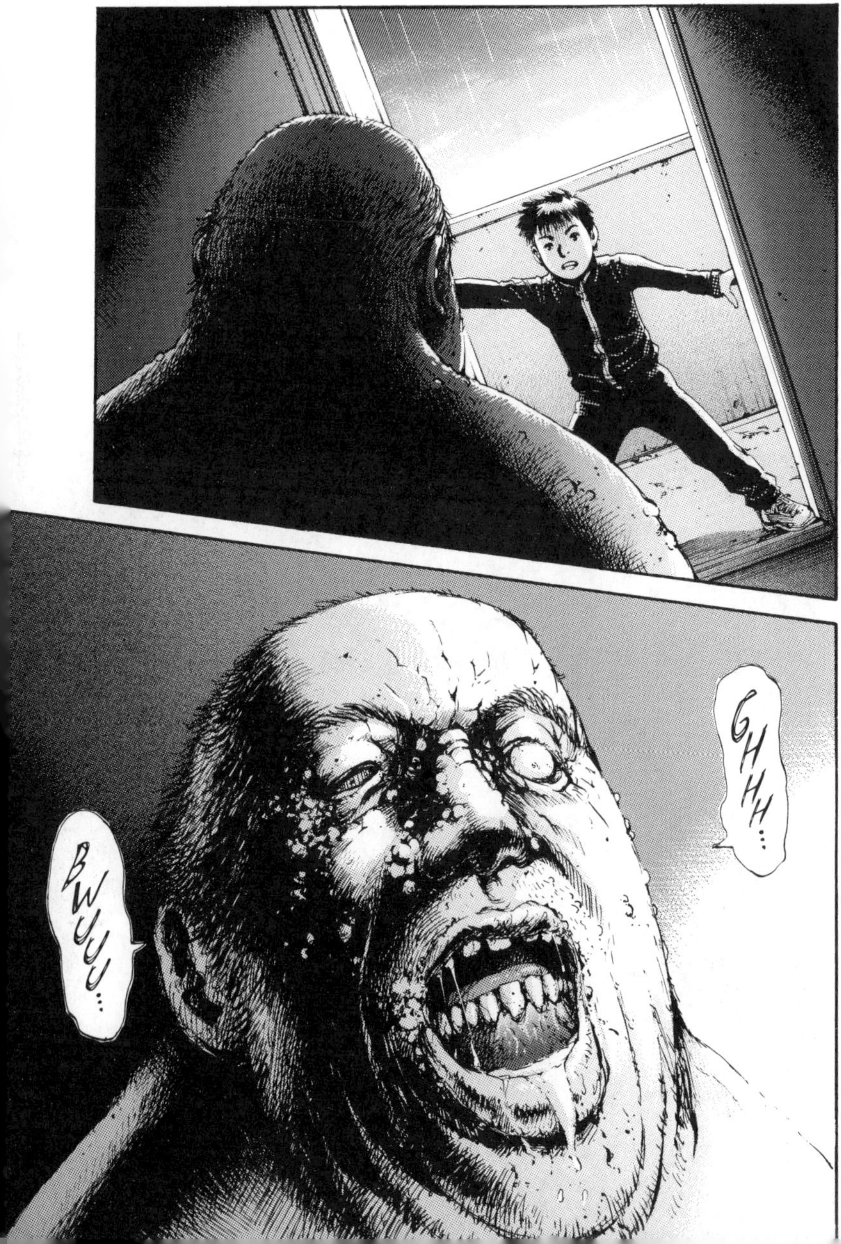
GHHH...
BWUUU...

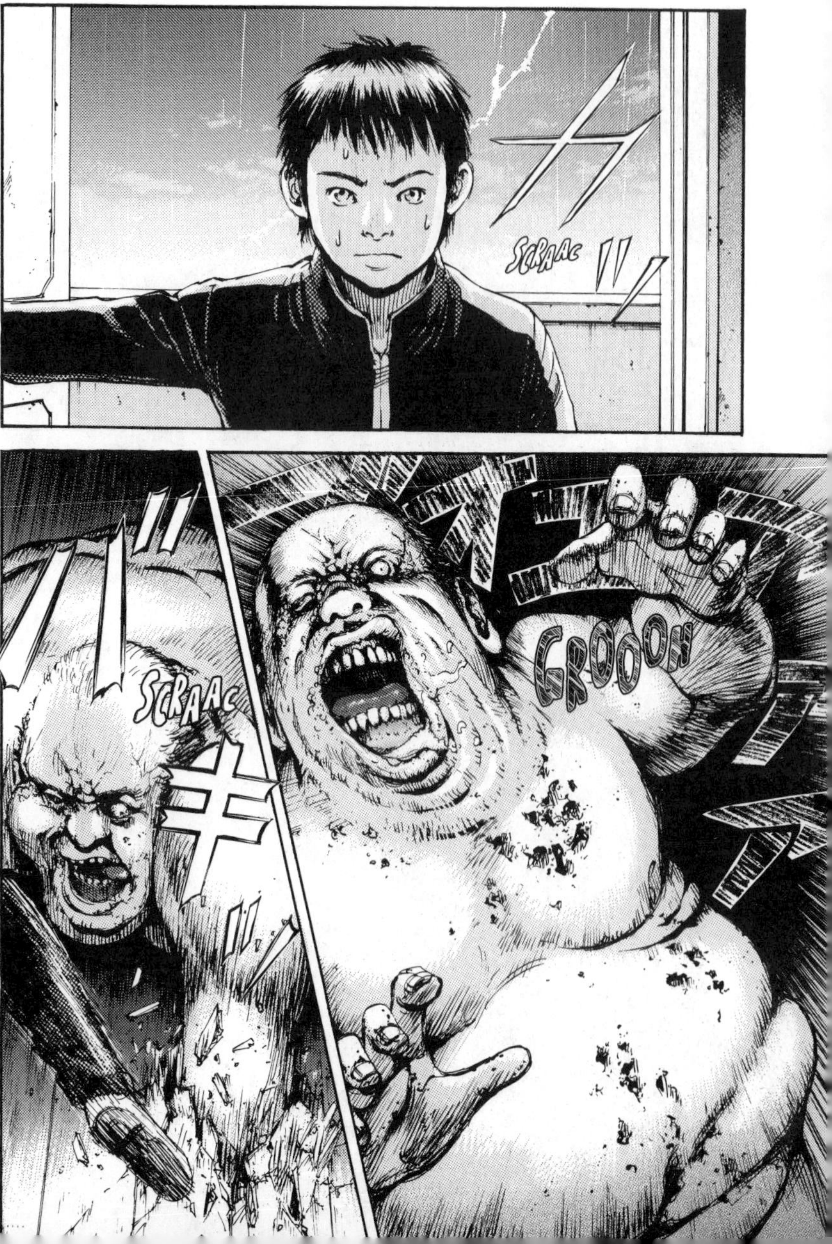
SCRAAC
GROOOH
SCRAAC

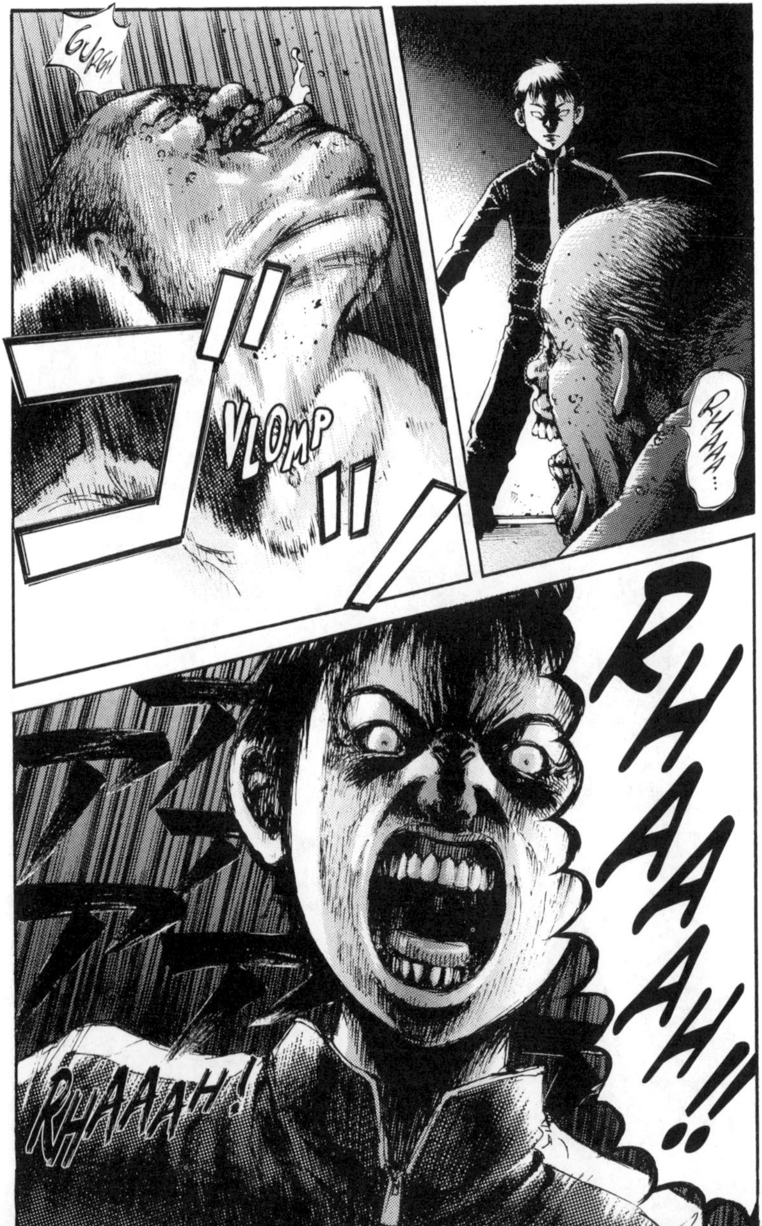
RHAAA...
GURGH
VLOMP!!
RHAAAAH!!
RHAAAH!

AUUH...
UUUH...
STAP!

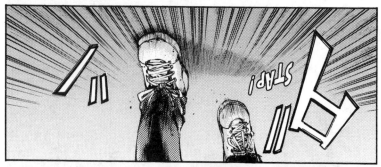

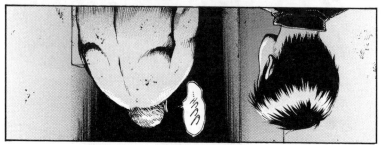

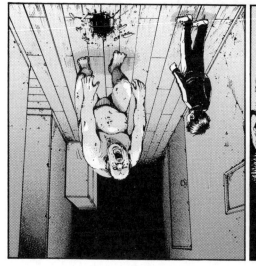

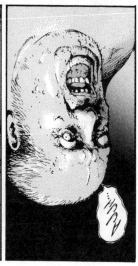

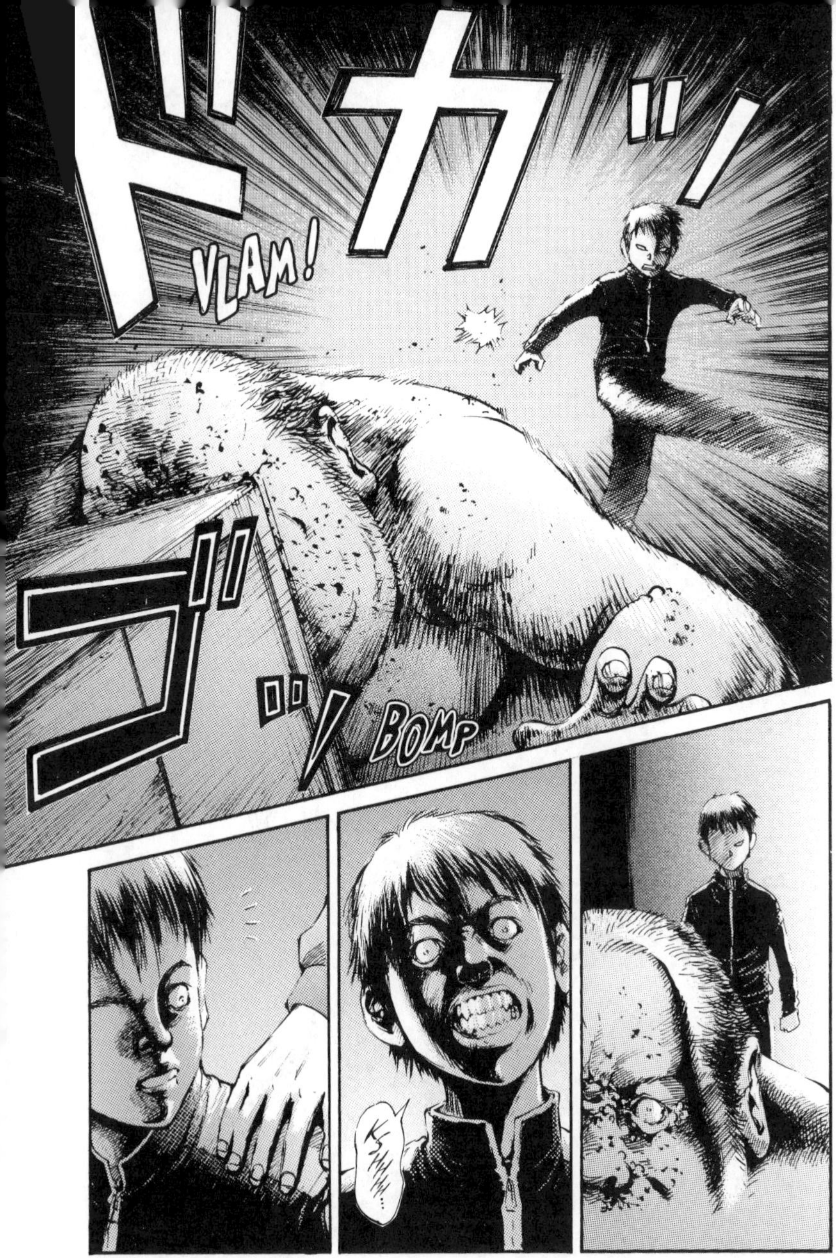
ドガッ
VLAM!
ゴッ
BOMP
KSHHH...

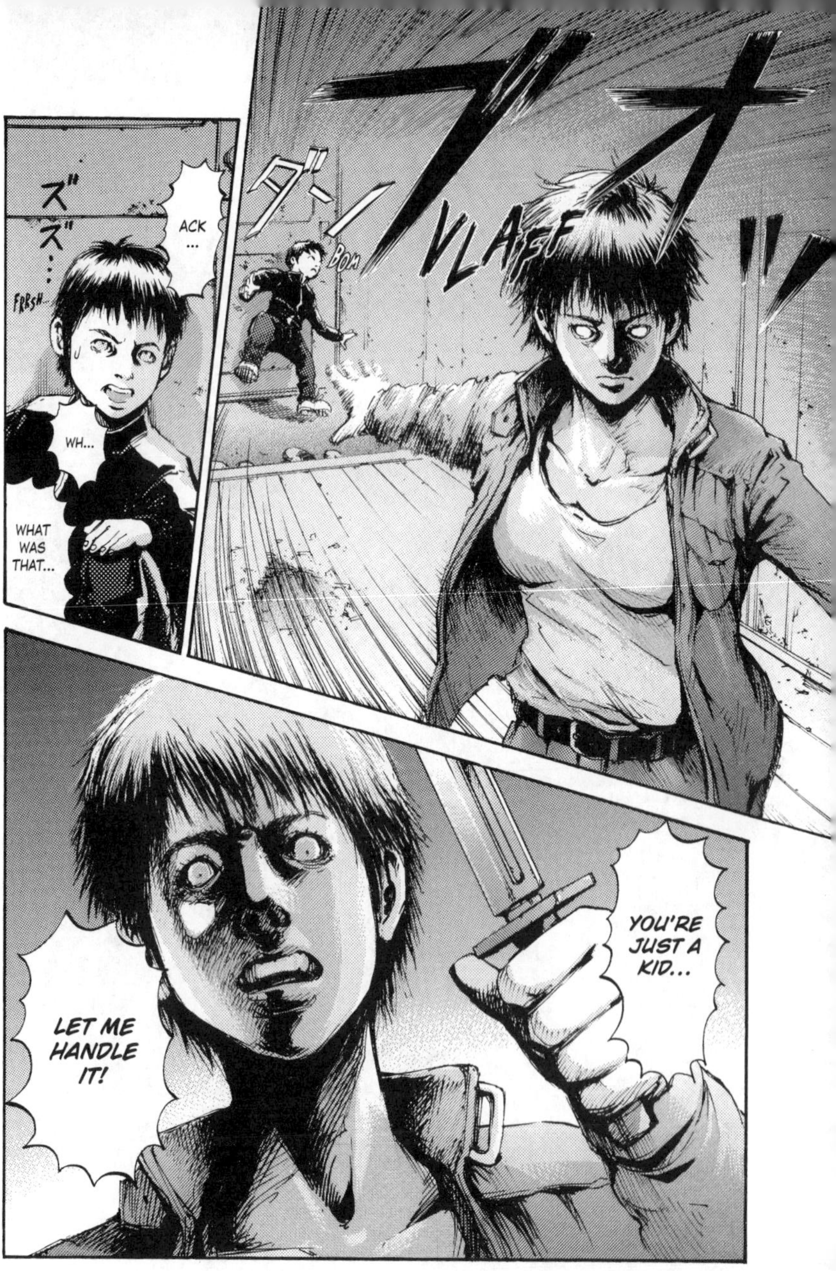
ブオッ
VLAFF
ダン
BOM
ズズ…
FRRSH…
ACK
...
WH...
WHAT WAS THAT...
YOU'RE JUST A KID...
LET ME HANDLE IT!

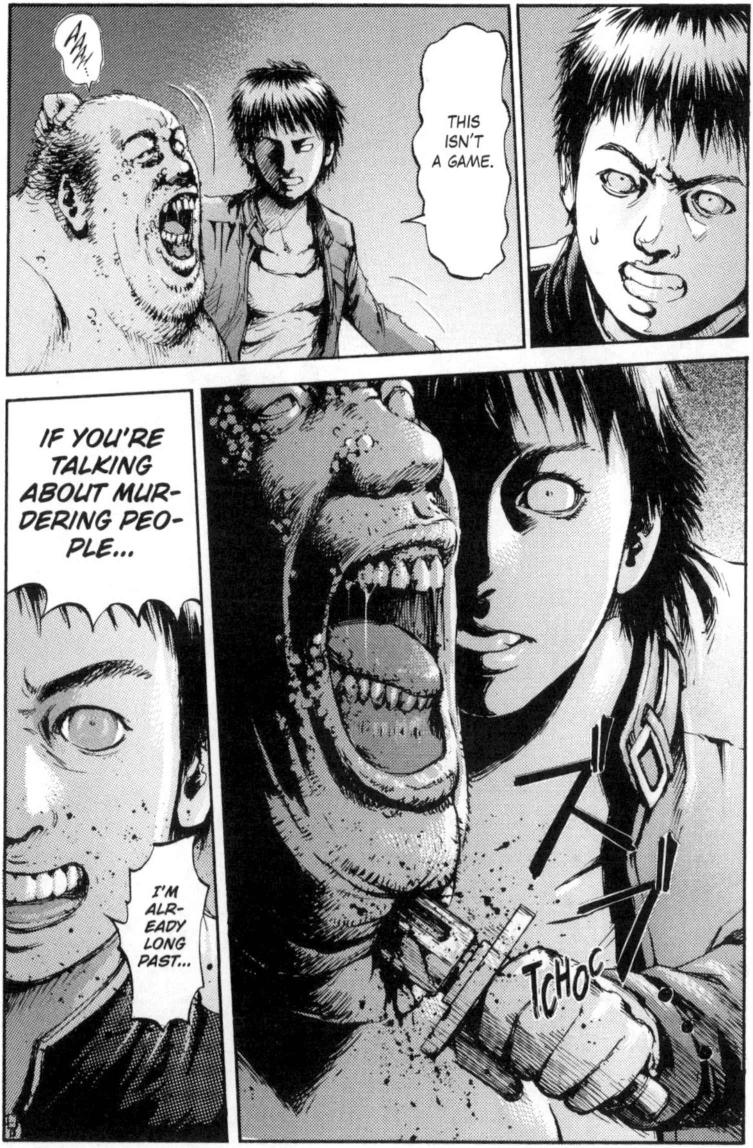
THIS ISN'T A GAME.
AAAH...
TCHOC
IF YOU'RE TALKING ABOUT MUR-DERING PEO-PLE...
I'M ALR-EADY LONG PAST...

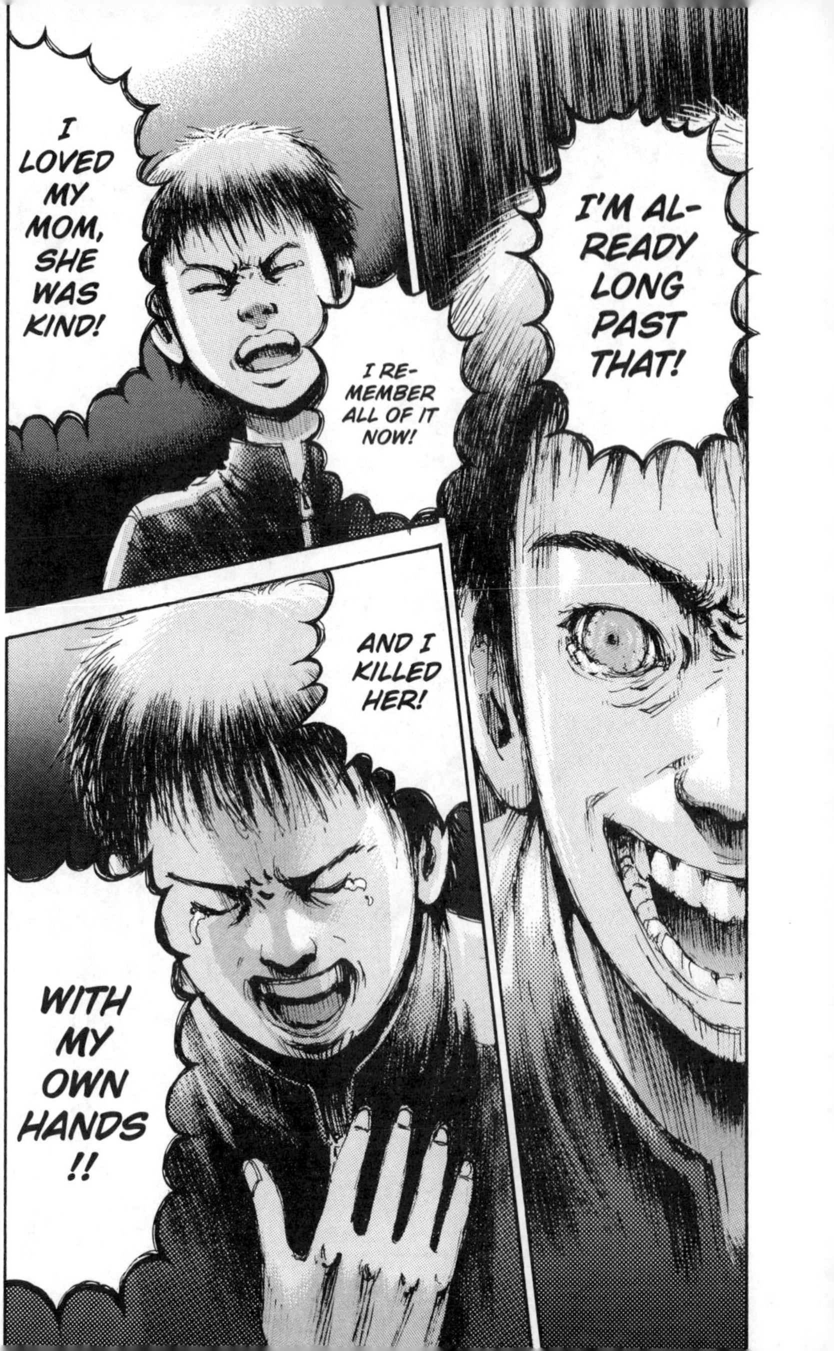
I'M AL-READY LONG PAST THAT!
I LOVED MY MOM, SHE WAS KIND!
I RE-MEMBER ALL OF IT NOW!
AND I KILLED HER!
WITH MY OWN HANDS !!

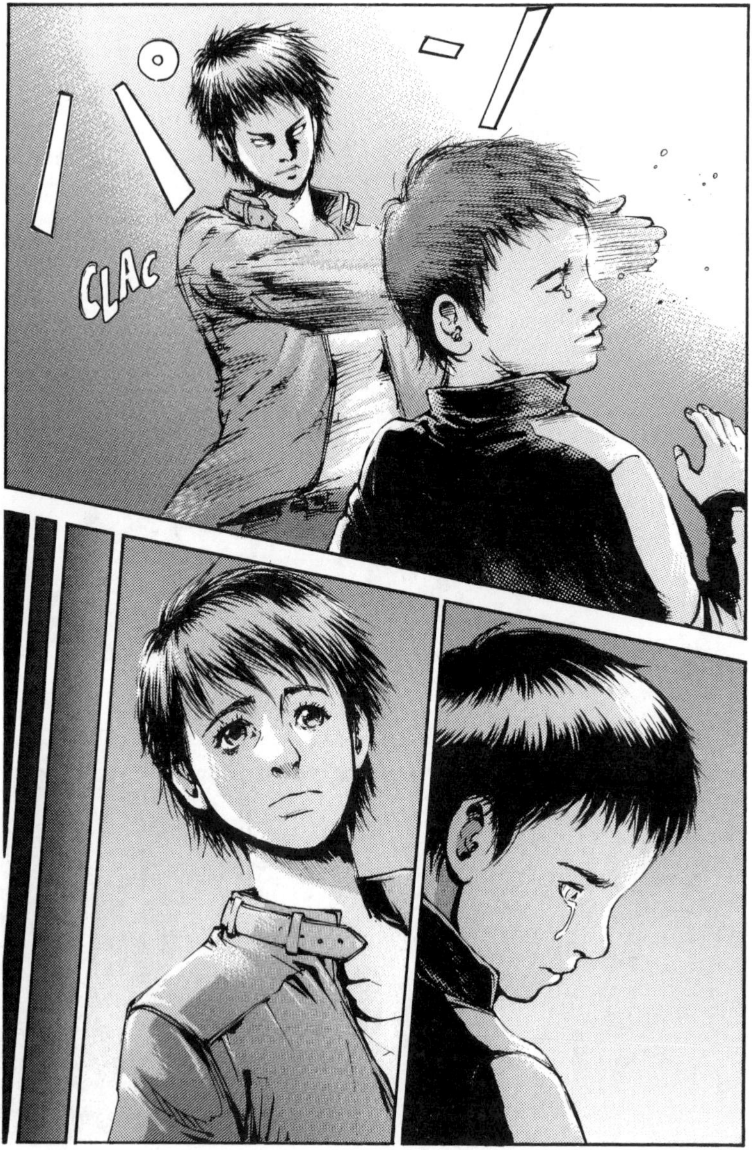
CLAC

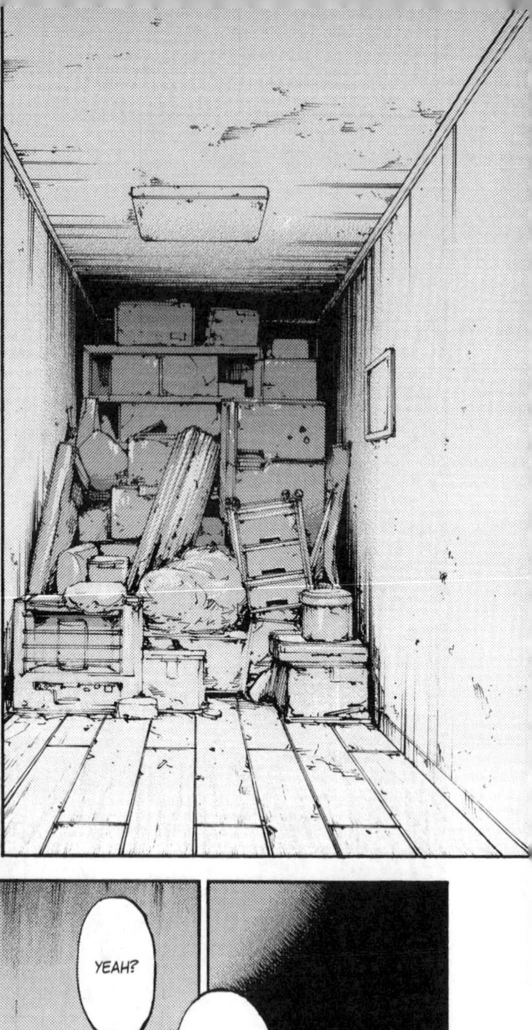

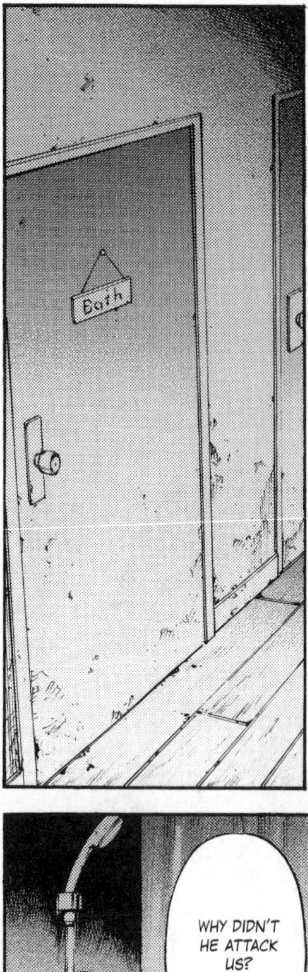
Bath

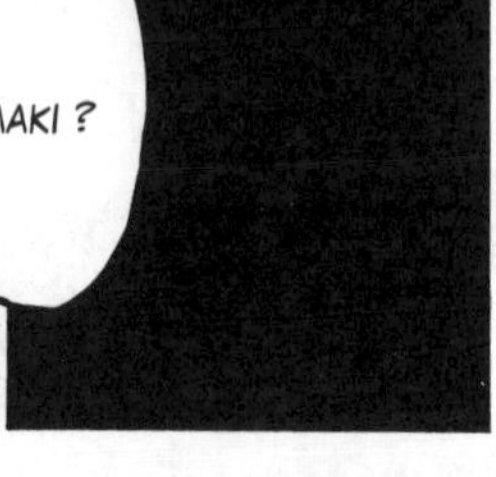
MAKI ?

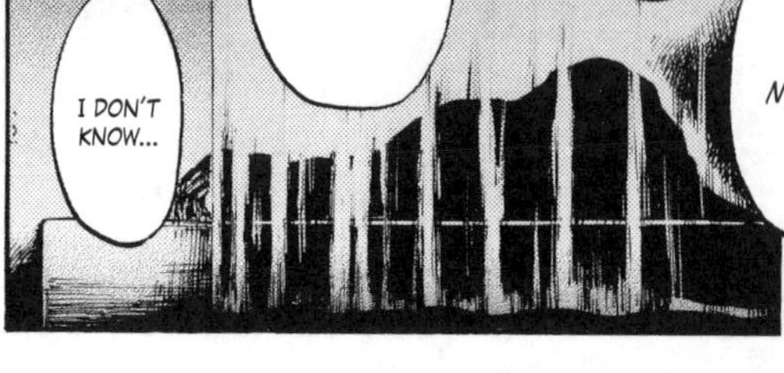
YEAH?
WHY DIDN'T HE ATTACK US?
I DON'T KNOW...

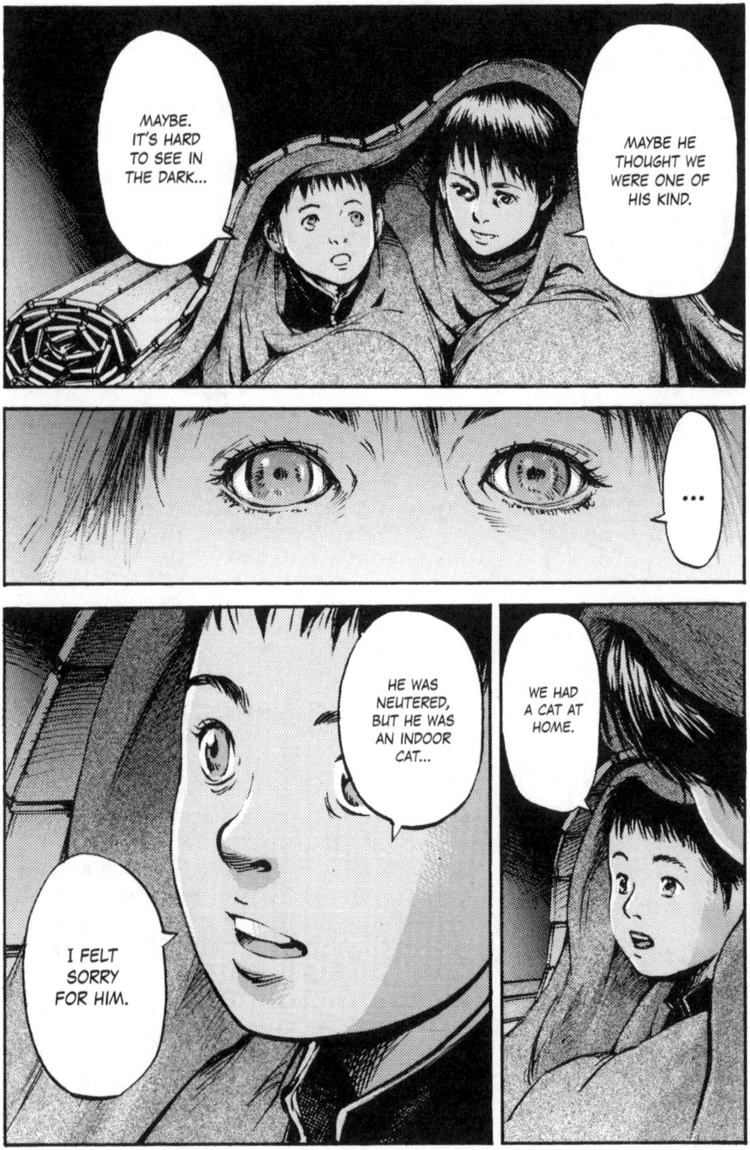
MAYBE HE THOUGHT WE WERE ONE OF HIS KIND.
MAYBE. IT'S HARD TO SEE IN THE DARK...
...
WE HAD A CAT AT HOME.
HE WAS NEUTERED, BUT HE WAS AN INDOOR CAT...
I FELT SORRY FOR HIM.

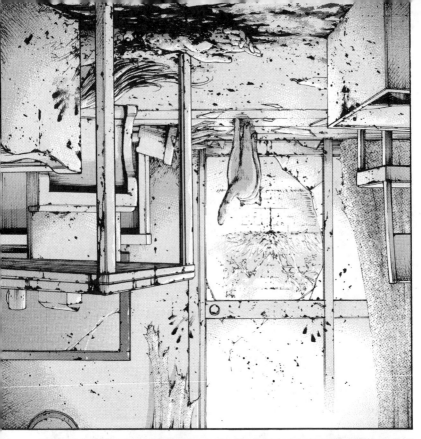

I WONDER IF HE'S WANDERING AROUND OUTSIDE RIGHT NOW....

CHAPTER 3

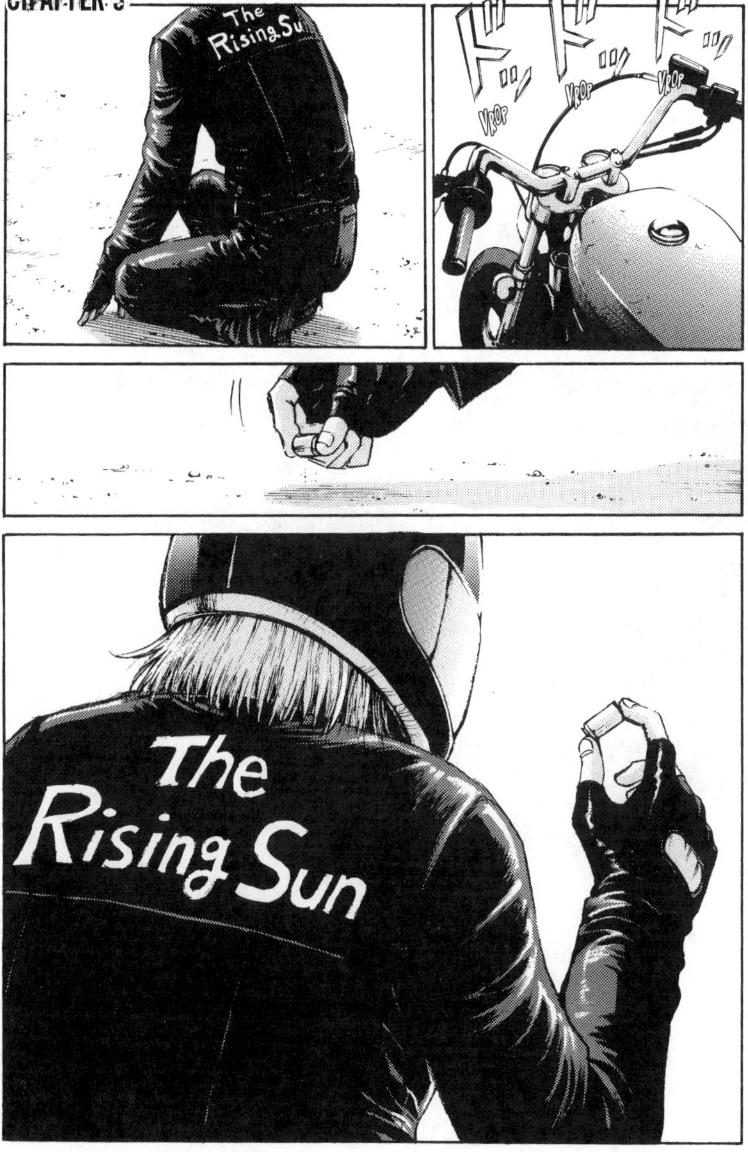

ドッ
ドッ
ドッ
VROP
VROP
VROP
The Rising Su
The Rising Sun

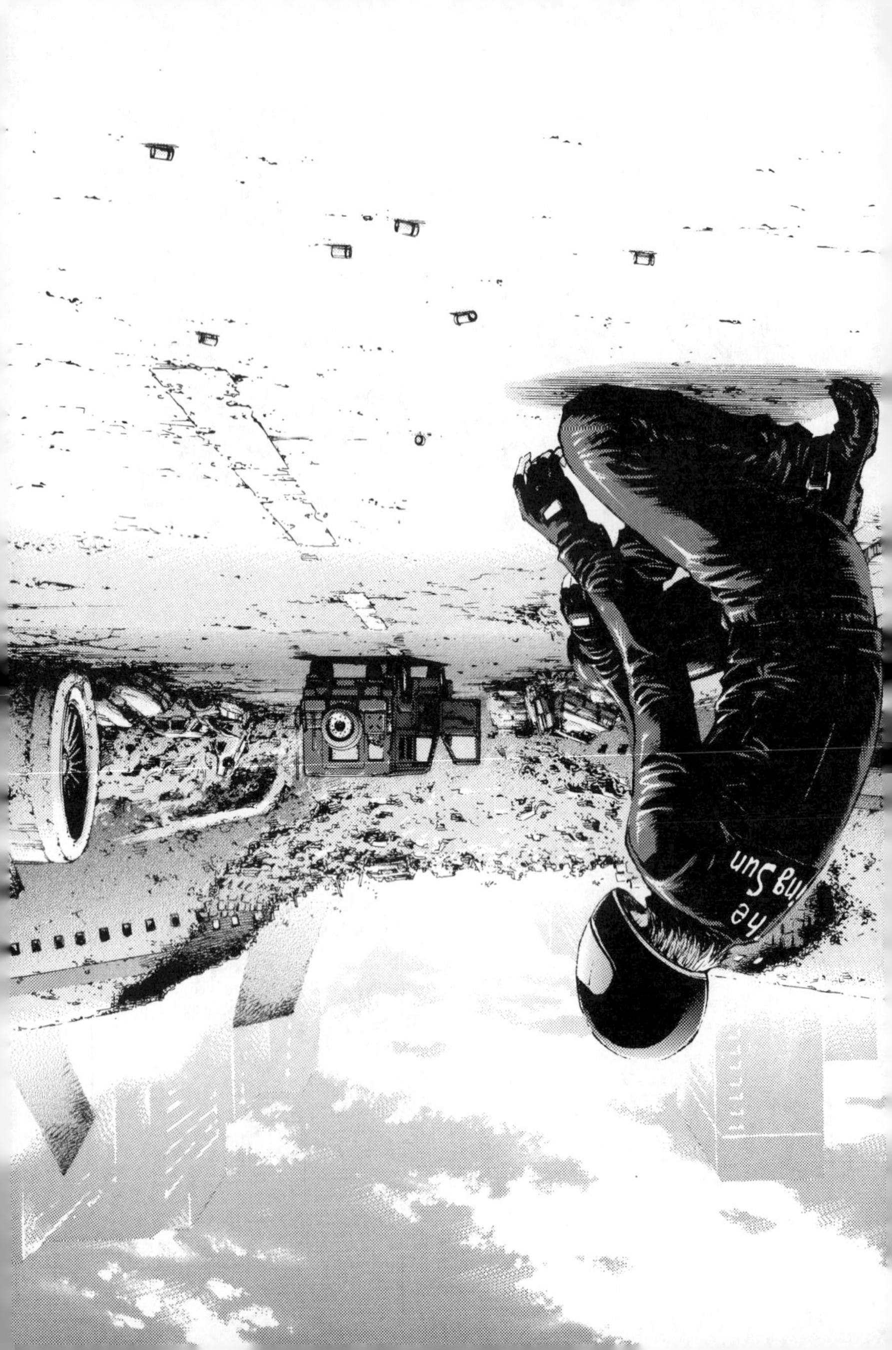

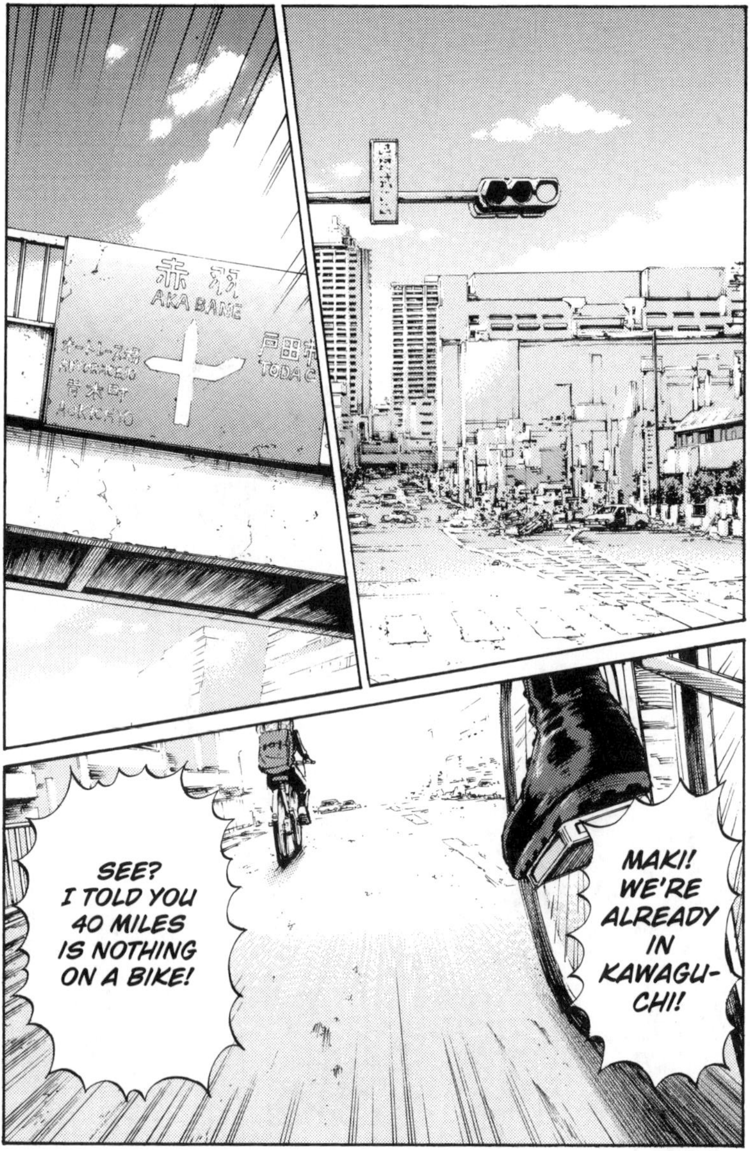
赤羽
AKA BANE
MAKI! WE'RE ALREADY IN KAWAGU-CHI!
SEE? I TOLD YOU 40 MILES IS NOTHING ON A BIKE!

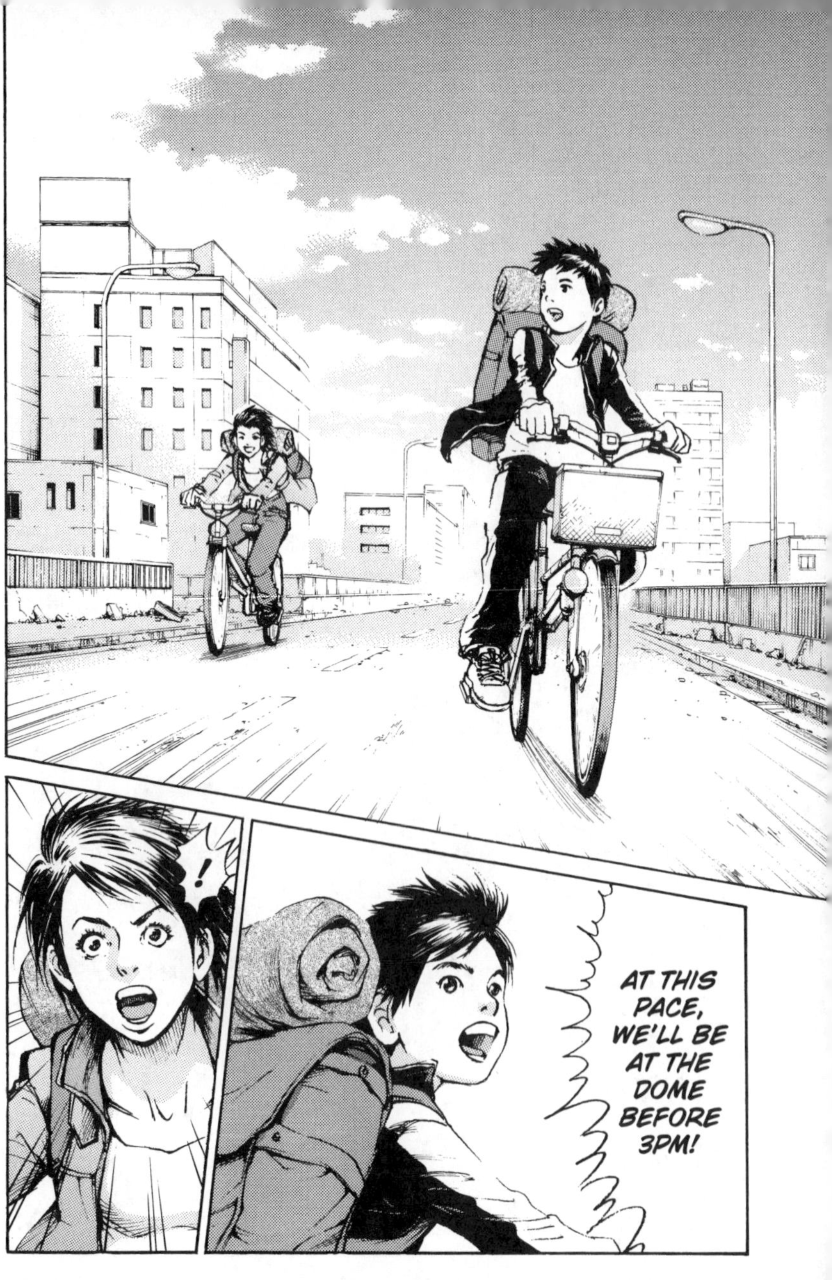
AT THIS PACE, WE'LL BE AT THE DOME BEFORE 3PM!
!

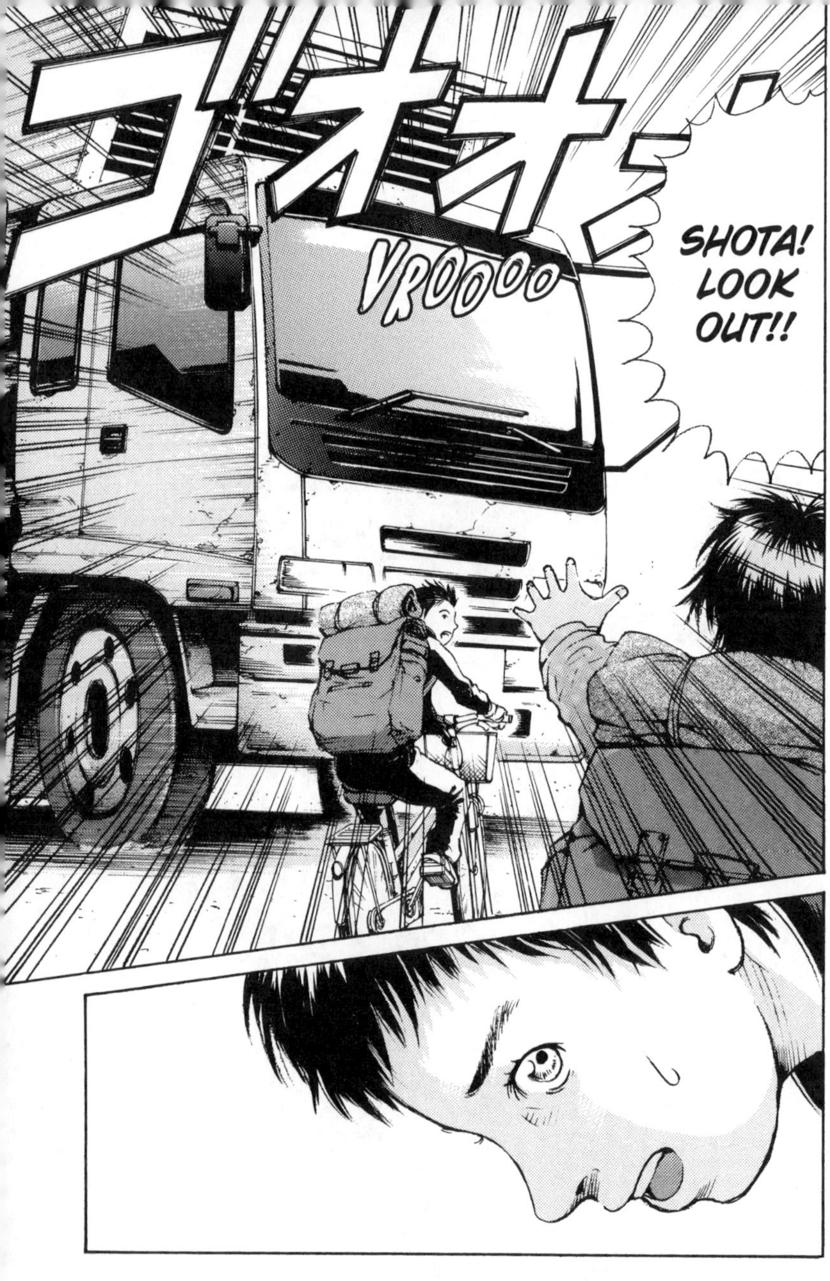
SHOTA! LOOK OUT!!
VROOOO

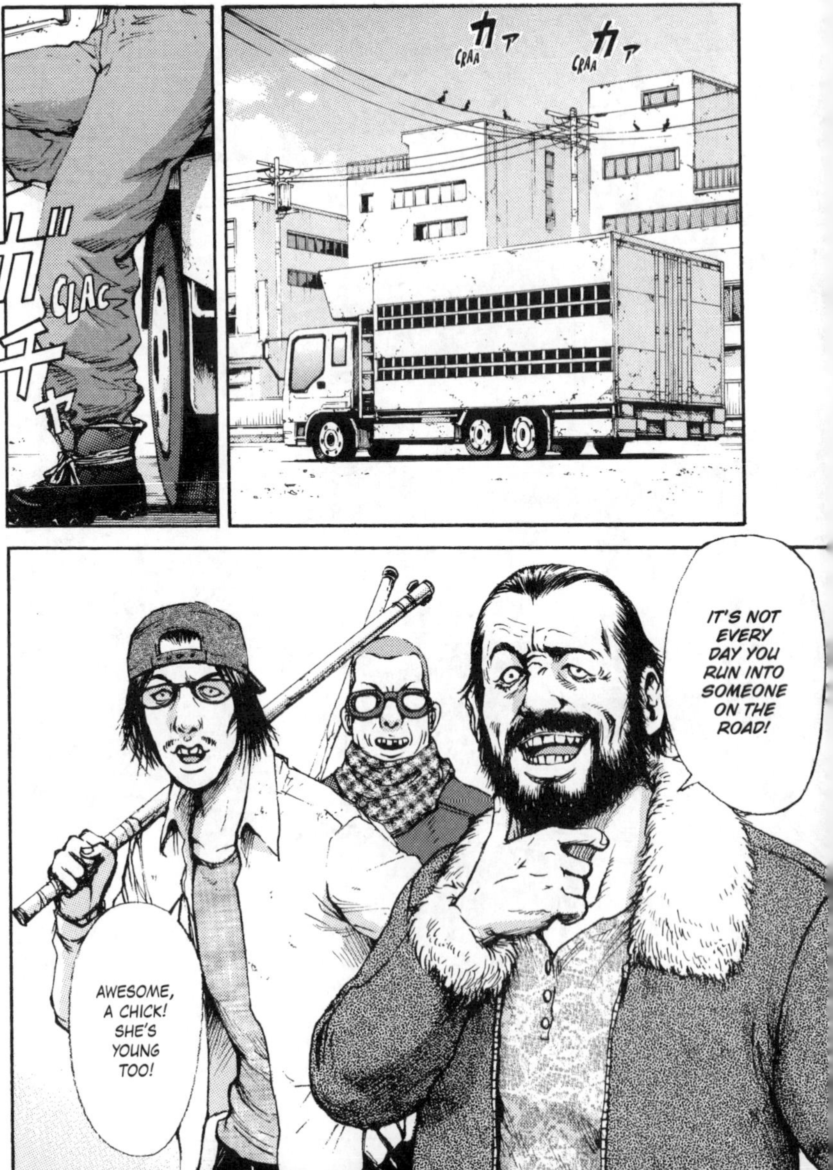
カァ CRAA
カァ CRAA
ガチャ CLAC
IT'S NOT EVERY DAY YOU RUN INTO SOMEONE ON THE ROAD!
AWESOME, A CHICK! SHE'S YOUNG TOO!

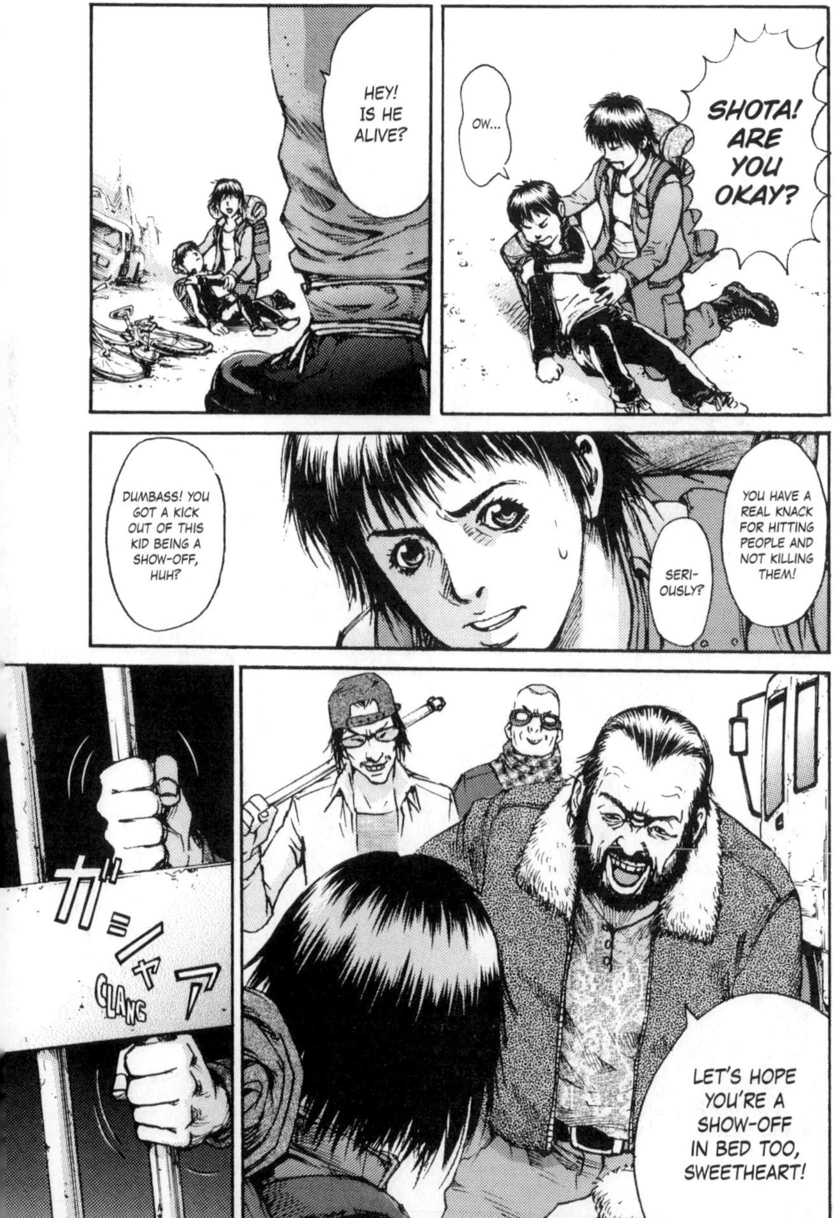
SHOTA! ARE YOU OKAY?
OW...
HEY! IS HE ALIVE?
YOU HAVE A REAL KNACK FOR HITTING PEOPLE AND NOT KILLING THEM!
SERI- OUSLY?
DUMBASS! YOU GOT A KICK OUT OF THIS KID BEING A SHOW-OFF, HUH?
LET'S HOPE YOU'RE A SHOW-OFF IN BED TOO, SWEETHEART!
ガシャア
CLANG

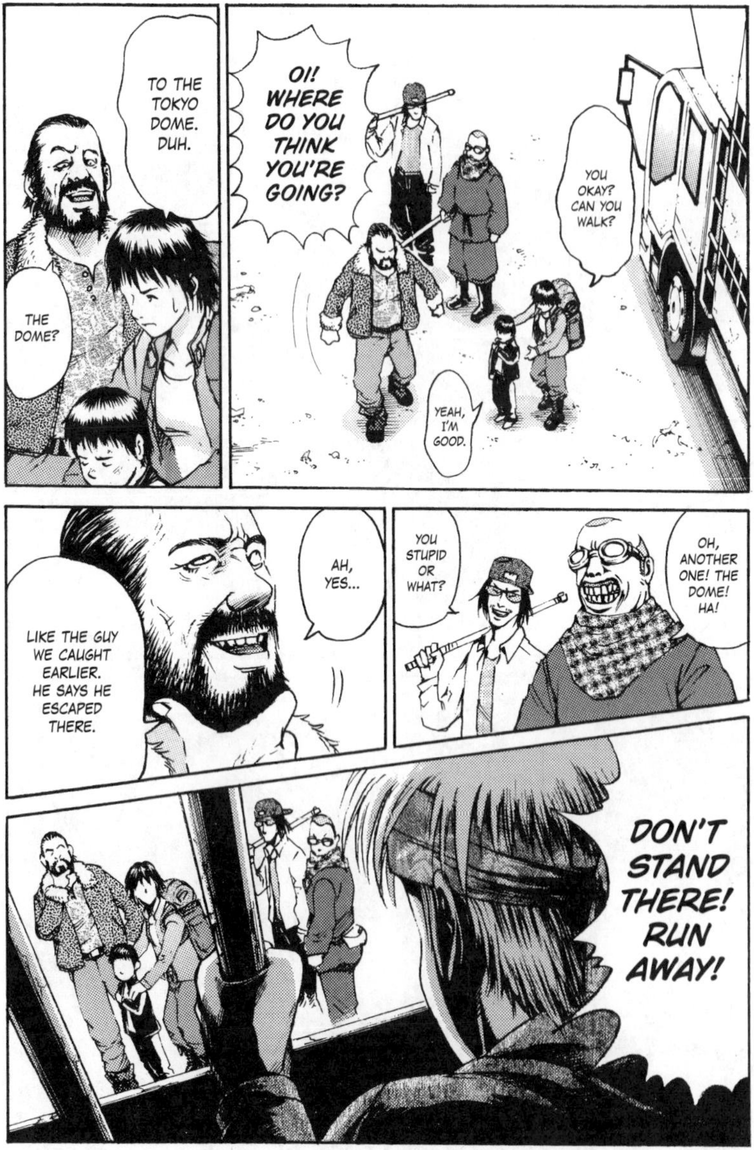

YOU OKAY? CAN YOU WALK?
OI! WHERE DO YOU THINK YOU'RE GOING?
YEAH, I'M GOOD.
TO THE TOKYO DOME. DUH.
THE DOME?
OH, ANOTHER ONE! THE DOME! HA!
YOU STUPID OR WHAT?
AH, YES...
LIKE THE GUY WE CAUGHT EARLIER. HE SAYS HE ESCAPED THERE.
DON'T STAND THERE! RUN AWAY!

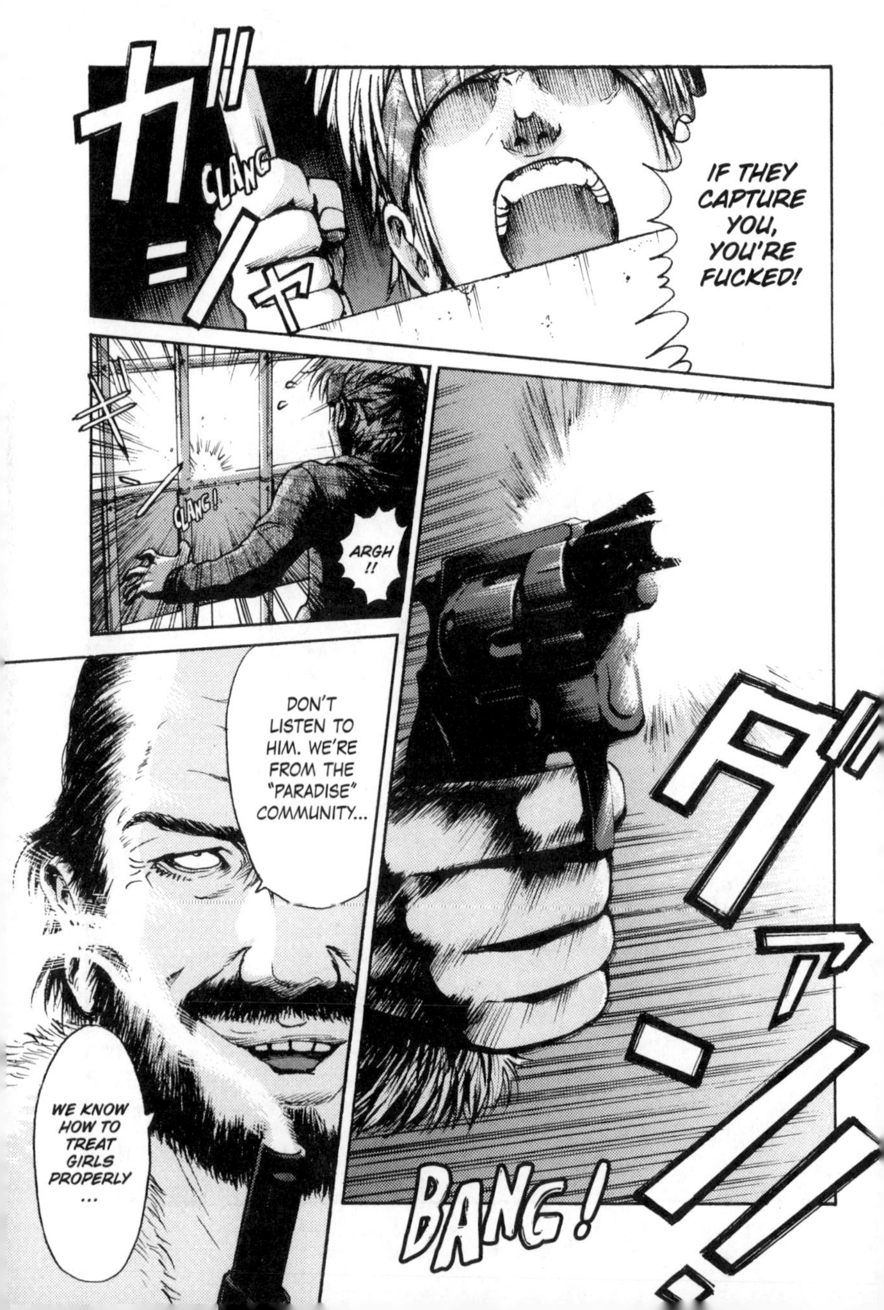

IF THEY CAPTURE YOU, YOU'RE FUCKED!
CLANG
BANG!
CLANG!
ARGH !!
DON'T LISTEN TO HIM. WE'RE FROM THE "PARADISE" COMMUNITY...
WE KNOW HOW TO TREAT GIRLS PROPERLY ...

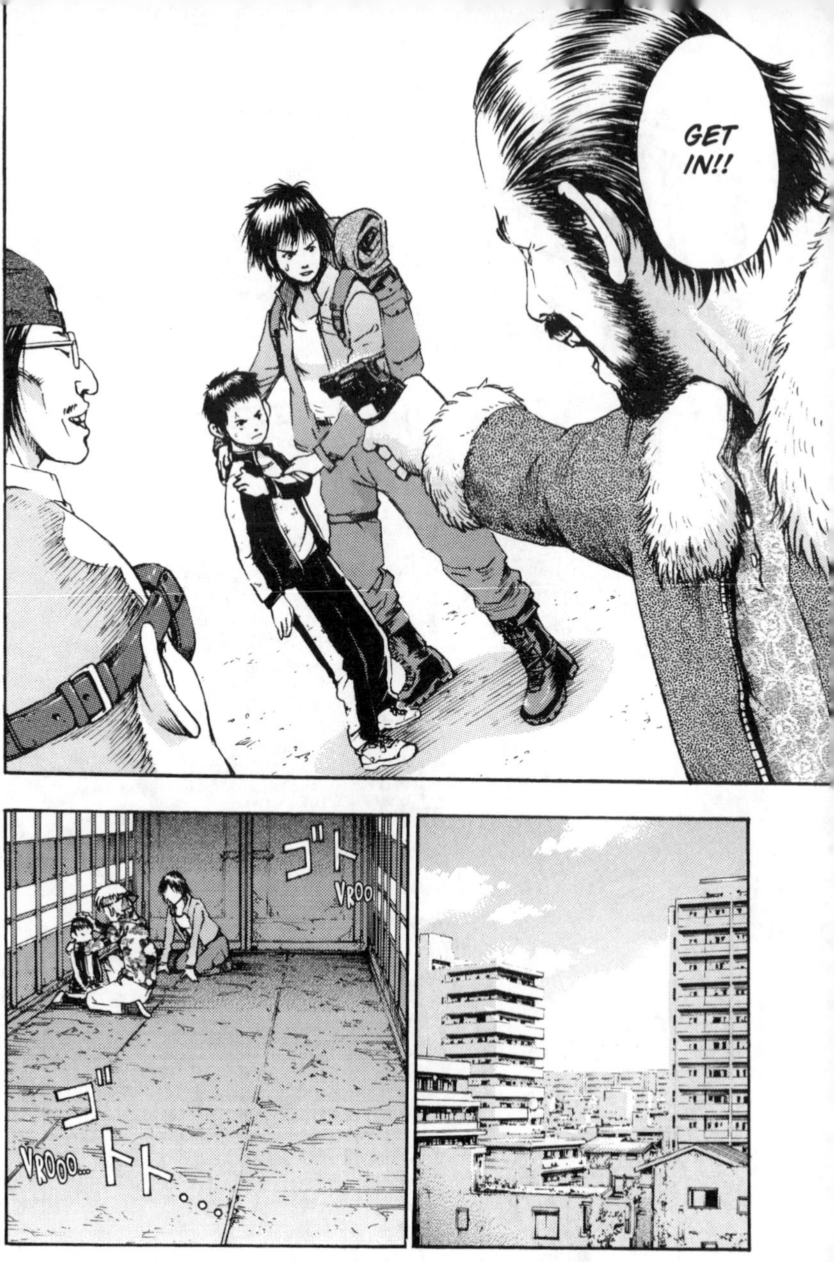
GET IN!!
ゴト
VROO
ゴトト…
VROOO...

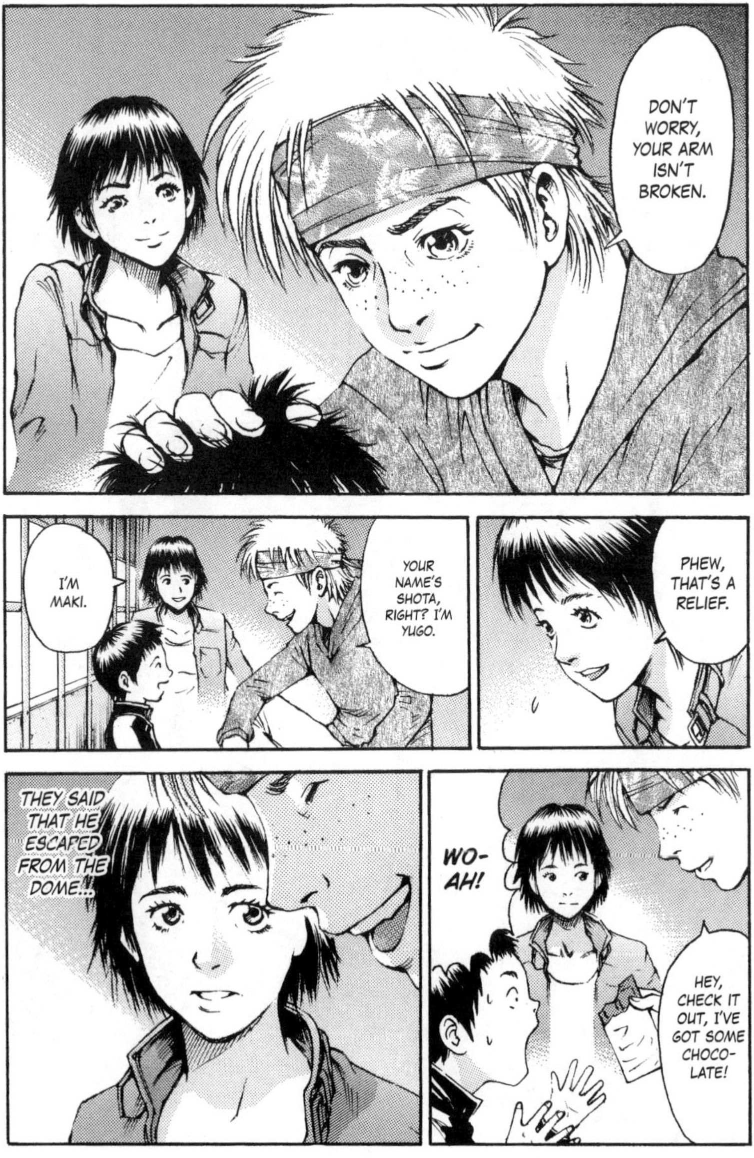
DON'T WORRY, YOUR ARM ISN'T BROKEN.
PHEW, THAT'S A RELIEF.
YOUR NAME'S SHOTA, RIGHT? I'M YUGO.
I'M MAKI.
HEY, CHECK IT OUT, I'VE GOT SOME CHOCO-LATE!
WO-AH!
THEY SAID THAT HE ESCAPED FROM THE DOME...

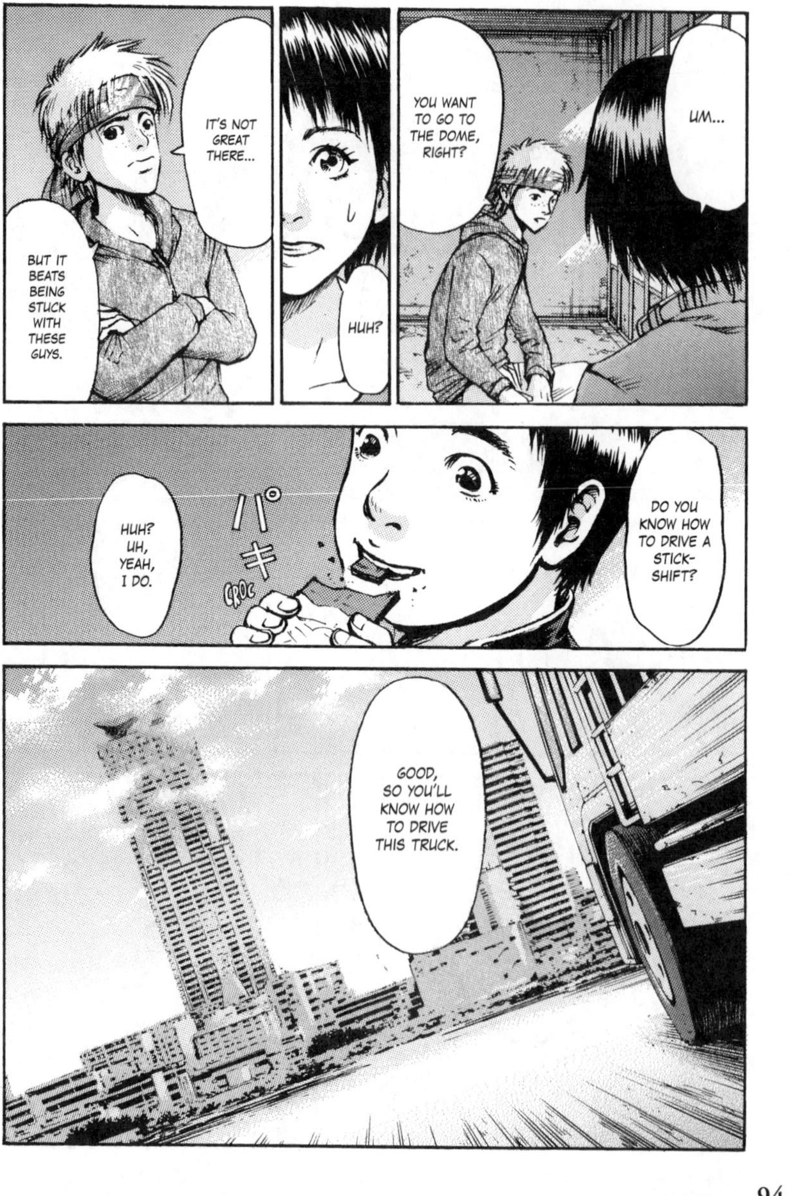
UM...
YOU WANT TO GO TO THE DOME, RIGHT?
HUH?
IT'S NOT GREAT THERE...
BUT IT BEATS BEING STUCK WITH THESE GUYS.
DO YOU KNOW HOW TO DRIVE A STICK-SHIFT?
パキ
CROC
HUH? UH, YEAH, I DO.
GOOD, SO YOU'LL KNOW HOW TO DRIVE THIS TRUCK.

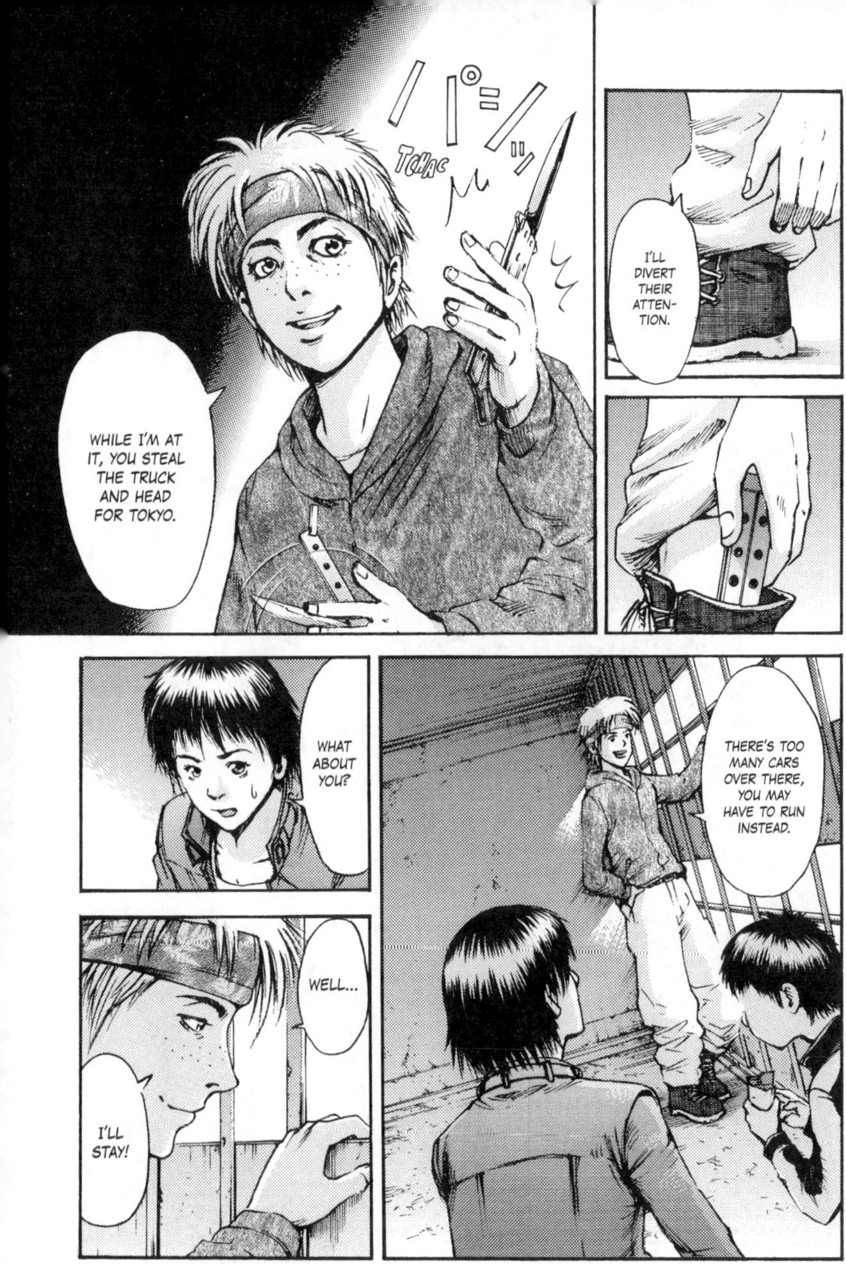
I'LL DIVERT THEIR ATTEN- TION.
TCHAC
WHILE I'M AT IT, YOU STEAL THE TRUCK AND HEAD FOR TOKYO.
THERE'S TOO MANY CARS OVER THERE, YOU MAY HAVE TO RUN INSTEAD.
WHAT ABOUT YOU?
WELL...
I'LL STAY!

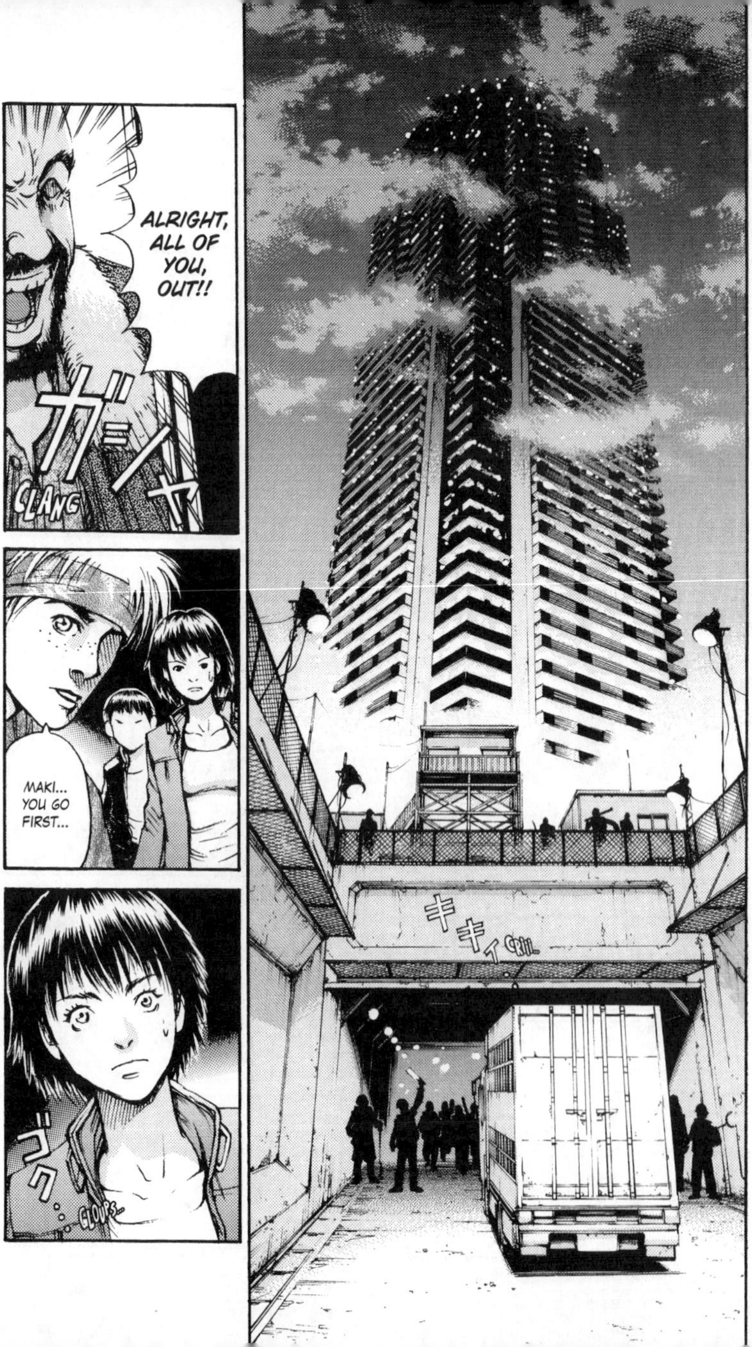
CRIII...
ALRIGHT, ALL OF YOU, OUT!!
CLANG
MAKI... YOU GO FIRST...
GLOUPS...

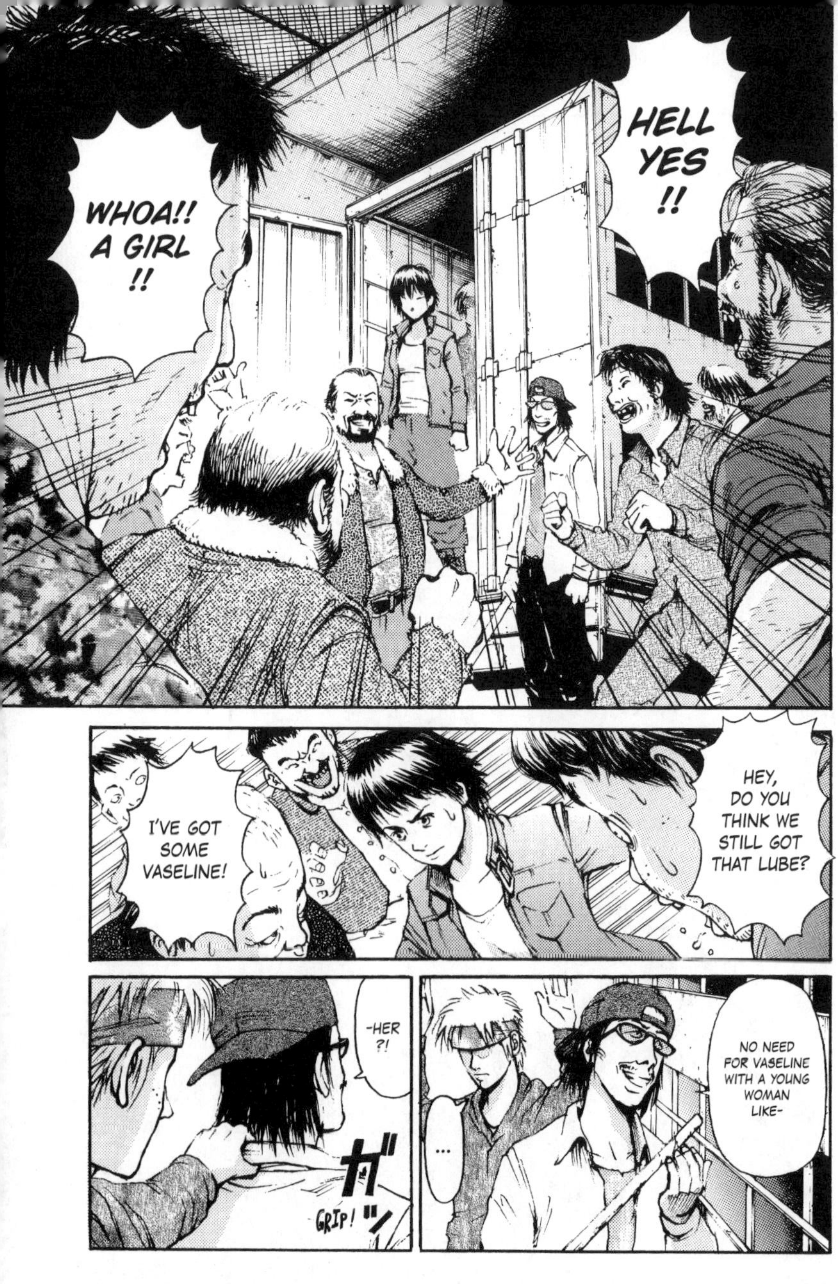
HELL YES !!
WHOA!! A GIRL !!
HEY, DO YOU THINK WE STILL GOT THAT LUBE?
I'VE GOT SOME VASELINE!
NO NEED FOR VASELINE WITH A YOUNG WOMAN LIKE-
...
-HER ?!
GRIP!

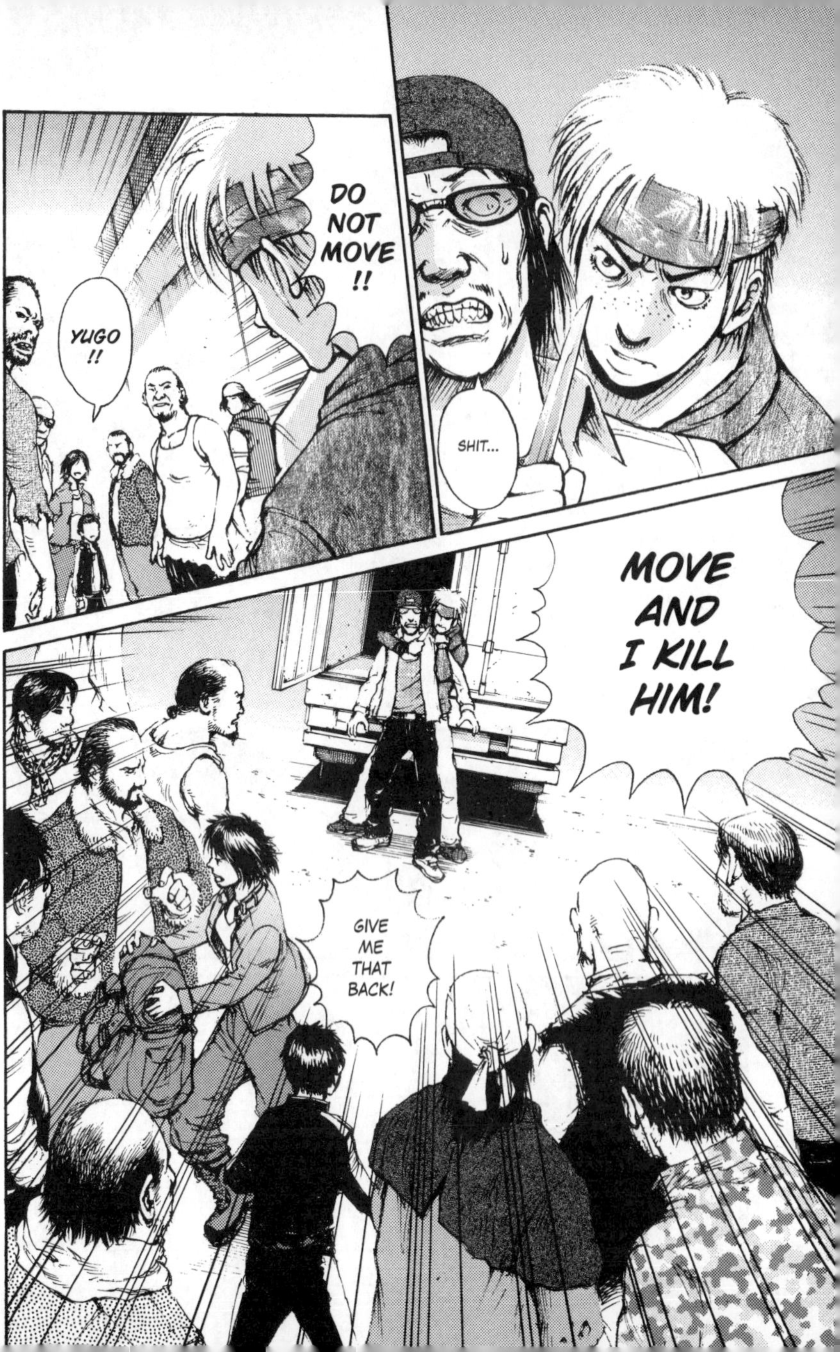
SHIT...
DO NOT MOVE !!
YUGO !!
MOVE AND I KILL HIM!
GIVE ME THAT BACK!

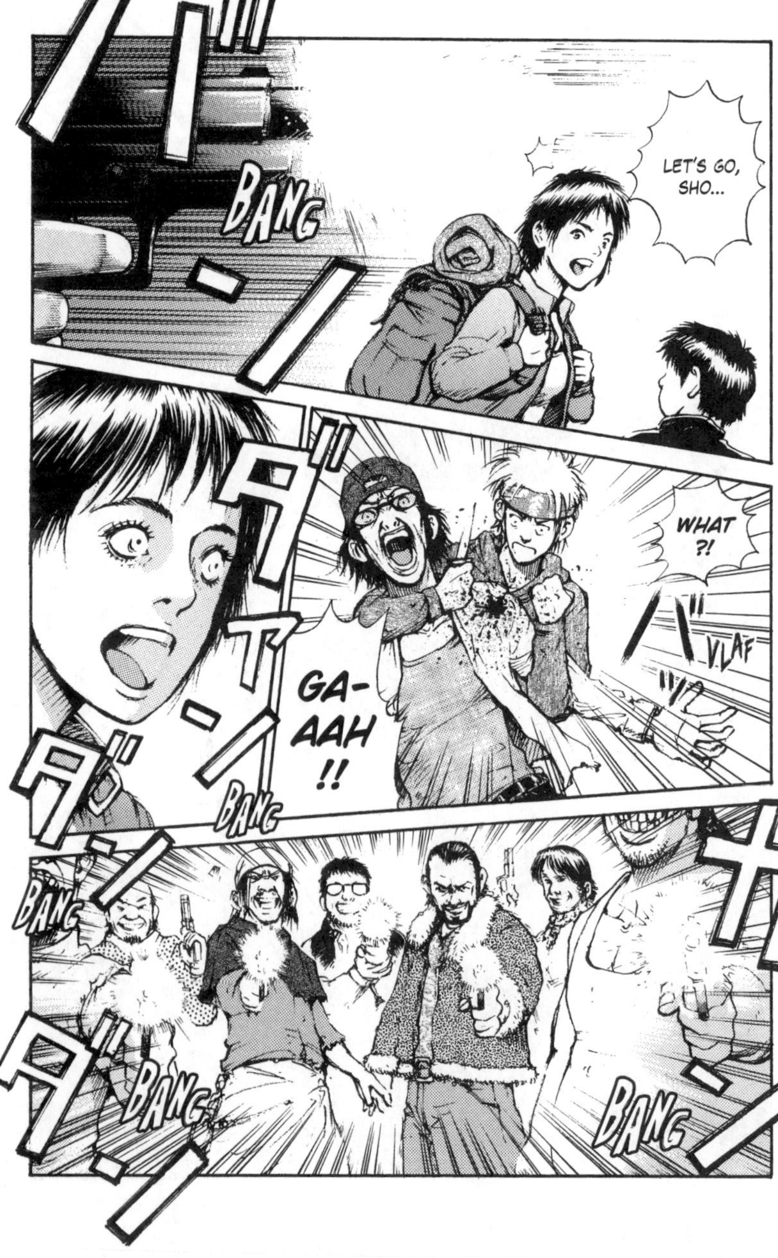
LET'S GO, SHO...
BANG
WHAT ?!
VLAF
GA-AAH !!
BANG
BANG
BANG
BANG

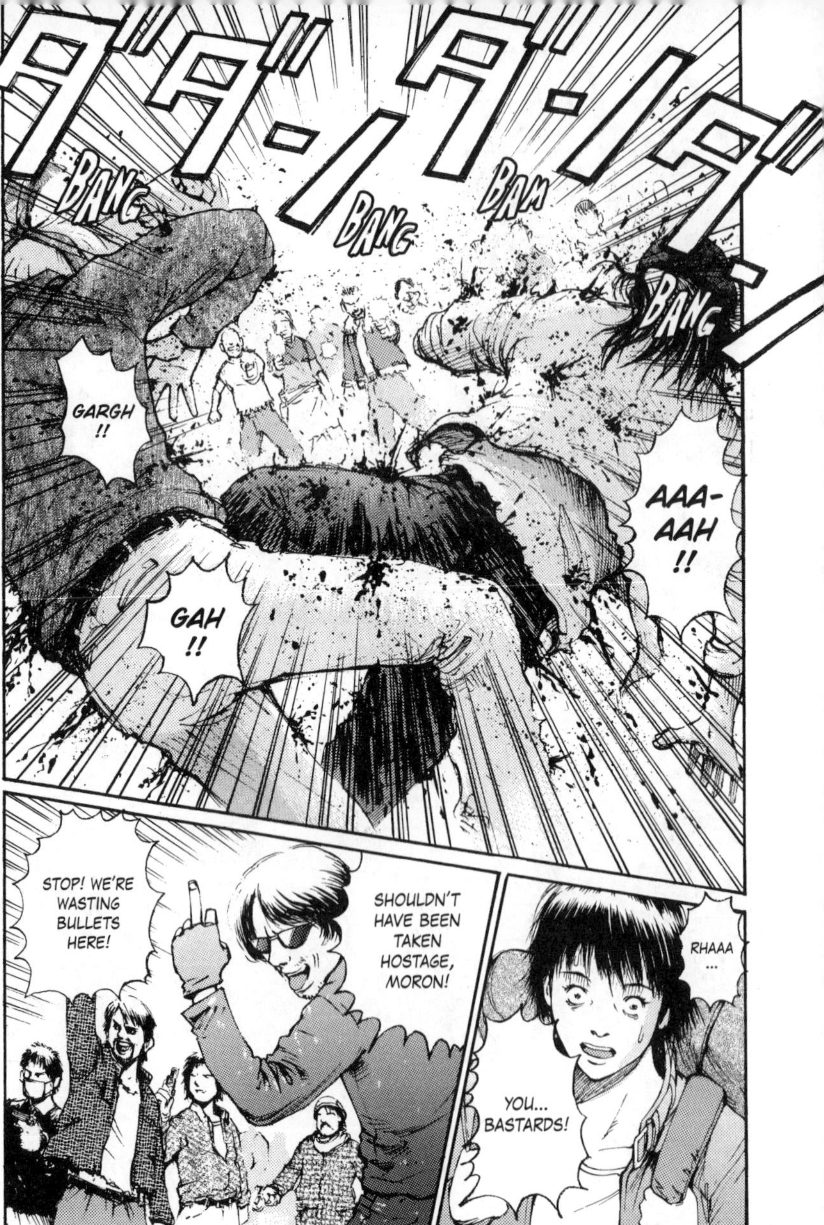
BANG
BAM
BANG
BANG
AAA-AAH!!
GARGH!!
GAH!!
RHAAA...
YOU... BASTARDS!
SHOULDN'T HAVE BEEN TAKEN HOSTAGE, MORON!
STOP! WE'RE WASTING BULLETS HERE!

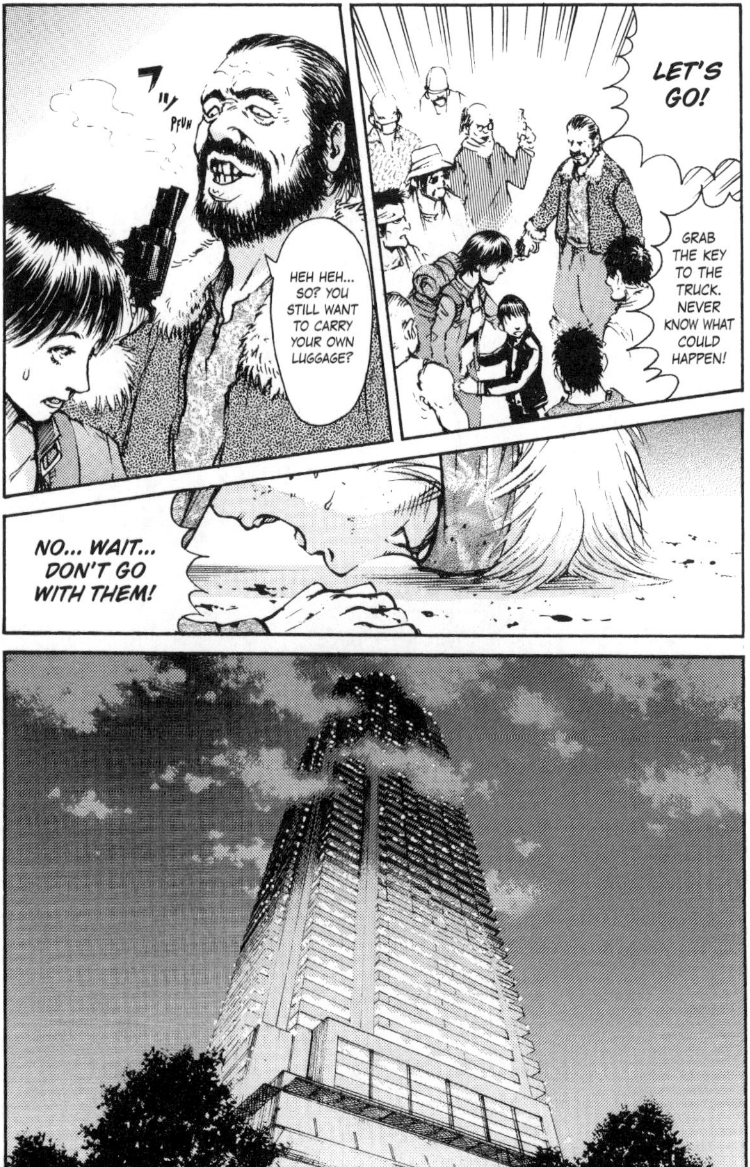
LET'S GO!
GRAB THE KEY TO THE TRUCK. NEVER KNOW WHAT COULD HAPPEN!
PFUH
HEH HEH... SO? YOU STILL WANT TO CARRY YOUR OWN LUGGAGE?
NO... WAIT... DON'T GO WITH THEM!

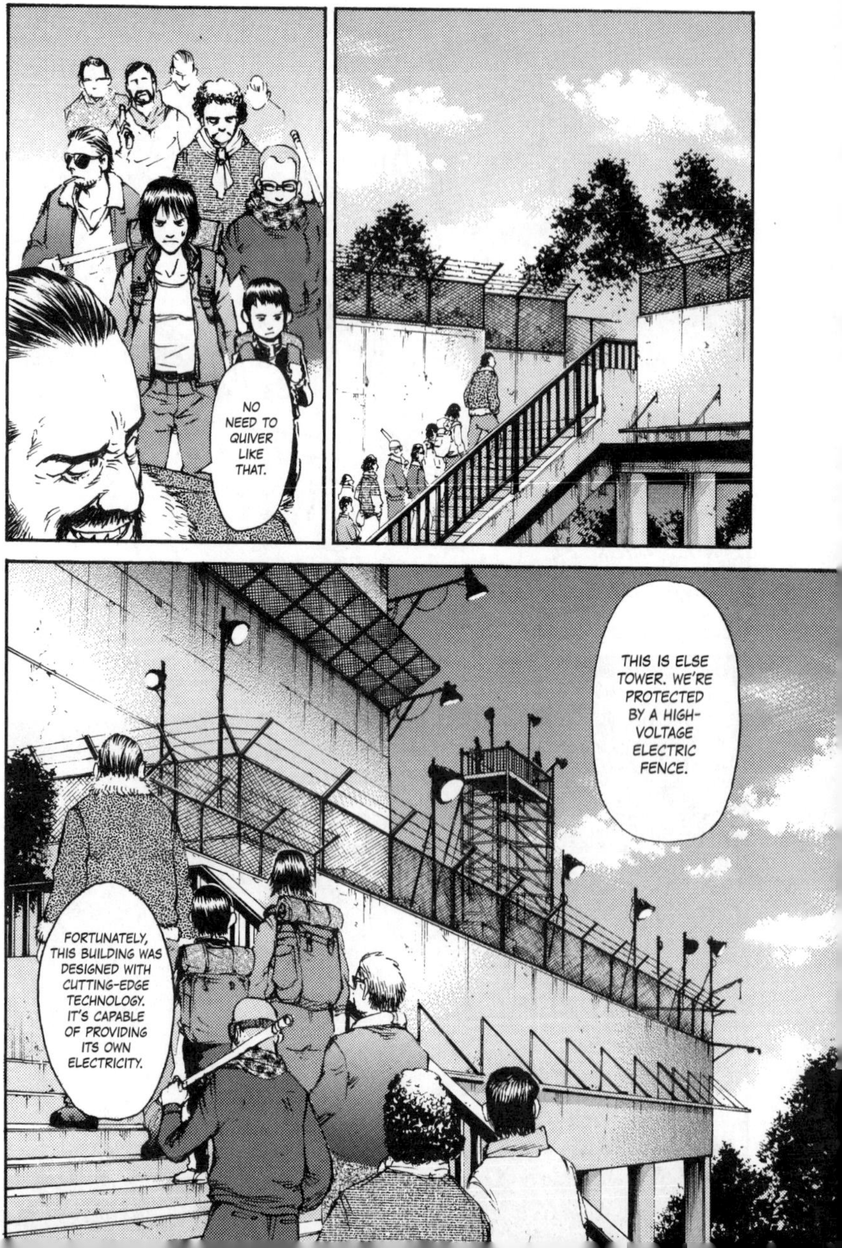
NO NEED TO QUIVER LIKE THAT.
THIS IS ELSE TOWER. WE'RE PROTECTED BY A HIGH-VOLTAGE ELECTRIC FENCE.
FORTUNATELY, THIS BUILDING WAS DESIGNED WITH CUTTING-EDGE TECHNOLOGY. IT'S CAPABLE OF PROVIDING ITS OWN ELECTRICITY.

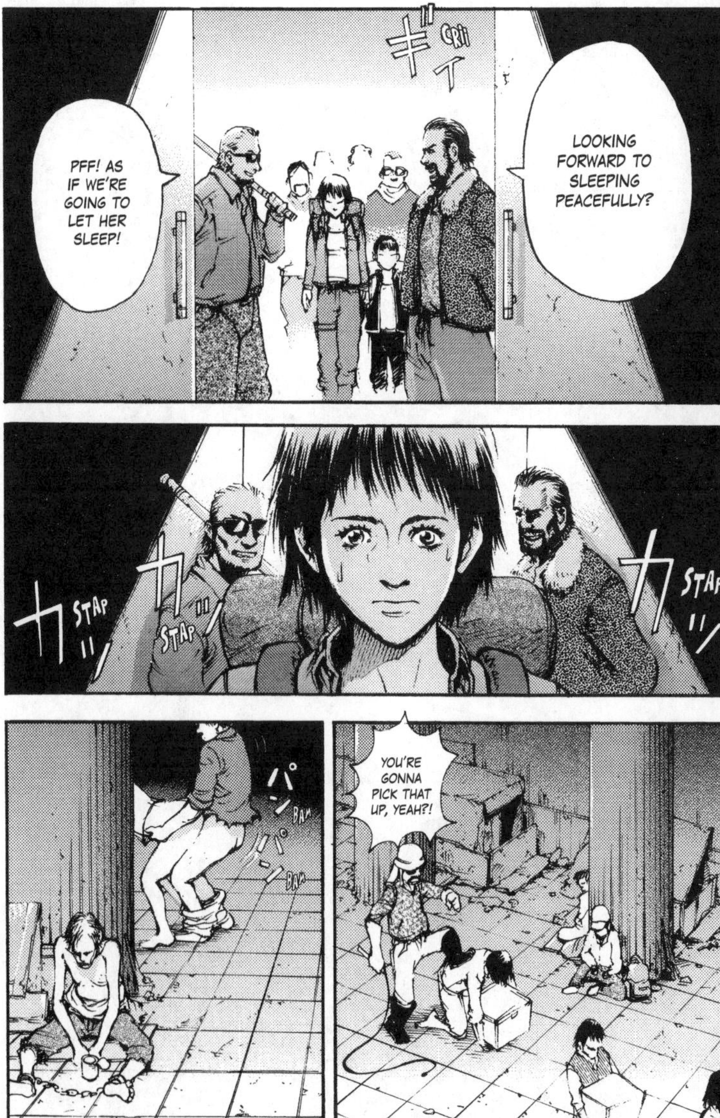
CRII
LOOKING FORWARD TO SLEEPING PEACEFULLY?
PFF! AS IF WE'RE GOING TO LET HER SLEEP!
STAP
STAP
STAP
YOU'RE GONNA PICK THAT UP, YEAH?!
BAM
BAM

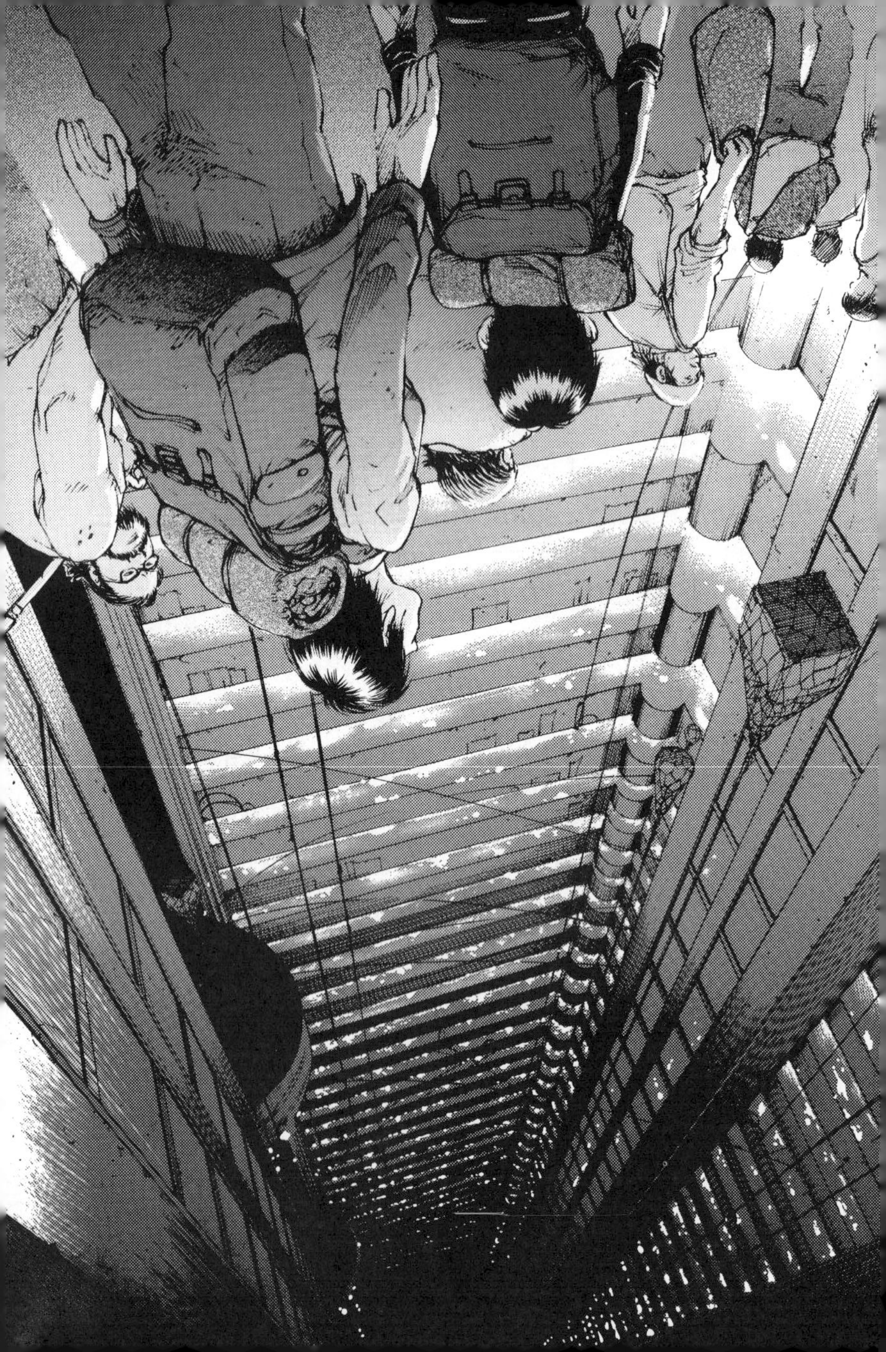

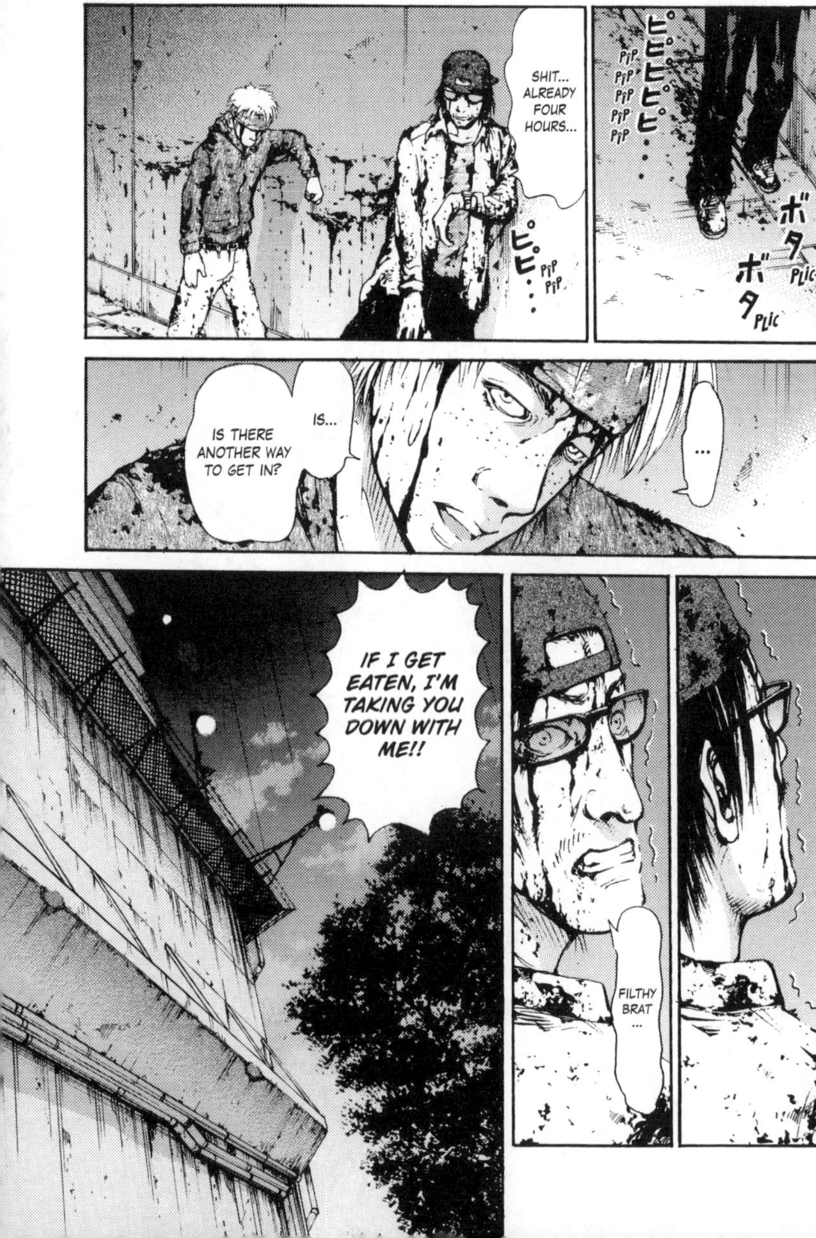
ピピピピピ・・・
PIP PIP PIP PIP PIP
ボタ PLIC
ボタ PLIC
SHIT... ALREADY FOUR HOURS...
ピピ・・・ PIP PIP
...
IS...
IS THERE ANOTHER WAY TO GET IN?
FILTHY BRAT ...
IF I GET EATEN, I'M TAKING YOU DOWN WITH ME!!

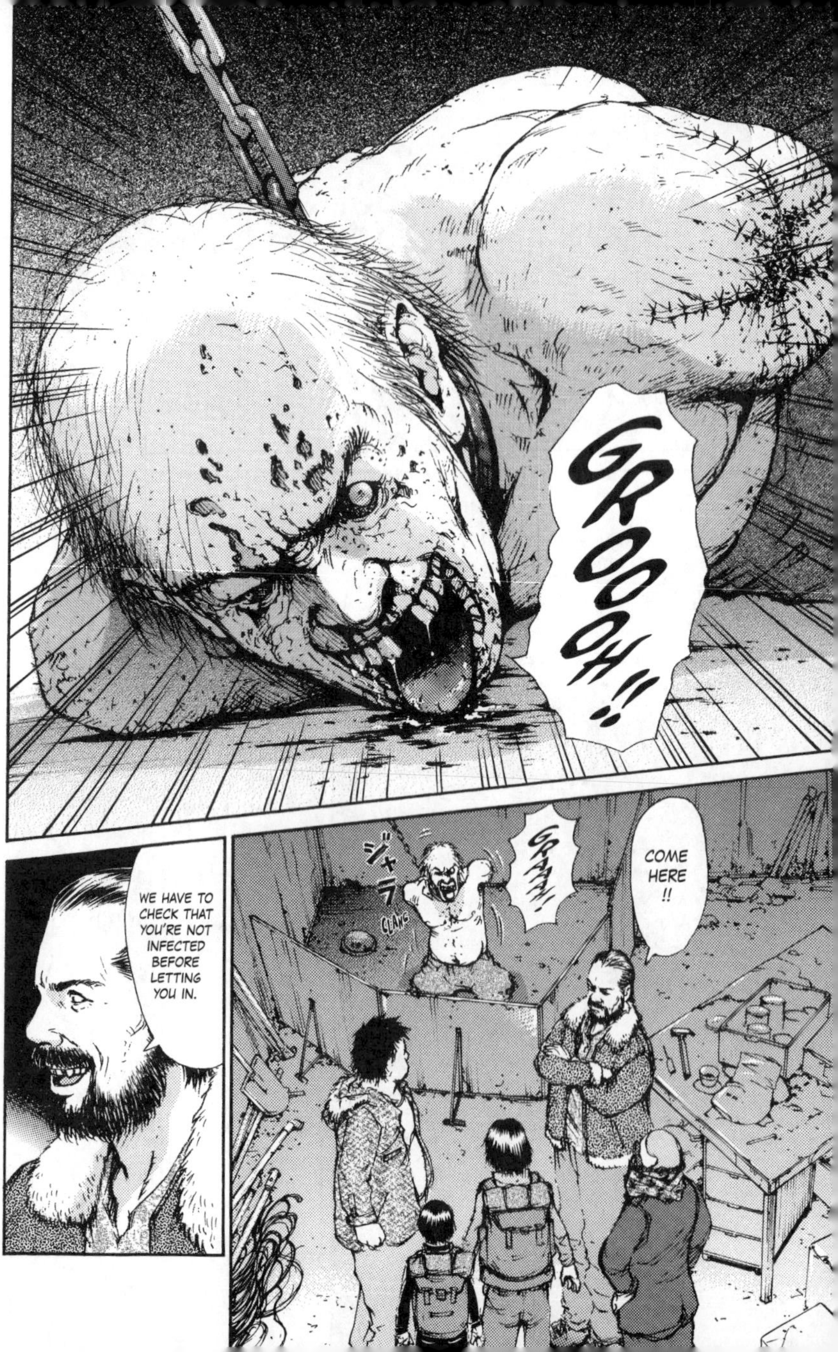
GROOOOH!!
COME HERE !!
GRAAAH!
ジャラ
CLANG
WE HAVE TO CHECK THAT YOU'RE NOT INFECTED BEFORE LETTING YOU IN.

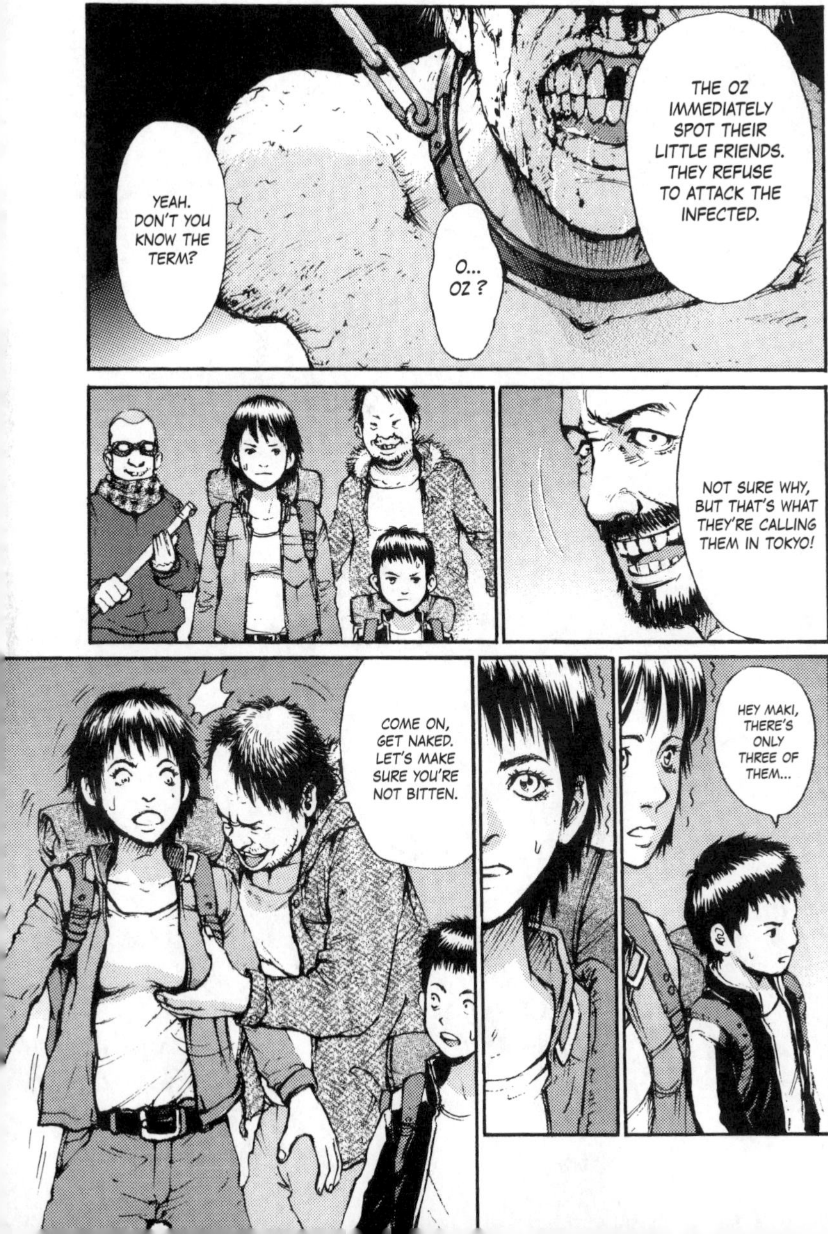
THE OZ IMMEDIATELY SPOT THEIR LITTLE FRIENDS. THEY REFUSE TO ATTACK THE INFECTED.
O... OZ ?
YEAH. DON'T YOU KNOW THE TERM?
NOT SURE WHY, BUT THAT'S WHAT THEY'RE CALLING THEM IN TOKYO!
HEY MAKI, THERE'S ONLY THREE OF THEM...
COME ON, GET NAKED. LET'S MAKE SURE YOU'RE NOT BITTEN.

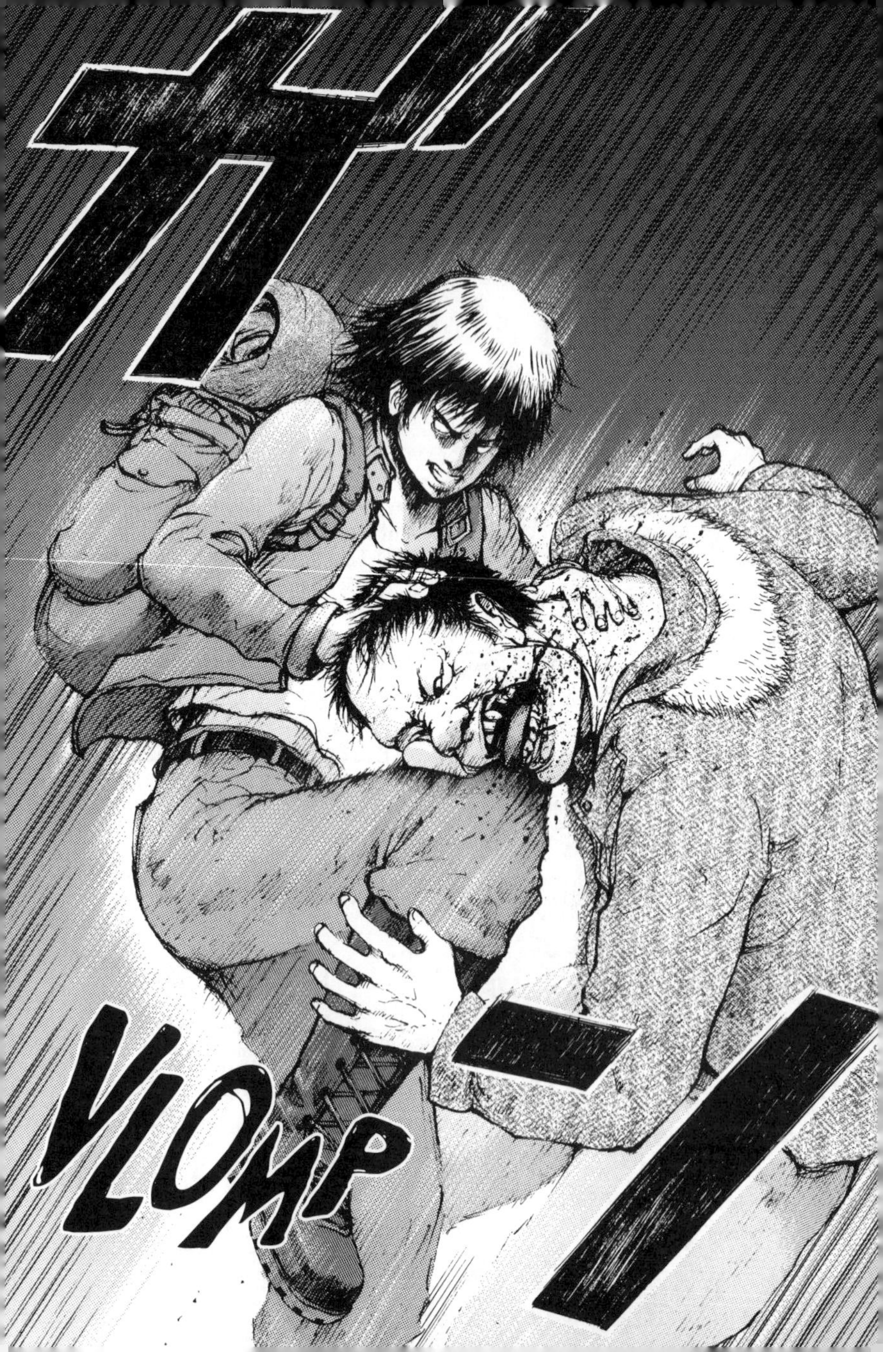
VLOMP

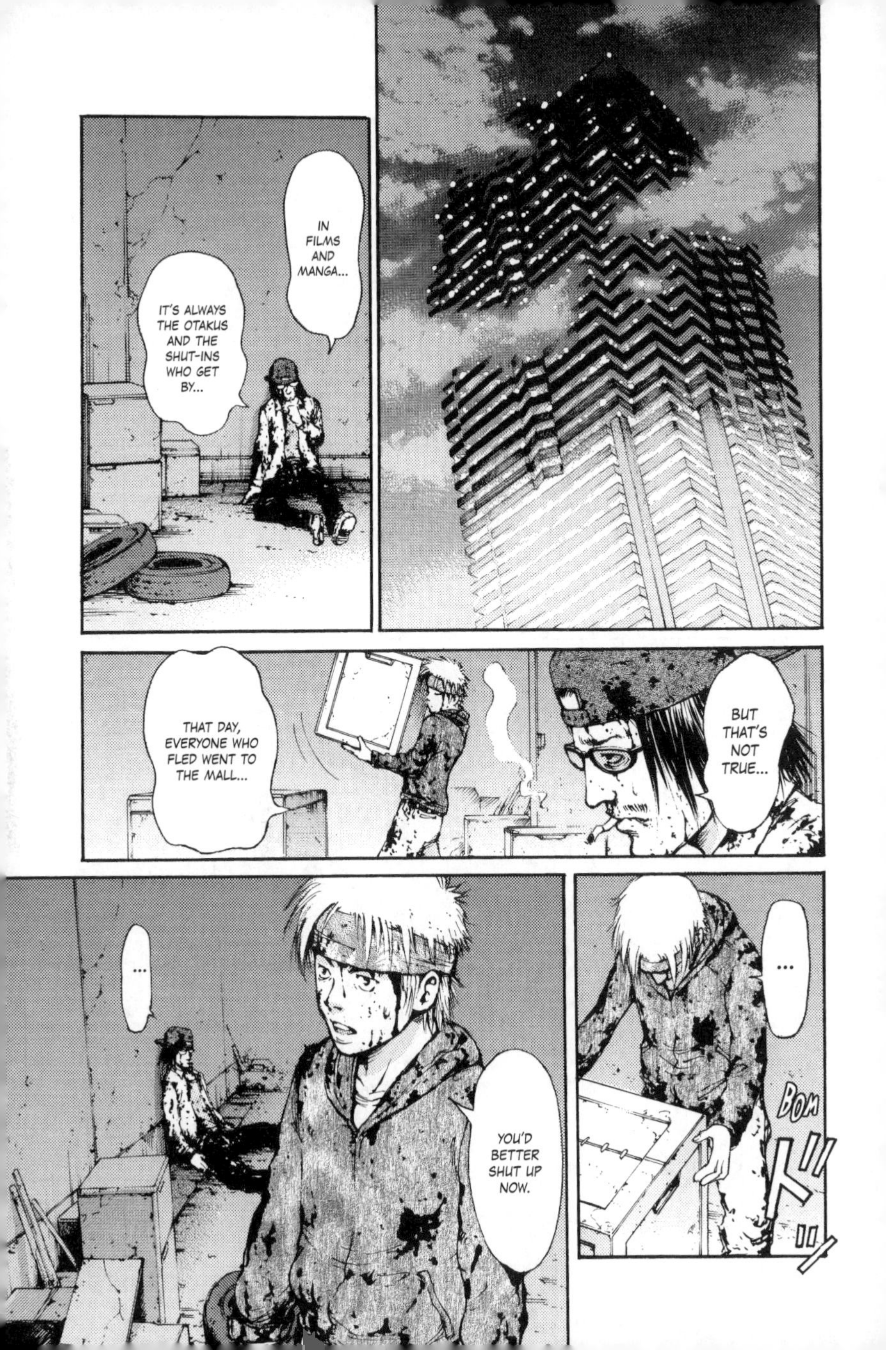
IN FILMS AND MANGA...
IT'S ALWAYS THE OTAKUS AND THE SHUT-INS WHO GET BY...
BUT THAT'S NOT TRUE...
THAT DAY, EVERYONE WHO FLED WENT TO THE MALL...
...
BOM
YOU'D BETTER SHUT UP NOW.
...

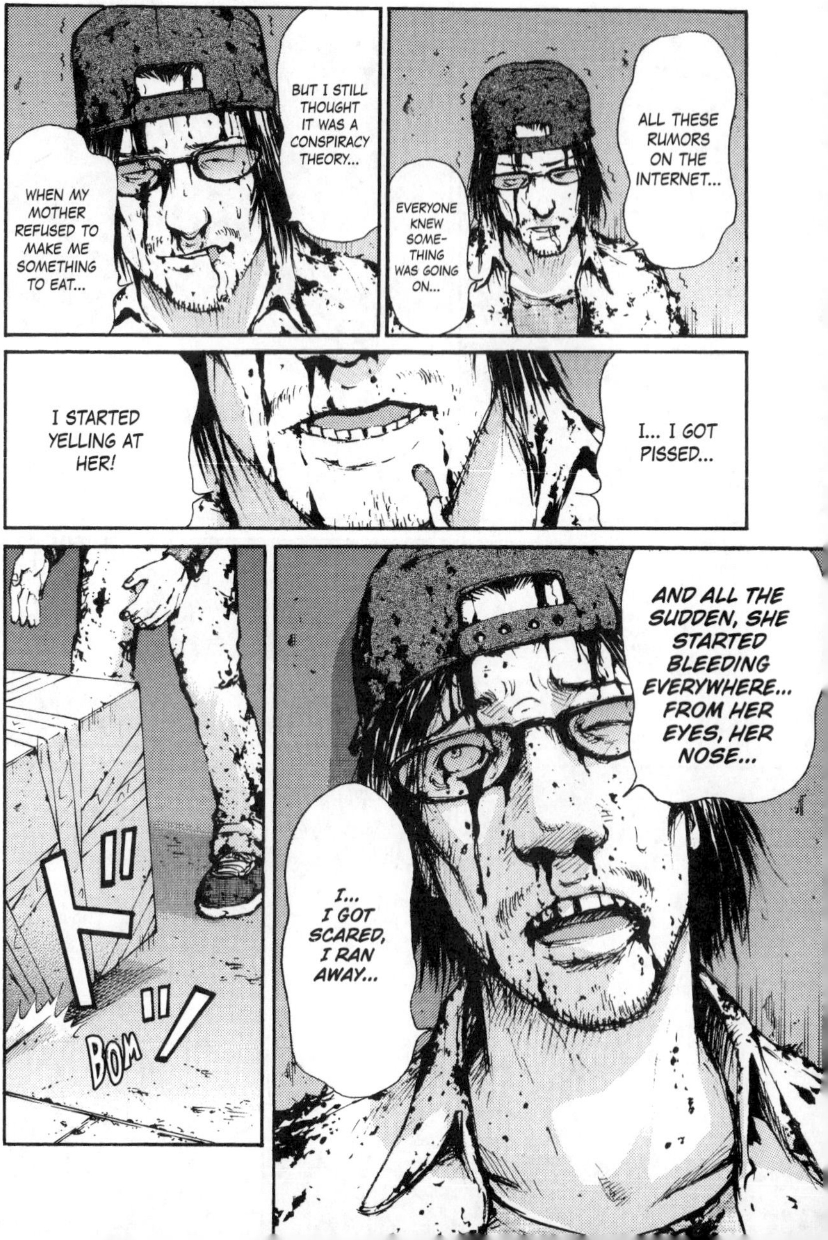
ALL THESE RUMORS ON THE INTERNET...
EVERYONE KNEW SOME-THING WAS GOING ON...
BUT I STILL THOUGHT IT WAS A CONSPIRACY THEORY...
WHEN MY MOTHER REFUSED TO MAKE ME SOMETHING TO EAT...
I... I GOT PISSED...
I STARTED YELLING AT HER!
AND ALL THE SUDDEN, SHE STARTED BLEEDING EVERYWHERE... FROM HER EYES, HER NOSE...
I... I GOT SCARED, I RAN AWAY...
BOM

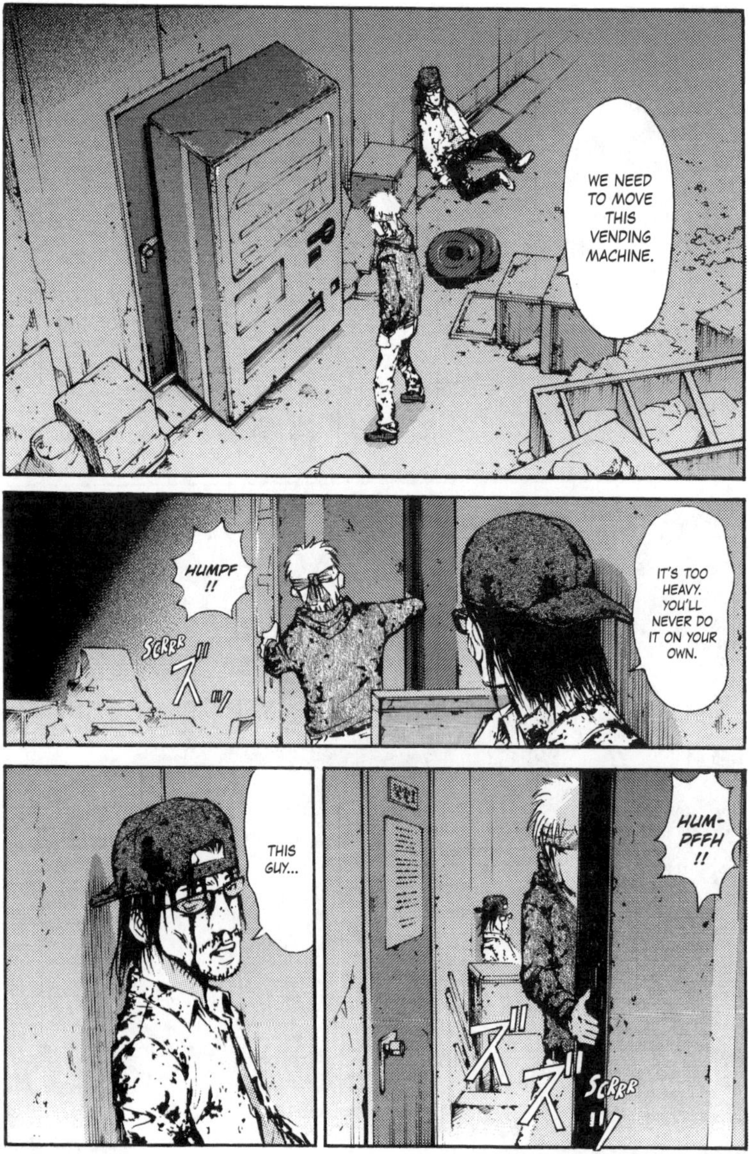
WE NEED TO MOVE THIS VENDING MACHINE.
IT'S TOO HEAVY. YOU'LL NEVER DO IT ON YOUR OWN.
HUMPF !!
SCRRR
HUM-PFFH !!
SCRRR
THIS GUY...

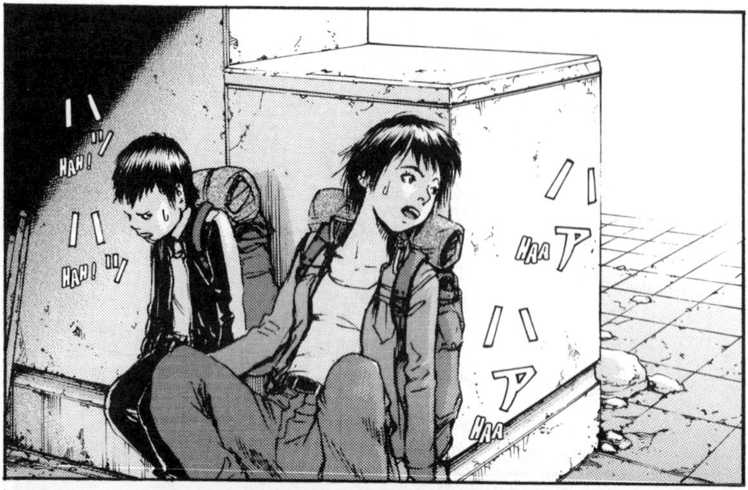
ハア HAA
ハア HAA
ハッ HAH!
ハッ HAH!

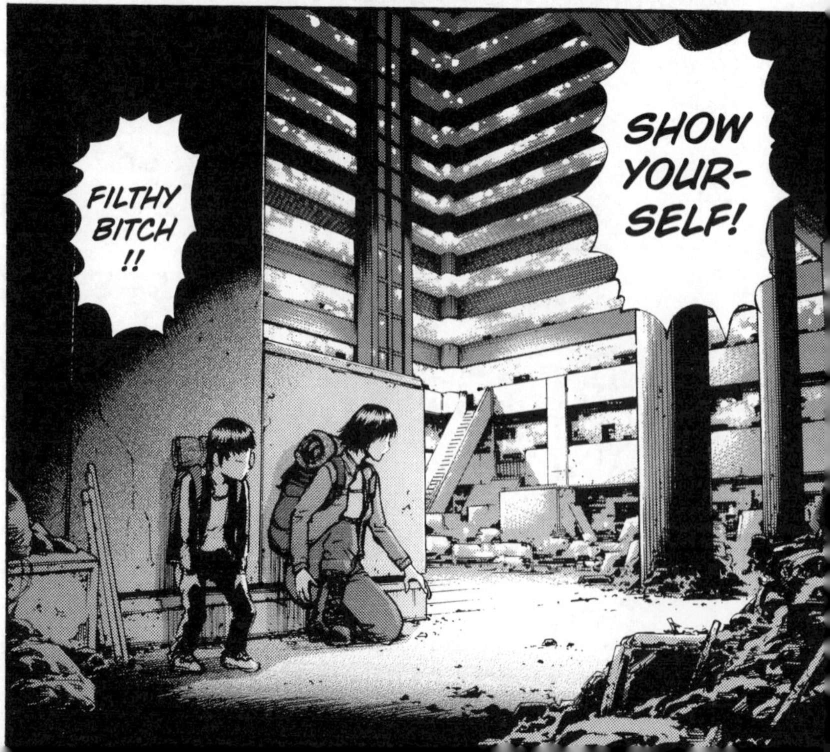
SHOW YOUR-SELF!
FILTHY BITCH !!

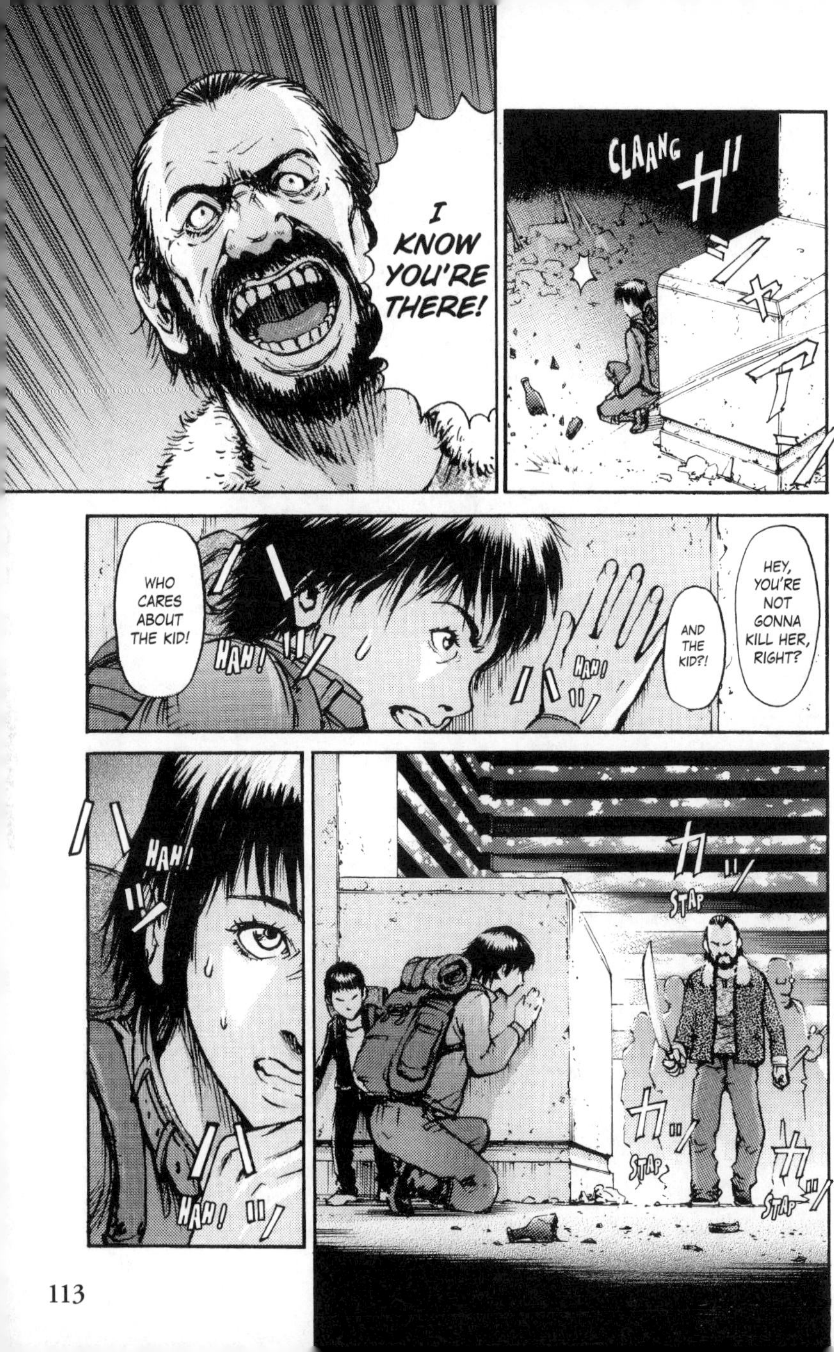
CLAANG
I KNOW YOU'RE THERE!
HEY, YOU'RE NOT GONNA KILL HER, RIGHT?
AND THE KID?!
HAH!
WHO CARES ABOUT THE KID!
HAH!
STAP
STAP
STAP
HAH!
HAH!

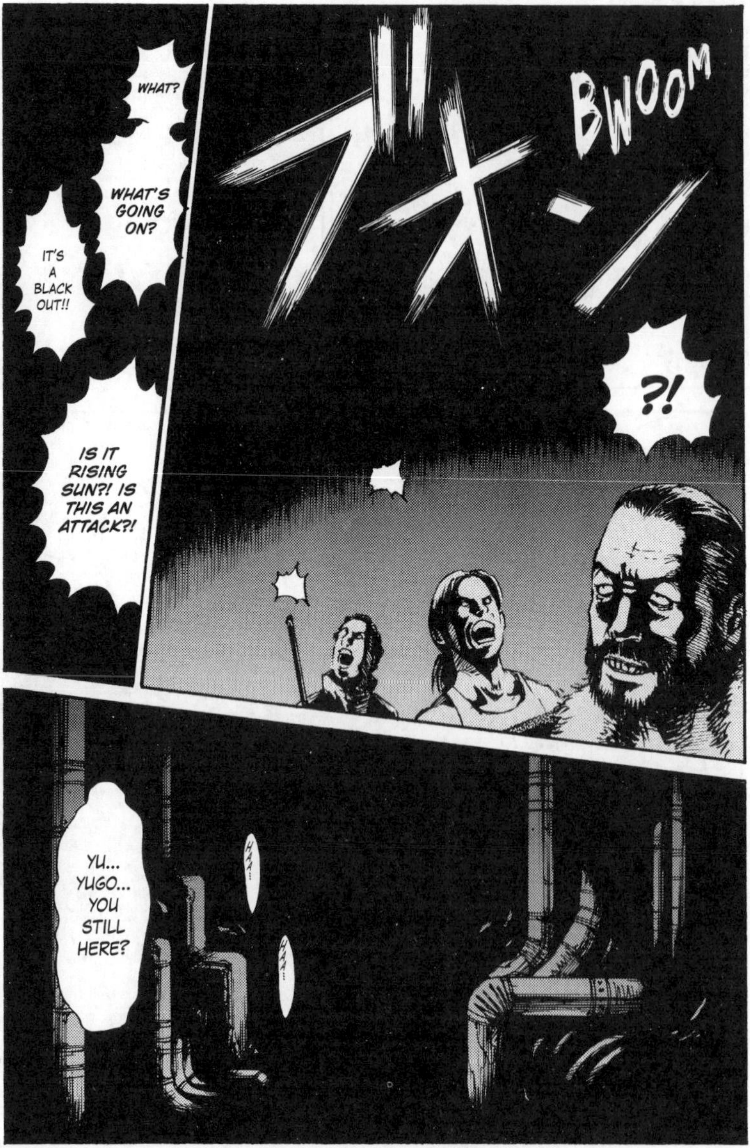
ブオーン
BWOOM
?!
WHAT?
WHAT'S GOING ON?
IT'S A BLACK OUT!!
IS IT RISING SUN?! IS THIS AN ATTACK?!
HAA...
HAA...
YU... YUGO... YOU STILL HERE?

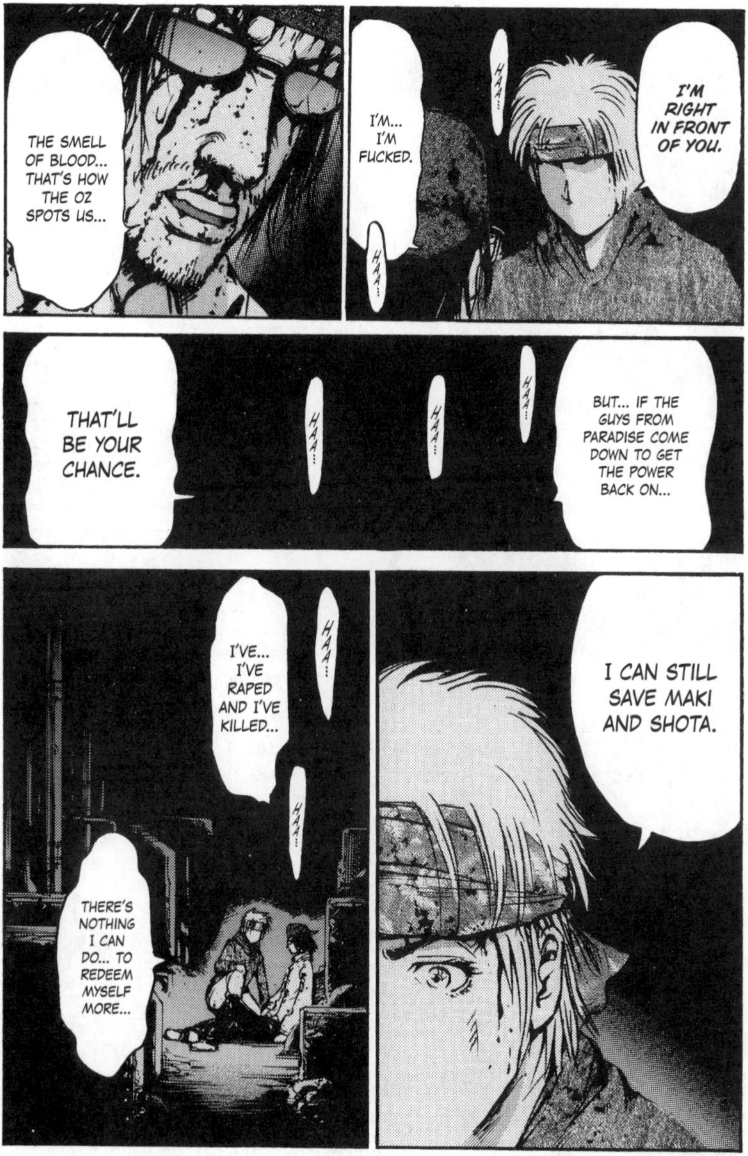
I'M RIGHT IN FRONT OF YOU.
HAA...
I'M... I'M FUCKED.
HAA...
THE SMELL OF BLOOD... THAT'S HOW THE OZ SPOTS US...
BUT... IF THE GUYS FROM PARADISE COME DOWN TO GET THE POWER BACK ON...
HAA...
HAA...
HAA...
THAT'LL BE YOUR CHANCE.
I CAN STILL SAVE MAKI AND SHOTA.
HAA...
I'VE... I'VE RAPED AND I'VE KILLED...
HAA...
THERE'S NOTHING I CAN DO... TO REDEEM MYSELF MORE...

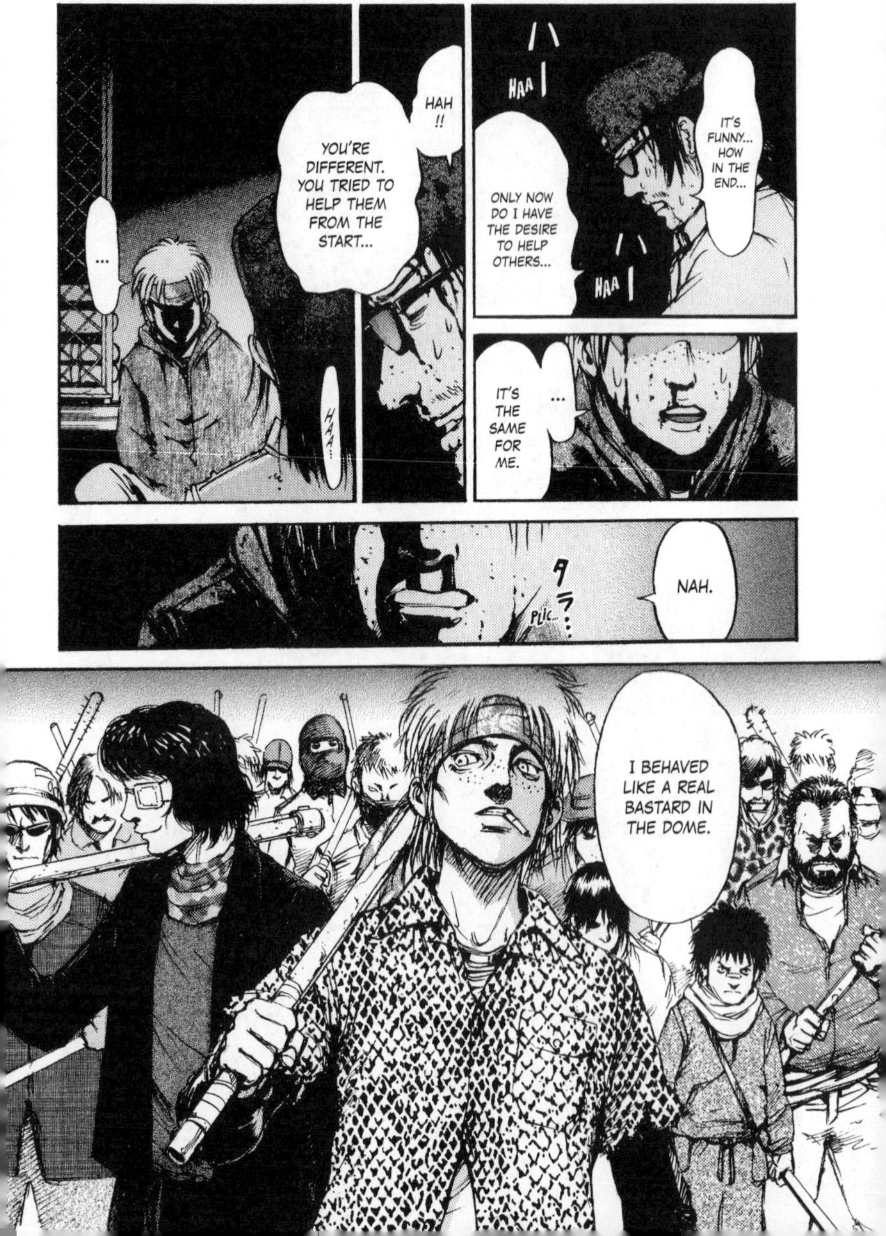
IT'S FUNNY... HOW IN THE END...
HAA
HAA
ONLY NOW DO I HAVE THE DESIRE TO HELP OTHERS...
...
IT'S THE SAME FOR ME.
HAH !!
YOU'RE DIFFERENT. YOU TRIED TO HELP THEM FROM THE START...
HAA...
...
NAH.
PLIC...
I BEHAVED LIKE A REAL BASTARD IN THE DOME.

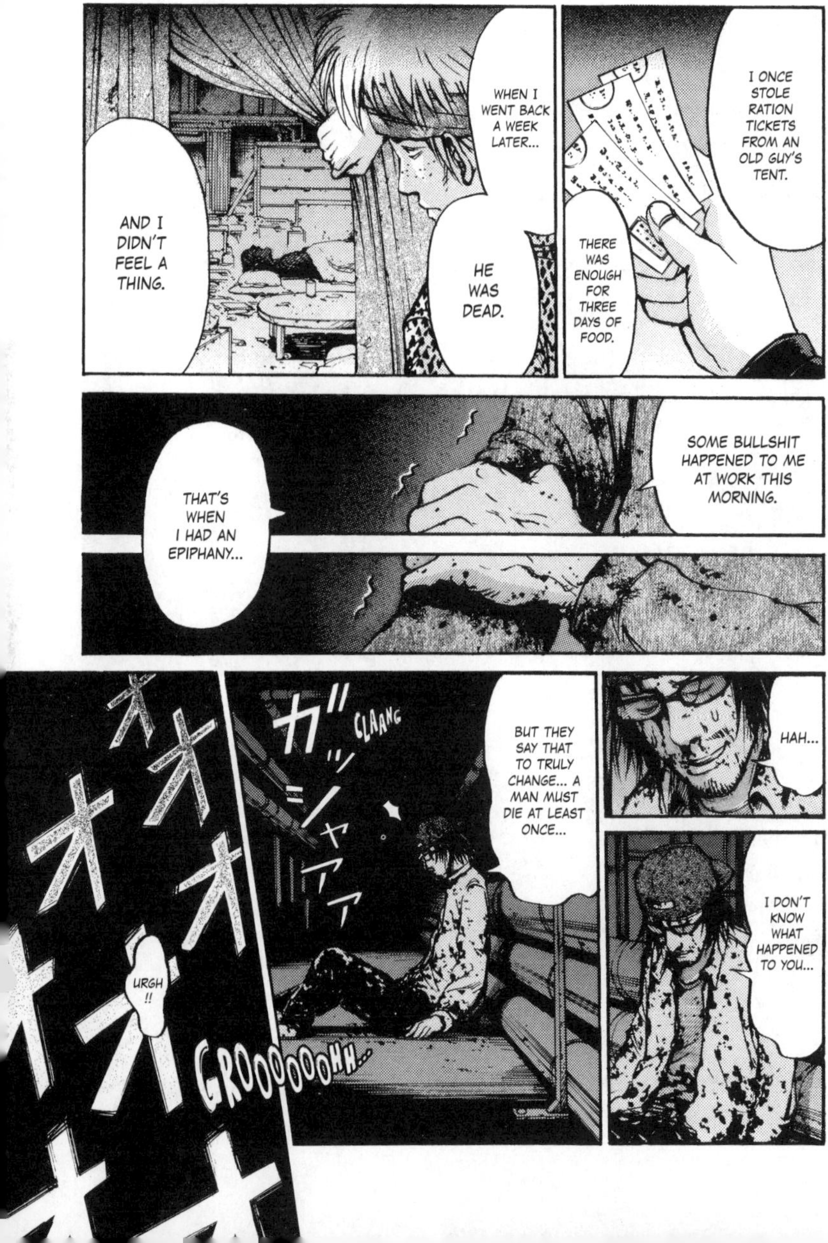
I ONCE STOLE RATION TICKETS FROM AN OLD GUY'S TENT.
THERE WAS ENOUGH FOR THREE DAYS OF FOOD.
WHEN I WENT BACK A WEEK LATER...
HE WAS DEAD.
AND I DIDN'T FEEL A THING.
SOME BULLSHIT HAPPENED TO ME AT WORK THIS MORNING.
THAT'S WHEN I HAD AN EPIPHANY...
HAH...
I DON'T KNOW WHAT HAPPENED TO YOU...
BUT THEY SAY THAT TO TRULY CHANGE... A MAN MUST DIE AT LEAST ONCE...
CLAANG
GROOOOOOHH...
URGH !!

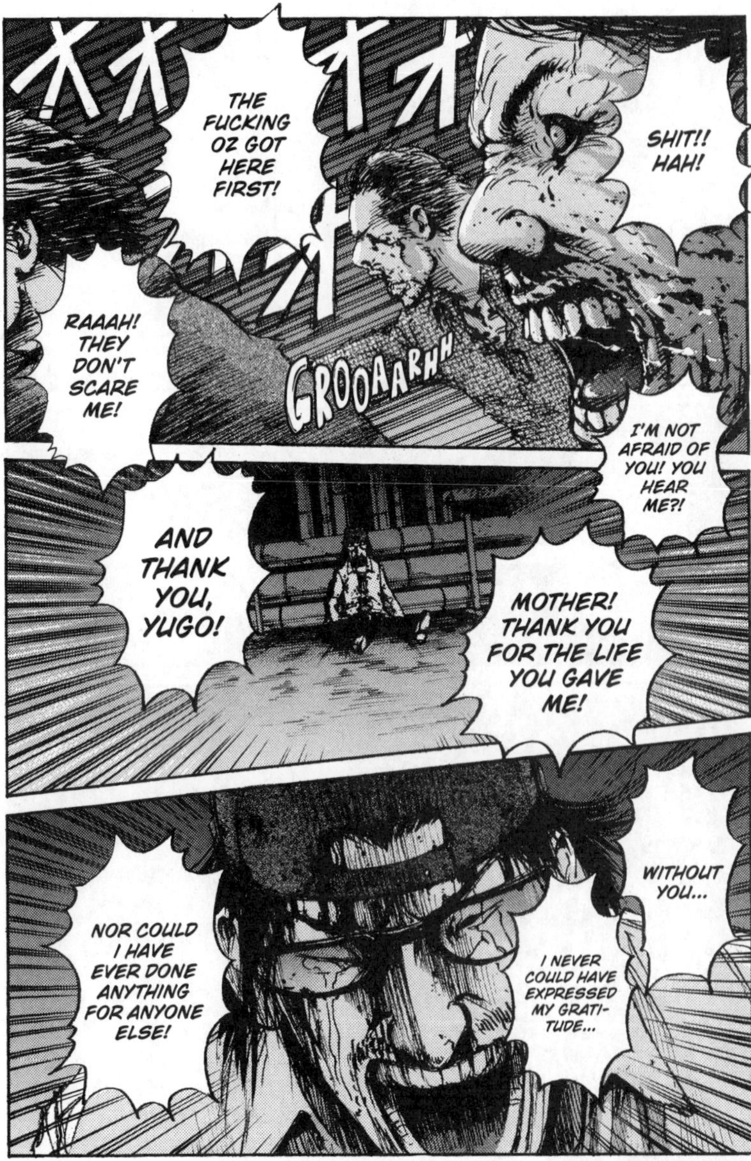
SHIT!! HAH!
THE FUCKING OZ GOT HERE FIRST!
GROOAARHH
RAAAH! THEY DON'T SCARE ME!
I'M NOT AFRAID OF YOU! YOU HEAR ME?!
MOTHER! THANK YOU FOR THE LIFE YOU GAVE ME!
AND THANK YOU, YUGO!
WITHOUT YOU...
I NEVER COULD HAVE EXPRESSED MY GRATI-TUDE...
NOR COULD I HAVE EVER DONE ANYTHING FOR ANYONE ELSE!

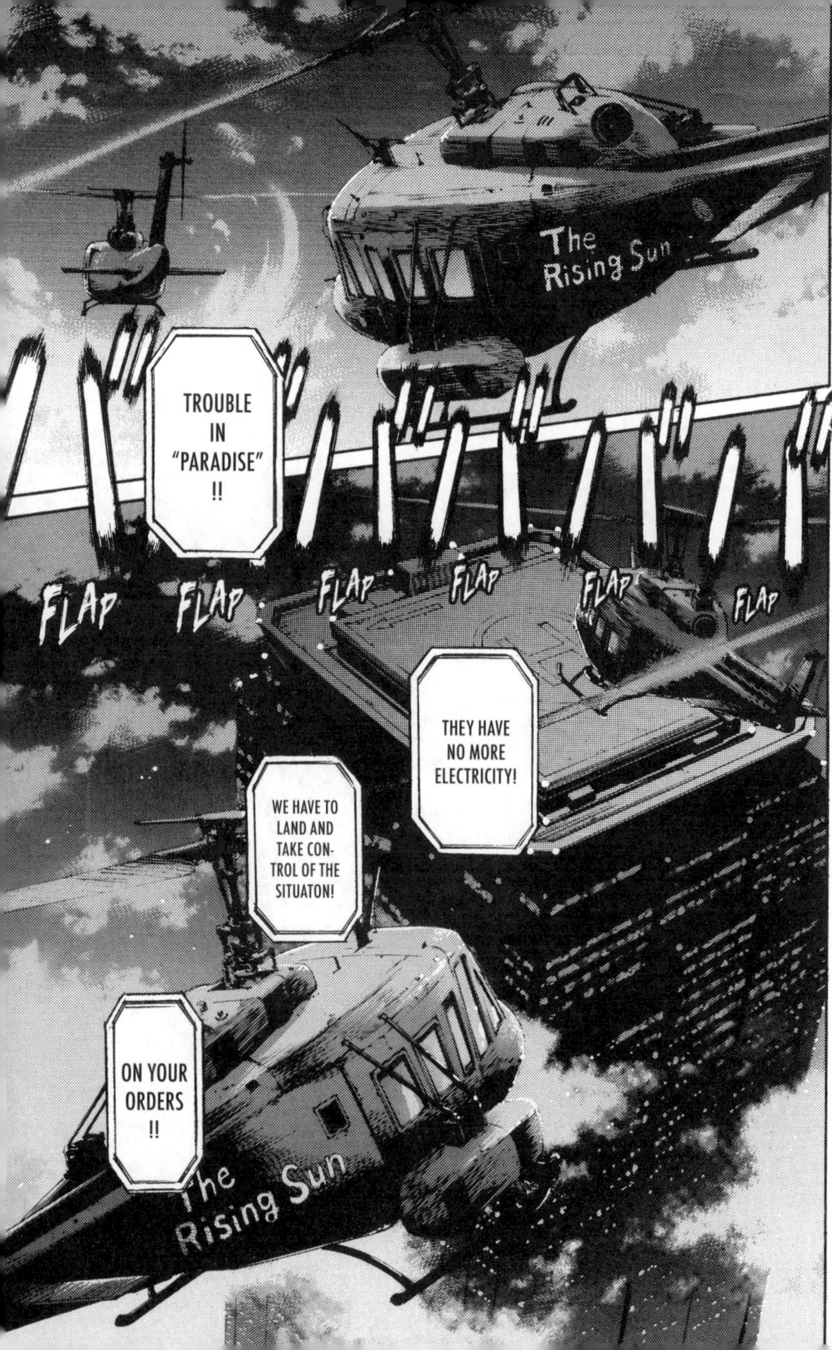
The Rising Sun
TROUBLE IN "PARADISE" !!
FLAP FLAP FLAP FLAP FLAP FLAP
THEY HAVE NO MORE ELECTRICITY!
WE HAVE TO LAND AND TAKE CONTROL OF THE SITUATON!
ON YOUR ORDERS !!
The Rising Sun

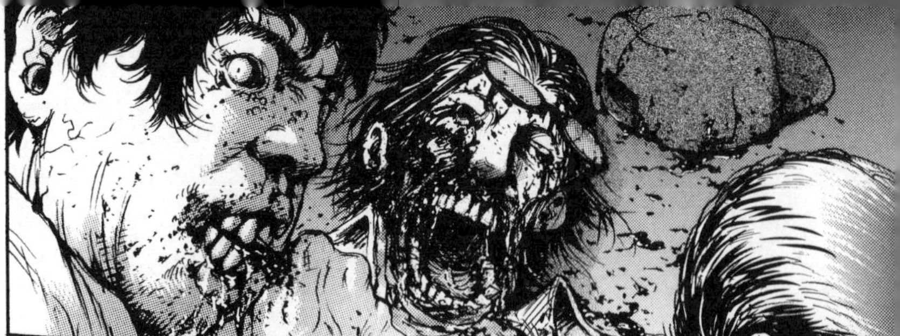
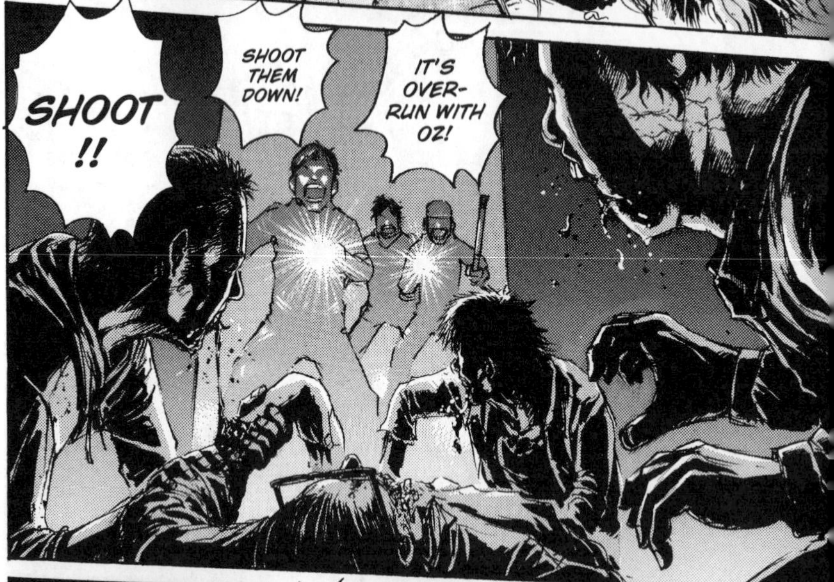
IT'S OVER-RUN WITH OZ!
SHOOT THEM DOWN!
SHOOT!!
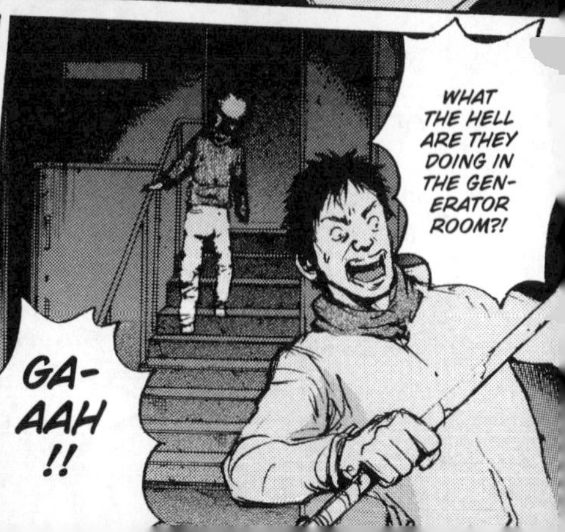
WHAT THE HELL ARE THEY DOING IN THE GEN-ERATOR ROOM?!
GA-AAH!!
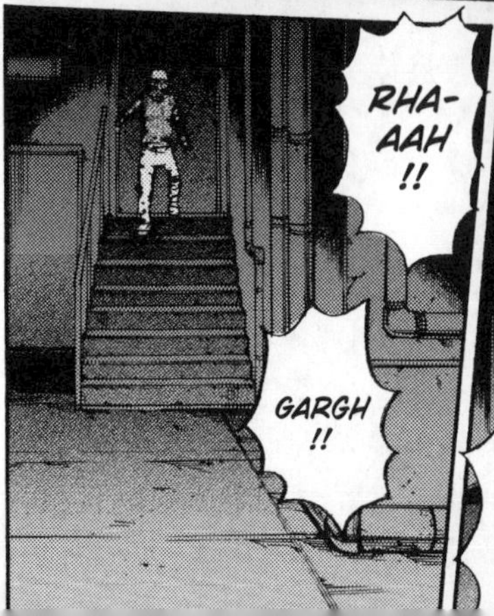
RHA-AAH!!
GARGH!!

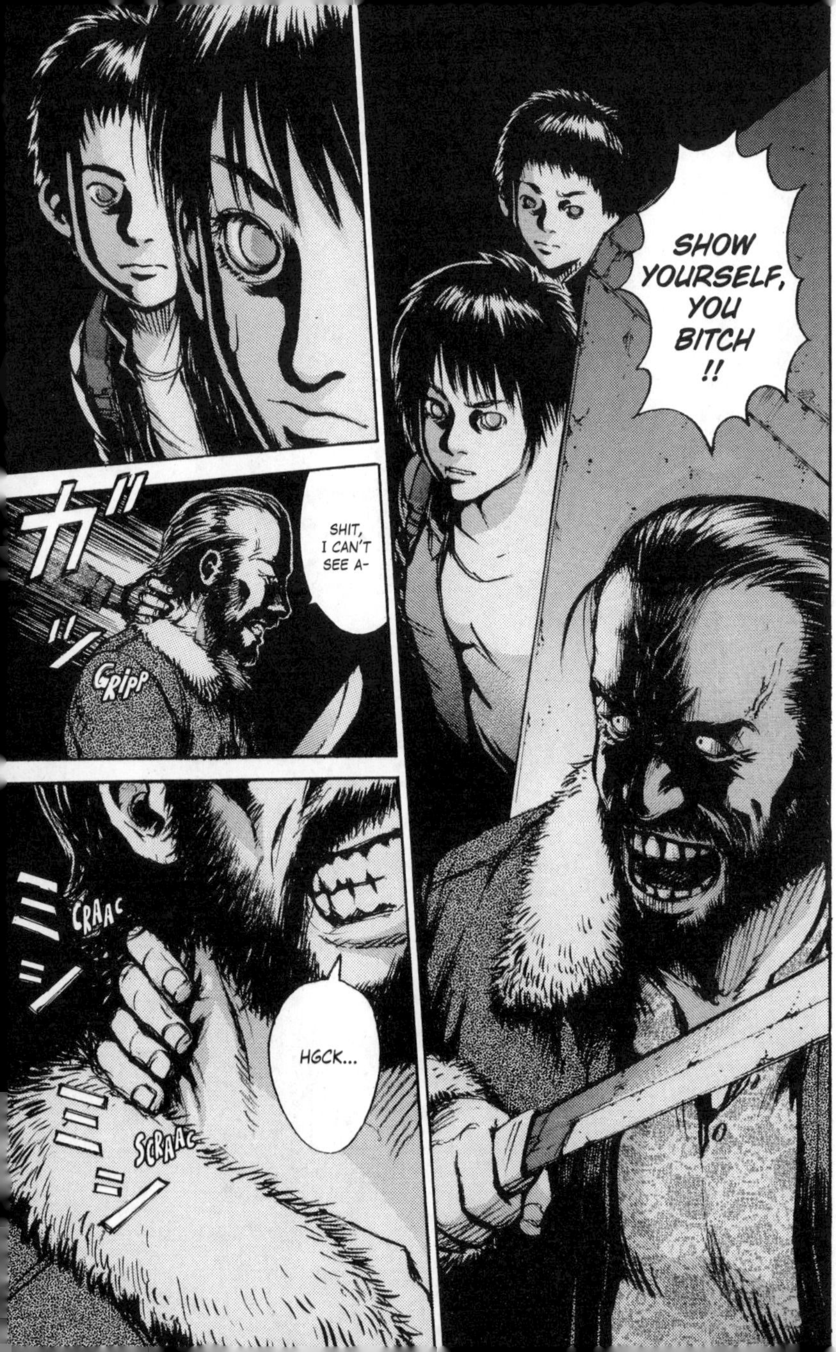
SHOW YOURSELF, YOU BITCH !!
SHIT, I CAN'T SEE A-
GRIPP
CRAAC
HGCK...
SCRAAC

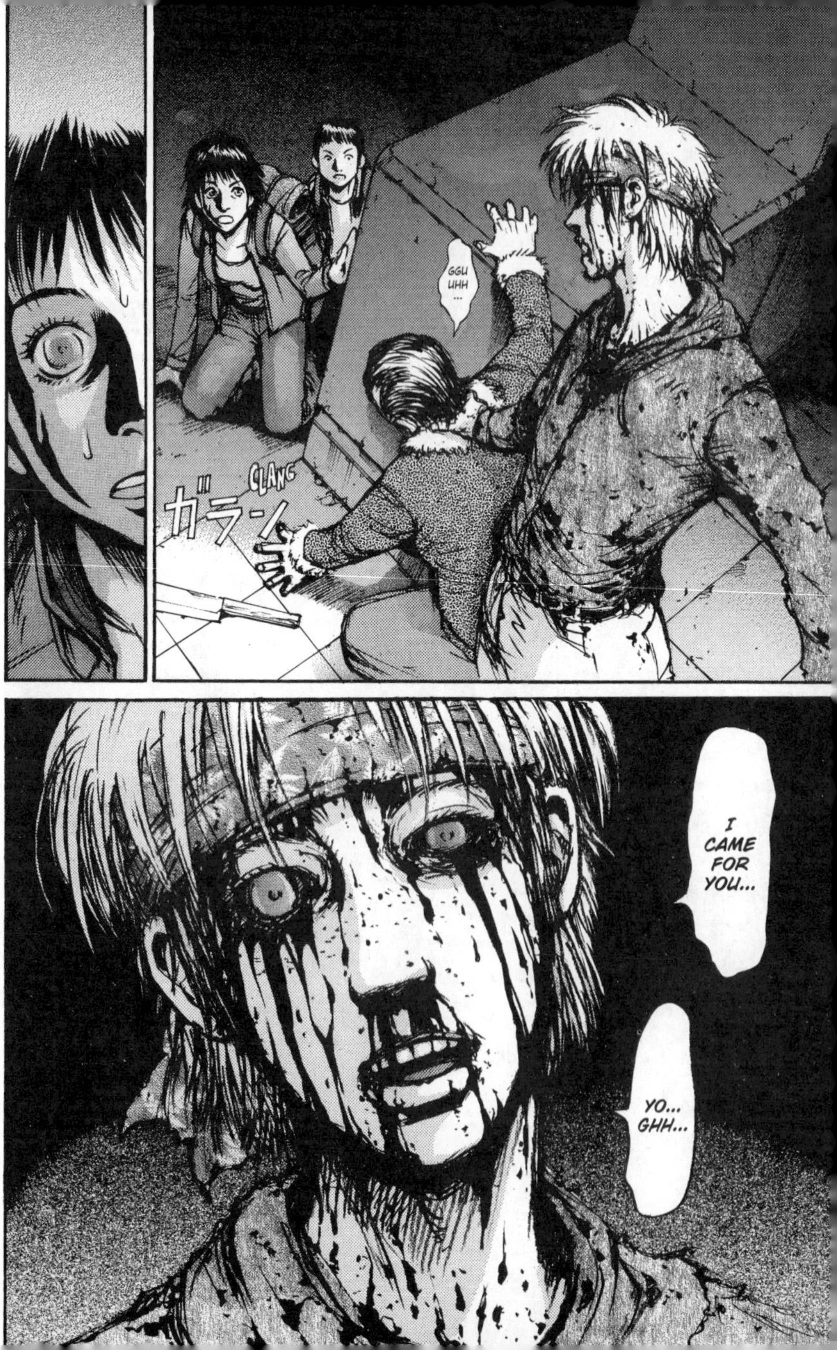
GGU UHH...
ガラーン
CLANG
I CAME FOR YOU...
YO... GHH...

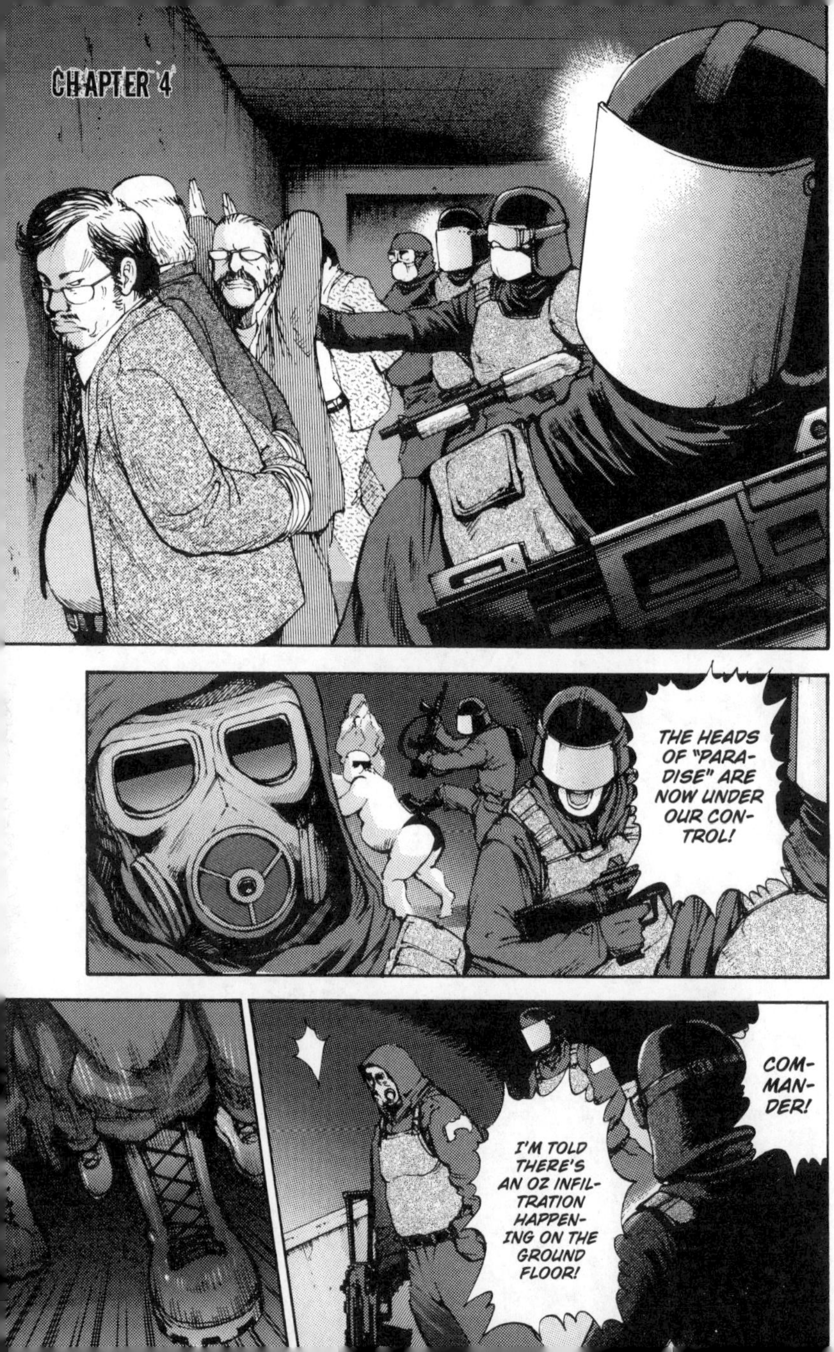
CHAPTER 4
THE HEADS OF "PARA-DISE" ARE NOW UNDER OUR CON-TROL!
COM-MAN-DER!
I'M TOLD THERE'S AN OZ INFIL-TRATION HAPPEN-ING ON THE GROUND FLOOR!

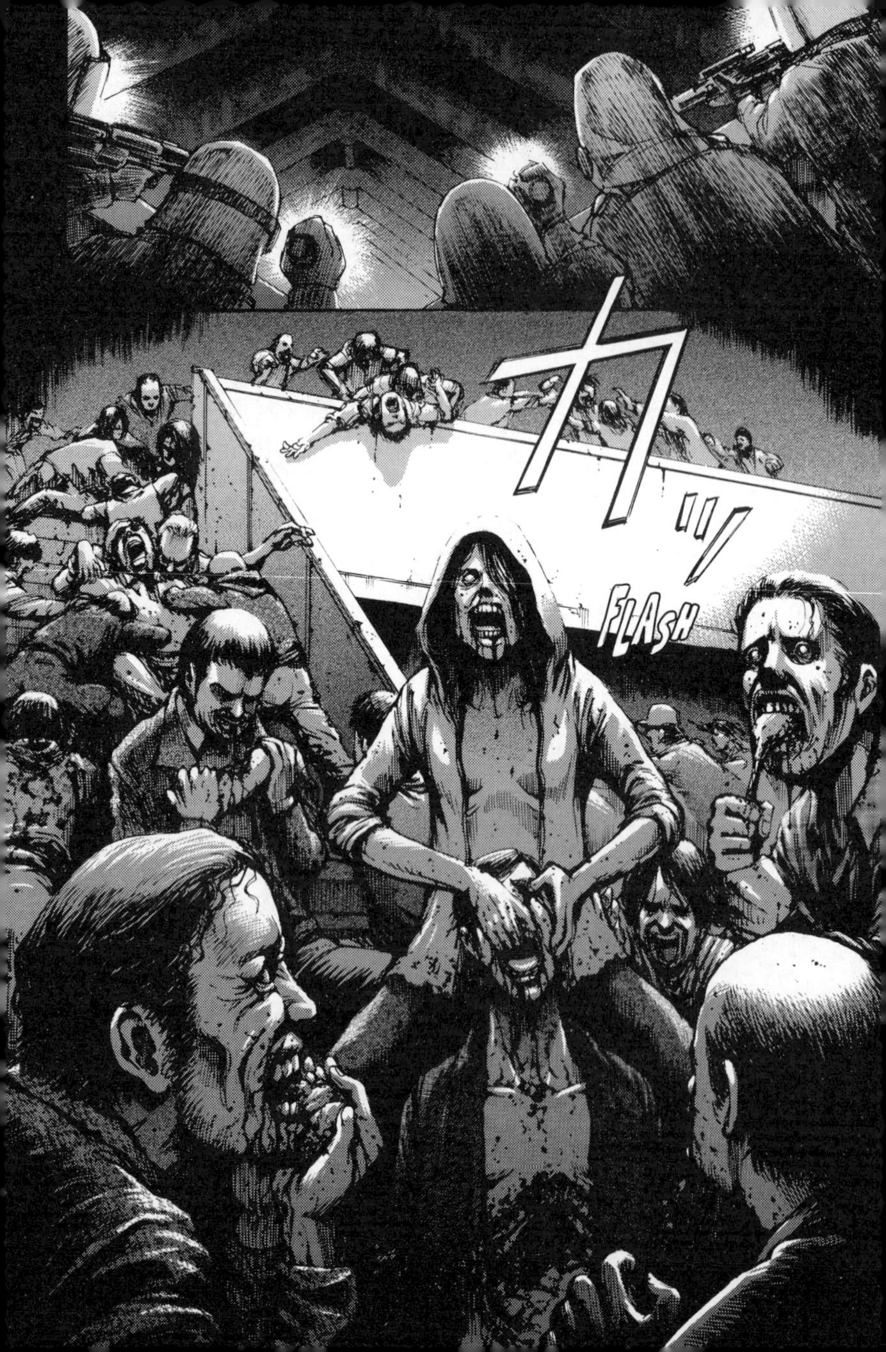
カッ
FLASH

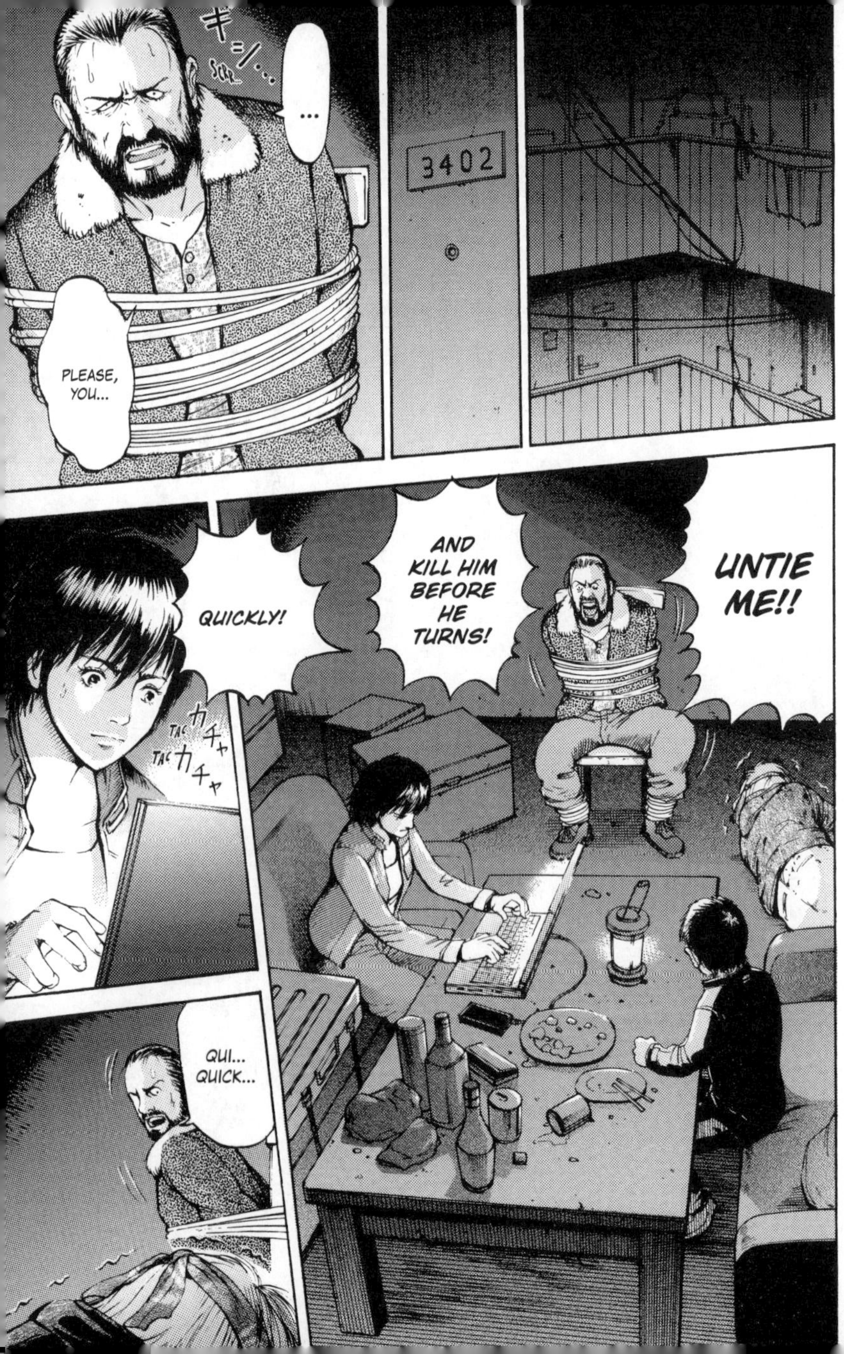
3402
ギシ…
SCRR...
...
PLEASE, YOU...
UNTIE ME!!
AND KILL HIM BEFORE HE TURNS!
QUICKLY!
カチャ TAC
カチャ TAC
QUI... QUICK...

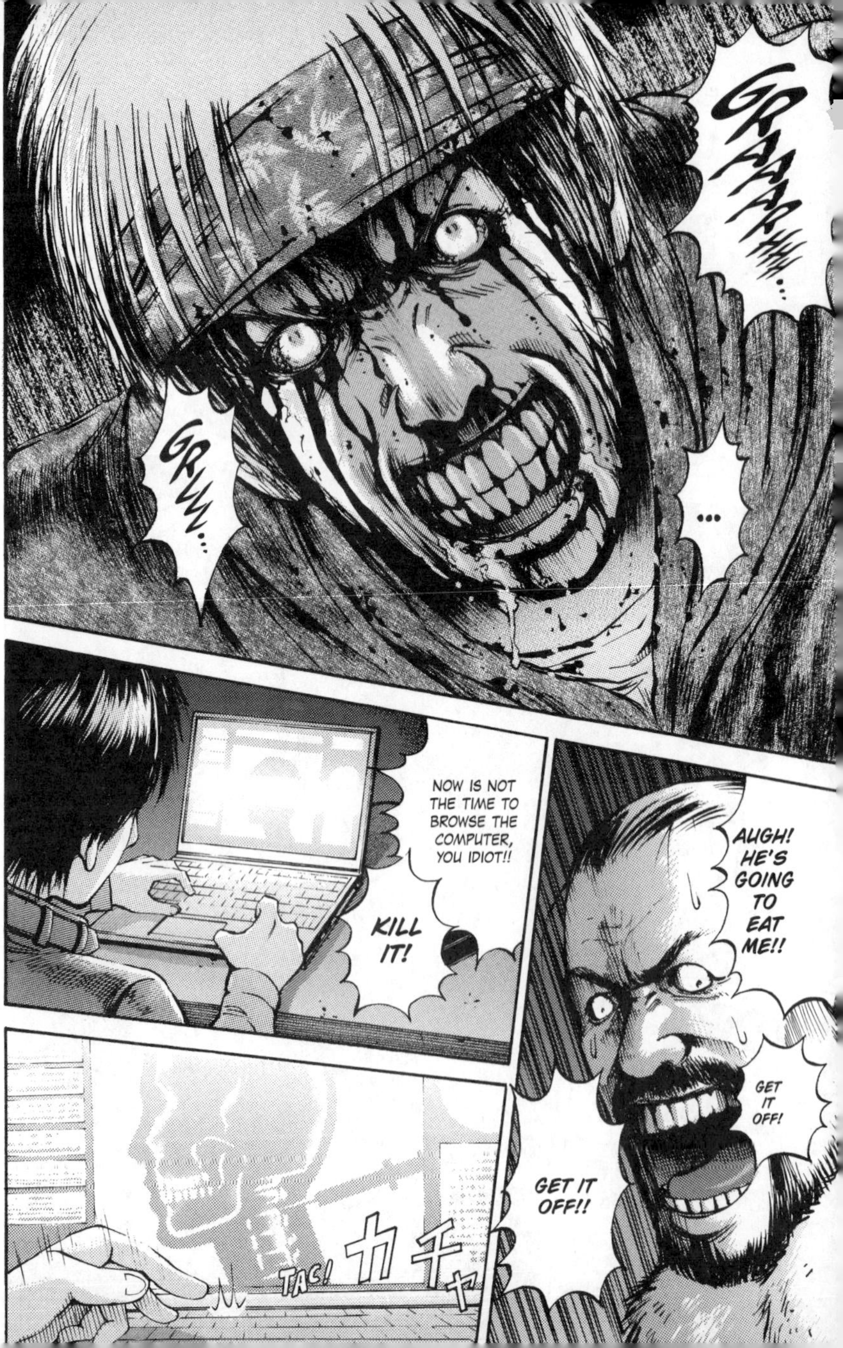
GRAAARHHH...
...
GRUUU...
AUGH! HE'S GOING TO EAT ME!!
GET IT OFF!
GET IT OFF!!
NOW IS NOT THE TIME TO BROWSE THE COMPUTER, YOU IDIOT!!
KILL IT!
TAC!
カチャ

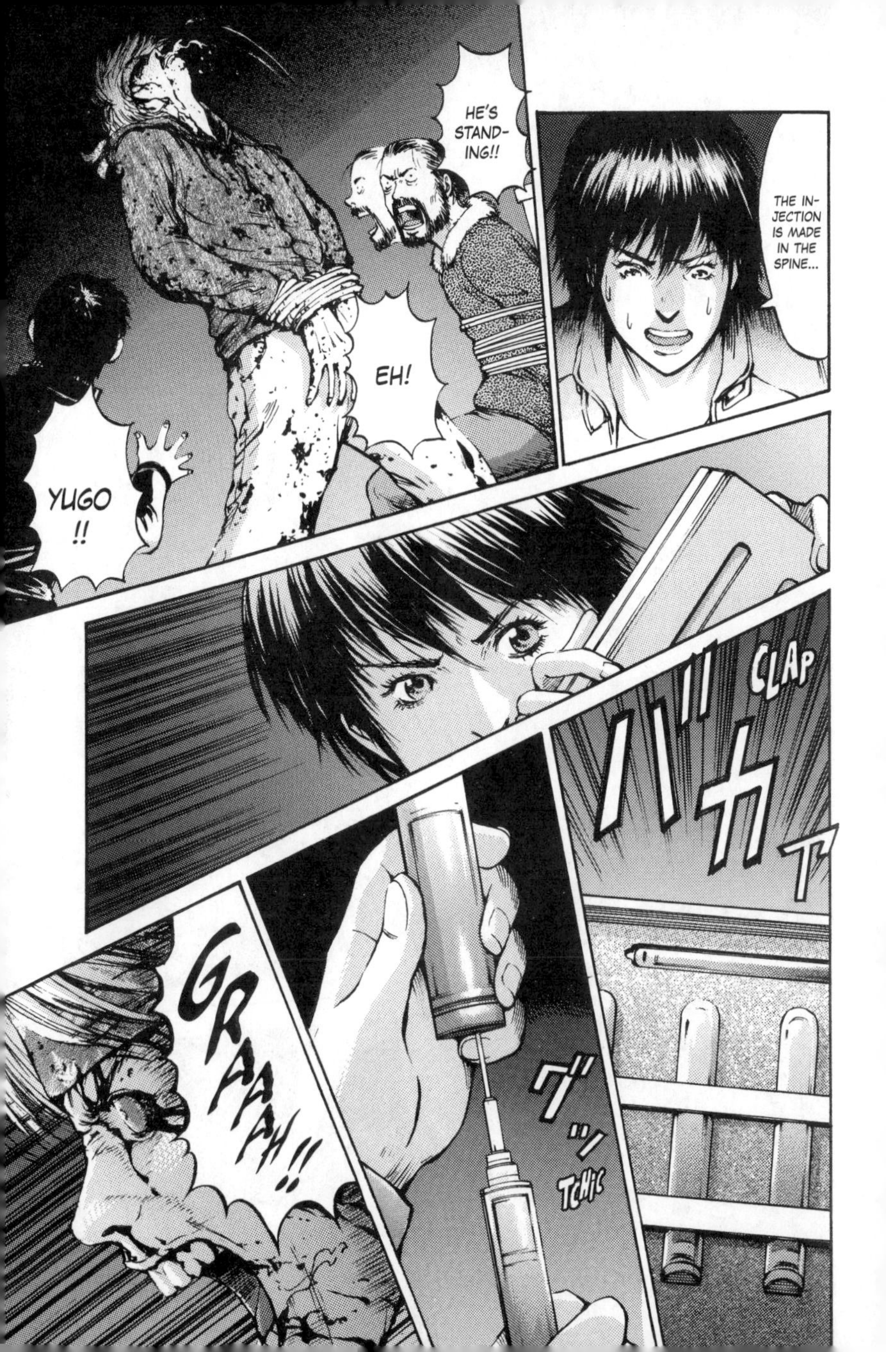
THE IN-JECTION IS MADE IN THE SPINE...
HE'S STAND-ING!!
EH!
YUGO !!
CLAP
TCHIC
GRAAAH!!

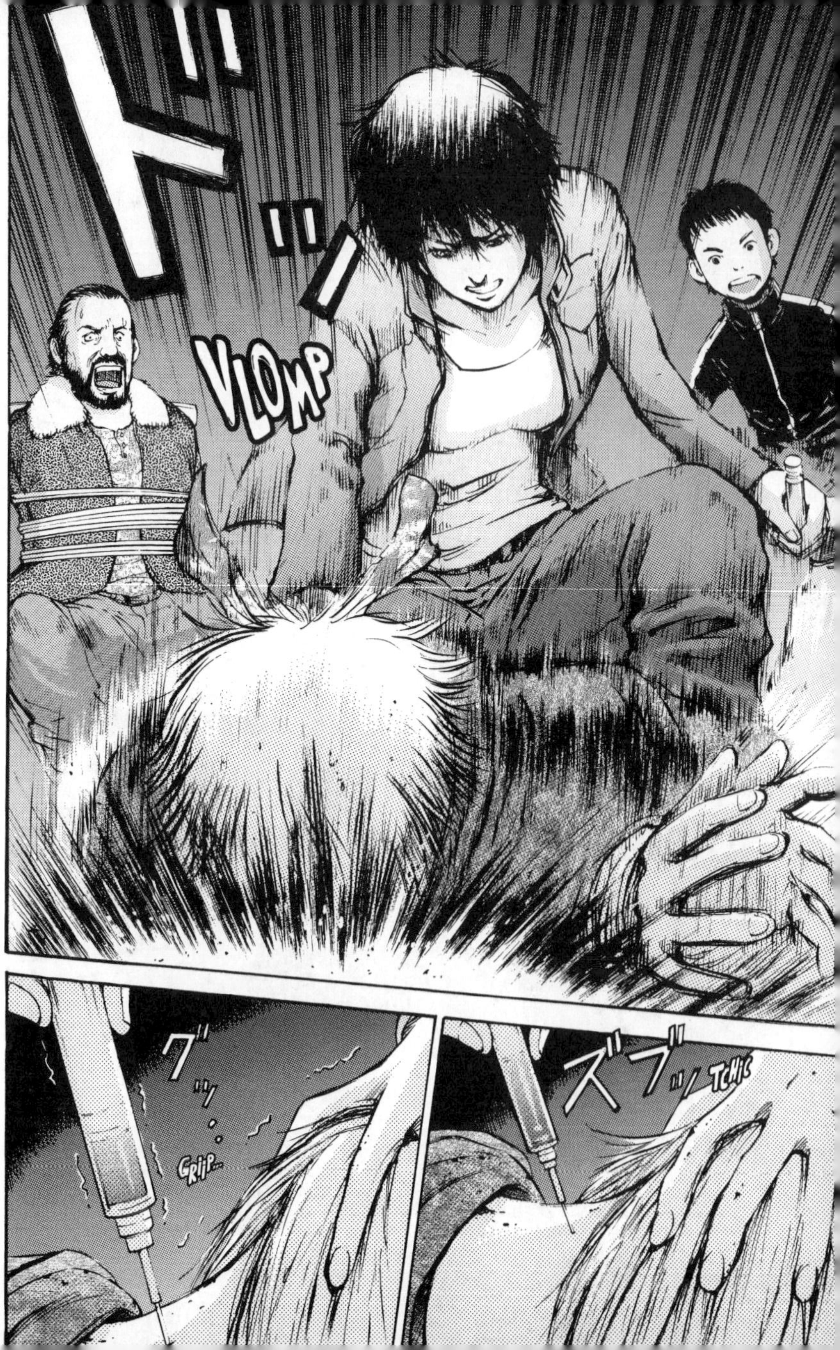
ドッ
VLOMP
ズブッ
TCHIC
グッ…
GRIIP...

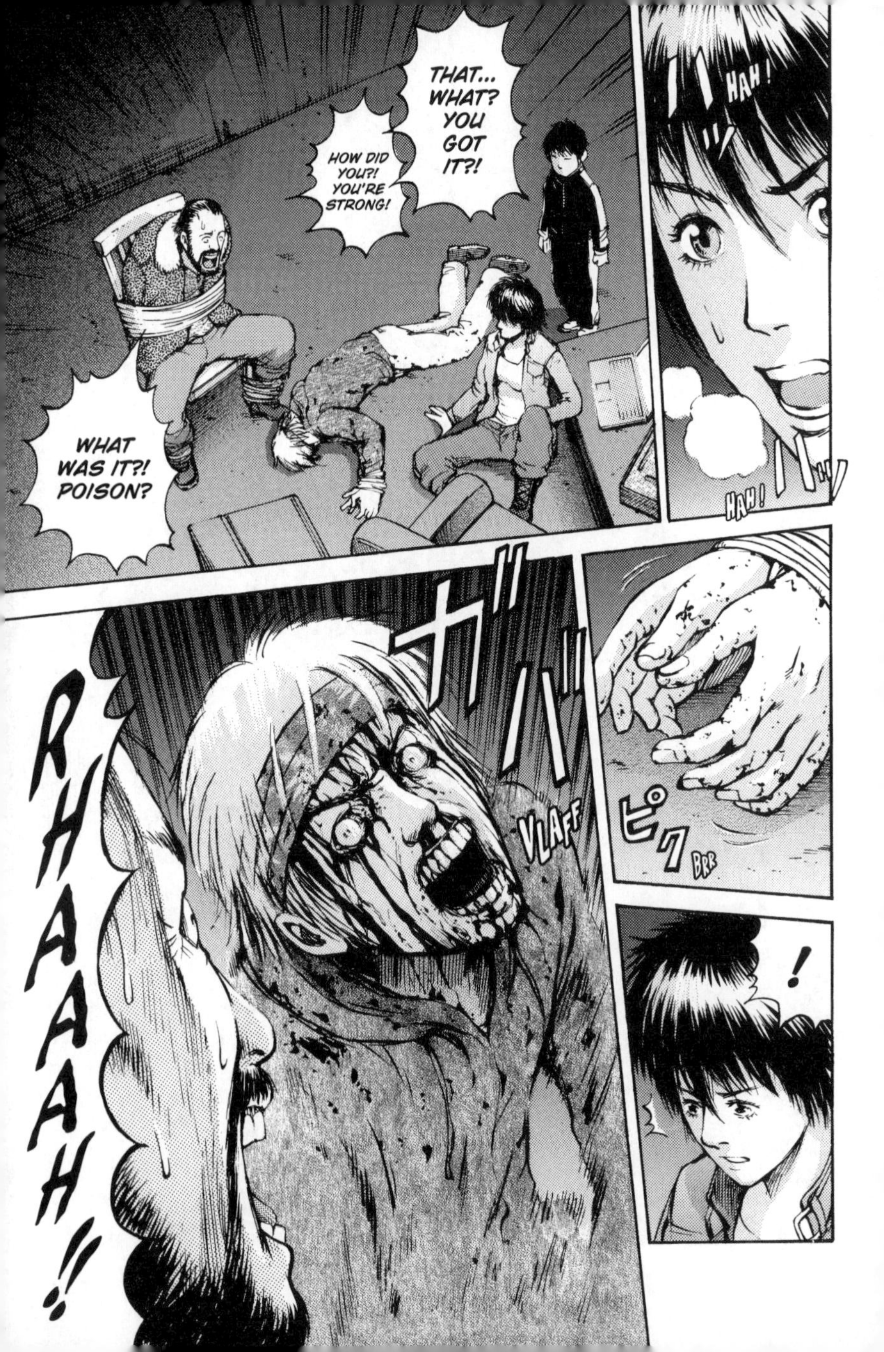
HAH!
HAH!
THAT... WHAT? YOU GOT IT?!
HOW DID YOU?! YOU'RE STRONG!
WHAT WAS IT?! POISON?
ピク
BRR
!
ガバ
VLAFF
RHAAAH!!

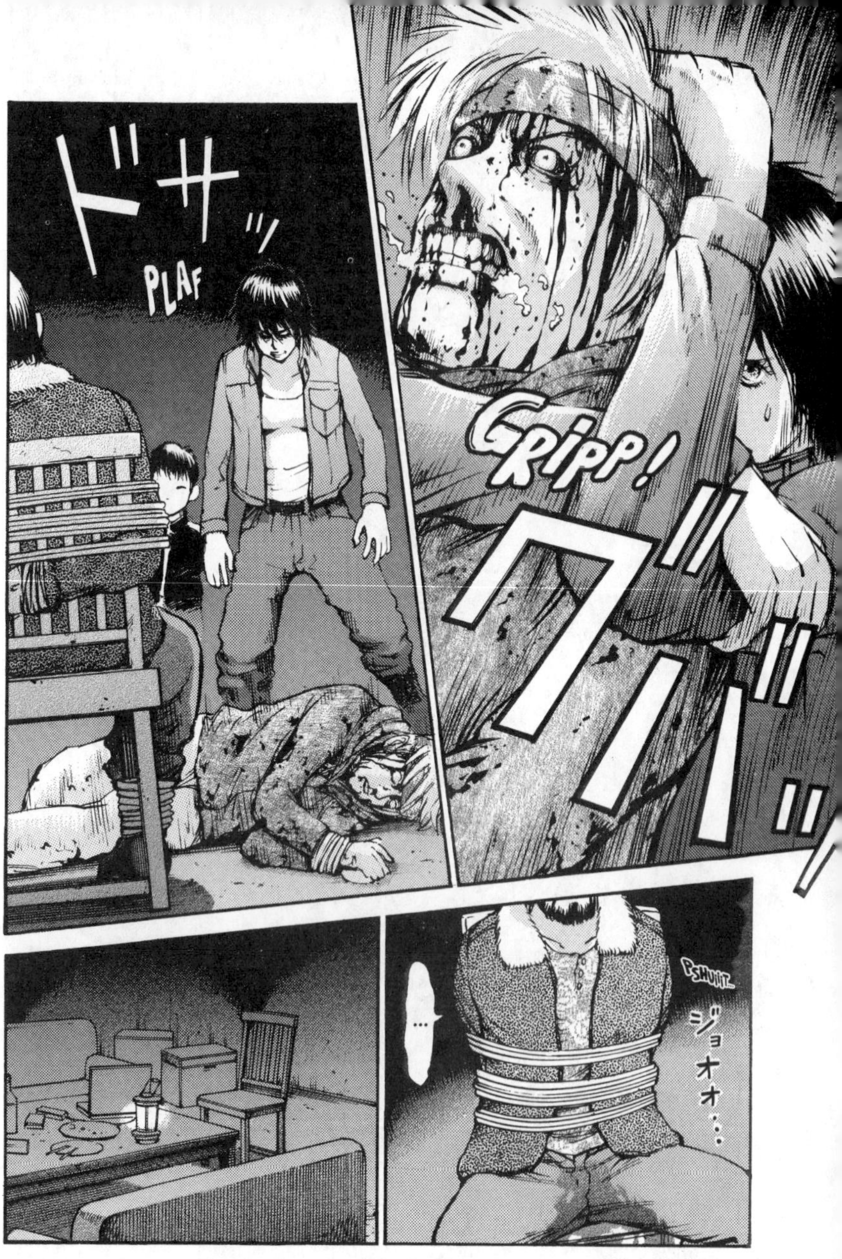
GRIPP!
グッ
ドサッ
PLAF
PSHUIIT...
ジョオオ...
...

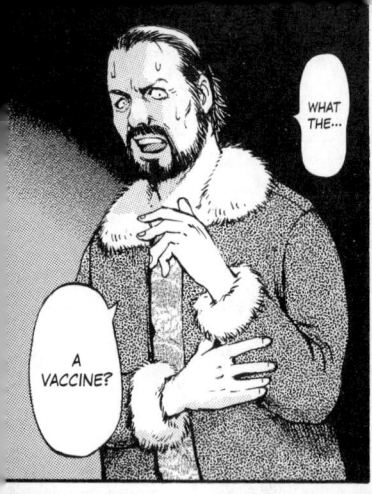

WHAT THE...

A VACCINE?

HE'LL BECOME HUMAN AGAIN?

ハァ HAA

ハァ HAA

WE HAVE TO REACH TOKYO AT ALL COSTS.

YOU WERE BEING SERIOUS?!

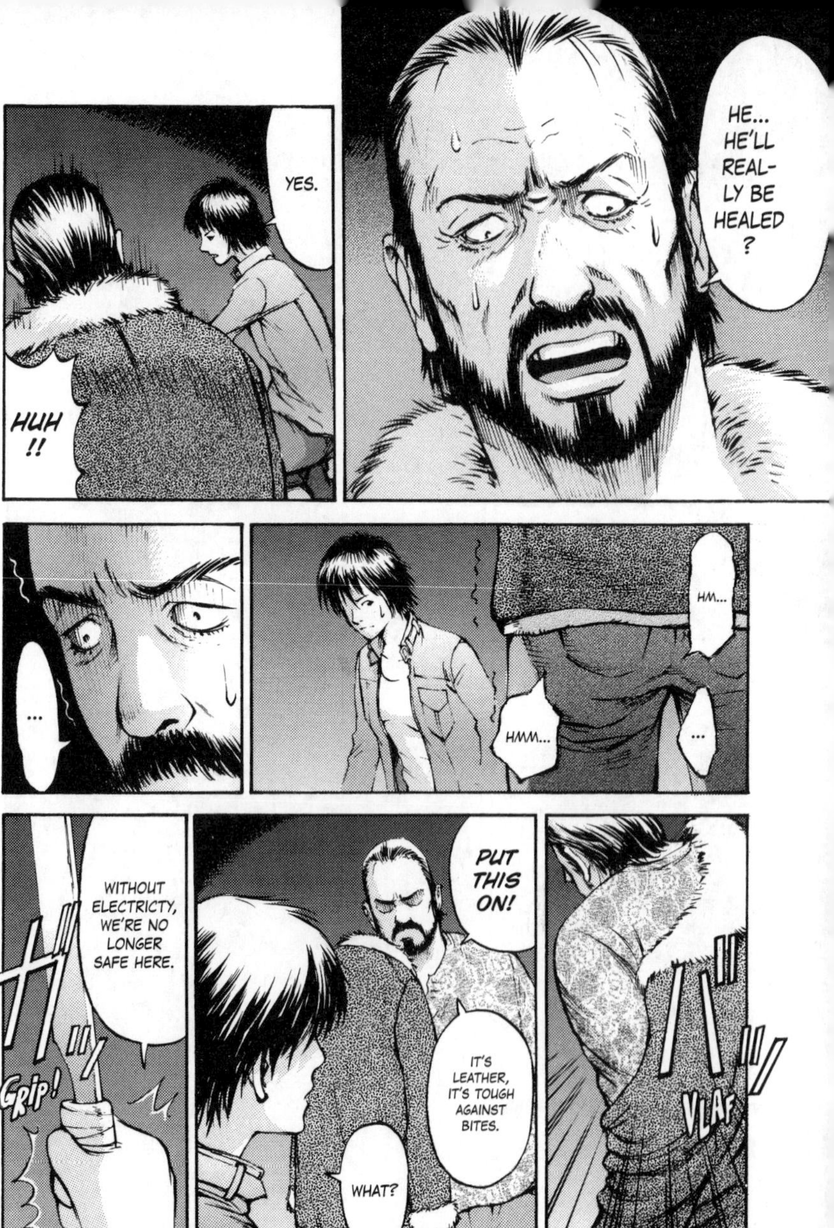
HE... HE'LL REAL-LY BE HEALED ?
YES.
HUH !!
HM...
...
HMM...
...
VLAF
PUT THIS ON!
IT'S LEATHER, IT'S TOUGH AGAINST BITES.
WHAT?
WITHOUT ELECTRICTY, WE'RE NO LONGER SAFE HERE.
GRIP!

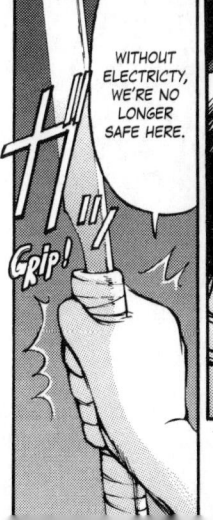

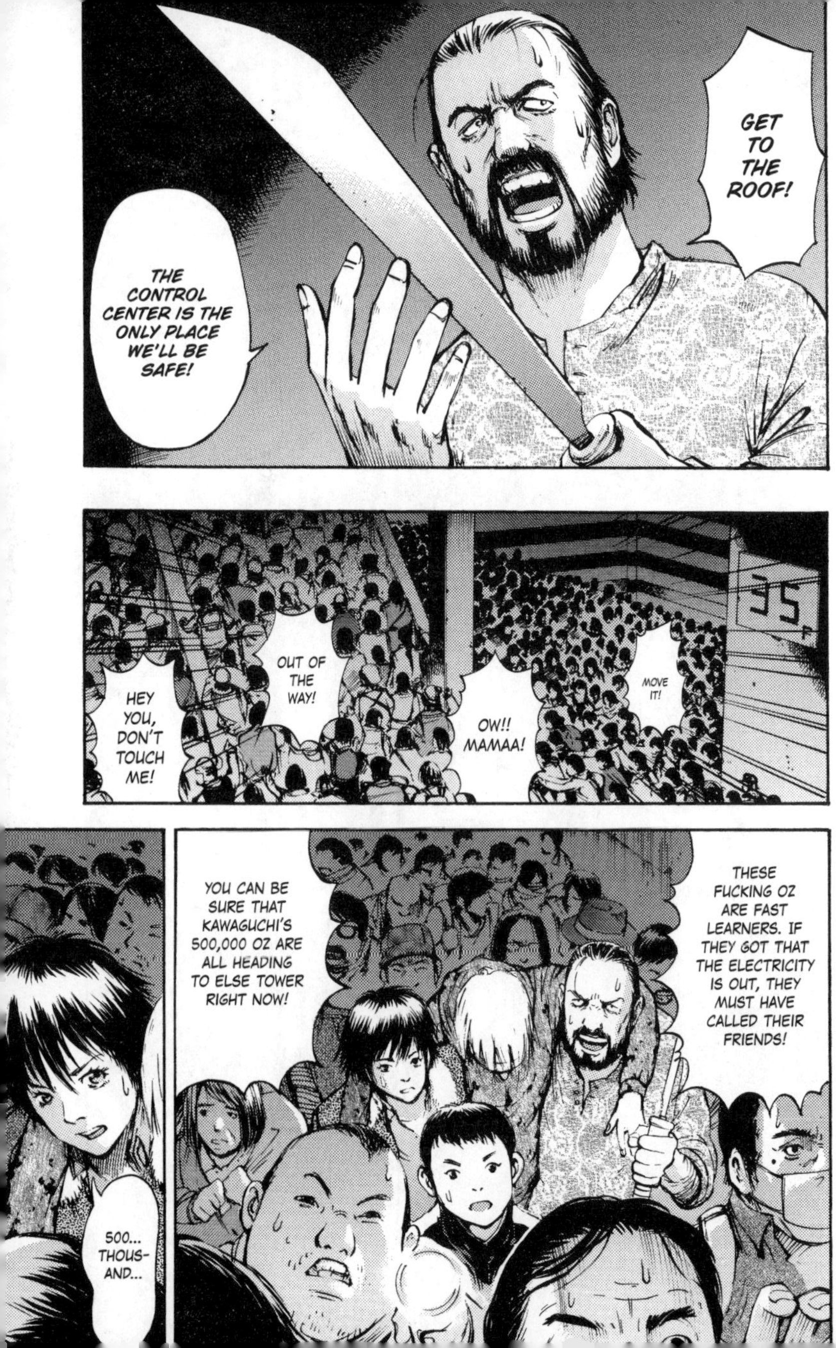
GET TO THE ROOF!
THE CONTROL CENTER IS THE ONLY PLACE WE'LL BE SAFE!
MOVE IT!
OW!! MAMAA!
OUT OF THE WAY!
HEY YOU, DON'T TOUCH ME!
THESE FUCKING OZ ARE FAST LEARNERS. IF THEY GOT THAT THE ELECTRICITY IS OUT, THEY MUST HAVE CALLED THEIR FRIENDS!
YOU CAN BE SURE THAT KAWAGUCHI'S 500,000 OZ ARE ALL HEADING TO ELSE TOWER RIGHT NOW!
500... THOUS-AND...

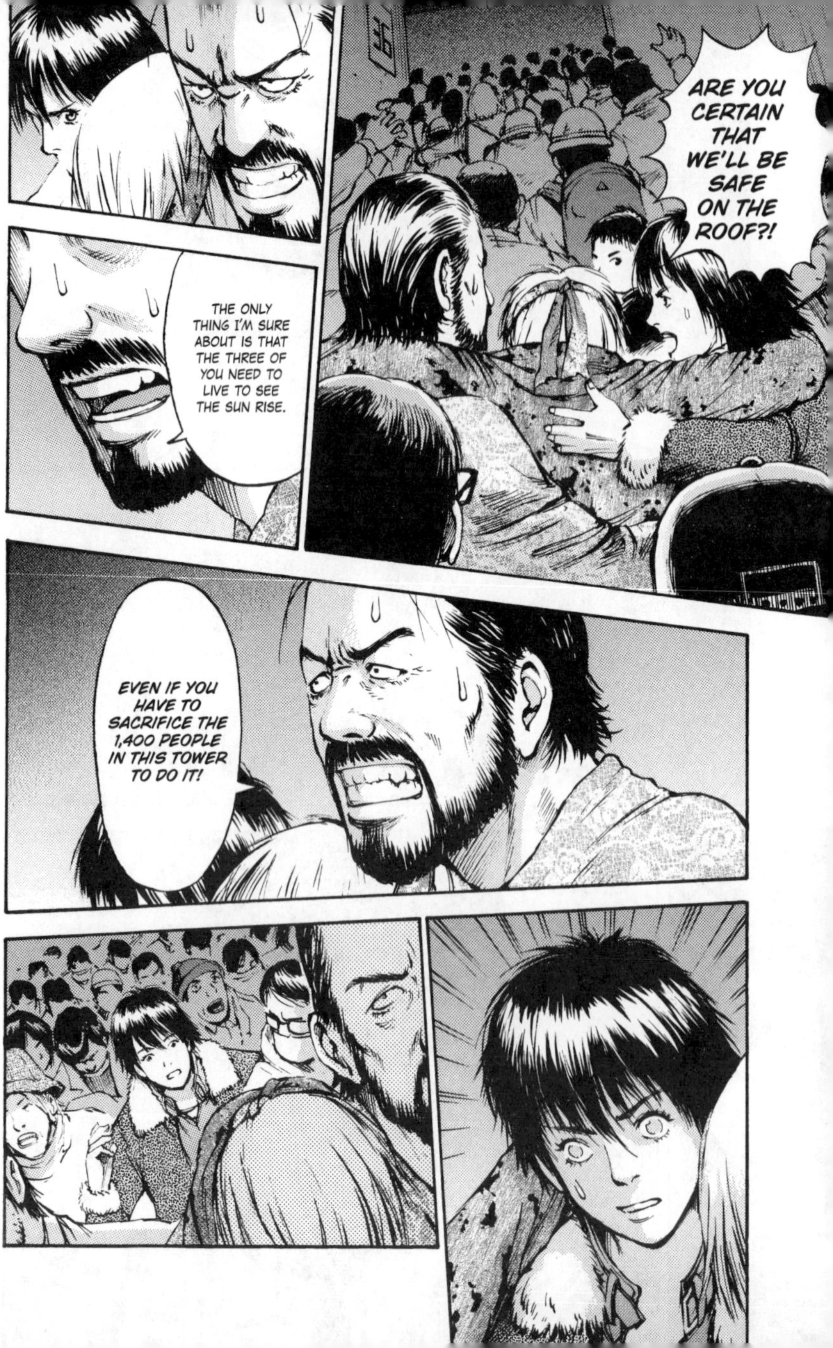
ARE YOU CERTAIN THAT WE'LL BE SAFE ON THE ROOF?!
THE ONLY THING I'M SURE ABOUT IS THAT THE THREE OF YOU NEED TO LIVE TO SEE THE SUN RISE.
EVEN IF YOU HAVE TO SACRIFICE THE 1,400 PEOPLE IN THIS TOWER TO DO IT!

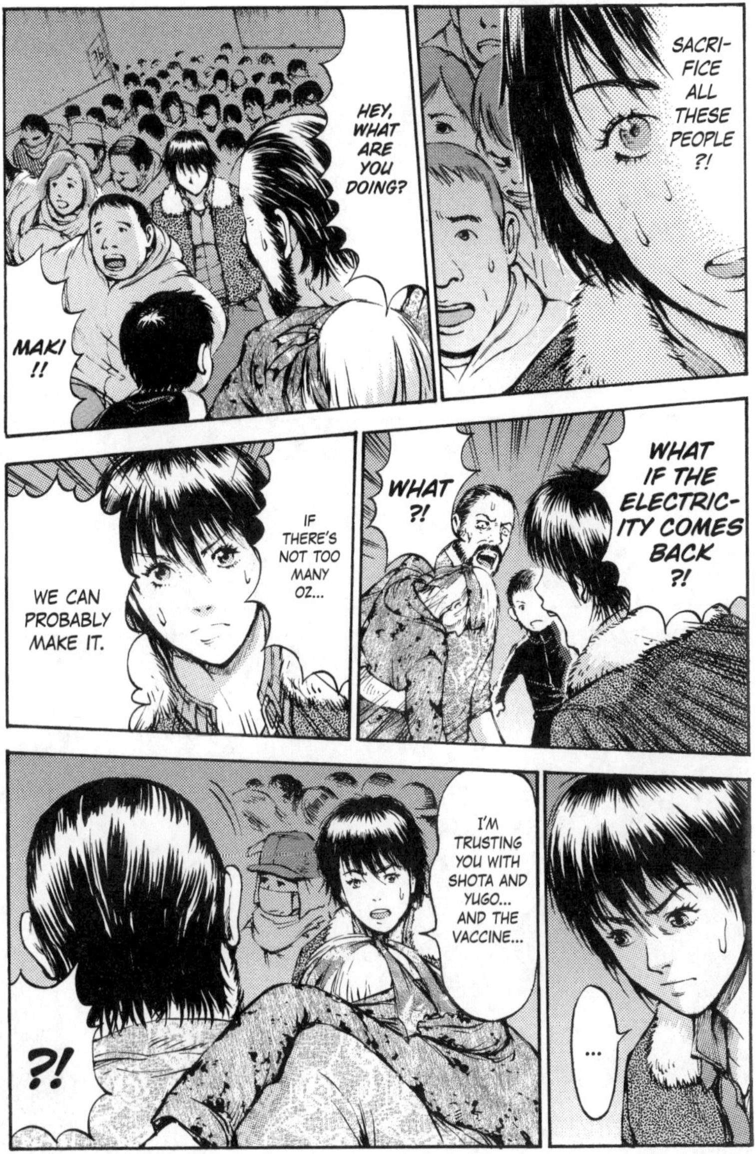
SACRIFICE ALL THESE PEOPLE ?!
HEY, WHAT ARE YOU DOING?
MAKI !!
WHAT IF THE ELECTRICITY COMES BACK ?!
WHAT ?!
IF THERE'S NOT TOO MANY OZ...
WE CAN PROBABLY MAKE IT.
...
I'M TRUSTING YOU WITH SHOTA AND YUGO... AND THE VACCINE...
?!

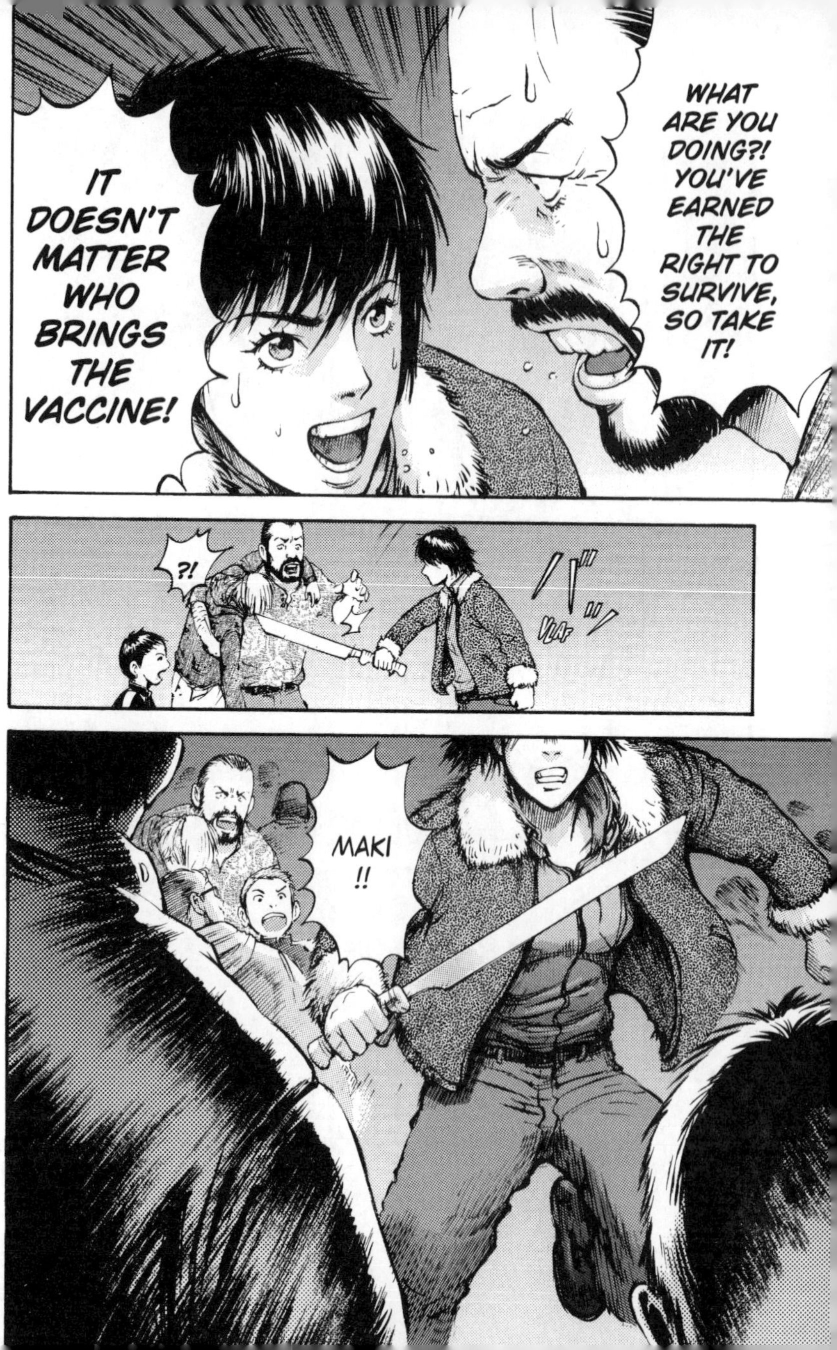
WHAT ARE YOU DOING?! YOU'VE EARNED THE RIGHT TO SURVIVE, SO TAKE IT!
IT DOESN'T MATTER WHO BRINGS THE VACCINE!
VLAF
?!
MAKI !!

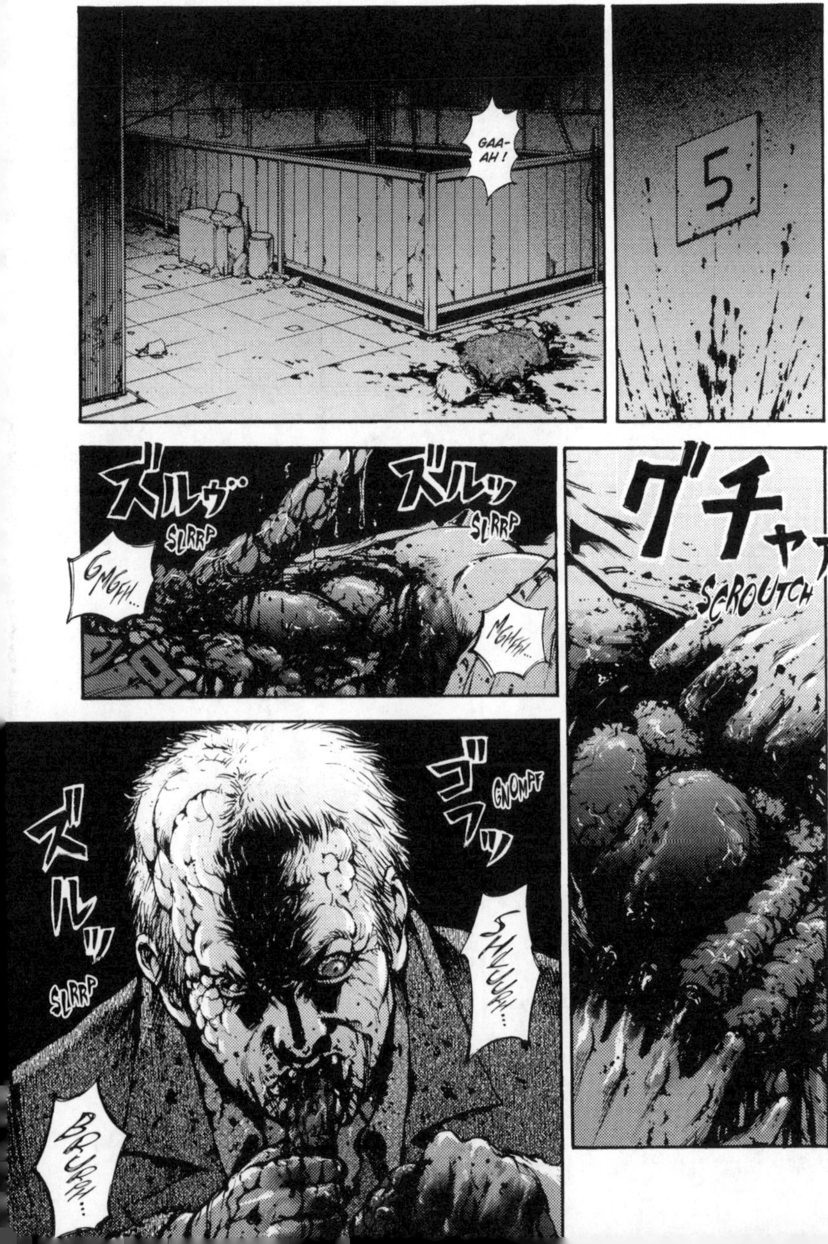
5
GAA-AH!
グチャア
SCROUTCH
ズルッ
SLRRP
MGHHH...
ズルヴ
SLRRP
GMGHH...
ゴフッ
GNOMPF
SHHUUUH...
ズルッ
SLRRP
BRUHHH...

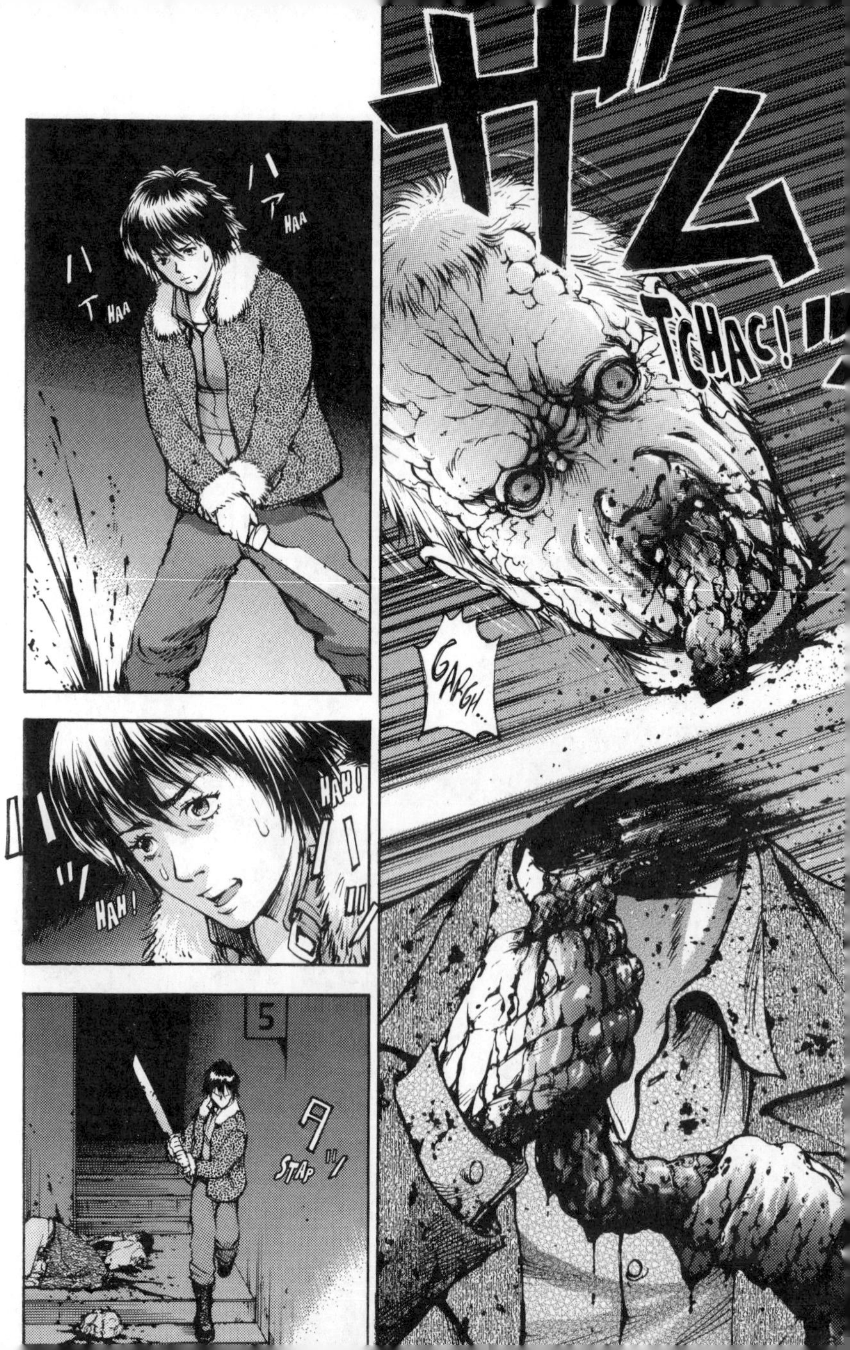

TCHAC!!
GARGH...
HAA
HAA
HAH!
HAH!
STAP

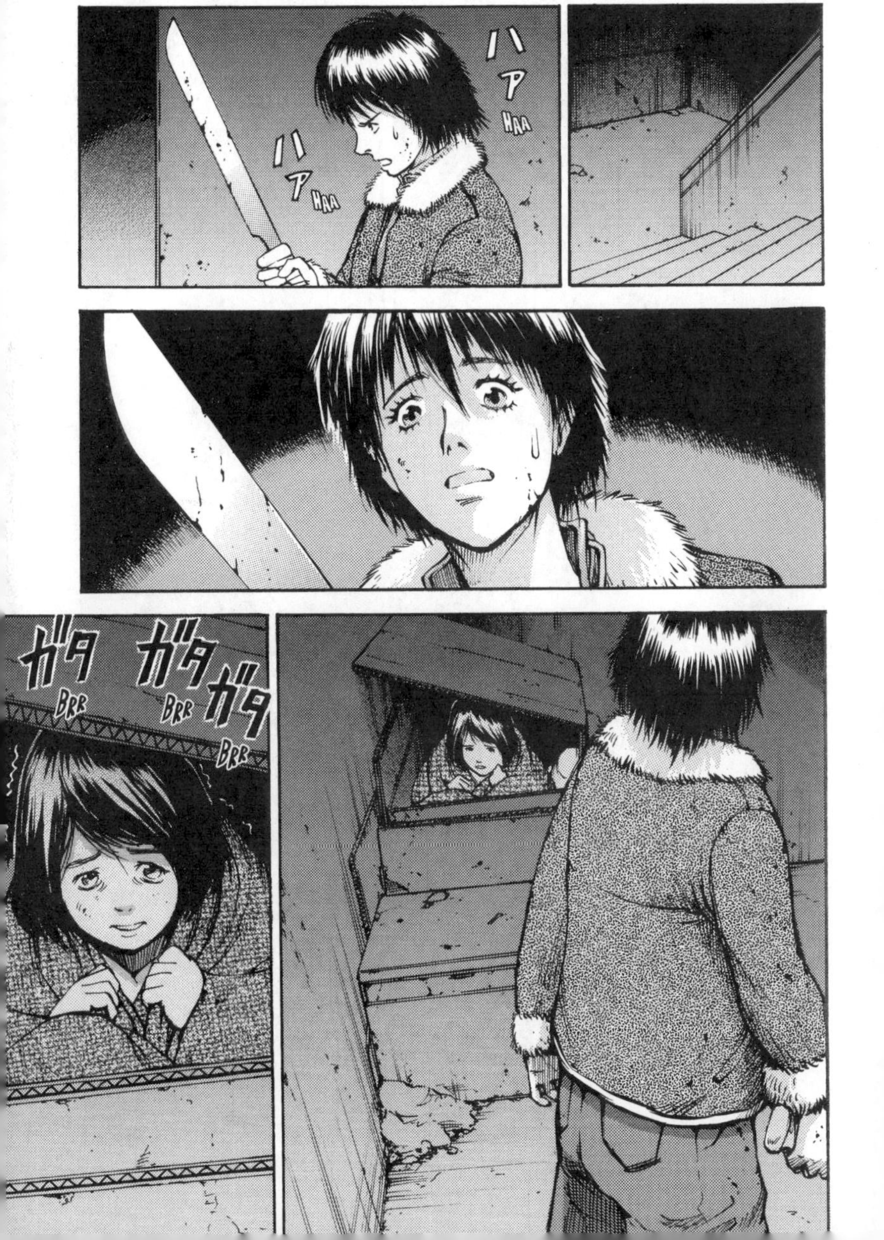

ハア
HAA
ハア
HAA
ガタ
BRR
ガタ
BRR
ガタ
BRR

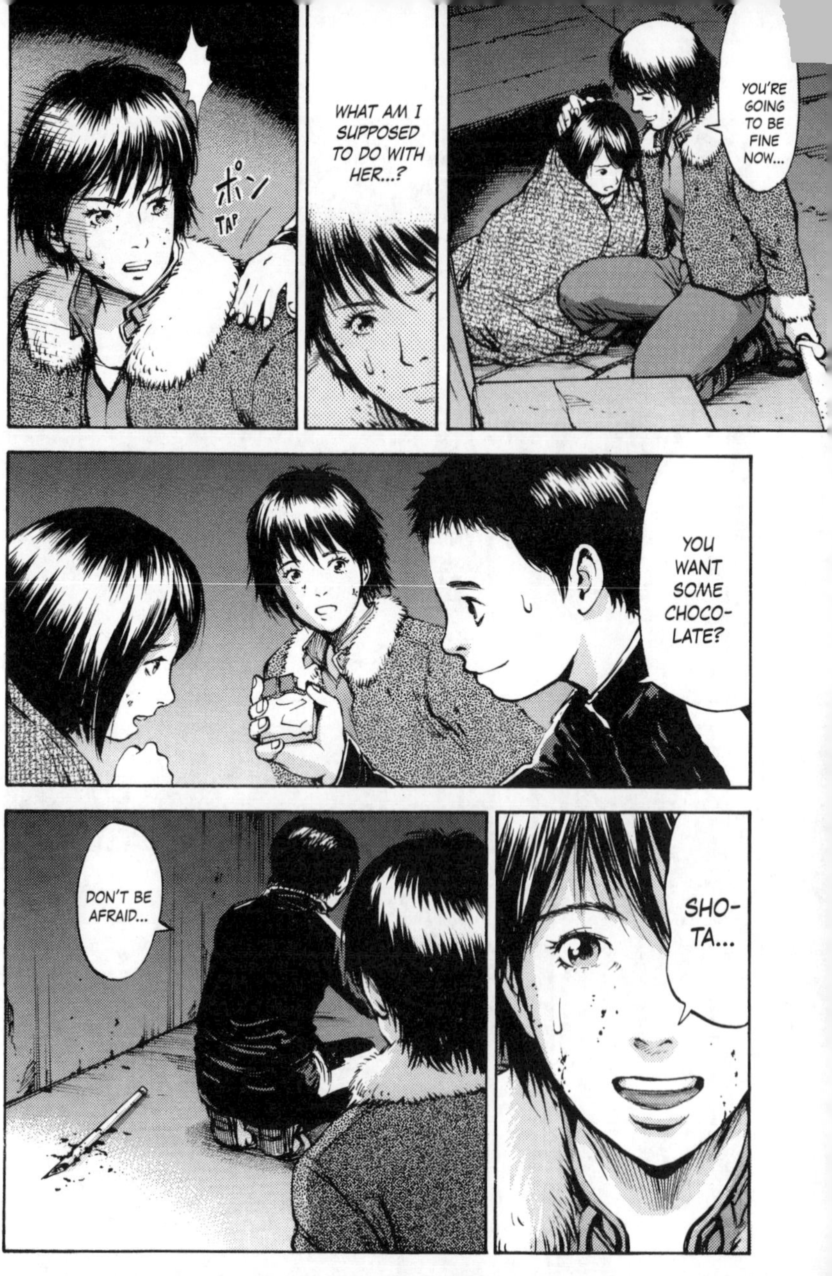
YOU'RE GOING TO BE FINE NOW...
WHAT AM I SUPPOSED TO DO WITH HER...?
ポン
TAP
YOU WANT SOME CHOCO-LATE?
SHO-TA...
DON'T BE AFRAID...

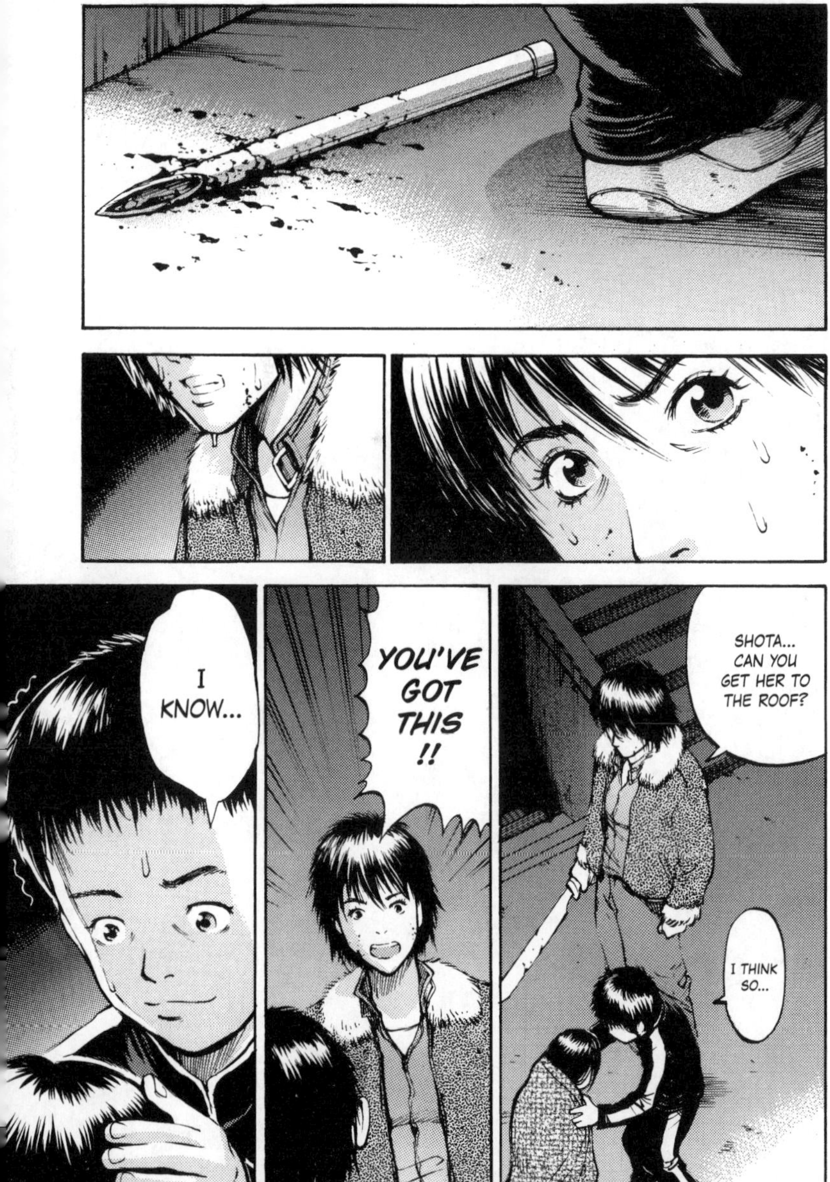

SHOTA... CAN YOU GET HER TO THE ROOF?
I THINK SO...
YOU'VE GOT THIS !!
I KNOW...

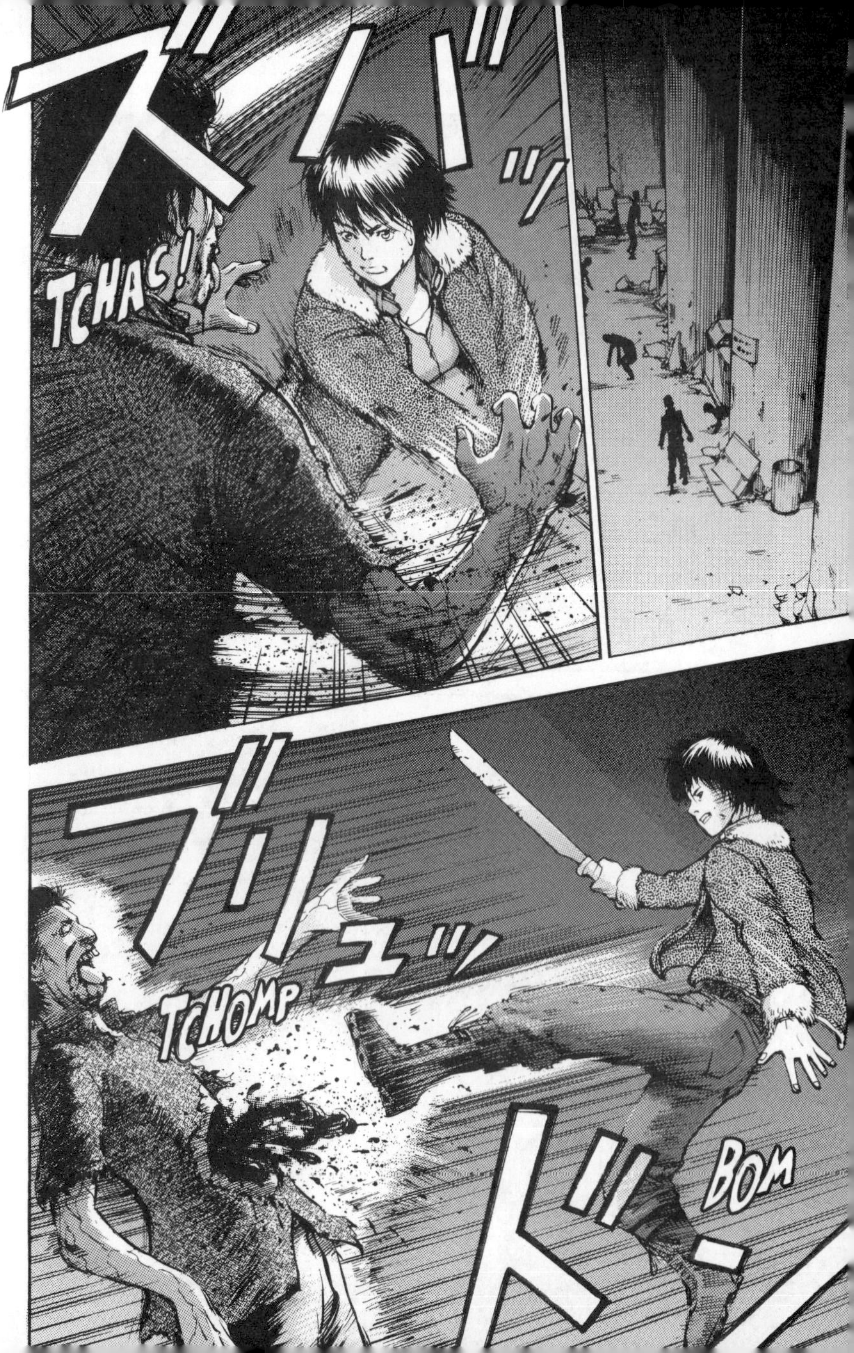
ズバッ
TCHAC!
ドッ
BOM
ブリュッ
TCHOMP

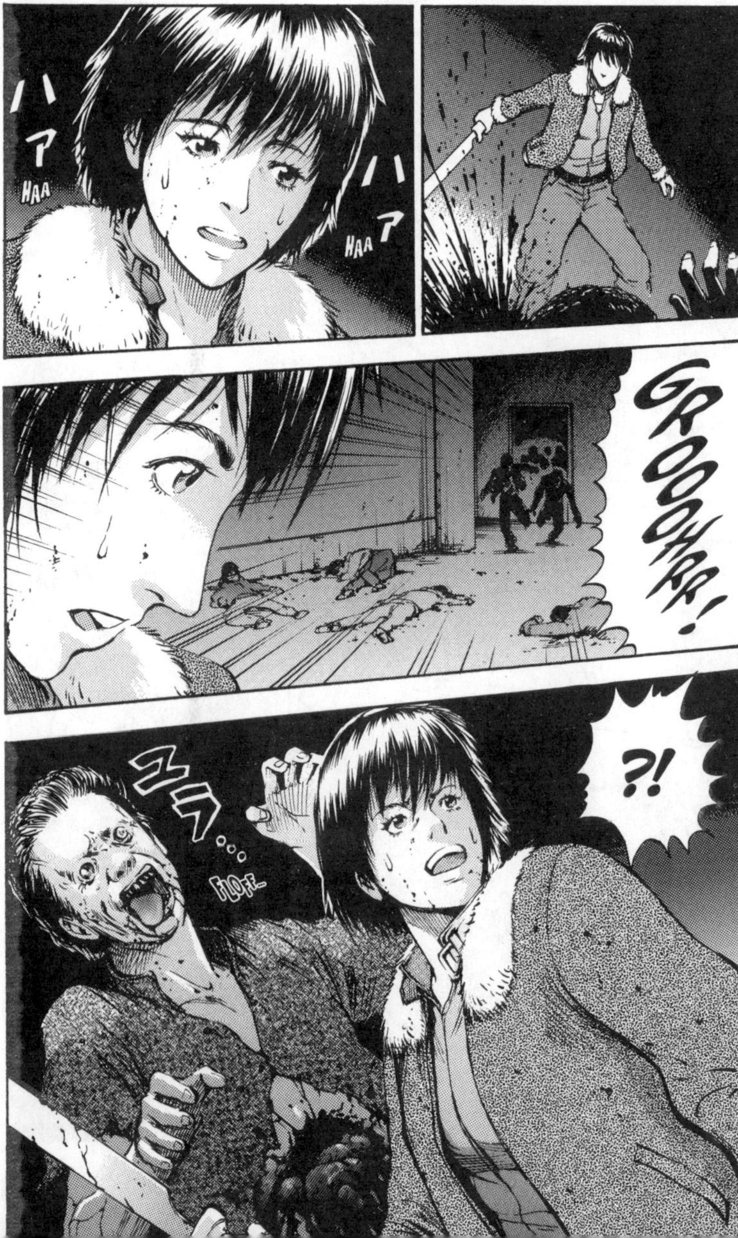
ハア
HAA
ハア
HAA
GROOOOHRR!
?!
ユラ。。。
FLOFF...

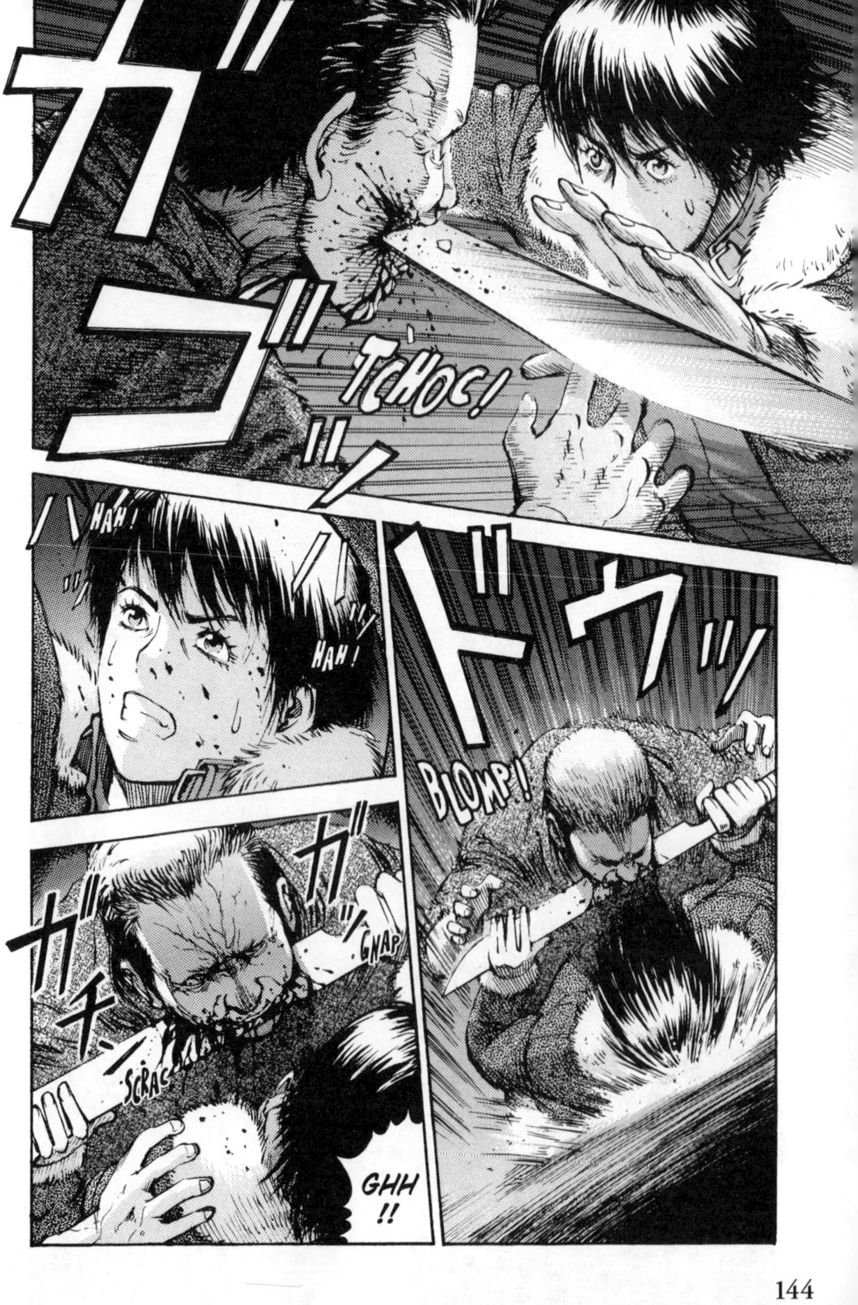
ガゴッ
TCHOC!
ドウッ
BLOMP!
ハッ HAH!
ハッ HAH!
ガッ GNAP
ガチッ SCRAC
GHH !!

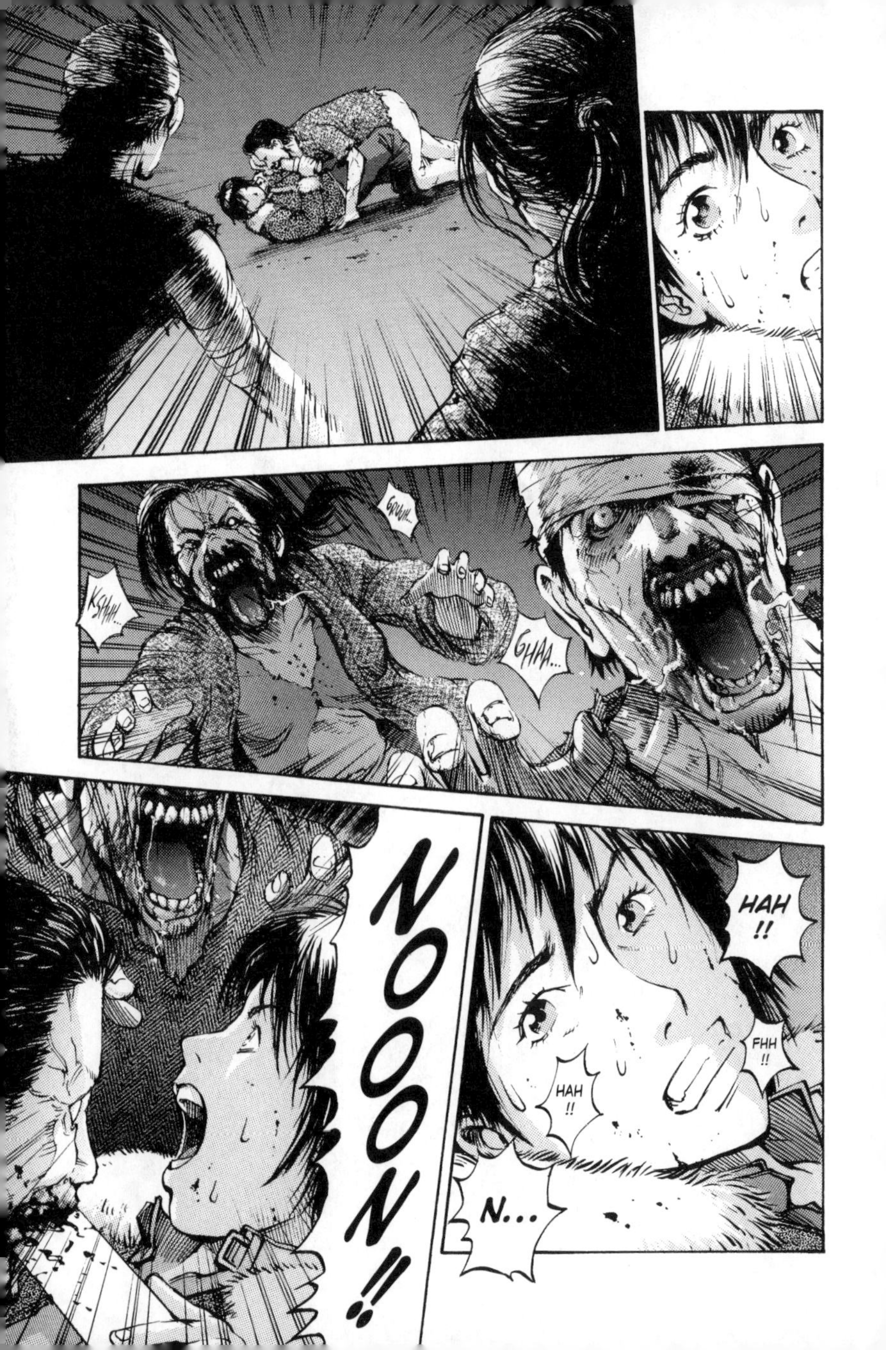
GRUUH...
GHAA...
KSHHH...
HAH !!
FHH !!
HAH !!
N...
NOOON!!

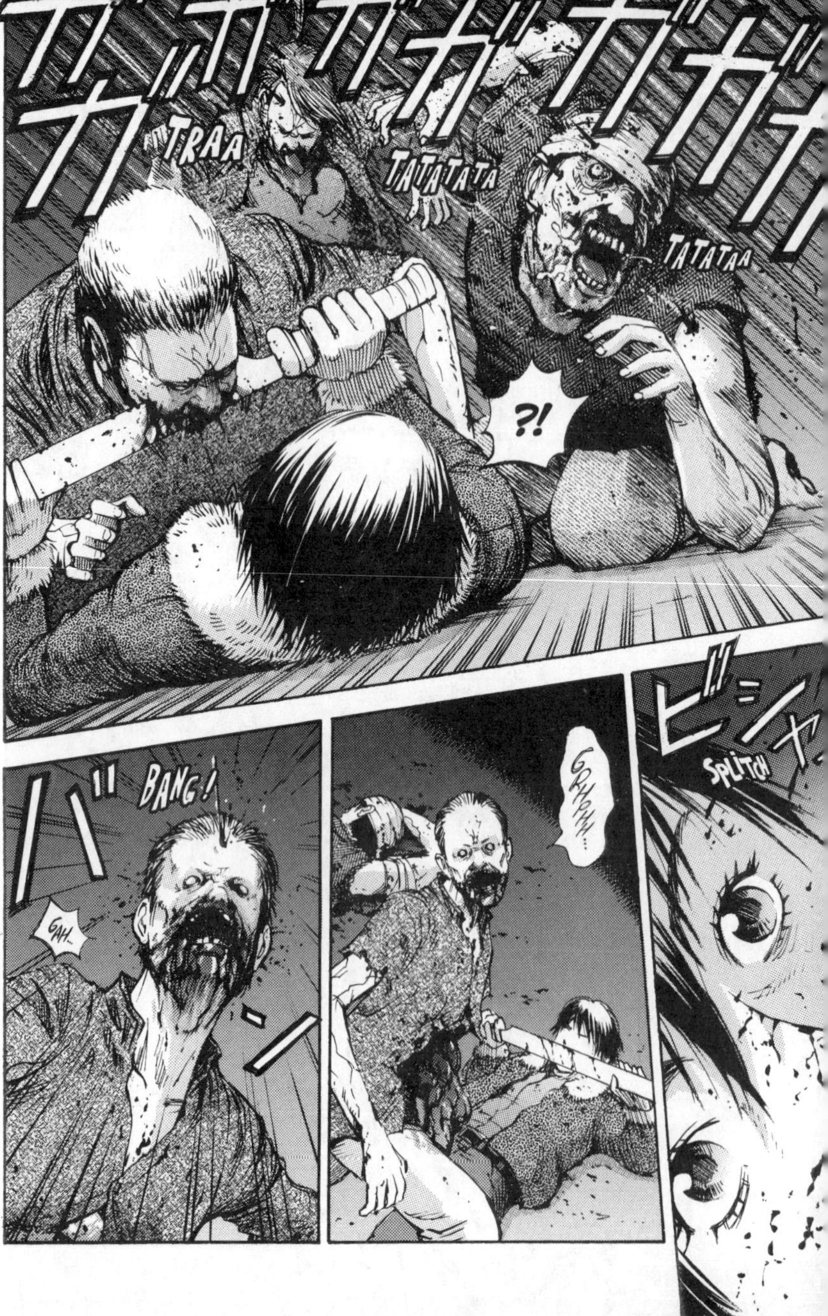
TATATAA
TATATATA
TRAA
?!
SPLITCH
GRPHH...
BANG!
GAH...

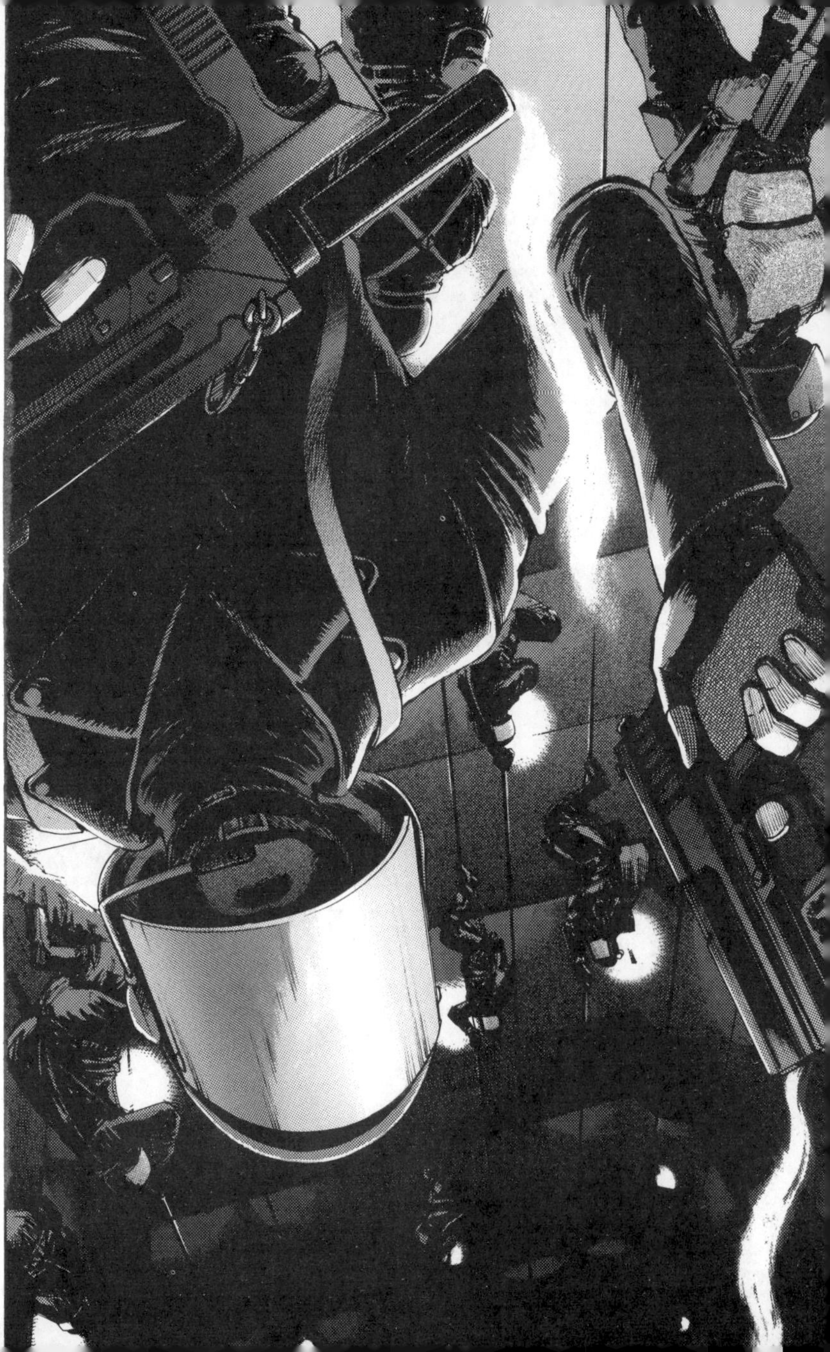

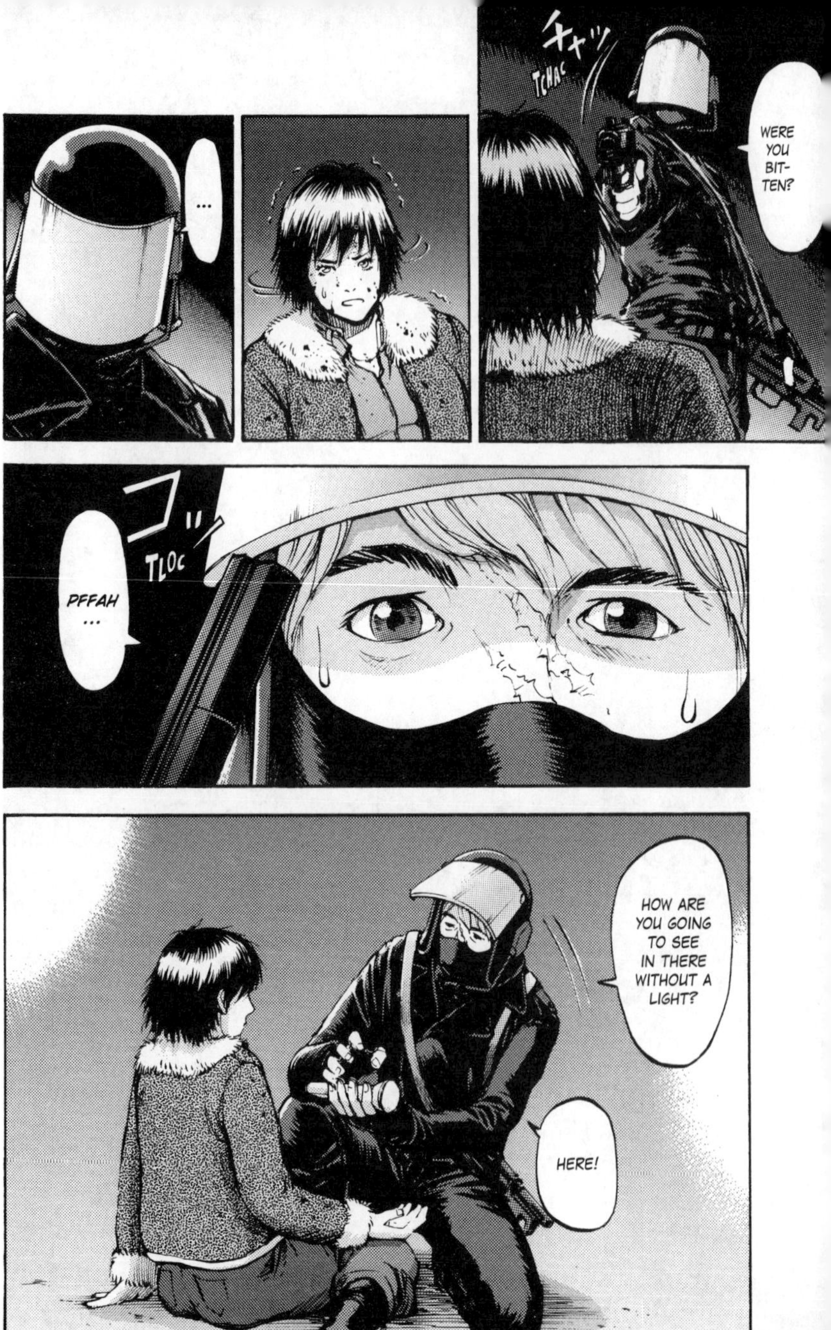
チャッ
TCHAC
WERE YOU BIT-TEN?
...
コッ
TLOC
PFFAH ...
HOW ARE YOU GOING TO SEE IN THERE WITHOUT A LIGHT?
HERE!

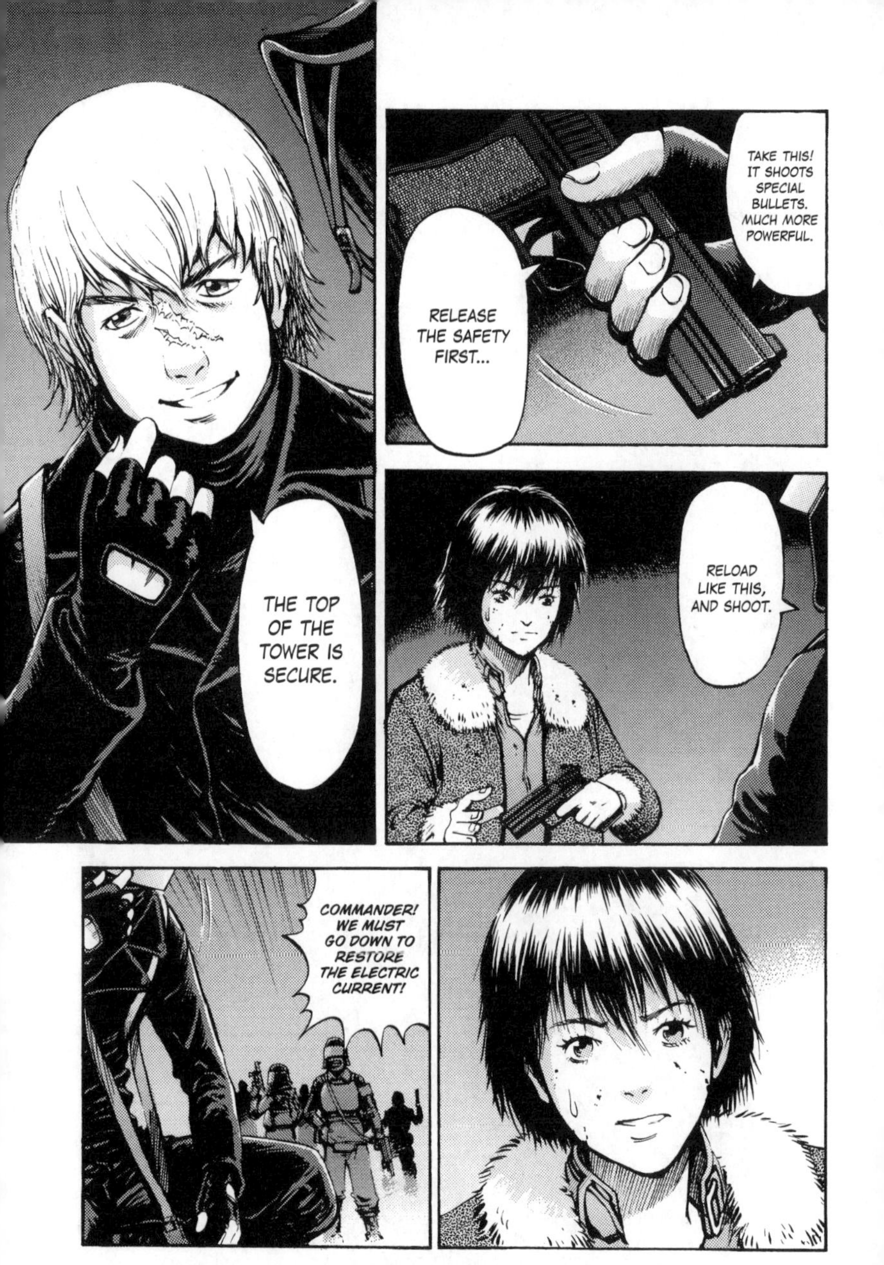
TAKE THIS! IT SHOOTS SPECIAL BULLETS. MUCH MORE POWERFUL.
RELEASE THE SAFETY FIRST...
RELOAD LIKE THIS, AND SHOOT.
THE TOP OF THE TOWER IS SECURE.
COMMANDER! WE MUST GO DOWN TO RESTORE THE ELECTRIC CURRENT!

I'LL BUY
YOU A DRINK
NEXT
TIME WE
MEET.

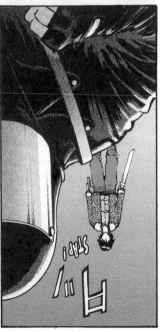

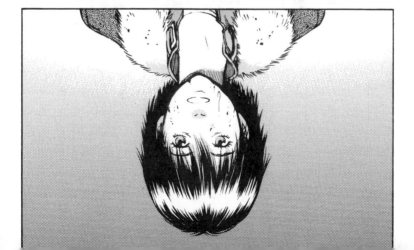

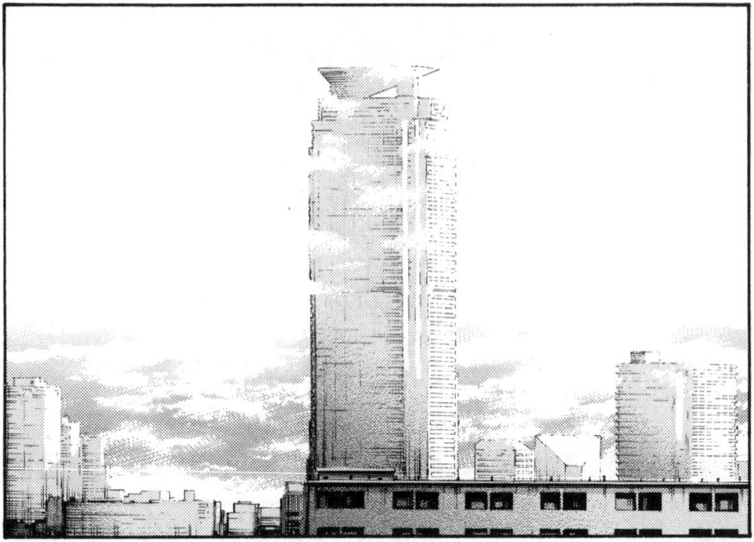

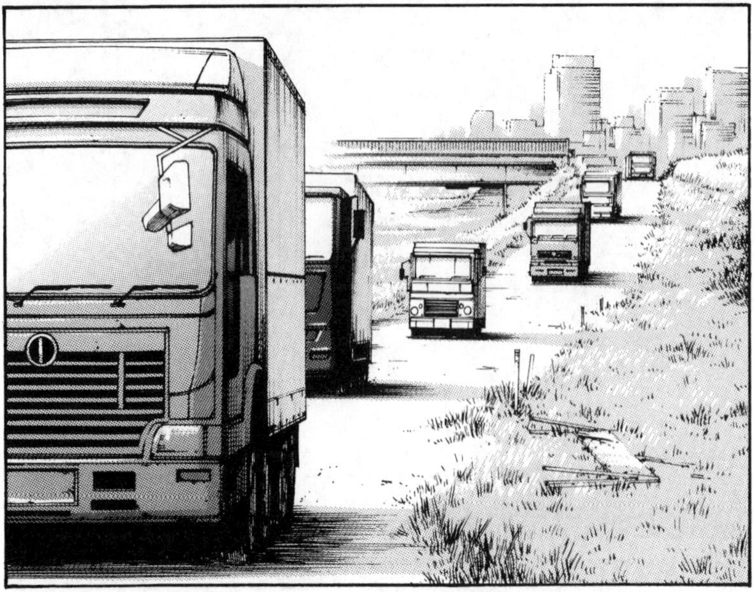

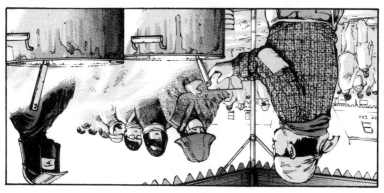

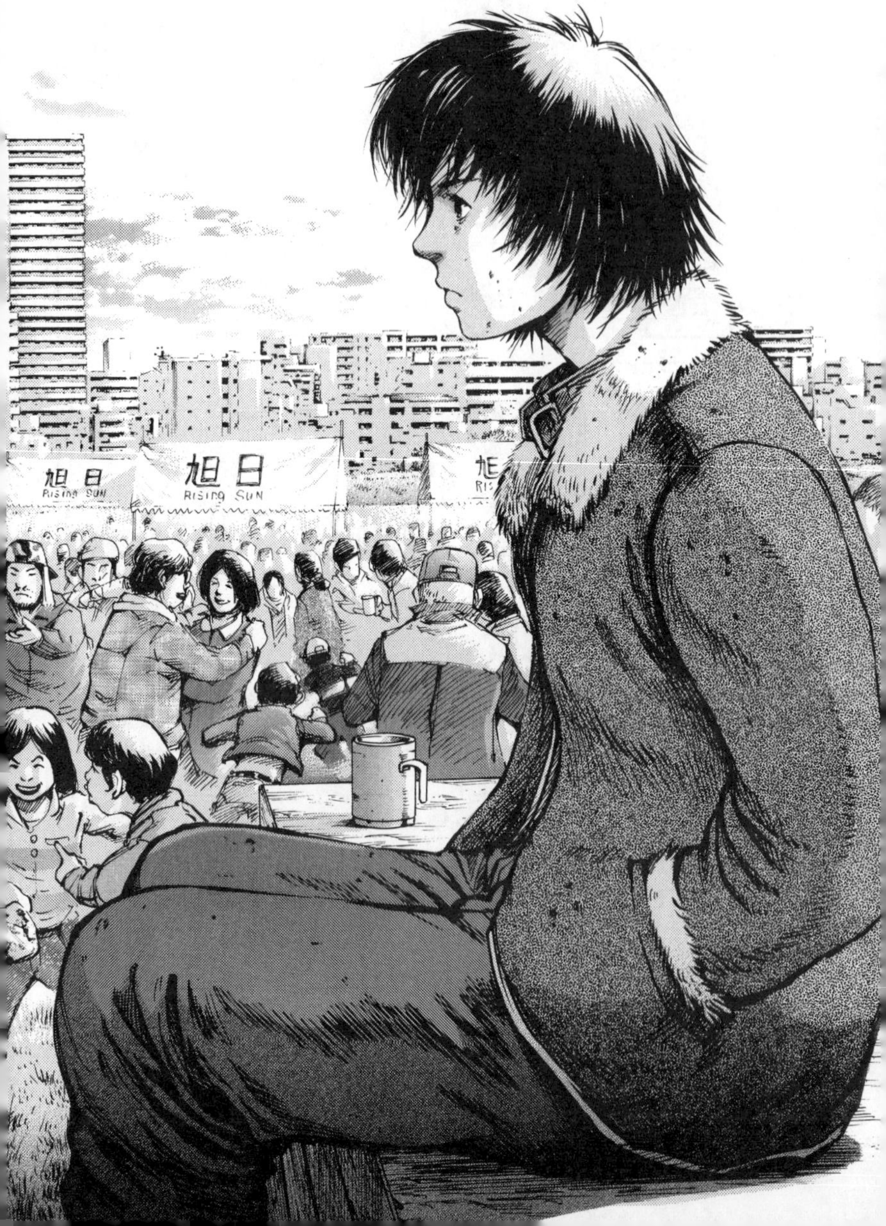
旭日
RISING SUN
旭日
RISING SUN

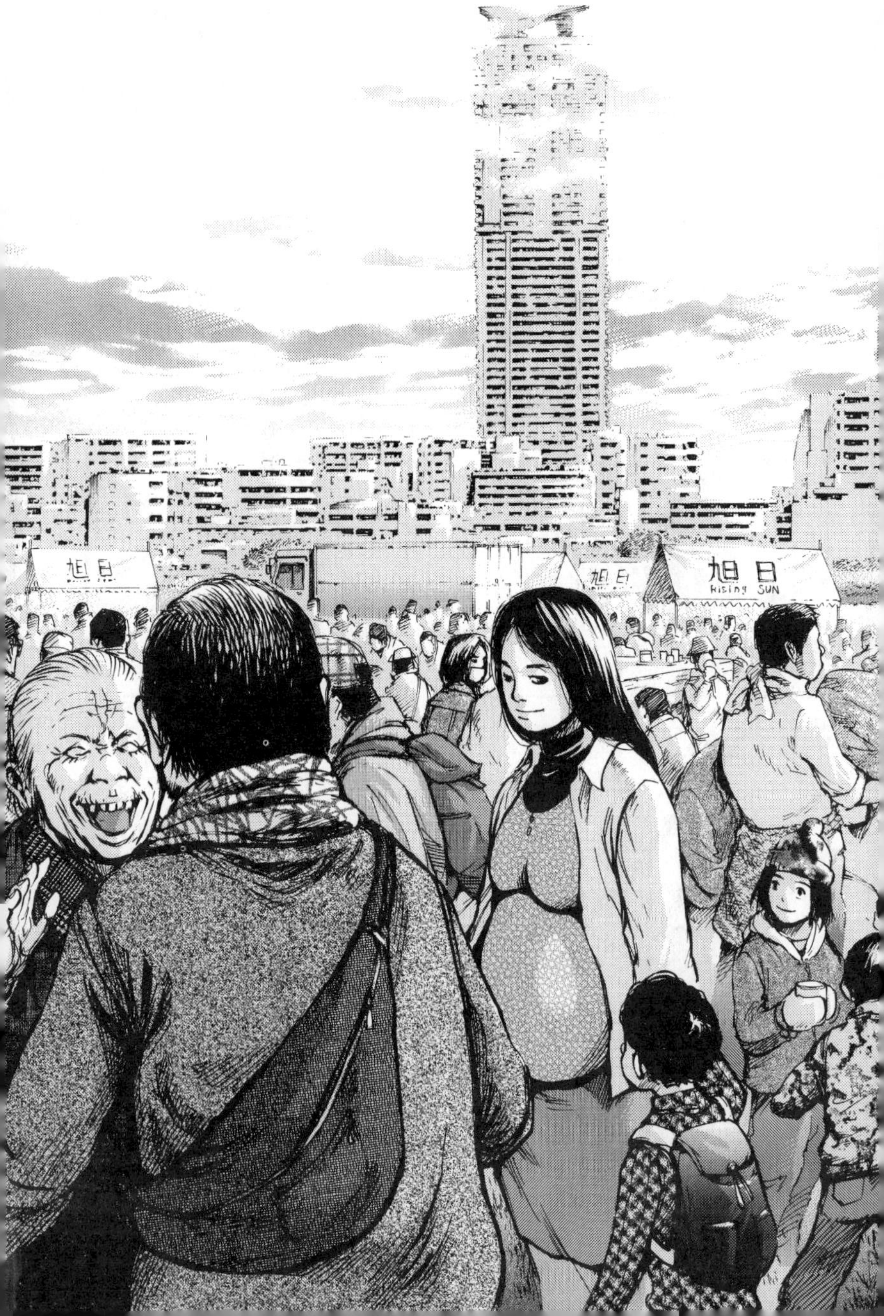
旭日
Rising SUN
旭日
旭日

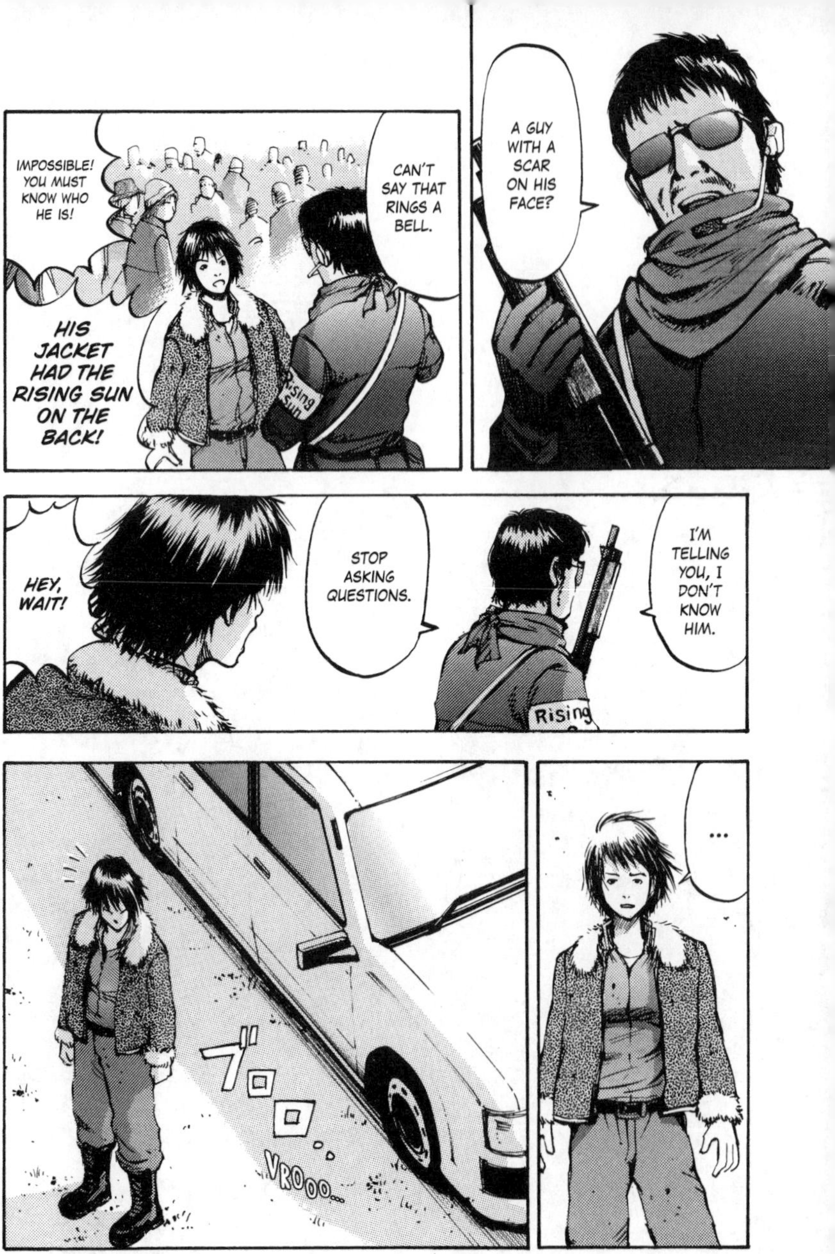
A GUY WITH A SCAR ON HIS FACE?
CAN'T SAY THAT RINGS A BELL.
IMPOSSIBLE! YOU MUST KNOW WHO HE IS!
HIS JACKET HAD THE RISING SUN ON THE BACK!
Rising Sun
I'M TELLING YOU, I DON'T KNOW HIM.
STOP ASKING QUESTIONS.
HEY, WAIT!
Rising
...
ブロロ
VROOO...

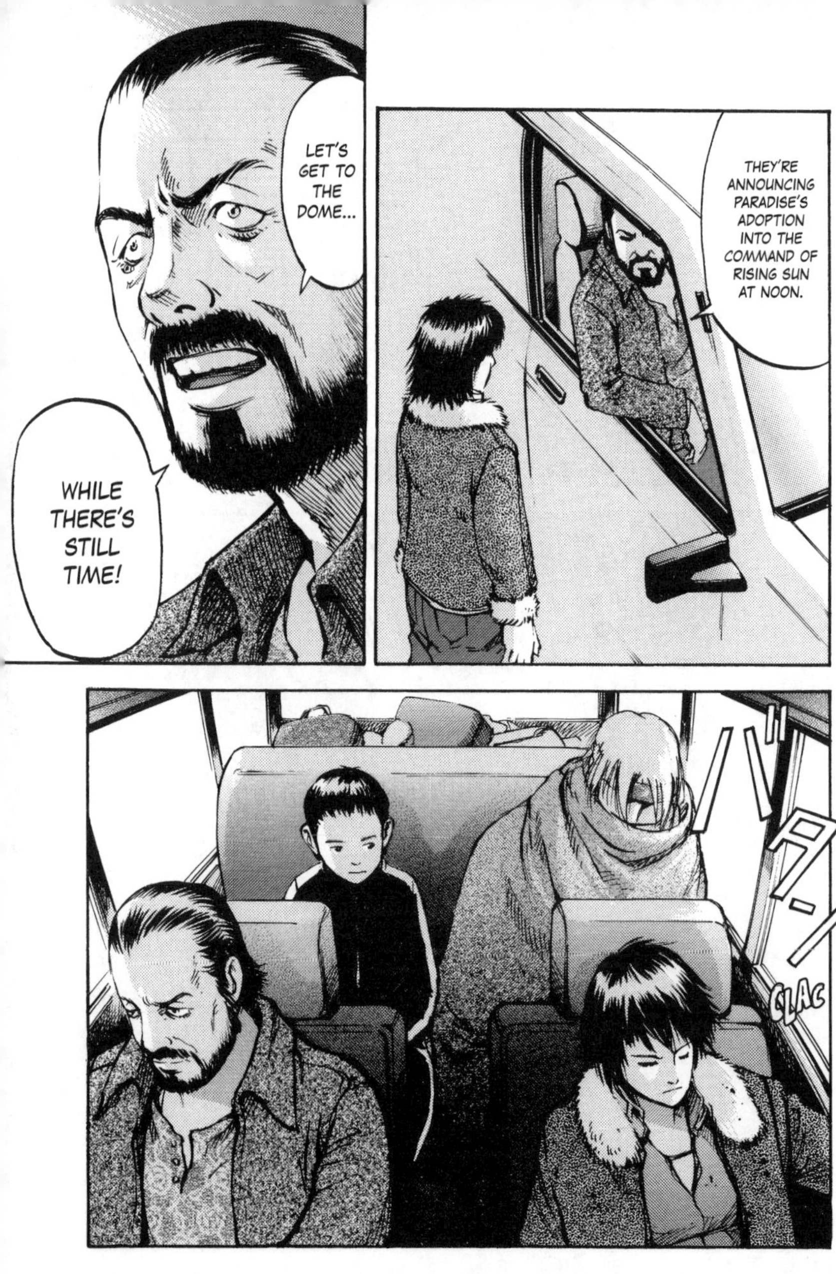
THEY'RE ANNOUNCING PARADISE'S ADOPTION INTO THE COMMAND OF RISING SUN AT NOON.
LET'S GET TO THE DOME...
WHILE THERE'S STILL TIME!
CLAC

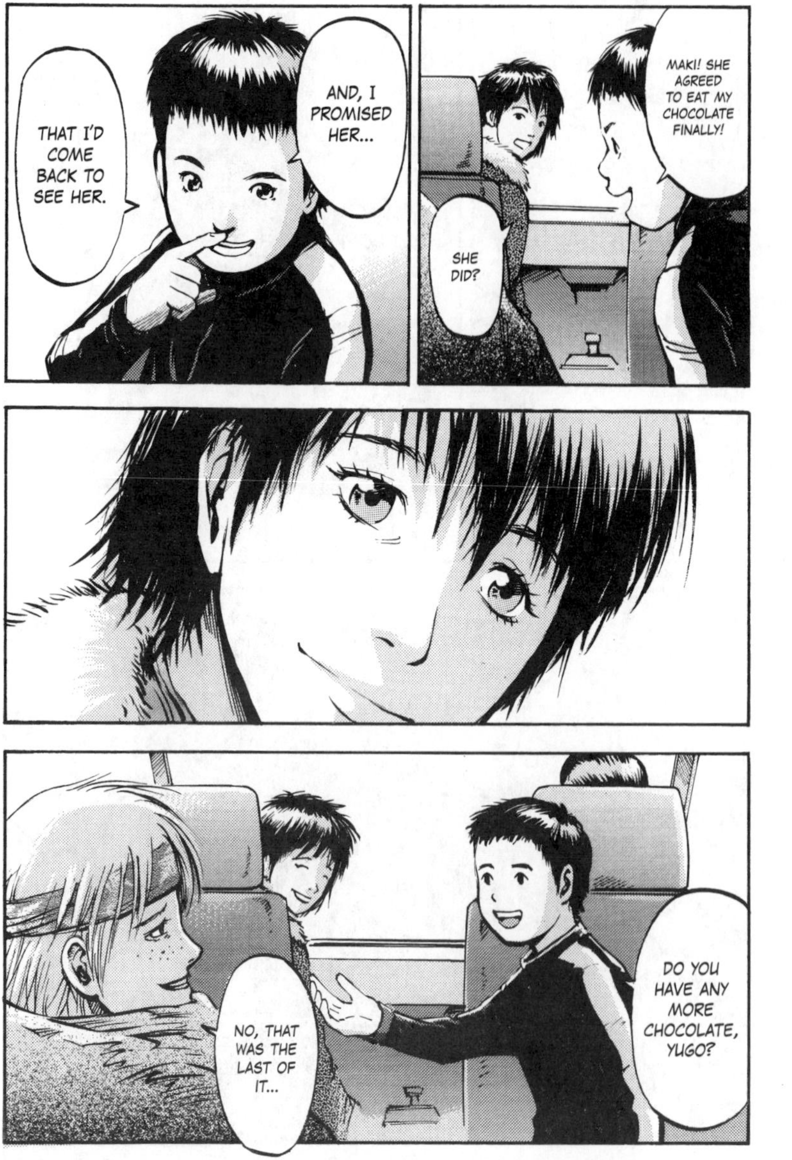
MAKI! SHE AGREED TO EAT MY CHOCOLATE FINALLY!
SHE DID?
AND, I PROMISED HER...
THAT I'D COME BACK TO SEE HER.
DO YOU HAVE ANY MORE CHOCOLATE, YUGO?
NO, THAT WAS THE LAST OF IT...

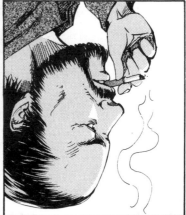

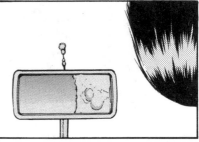

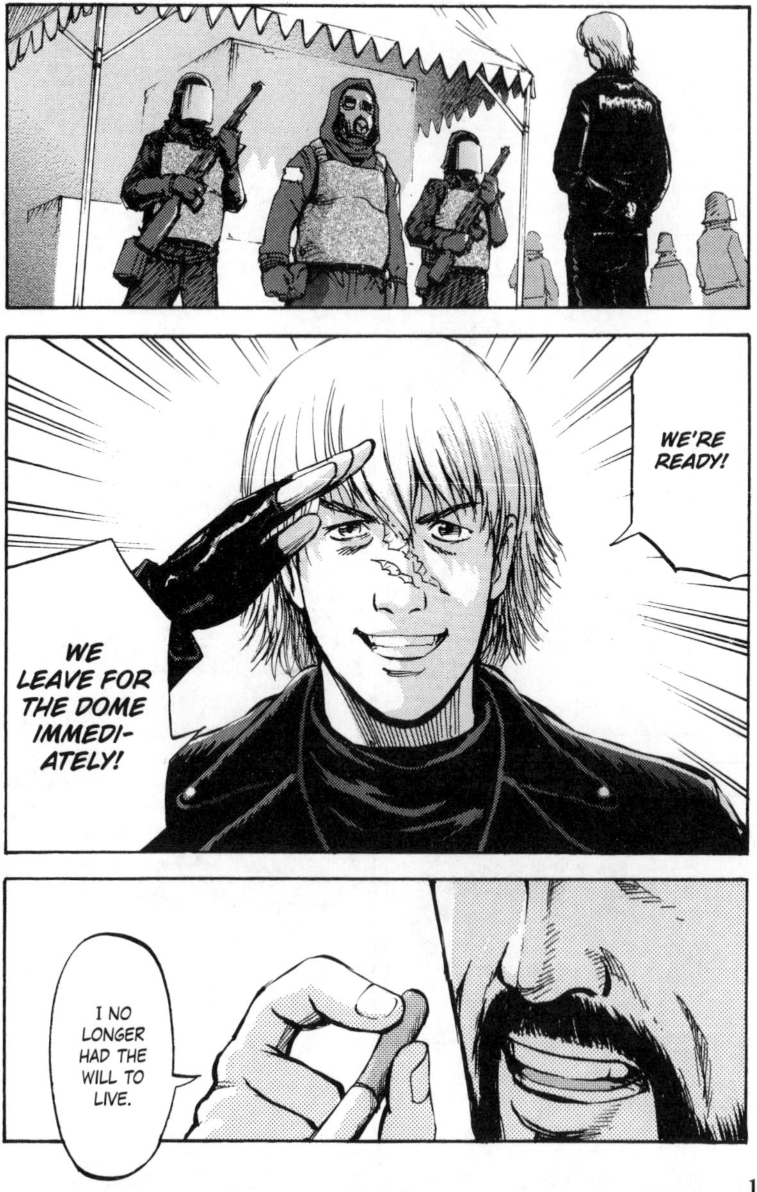
WE'RE READY!
WE LEAVE FOR THE DOME IMMEDI-ATELY!
I NO LONGER HAD THE WILL TO LIVE.

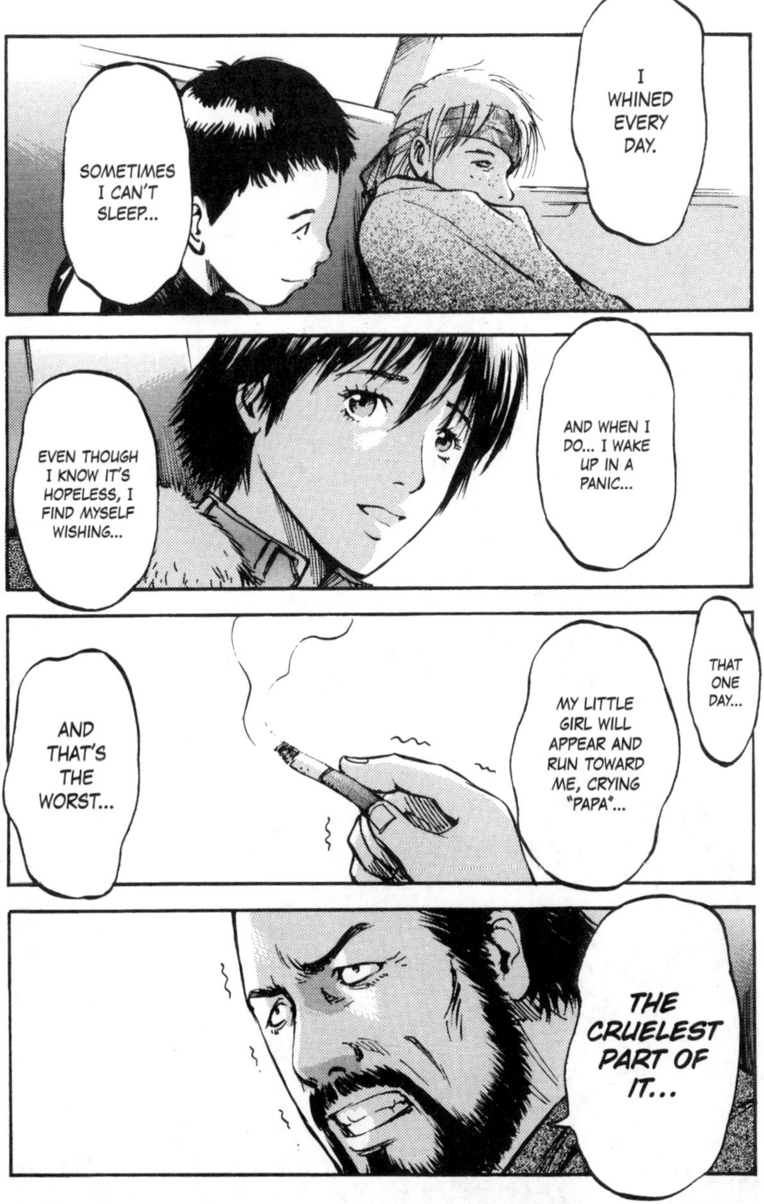
I WHINED EVERY DAY.
SOMETIMES I CAN'T SLEEP...
AND WHEN I DO... I WAKE UP IN A PANIC...
EVEN THOUGH I KNOW IT'S HOPELESS, I FIND MYSELF WISHING...
THAT ONE DAY...
MY LITTLE GIRL WILL APPEAR AND RUN TOWARD ME, CRYING "PAPA"...
AND THAT'S THE WORST...
THE CRUELEST PART OF IT...

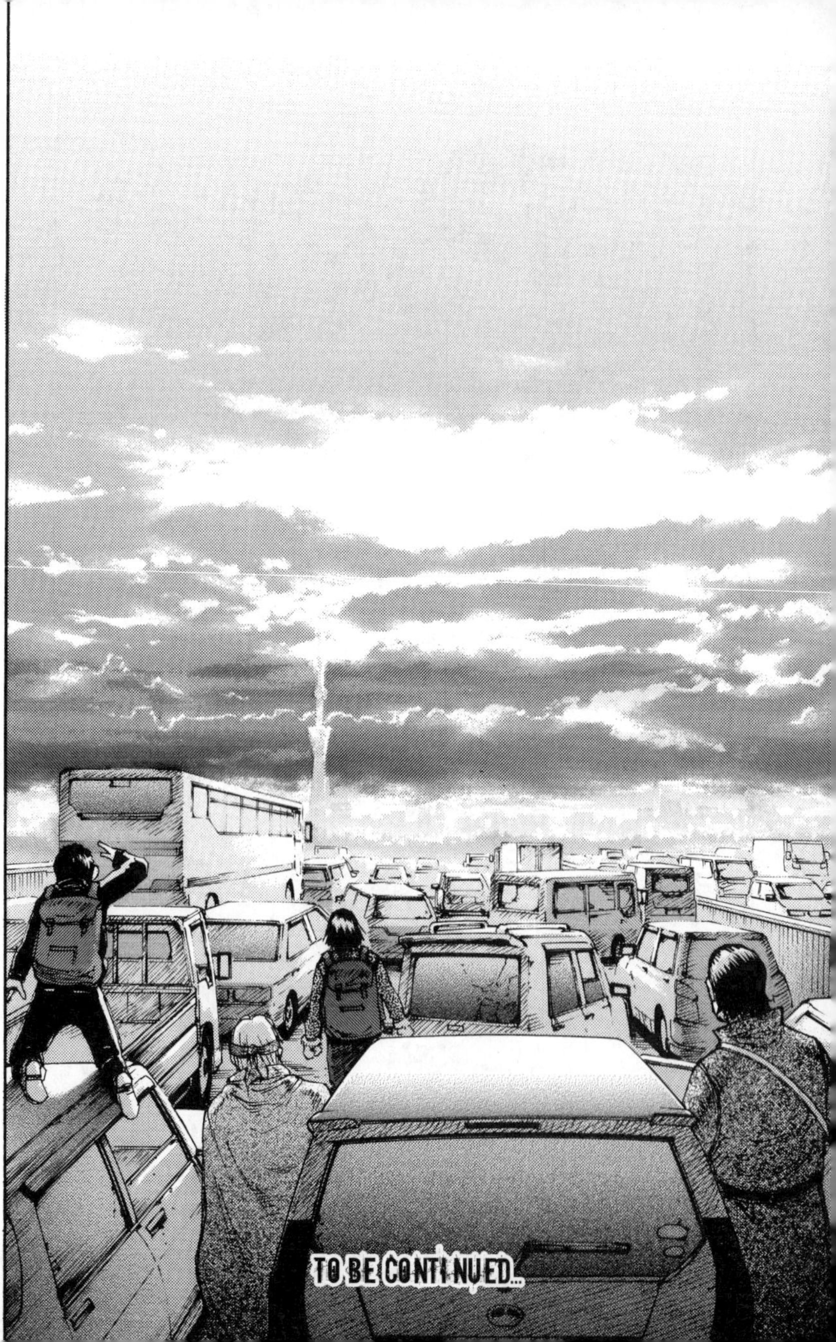
TO BE CONTINUED...

CRUELER THAN DEAD

CHAPTER ZERO

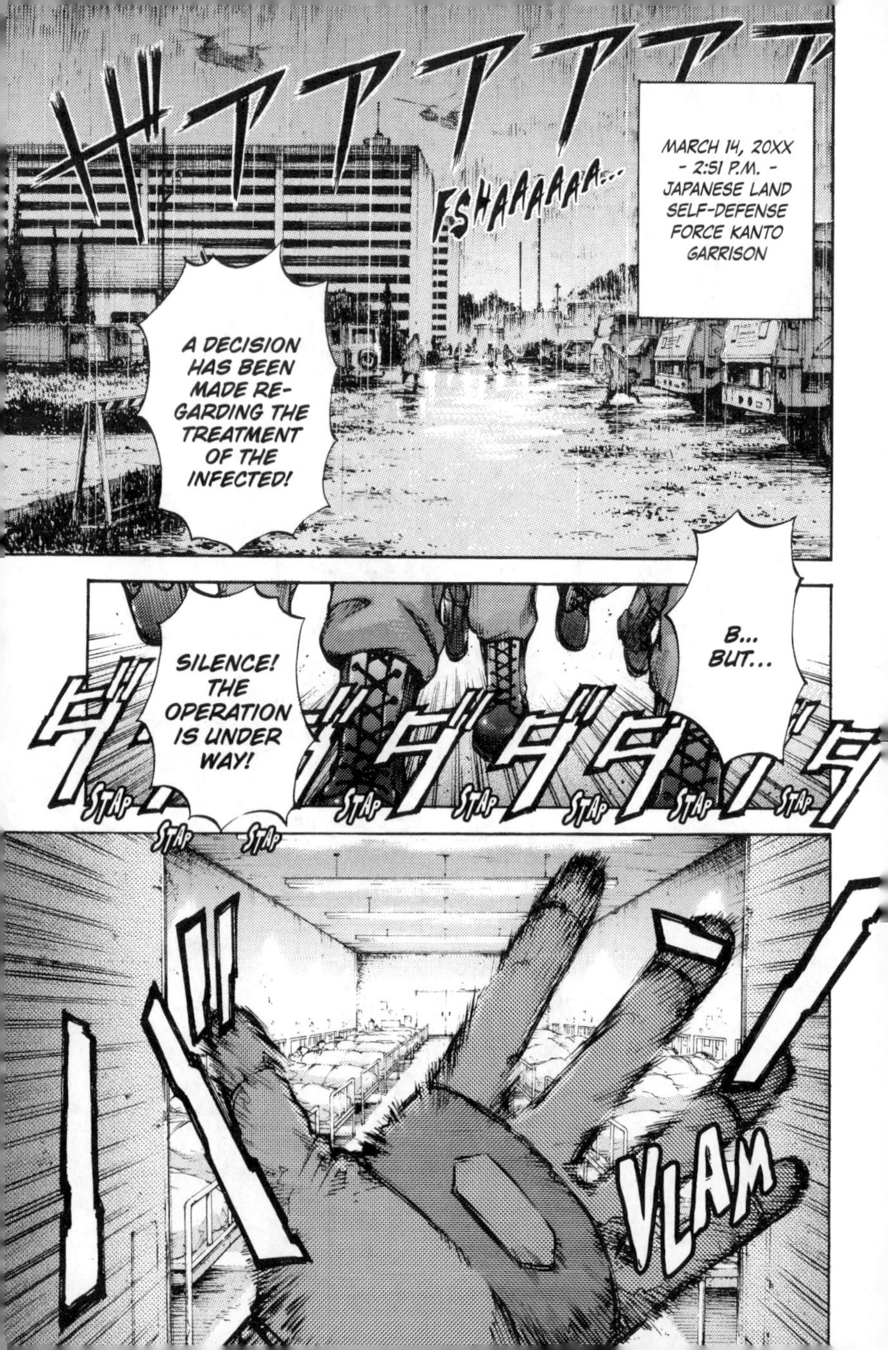
MARCH 14, 20XX
- 2:51 P.M. -
JAPANESE LAND SELF-DEFENSE FORCE KANTO GARRISON
FSHAAAAAA...
A DECISION HAS BEEN MADE RE-GARDING THE TREATMENT OF THE INFECTED!
B... BUT...
SILENCE! THE OPERATION IS UNDER WAY!
STAP STAP STAP STAP STAP STAP STAP STAP
VLAM

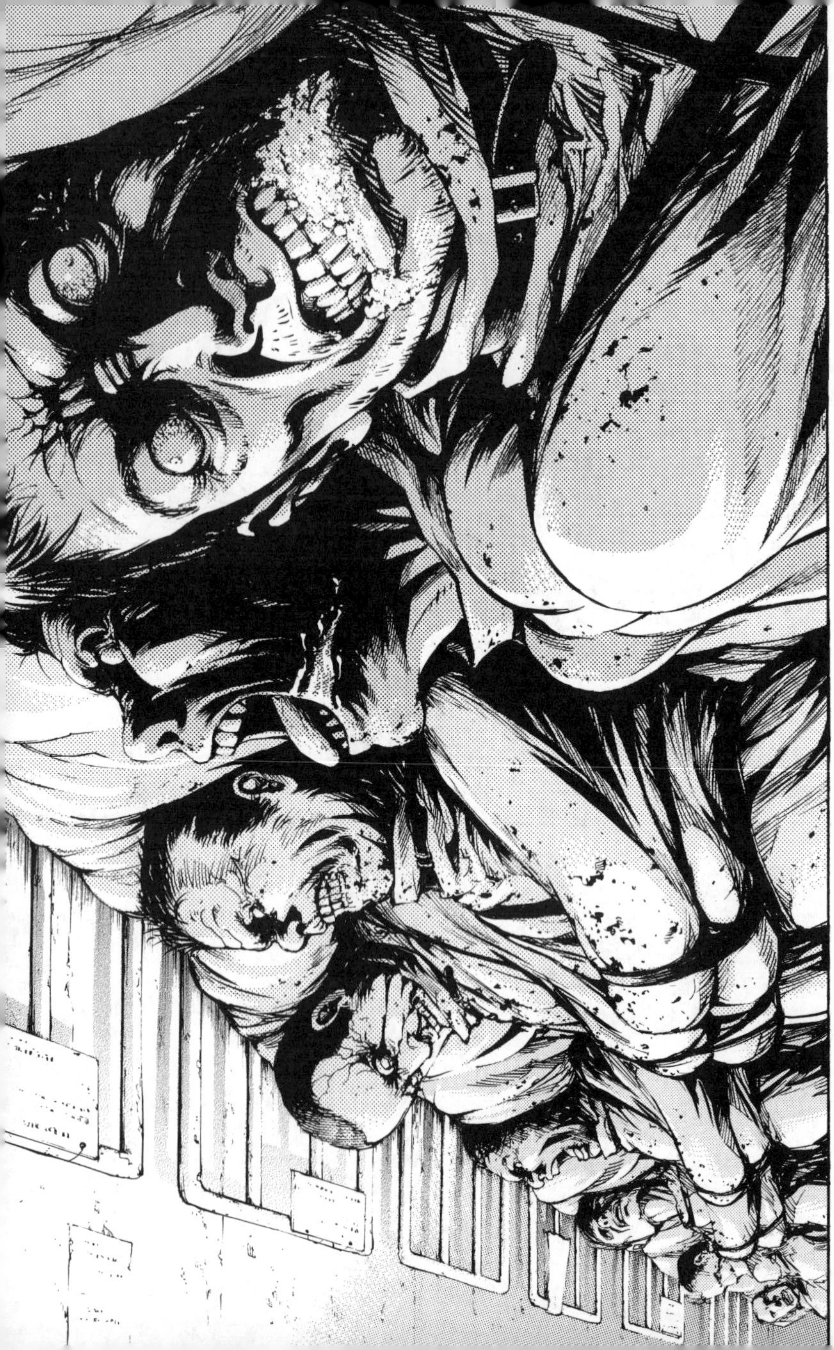

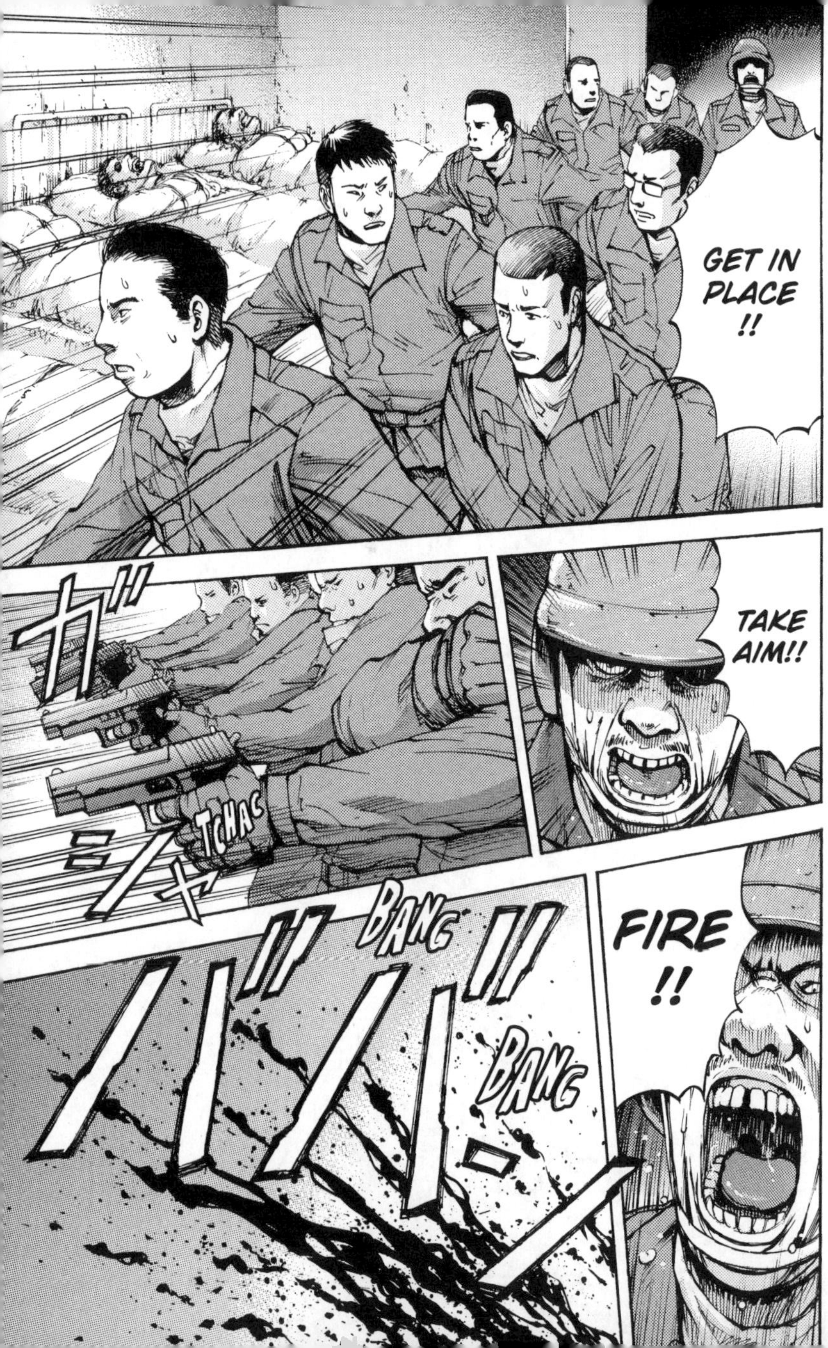
GET IN PLACE !!
TAKE AIM!!
TCHAC
FIRE !!
BANG !!
BANG

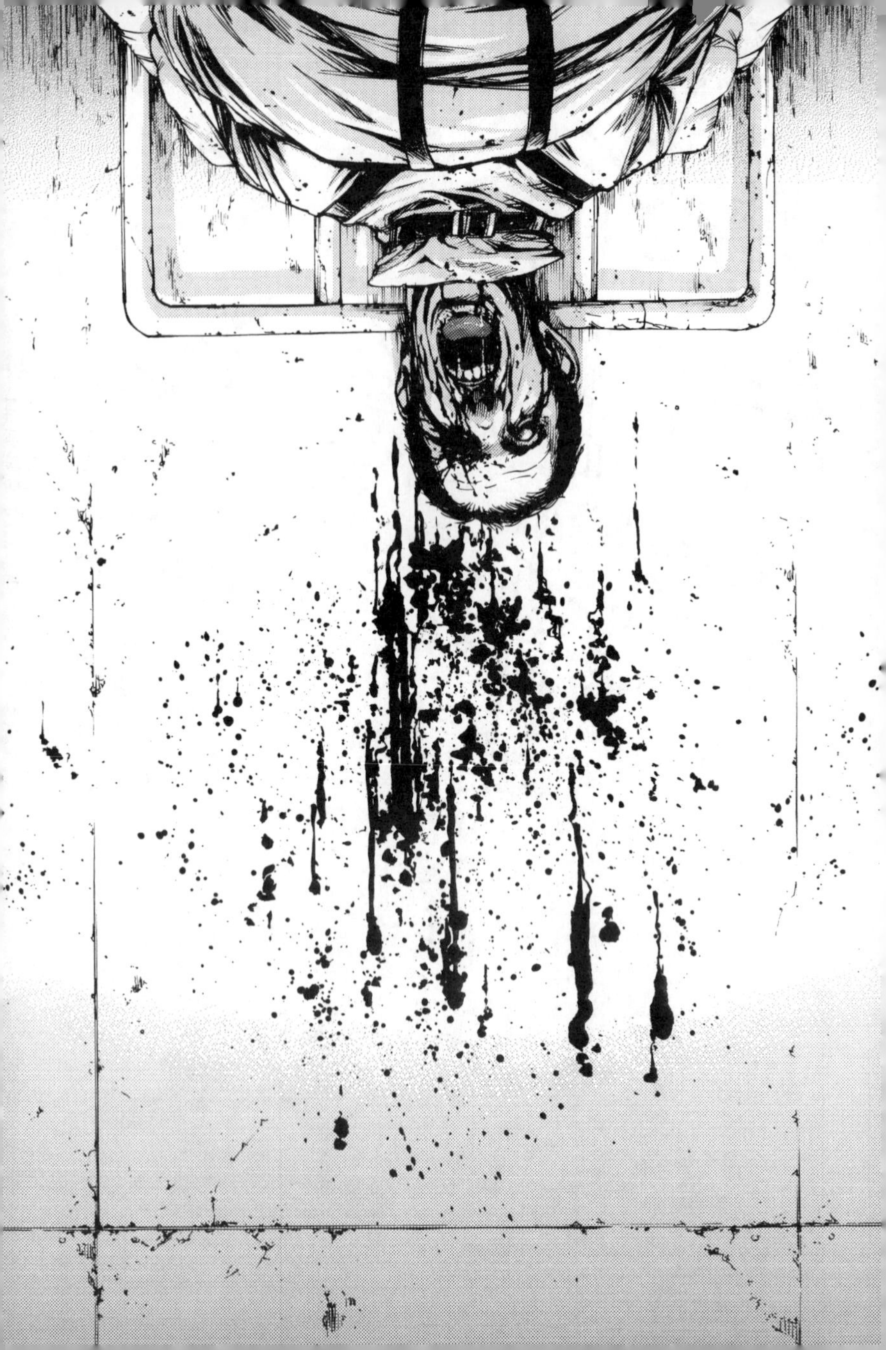

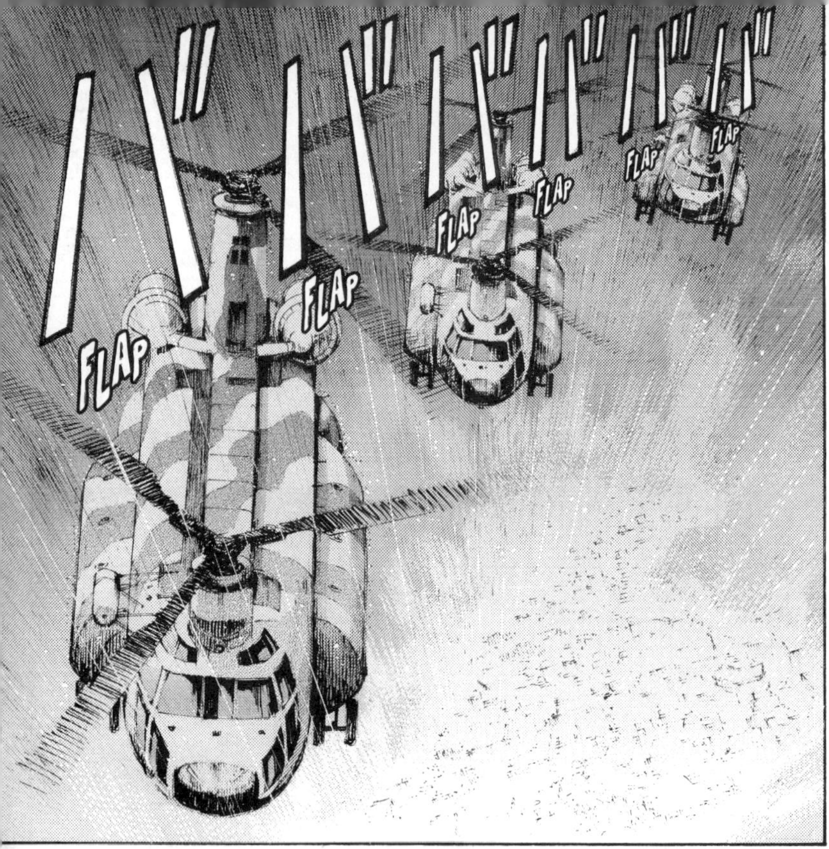
FLAP
FLAP
FLAP
FLAP
FLAP
FLAP

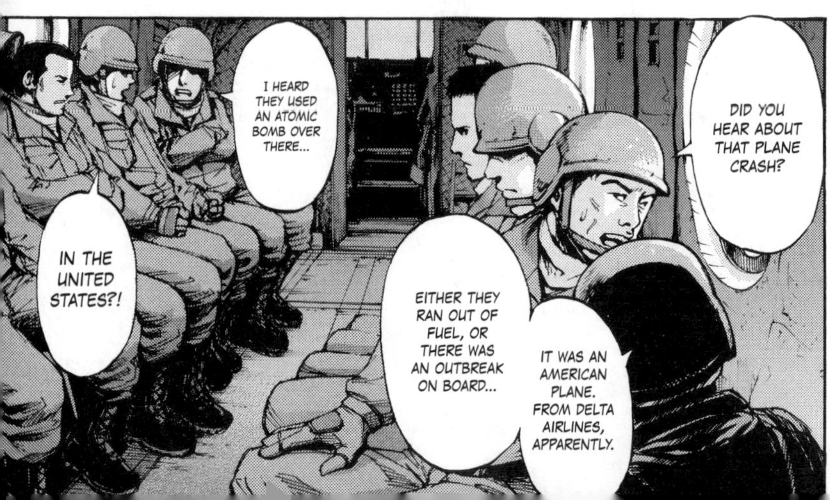
DID YOU HEAR ABOUT THAT PLANE CRASH?
IT WAS AN AMERICAN PLANE. FROM DELTA AIRLINES, APPARENTLY.
EITHER THEY RAN OUT OF FUEL, OR THERE WAS AN OUTBREAK ON BOARD...
I HEARD THEY USED AN ATOMIC BOMB OVER THERE...
IN THE UNITED STATES?!

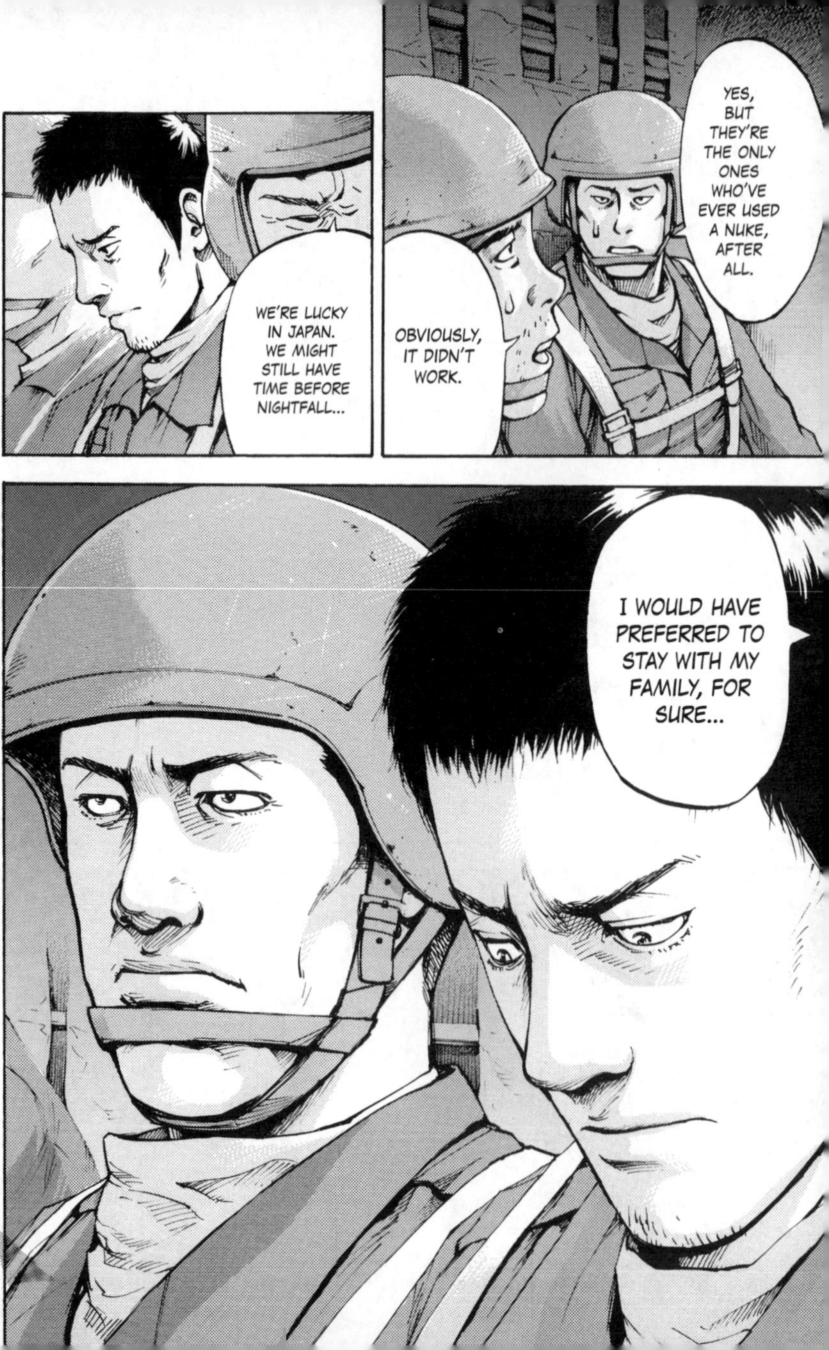
YES, BUT THEY'RE THE ONLY ONES WHO'VE EVER USED A NUKE, AFTER ALL.
OBVIOUSLY, IT DIDN'T WORK.
WE'RE LUCKY IN JAPAN. WE MIGHT STILL HAVE TIME BEFORE NIGHTFALL...
I WOULD HAVE PREFERRED TO STAY WITH MY FAMILY, FOR SURE...

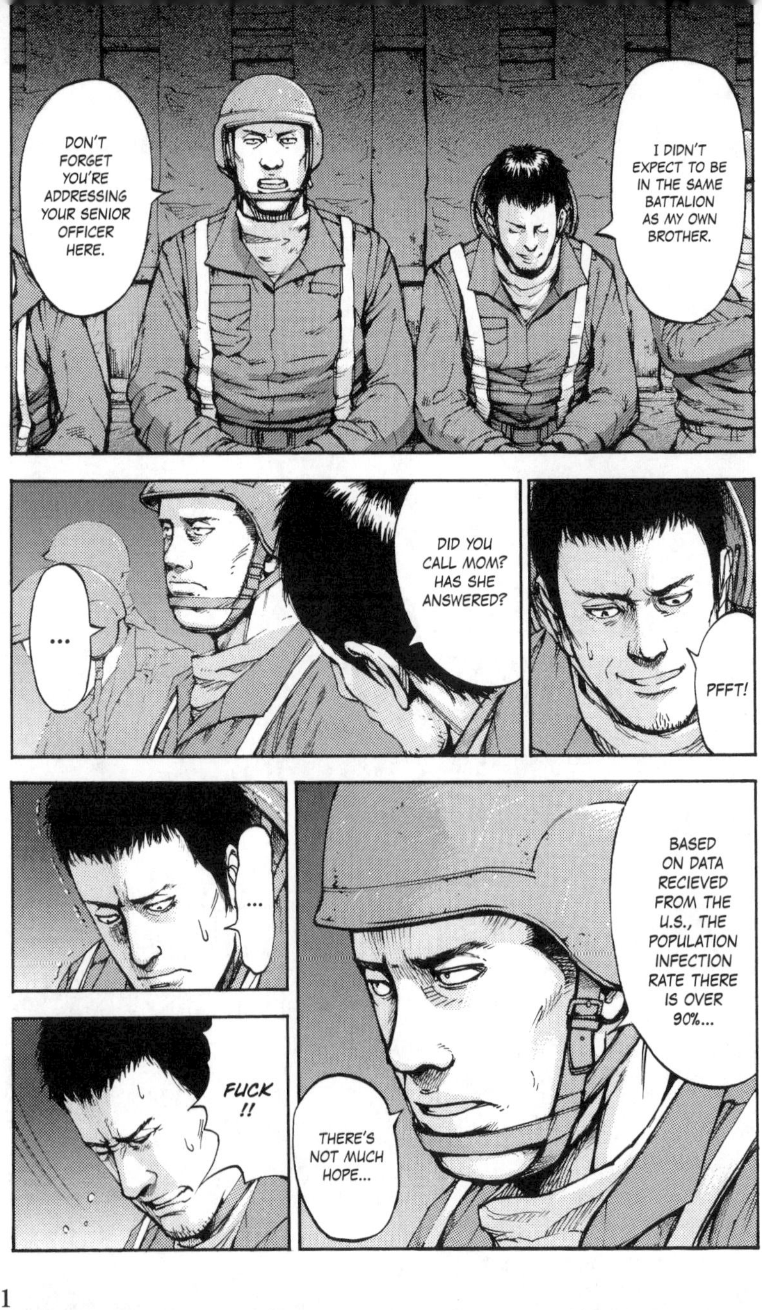
I DIDN'T EXPECT TO BE IN THE SAME BATTALION AS MY OWN BROTHER.
DON'T FORGET YOU'RE ADDRESSING YOUR SENIOR OFFICER HERE.
PFFT!
DID YOU CALL MOM? HAS SHE ANSWERED?
...
BASED ON DATA RECIEVED FROM THE U.S., THE POPULATION INFECTION RATE THERE IS OVER 90%...
THERE'S NOT MUCH HOPE...
...
FUCK !!

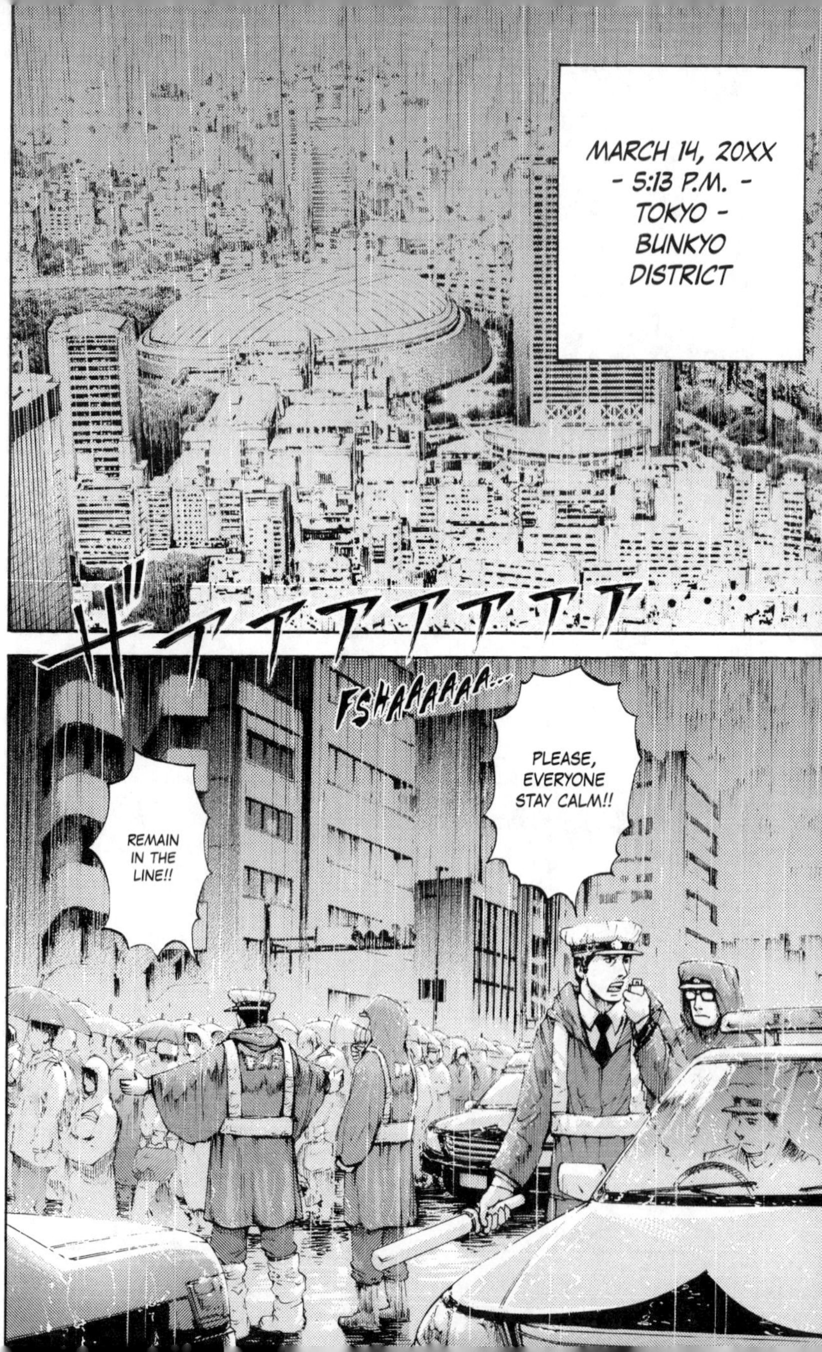
MARCH 14, 20XX
- 5:13 P.M. -
TOKYO -
BUNKYO
DISTRICT
ザァァァァァァァ
FSHAAAAAA...
PLEASE, EVERYONE STAY CALM!!
REMAIN IN THE LINE!!

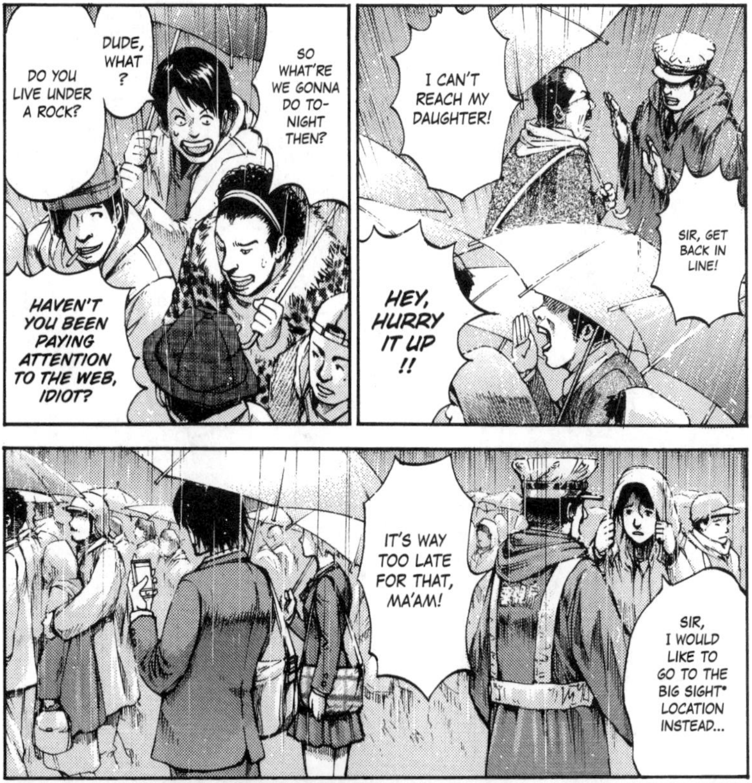
I CAN'T REACH MY DAUGHTER!
SIR, GET BACK IN LINE!
HEY, HURRY IT UP !!
DUDE, WHAT ?
DO YOU LIVE UNDER A ROCK?
SO WHAT'RE WE GONNA DO TO-NIGHT THEN?
HAVEN'T YOU BEEN PAYING ATTENTION TO THE WEB, IDIOT?
SIR, I WOULD LIKE TO GO TO THE BIG SIGHT* LOCATION INSTEAD...
IT'S WAY TOO LATE FOR THAT, MA'AM!

*A.N. : Big Sight is the nickname for the Toyko International Exhibition Center, a convention center located in Odaiba, Tokyo Bay.

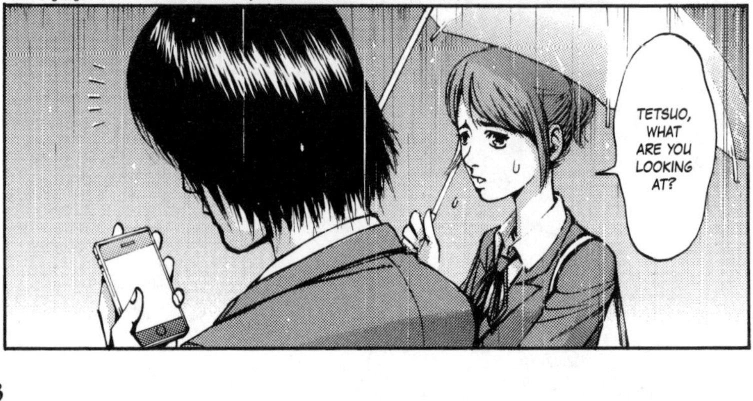
TETSUO, WHAT ARE YOU LOOKING AT?

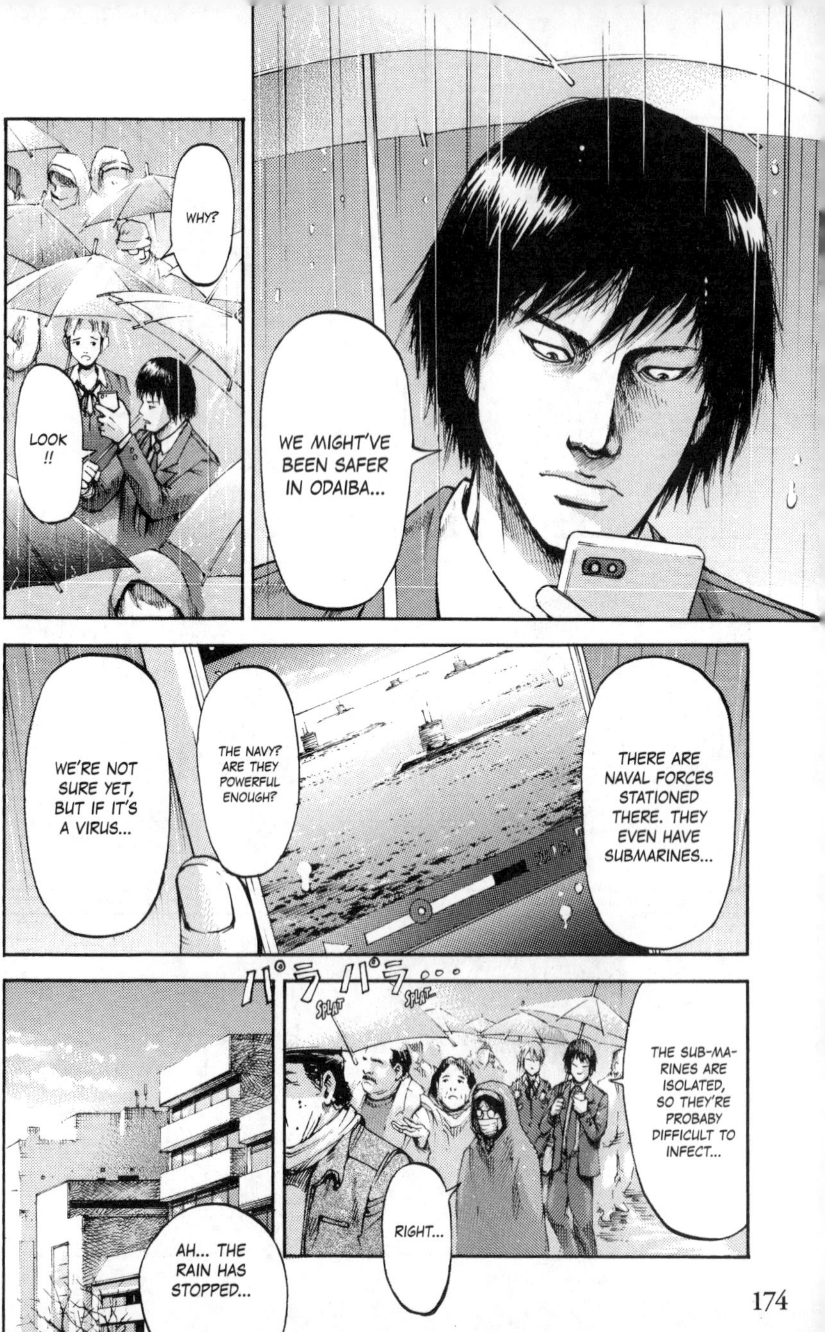
WE MIGHT'VE BEEN SAFER IN ODAIBA...
WHY?
LOOK !!
THERE ARE NAVAL FORCES STATIONED THERE. THEY EVEN HAVE SUBMARINES...
THE NAVY? ARE THEY POWERFUL ENOUGH?
WE'RE NOT SURE YET, BUT IF IT'S A VIRUS...
パラパラ...
SPLAT...
SPLAT
THE SUB-MA-RINES ARE ISOLATED, SO THEY'RE PROBABY DIFFICULT TO INFECT...
RIGHT...
AH... THE RAIN HAS STOPPED...

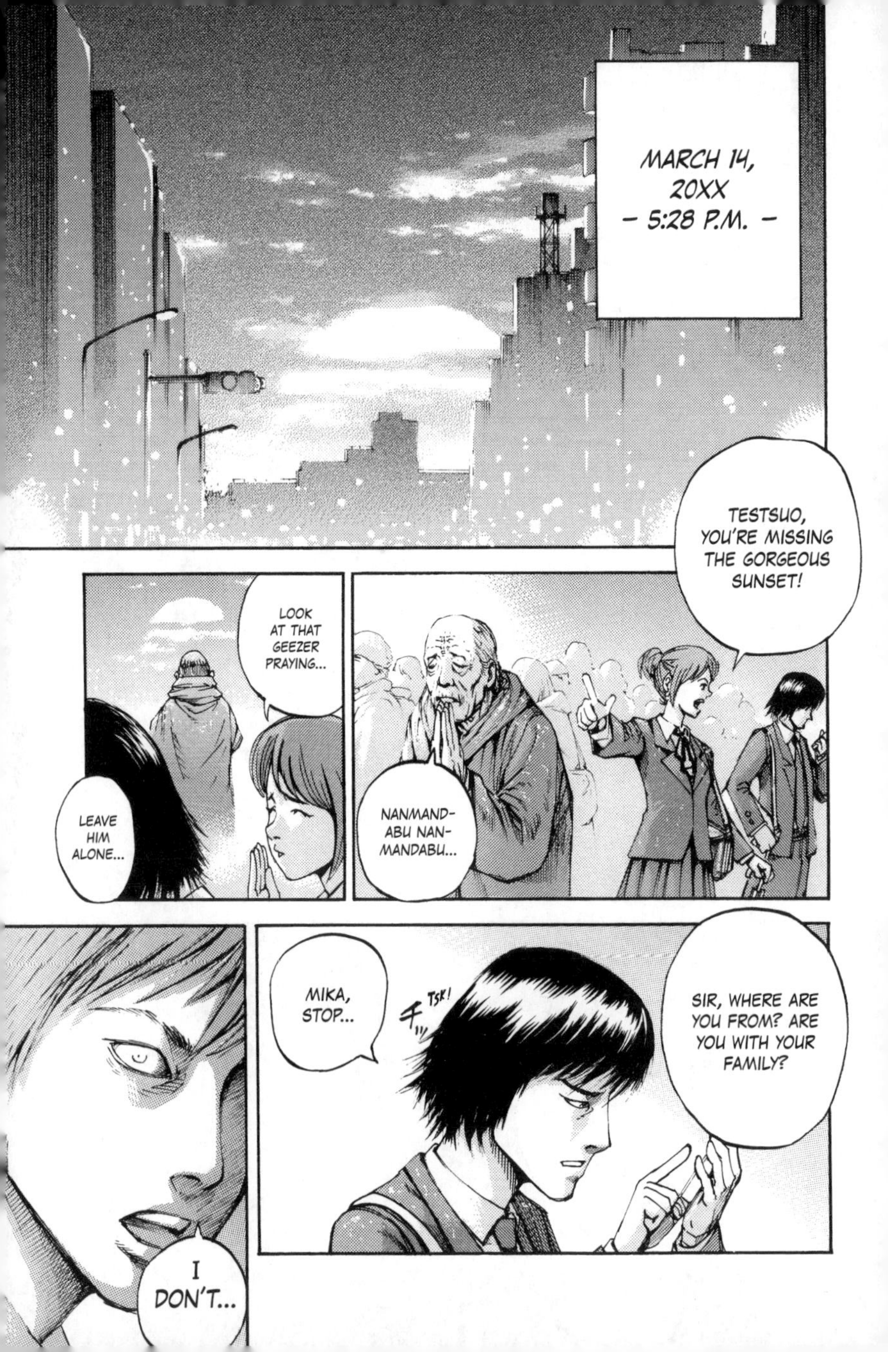
MARCH 14, 20XX - 5:28 P.M. -
TESTSUO, YOU'RE MISSING THE GORGEOUS SUNSET!
NANMAND-ABU NAN-MANDABU...
LOOK AT THAT GEEZER PRAYING...
LEAVE HIM ALONE...
SIR, WHERE ARE YOU FROM? ARE YOU WITH YOUR FAMILY?
TSK!
MIKA, STOP...
I DON'T...

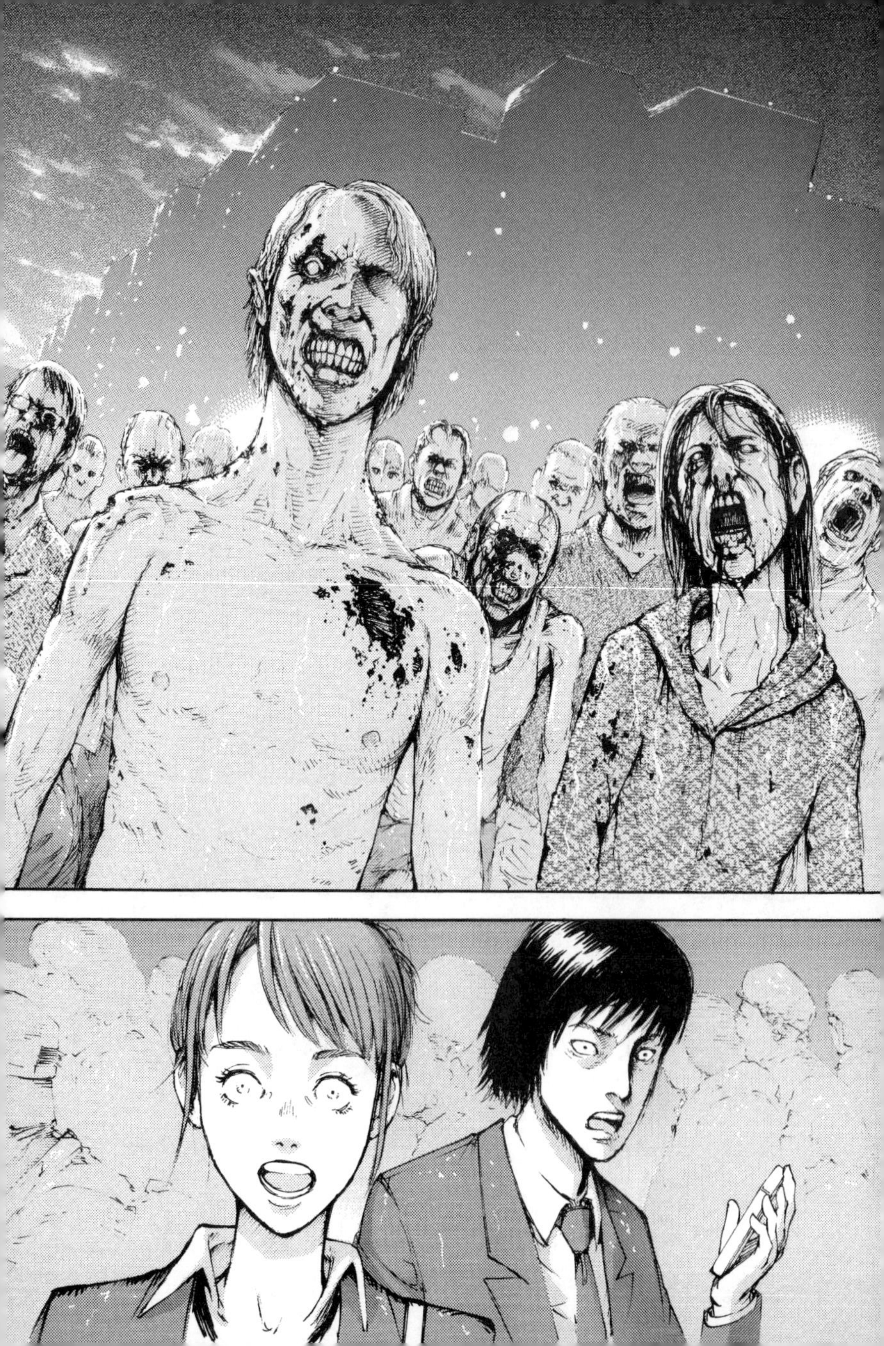

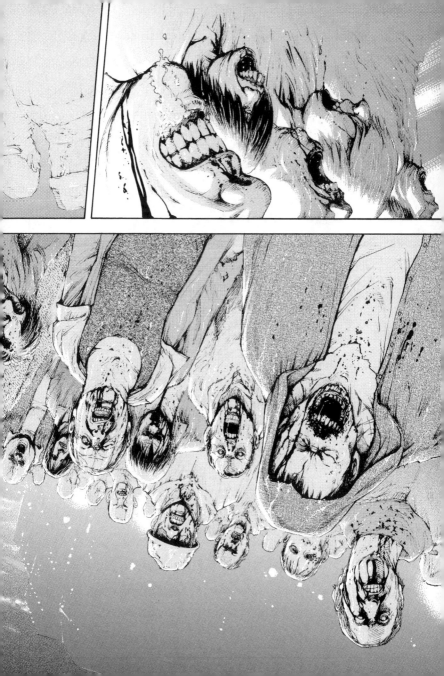

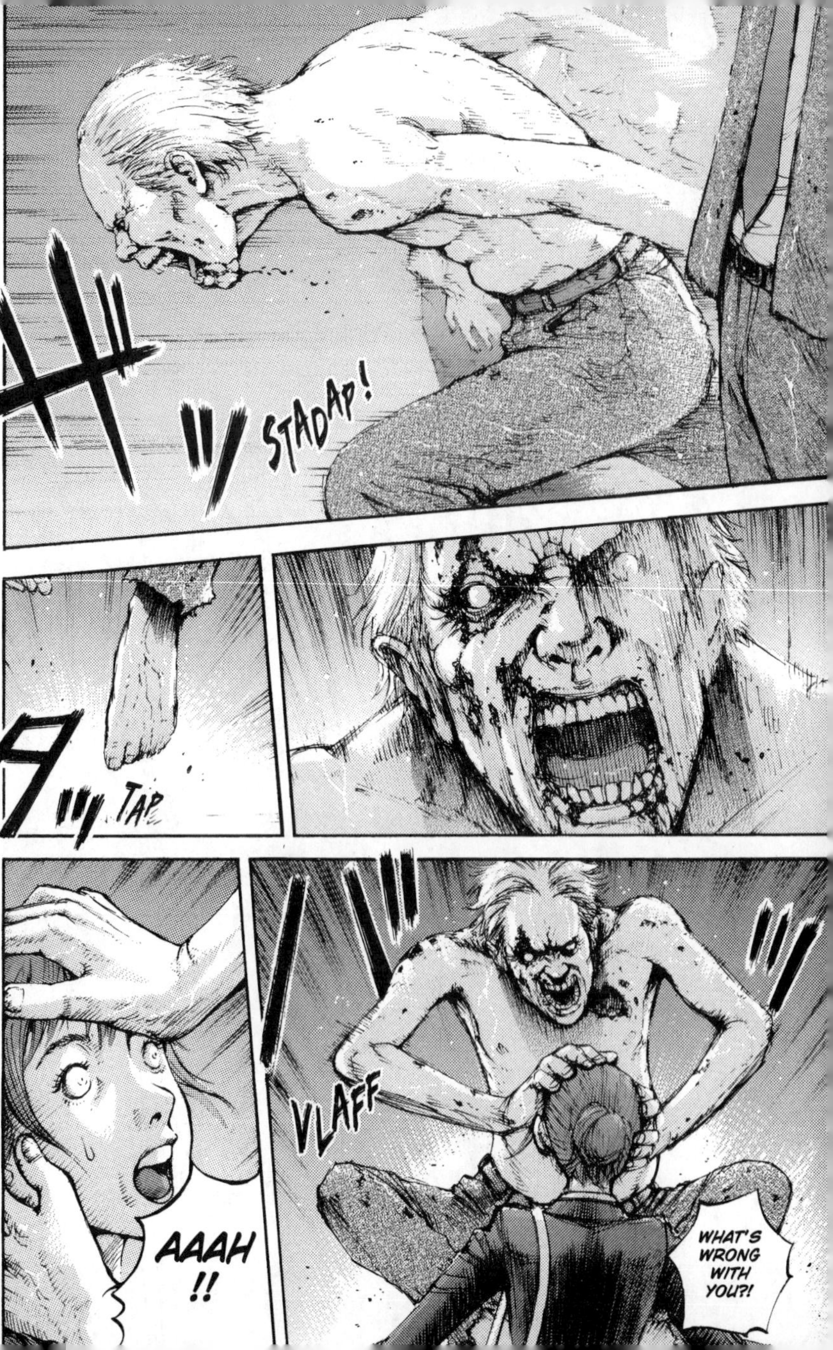
STADAP!
TAP
VLAFF
WHAT'S WRONG WITH YOU?!
AAAH!!

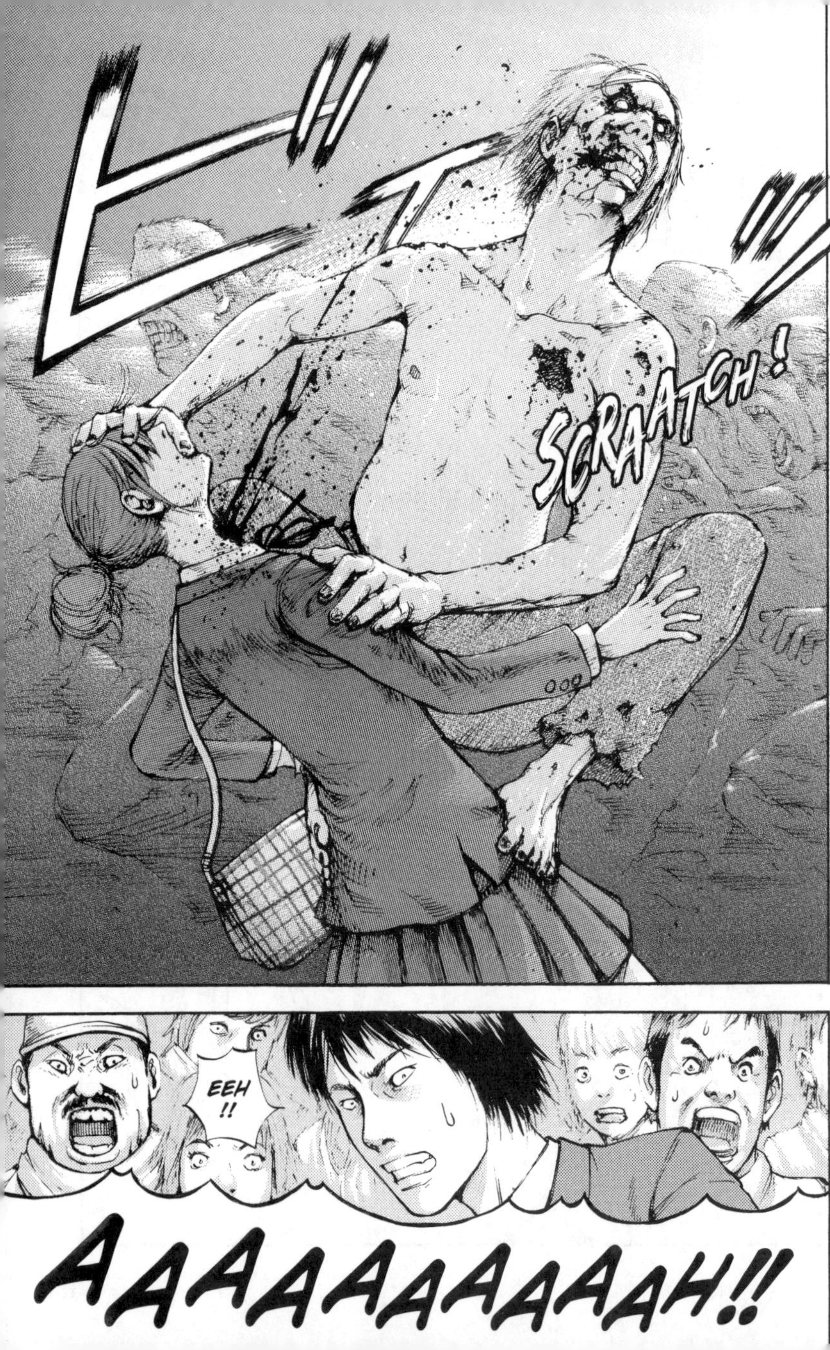
SCRAATCH!
EEH !!
AAAAAAAAAAH!!

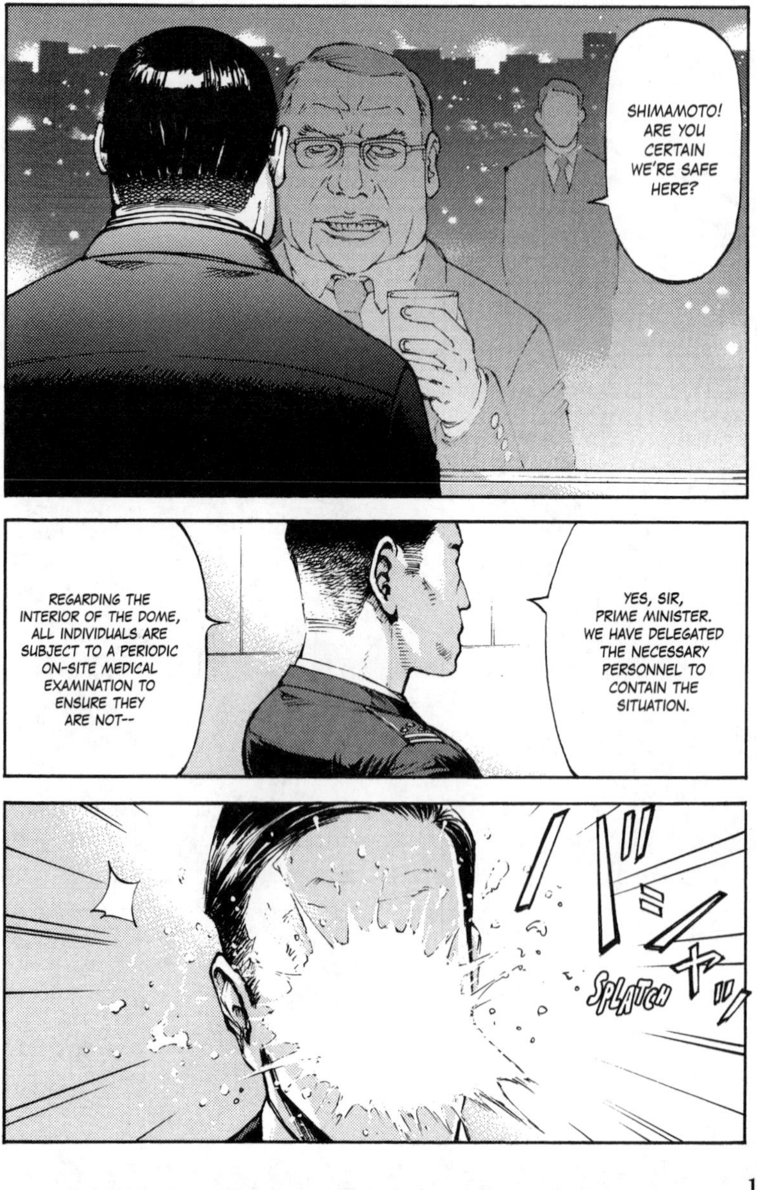
SHIMAMOTO! ARE YOU CERTAIN WE'RE SAFE HERE?
YES, SIR, PRIME MINISTER. WE HAVE DELEGATED THE NECESSARY PERSONNEL TO CONTAIN THE SITUATION.
REGARDING THE INTERIOR OF THE DOME, ALL INDIVIDUALS ARE SUBJECT TO A PERIODIC ON-SITE MEDICAL EXAMINATION TO ENSURE THEY ARE NOT--
SPLATCH

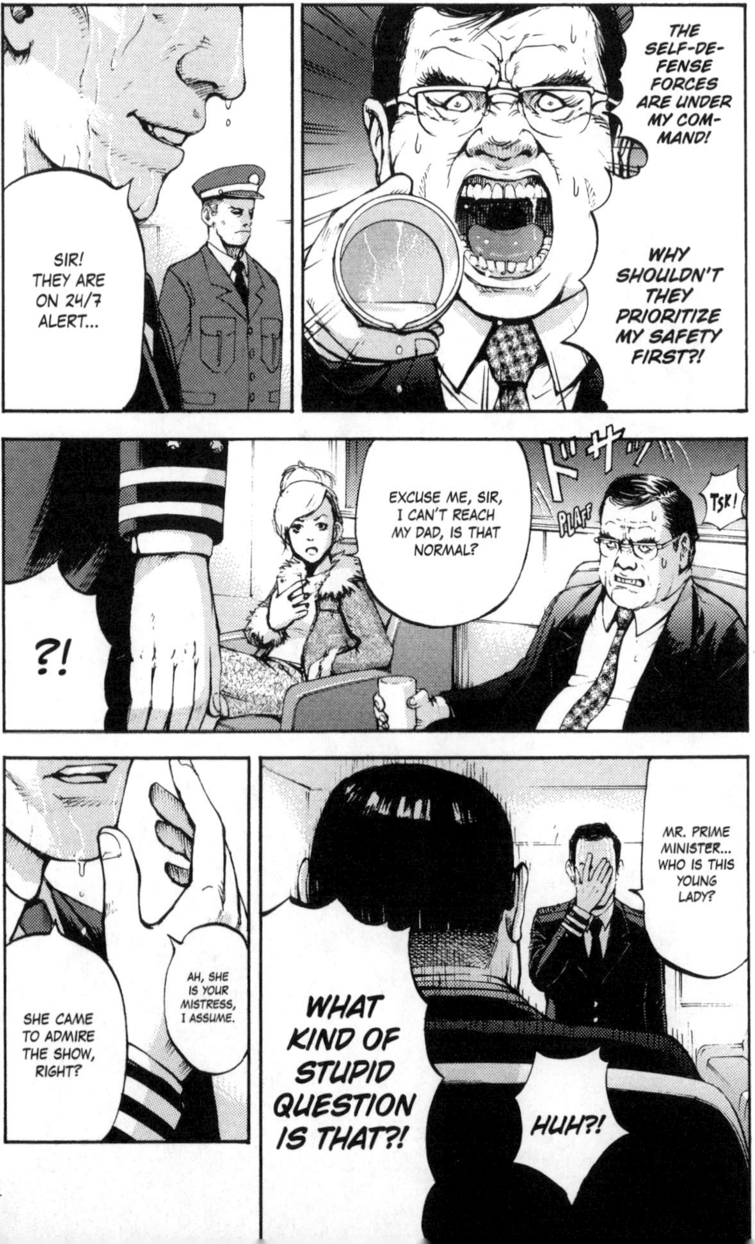
THE SELF-DE-FENSE FORCES ARE UNDER MY COM-MAND!
WHY SHOULDN'T THEY PRIORITIZE MY SAFETY FIRST?!
SIR! THEY ARE ON 24/7 ALERT...
TSK!
PLAFF
EXCUSE ME, SIR, I CAN'T REACH MY DAD, IS THAT NORMAL?
?!
MR. PRIME MINISTER... WHO IS THIS YOUNG LADY?
WHAT KIND OF STUPID QUESTION IS THAT?!
HUH?!
AH, SHE IS YOUR MISTRESS, I ASSUME.
SHE CAME TO ADMIRE THE SHOW, RIGHT?

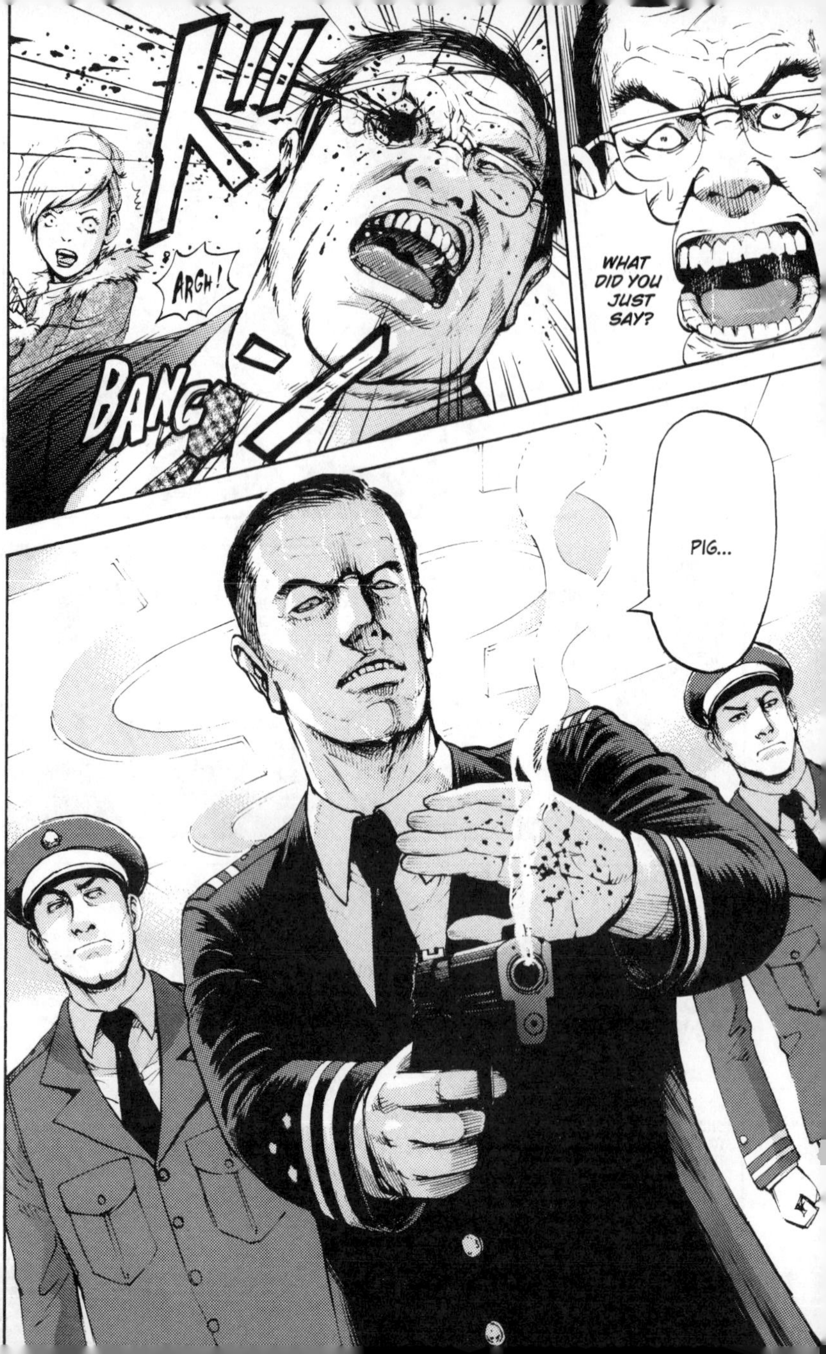
WHAT DID YOU JUST SAY?
BANG
ARGH!
PIG...

AAAAAH!!

I'D PRESUMED THAT THE SITUATION WOULD FORCE HIM TO SHOW AN OUNCE OF INTELLIGENCE...

BUT I SEE NOW I'VE WASTED MY TIME.

NOOO ...

AAH!

...

COLONEL? WHAT SHOULD WE DO WITH HER?

TAKE CARE OF HER... SHE MAY BE USEFUL LATER ON.

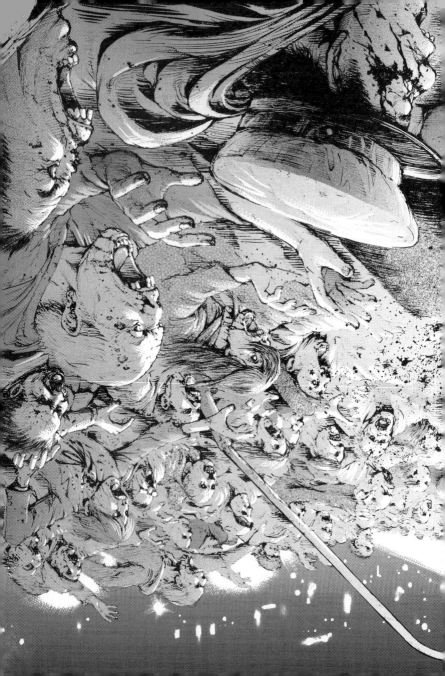

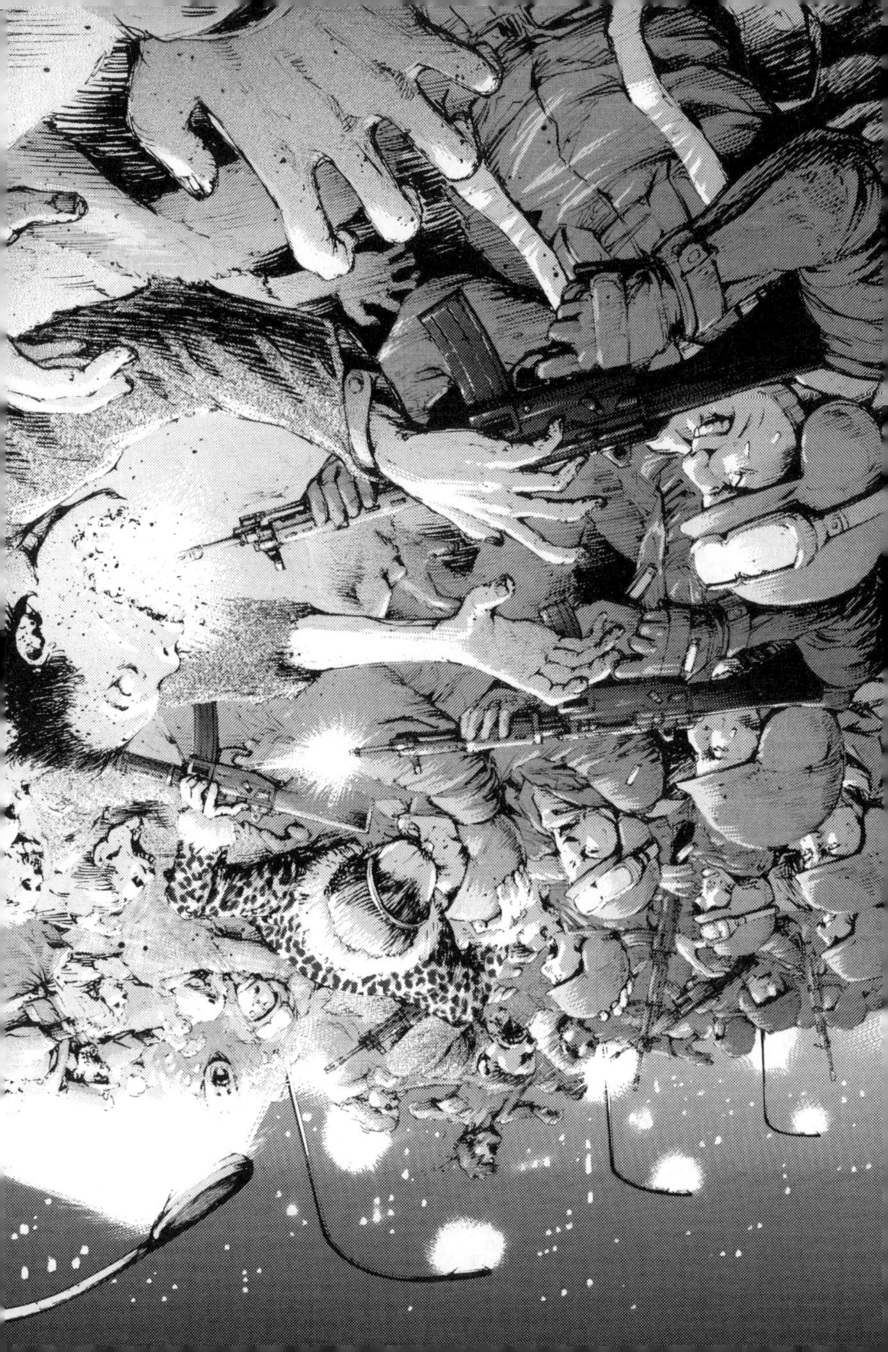

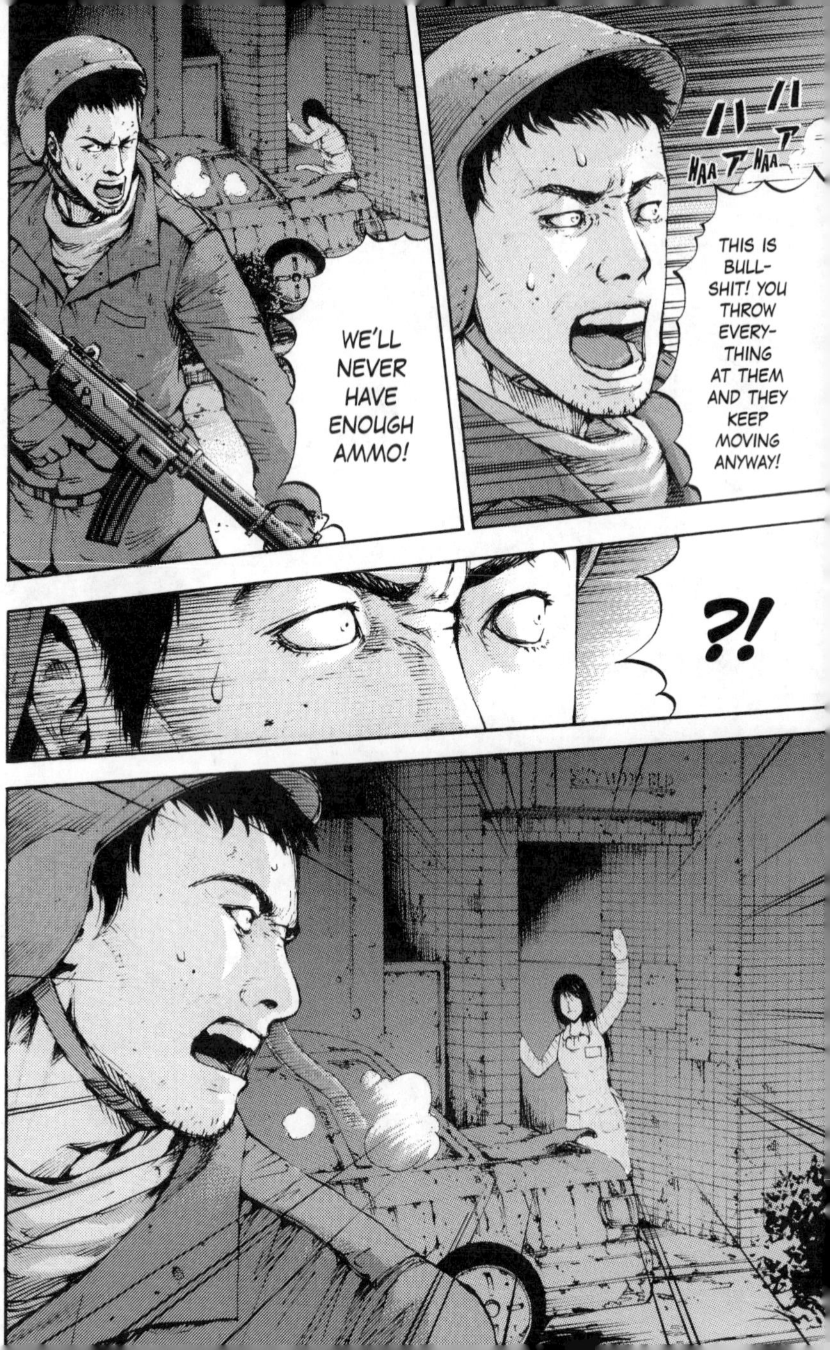
ハ ハ
HAA ア HAA ア
THIS IS BULL-SHIT! YOU THROW EVERY-THING AT THEM AND THEY KEEP MOVING ANYWAY!
WE'LL NEVER HAVE ENOUGH AMMO!
?!

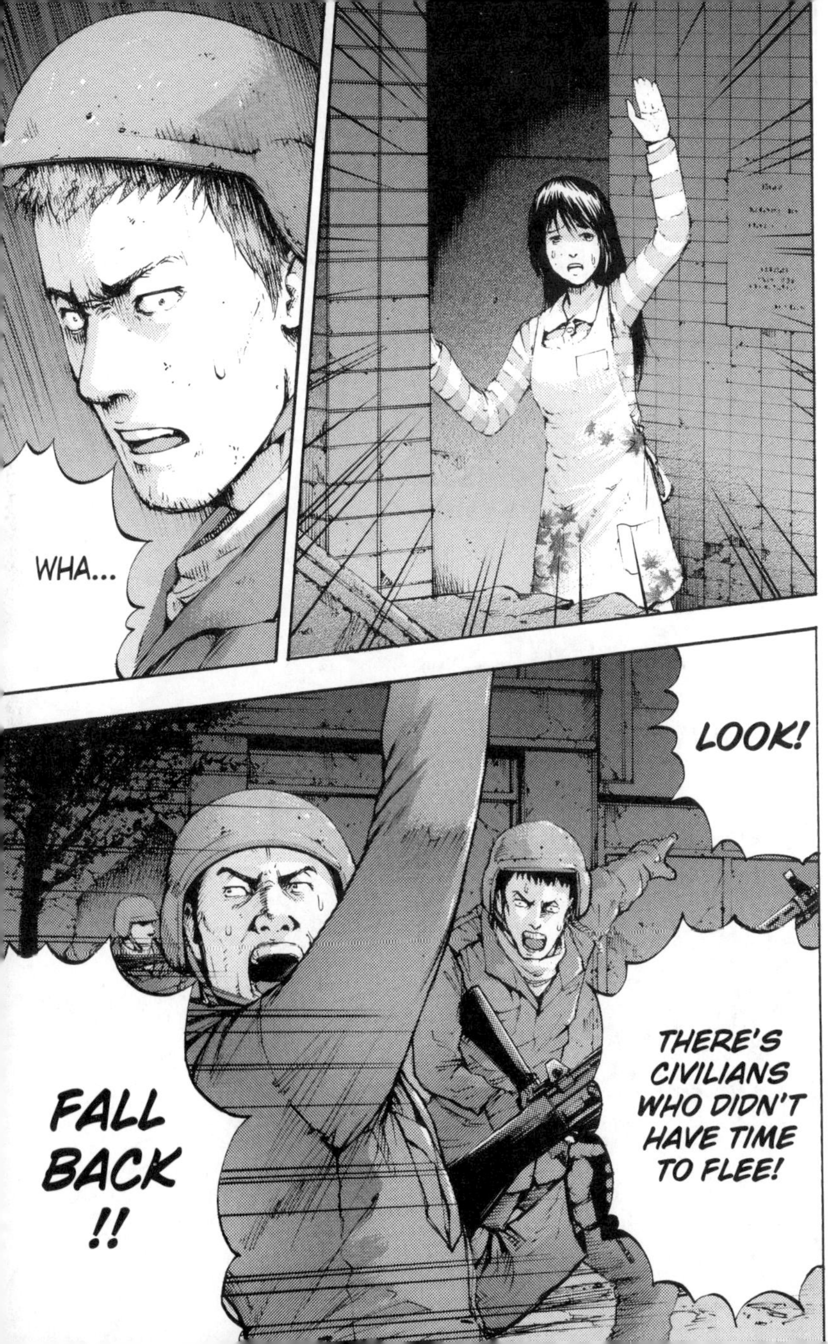
WHA...
LOOK!
THERE'S CIVILIANS WHO DIDN'T HAVE TIME TO FLEE!
FALL BACK !!

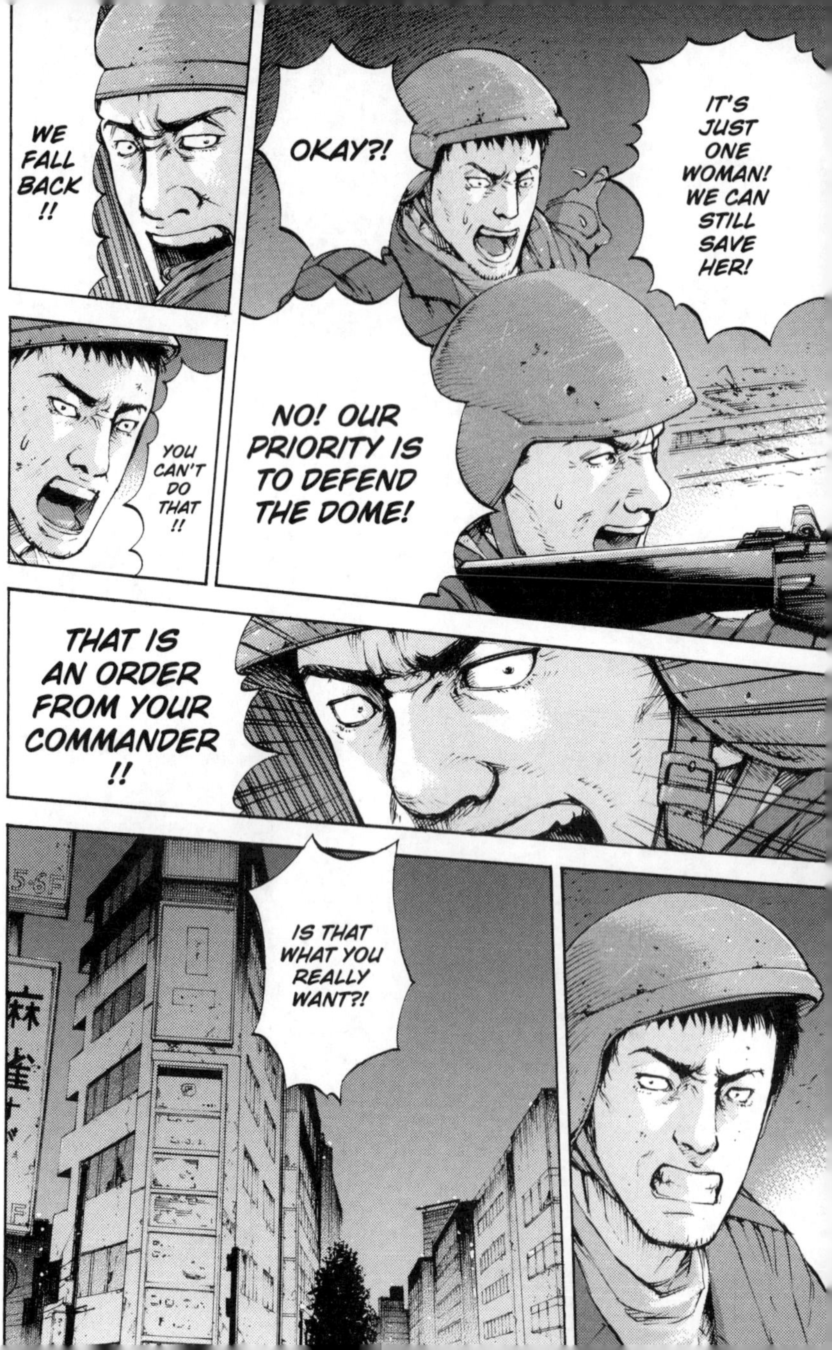
IT'S JUST ONE WOMAN! WE CAN STILL SAVE HER!
OKAY?!
WE FALL BACK !!
NO! OUR PRIORITY IS TO DEFEND THE DOME!
YOU CAN'T DO THAT !!
THAT IS AN ORDER FROM YOUR COMMANDER !!
IS THAT WHAT YOU REALLY WANT?!

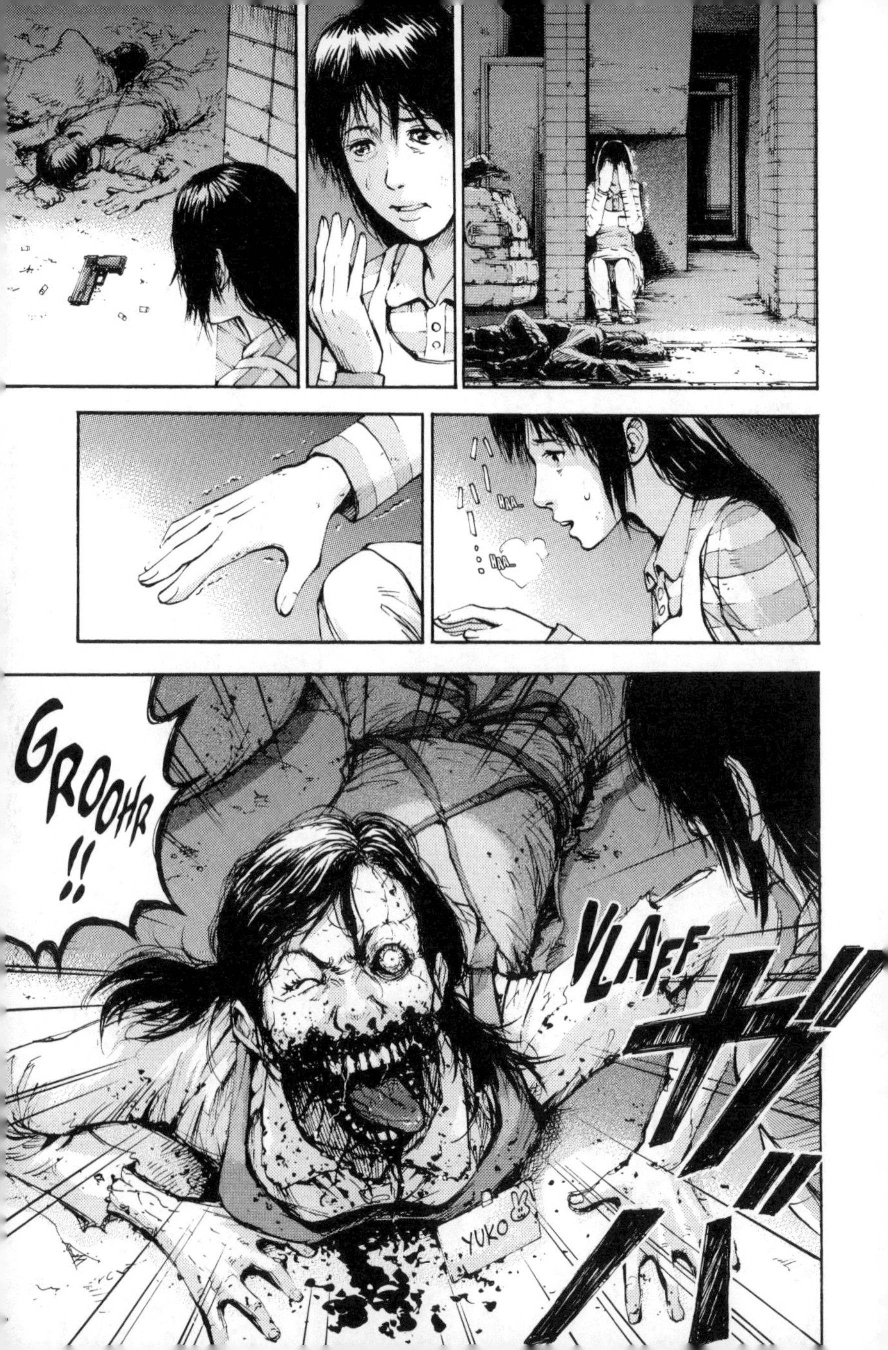
HAA...
HAA...
VLAFF
GROOHR !!
YUKO

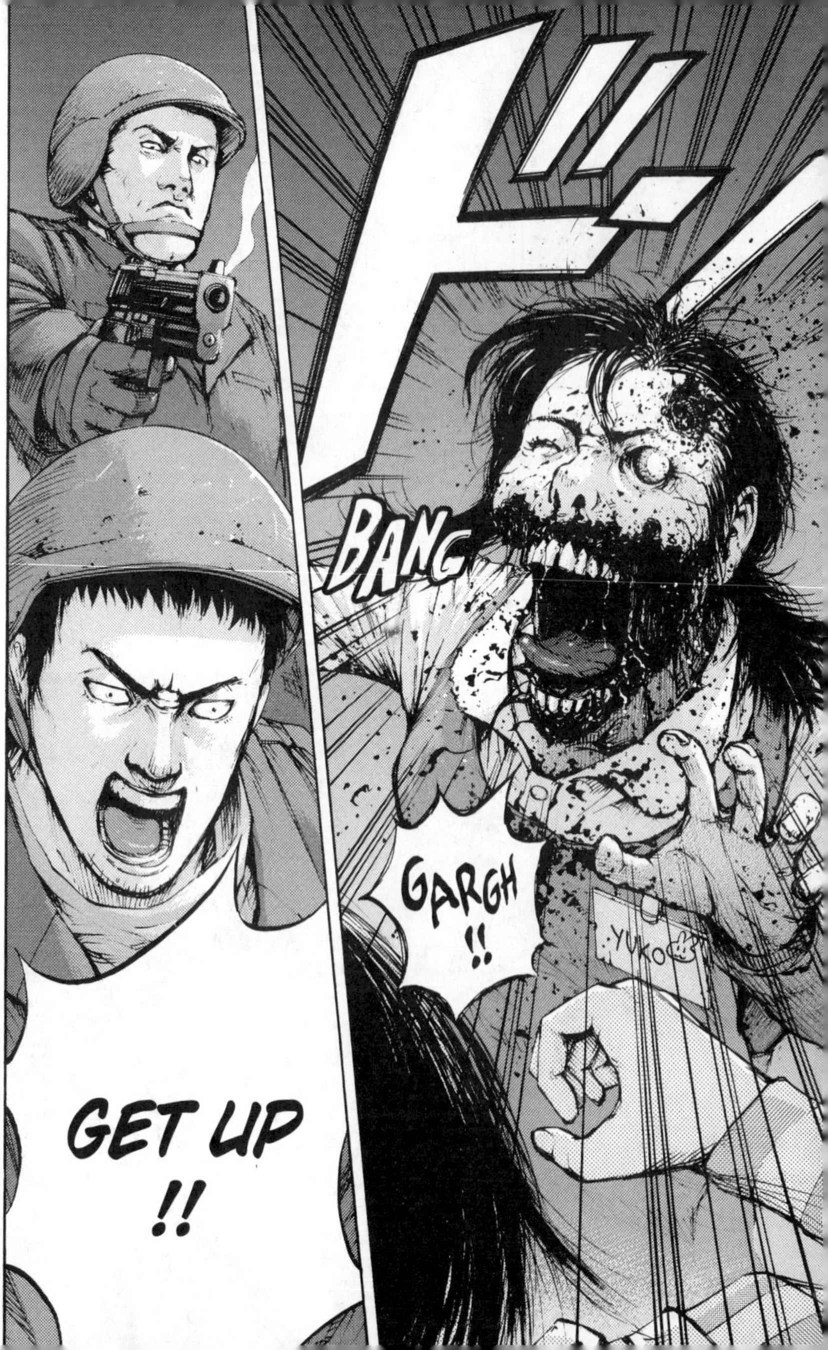
BANG
GARGH !!
YUKO
GET UP !!

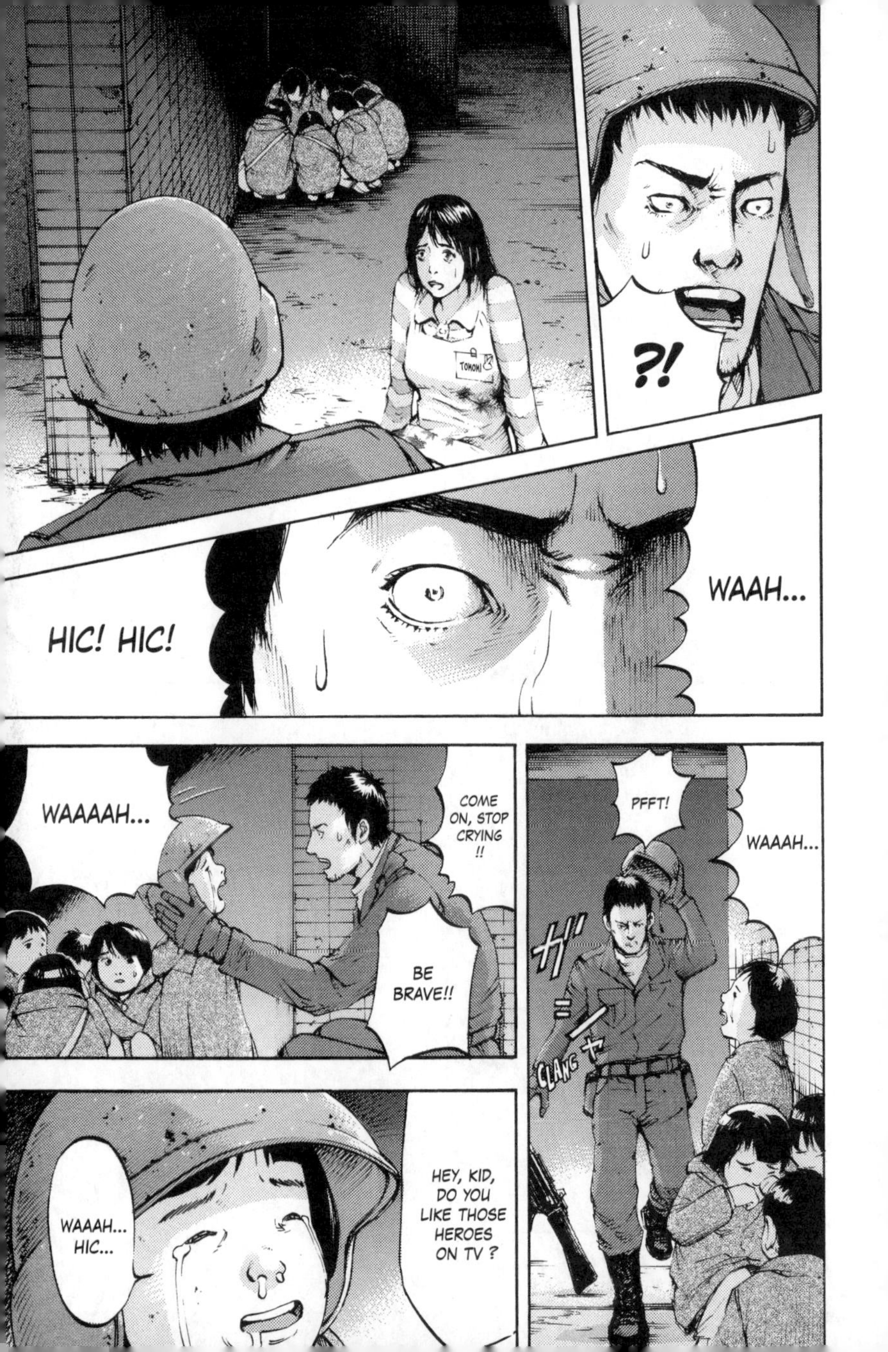
?!
TOMOMI
WAAH...
HIC! HIC!
PFFT!
WAAAH...
CLANG
COME ON, STOP CRYING !!
WAAAAH...
BE BRAVE!!
HEY, KID, DO YOU LIKE THOSE HEROES ON TV ?
WAAAH... HIC...

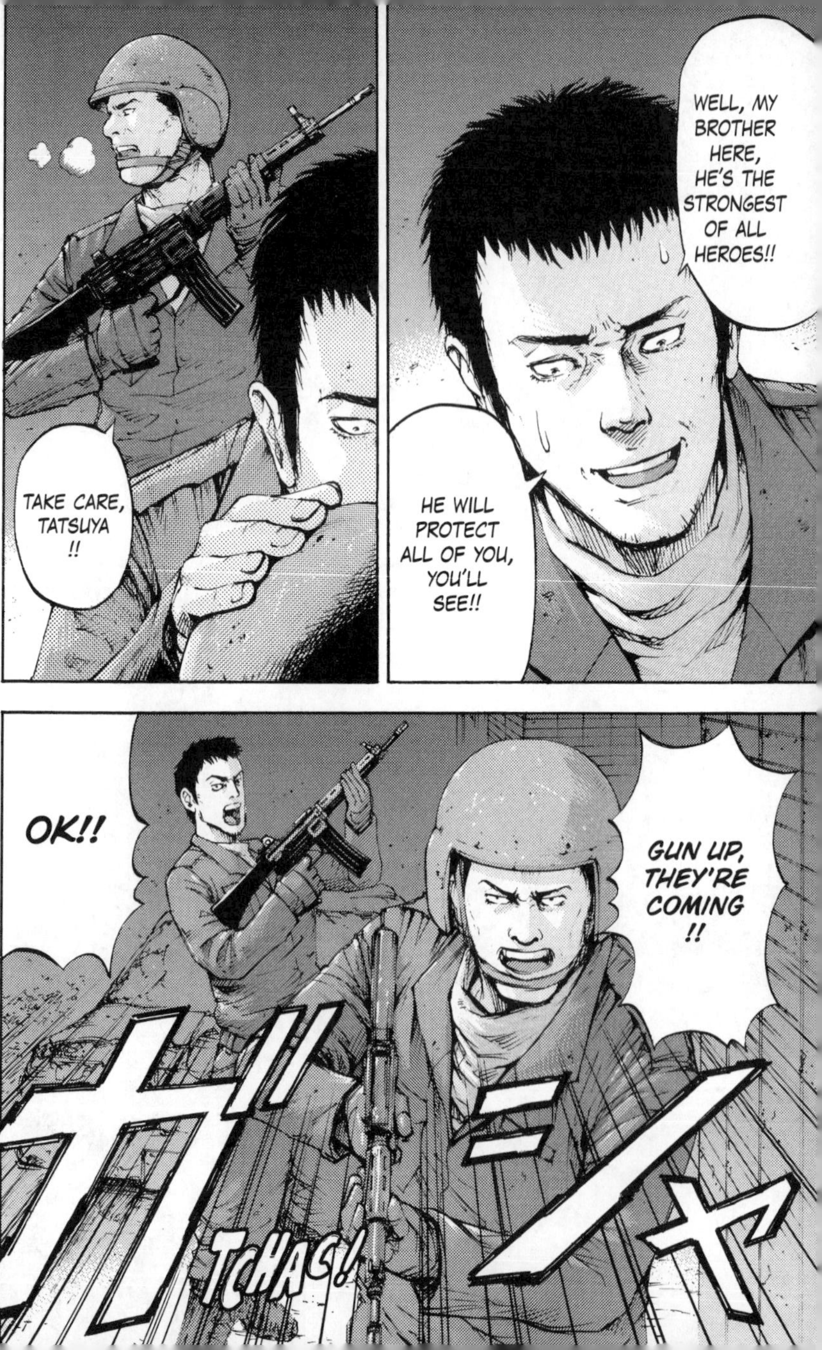
WELL, MY BROTHER HERE, HE'S THE STRONGEST OF ALL HEROES!!
HE WILL PROTECT ALL OF YOU, YOU'LL SEE!!
TAKE CARE, TATSUYA !!
GUN UP, THEY'RE COMING !!
OK!!
TCHAC!

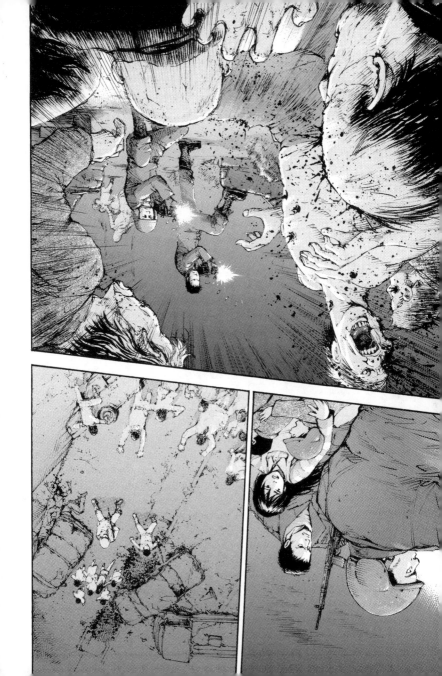

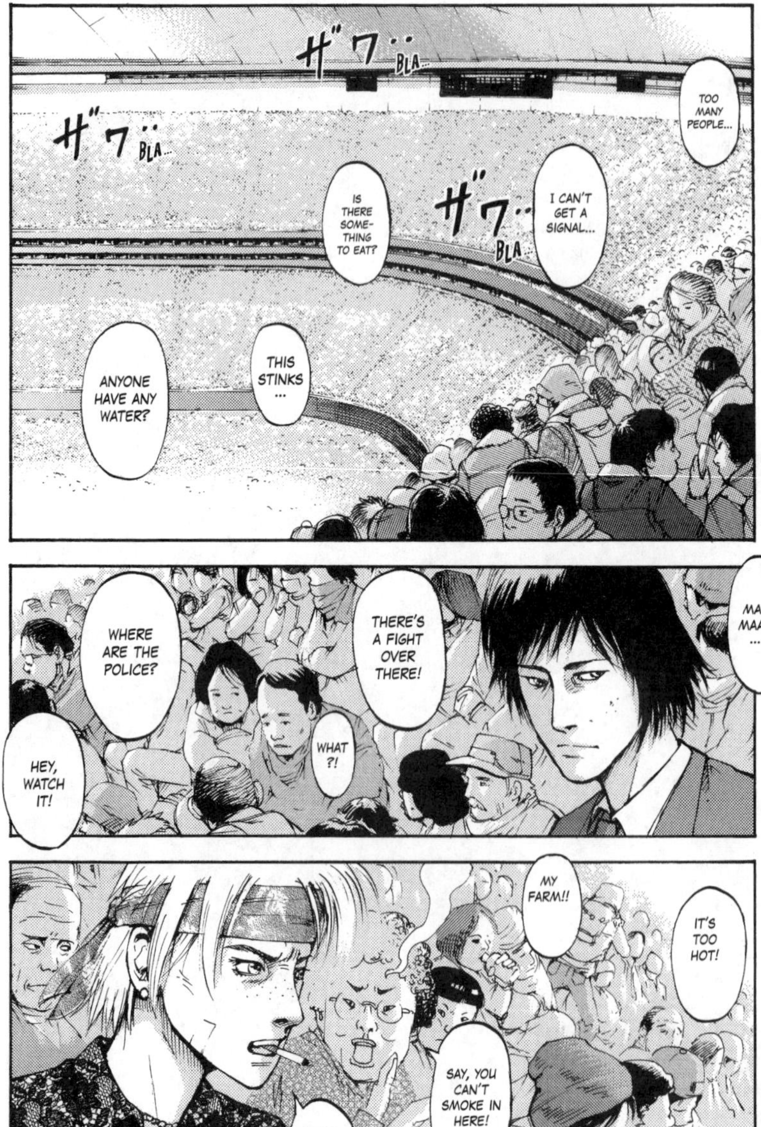
TOO MANY PEOPLE...
ザワ‥ BLA...
I CAN'T GET A SIGNAL...
ザワ‥ BLA...
IS THERE SOME-THING TO EAT?
ザワ‥ BLA...
THIS STINKS ...
ANYONE HAVE ANY WATER?
MA-MAAA ...
THERE'S A FIGHT OVER THERE!
WHAT ?!
WHERE ARE THE POLICE?
HEY, WATCH IT!
IT'S TOO HOT!
MY FARM!!
SAY, YOU CAN'T SMOKE IN HERE!
SHUT IT, OLD HAG!

GET GOING, TATSUYA!!
THAT'S IT!!
バーン
BANG!
I'M NOT GOING TO ABANDON MY COM-MANDING OFFICER!
IT'S UP TO YOU TO PROTECT THEM NOW!
I'M COUNT-ING ON YOU!!

CLAC

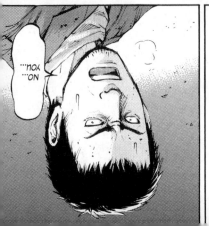

NO... YOU...

GET OUT OF HERE !!

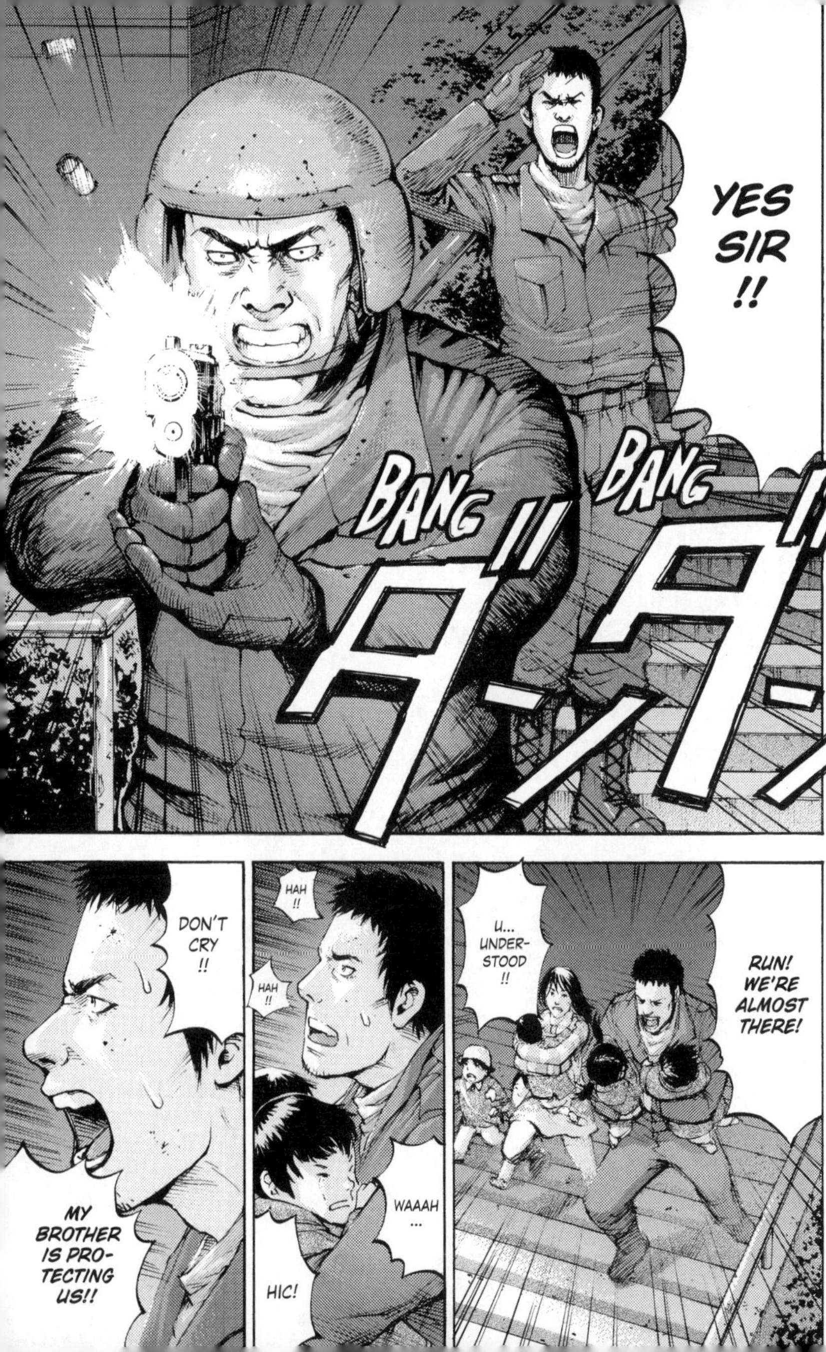
YES SIR !!
BANG !!
BANG !!
ダーダー
RUN! WE'RE ALMOST THERE!
U... UNDER-STOOD !!
HAH !!
HAH !!
WAAAH ...
HIC!
DON'T CRY !!
MY BROTHER IS PRO-TECTING US!!

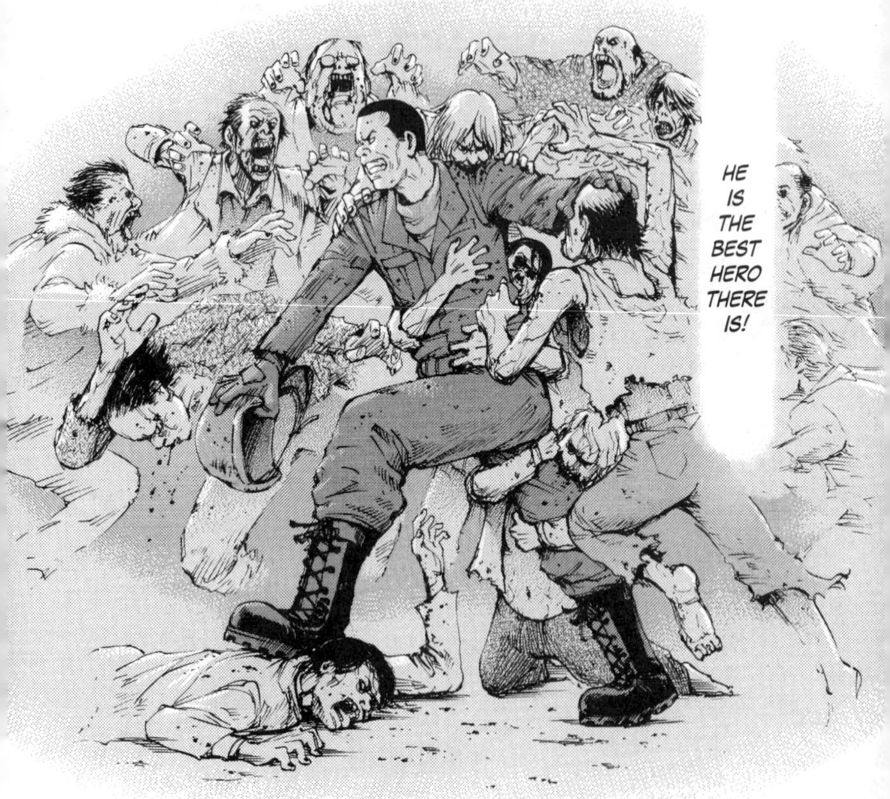
HE IS THE BEST HERO THERE IS!

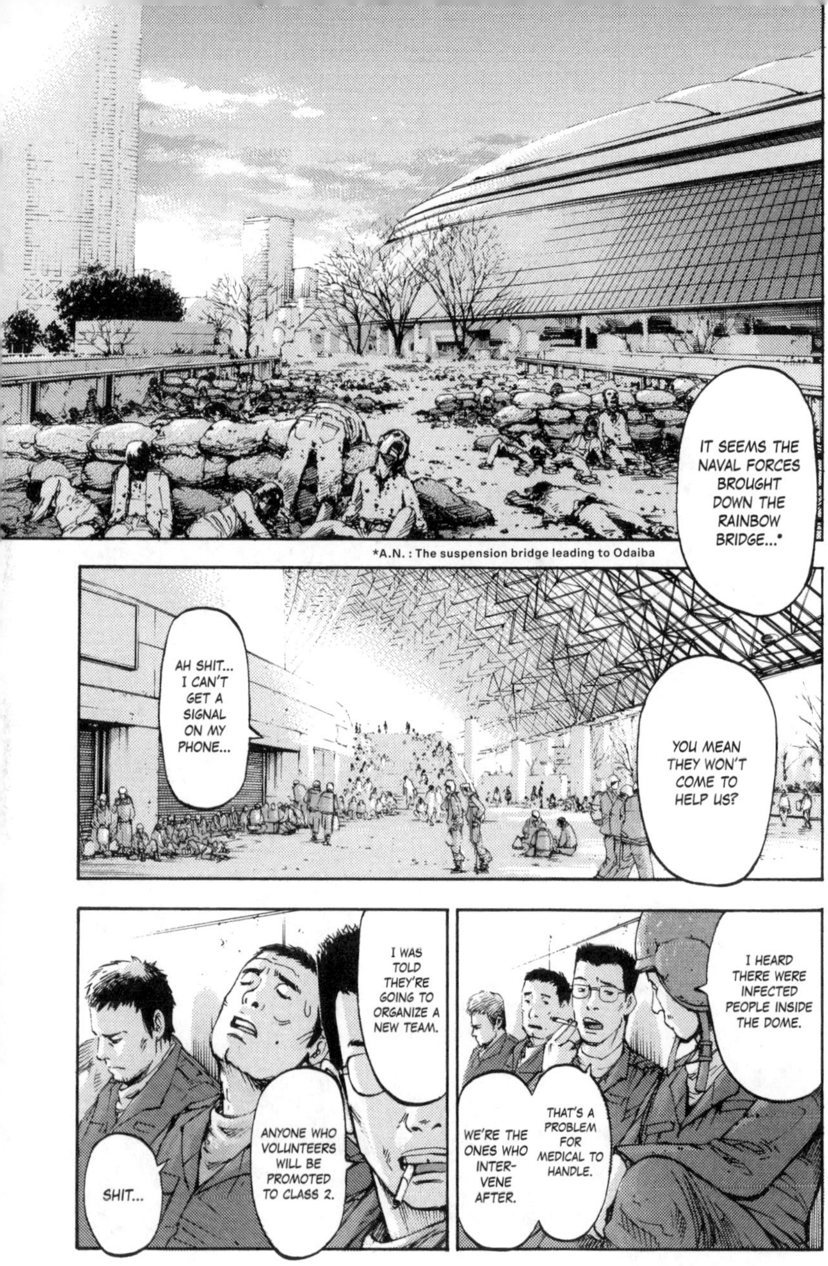
IT SEEMS THE NAVAL FORCES BROUGHT DOWN THE RAINBOW BRIDGE...*
YOU MEAN THEY WON'T COME TO HELP US?
AH SHIT... I CAN'T GET A SIGNAL ON MY PHONE...
I HEARD THERE WERE INFECTED PEOPLE INSIDE THE DOME.
THAT'S A PROBLEM FOR MEDICAL TO HANDLE.
WE'RE THE ONES WHO INTER-VENE AFTER.
I WAS TOLD THEY'RE GOING TO ORGANIZE A NEW TEAM.
ANYONE WHO VOLUNTEERS WILL BE PROMOTED TO CLASS 2.
SHIT...
*A.N. : The suspension bridge leading to Odaiba

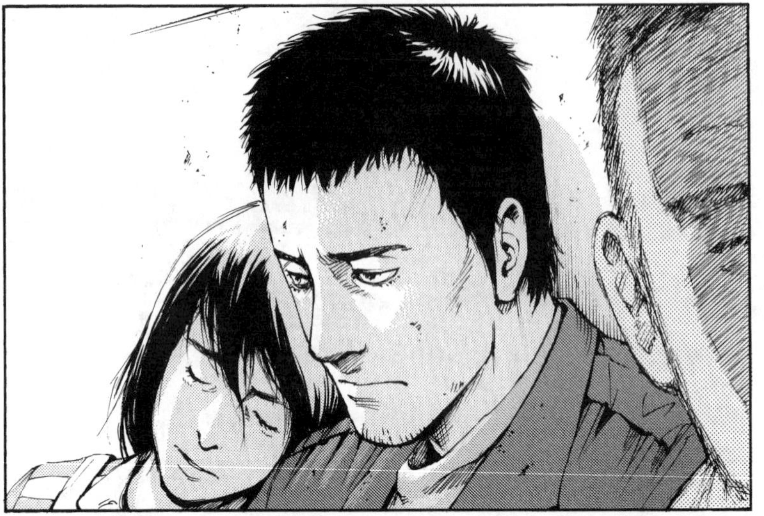
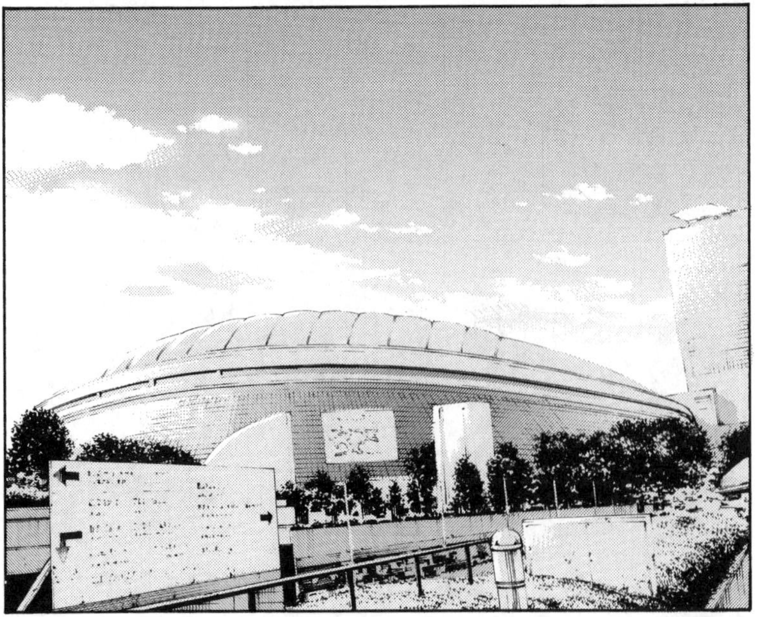

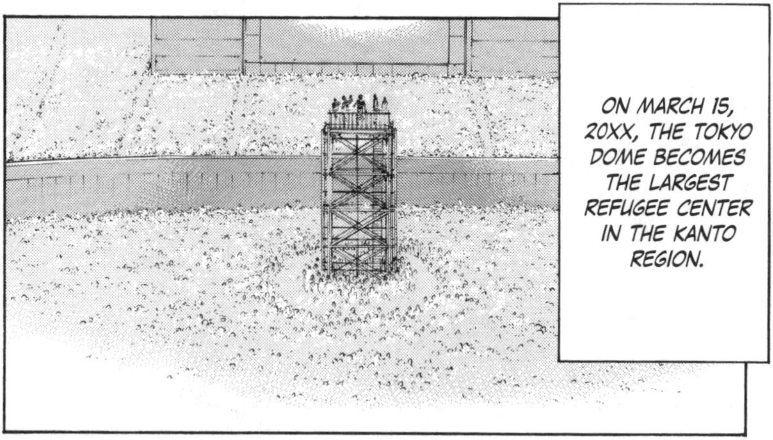
ON MARCH 15, 20XX, THE TOKYO DOME BECOMES THE LARGEST REFUGEE CENTER IN THE KANTO REGION.

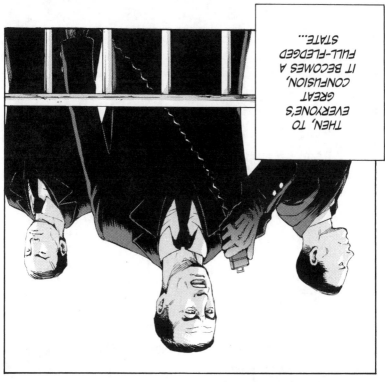

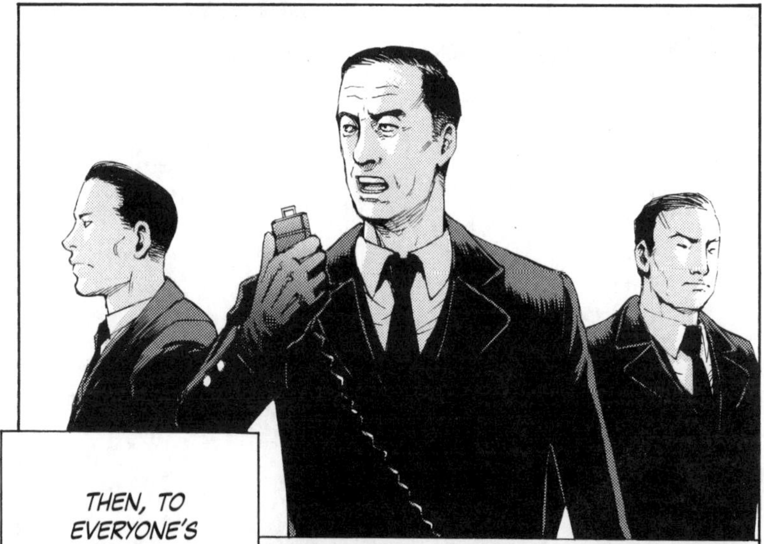
THEN, TO EVERYONE'S GREAT CONFUSION, IT BECOMES A FULL-FLEDGED STATE...

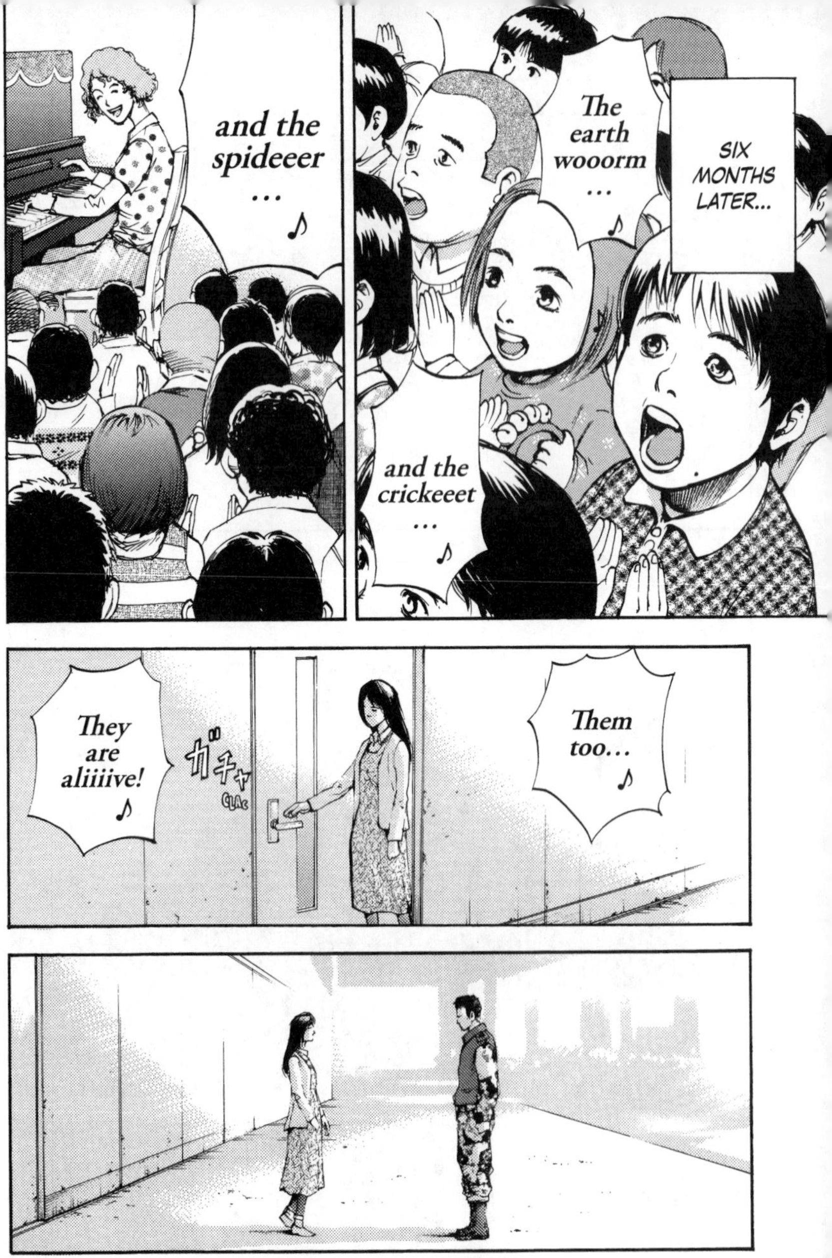
SIX MONTHS LATER...
The earth wooorm ... ♪
and the crickeeet ... ♪
and the spideeer ... ♪
Them too... ♪
ガチャ
CLAC
They are aliiiive! ♪

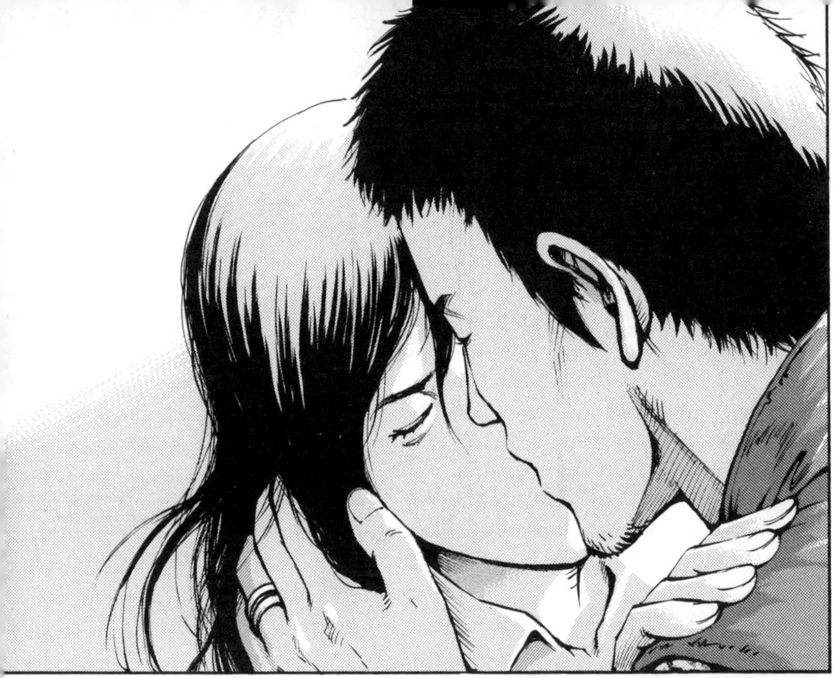

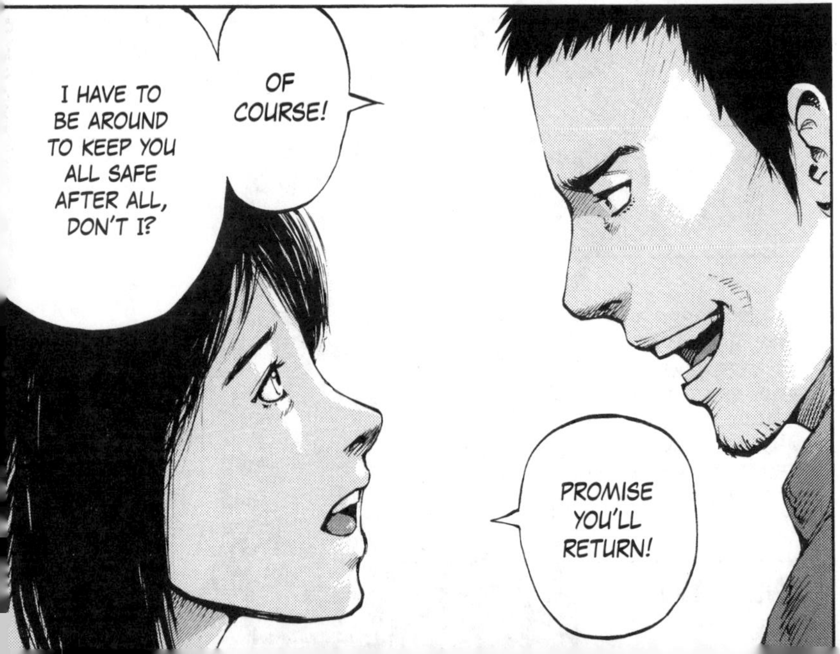
PROMISE YOU'LL RETURN!
OF COURSE!
I HAVE TO BE AROUND TO KEEP YOU ALL SAFE AFTER ALL, DON'T I?

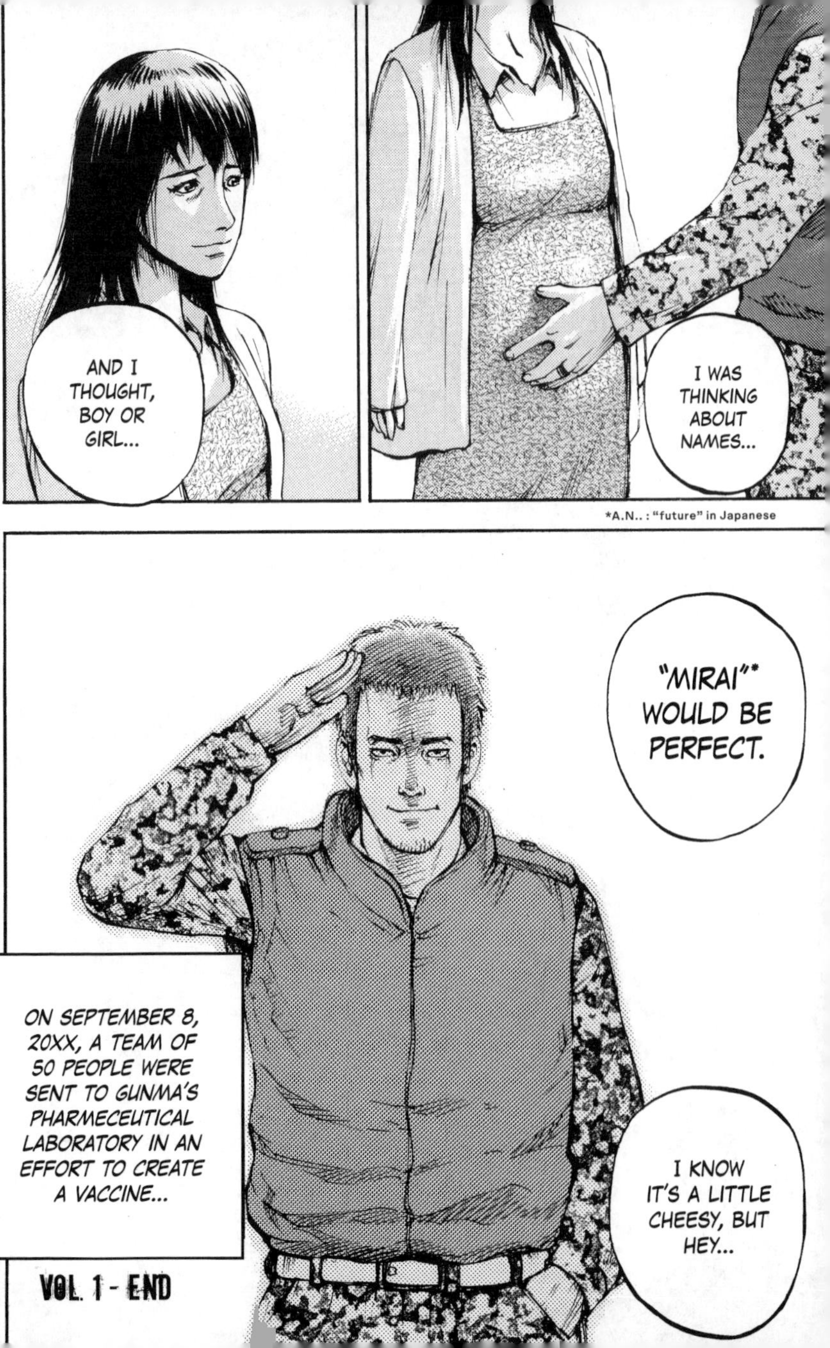
I WAS THINKING ABOUT NAMES...
AND I THOUGHT, BOY OR GIRL...
"MIRAI"* WOULD BE PERFECT.
I KNOW IT'S A LITTLE CHEESY, BUT HEY...
ON SEPTEMBER 8, 20XX, A TEAM OF 50 PEOPLE WERE SENT TO GUNMA'S PHARMECEUTICAL LABORATORY IN AN EFFORT TO CREATE A VACCINE...
VOL. 1 - END

*A.N.. : "future" in Japanese

CRUELER THAN DEAD
by Tsukasa Saimura and Kozo Takahashi

Translated and lettered by:
FairSquare Comics (Fabrice Sapolsky, Lilliah Campagna)

FOR ABLAZE

Managing Editor:
Rich Young

Editor:
Kevin Ketner

Designer:
Rodolfo Muraguchi

Publisher's Cataloging-in-Publication data

Names: Saimura, Tsukasa, author. | Takahashi, Kozo, illustrator.
Title: Crueler than dead / Tsukasa Saimura ; Kozo Takahashi.
Description: Portland, OR: Ablaze Publishing, 2021.
Identifiers: ISBN 978-1-950912-41-4
Subjects: LCSH Zombies—Fiction. | Tokyo—Fiction. | Horror. | Graphic novels. | BISAC COMICS & GRAPHIC NOVELS / Manga / Horror | COMICS & GRAPHIC NOVELS / Horror
Classification: LCC PN6790.J33 .S25 2021 | DDC 741.5—dc23

 /ablazepub   @AblazePub   @AblazePub

ablazepublishing.com

To find a comics shop in your area go to:
www.comicshoplocator.com

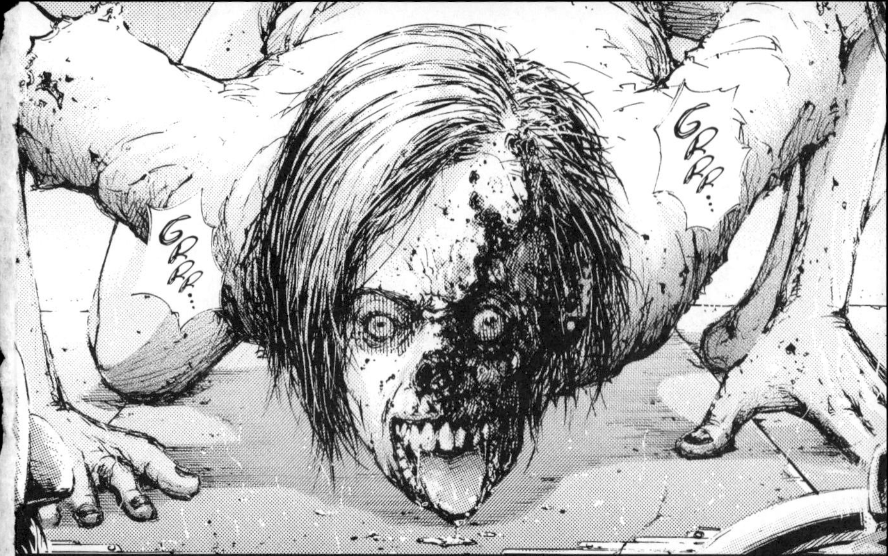
GRRR...
GRRR...

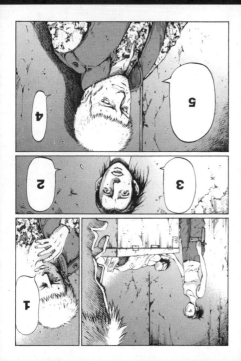

STOP!

THIS IS THE BACK OF THE BOOK!

This manga collection is translated into English, but arranged in right-to-left reading format to maintain the artwork's visual orientation as originally drawn and published in Japan. Start in the upper right-hand corner and read each word balloon and panel right-to-left.

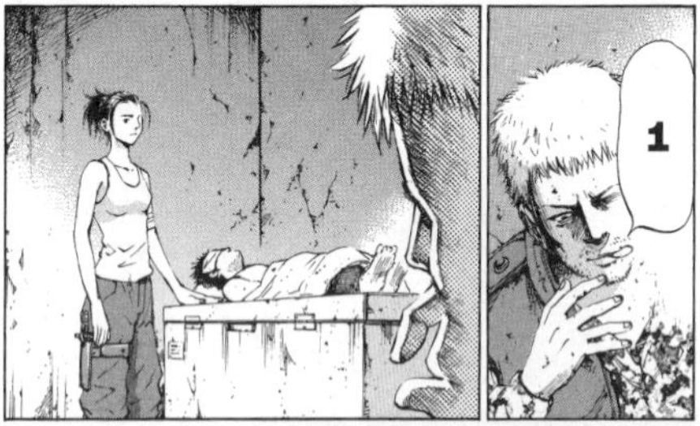
1
2
3
4
5